PENGUIN BO

BOSWELL'S PRESUMPTUOUS TASK

Adam Sisman is the author of *A.J.P. Taylor: A Biography*. He lives near Bath, England, with his wife, the novelist Robyn Sisman, and their two children. *Boswell's Presumptuous Task* was the winner of the National Book Critics Circle Award for Biography, and was a finalist for the *Los Angeles Times* Book Prize. It was named a *New York Times* Notable Book and a *Library Journal* Best Book of the Year.

BOSWELL'S PRESUMPTUOUS TASK

The Making of the Life of Dr. Johnson

ADAM SISMAN

PENGUIN BOOKS

PENGUIN BOOKS

Published by the Penguin Group
Penguin Putnam Inc., 375 Hudson Street,
New York, New York 10014, U.S.A.
Penguin Books Ltd, 80 Strand, London WC2R 0RL, England
Penguin Books Australia Ltd, 250 Camberwell Road,
Camberwell, Victoria 3124, Australia
Penguin Books Canada Ltd, 10 Alcorn Avenue,
Toronto, Ontario, Canada M4V 3B2
Penguin Books India (P) Ltd, 11 Community Centre,
Panchsheel Park, New Delhi – 110 017, India
Penguin Books (N.Z.) Ltd, Cnr Rosedale and Airborne Roads,
Albany, Auckland, New Zealand
Penguin Books (South Africa) (Pty) Ltd, 24 Sturdee Avenue,
Rosebank, Johannesburg 2196, South Africa

Penguin Books Ltd, Registered Offices:
Harmondsworth, Middlesex, England

First published in Great Britain by Hamish Hamilton 2000
First published in the United States of America by Farrar, Straus and Giroux 2001
Published in Penguin Books 2002

1 3 5 7 9 10 8 6 4 2

THE LIBRARY OF CONGRESS HAS CATALOGED THE
AMERICAN HARDCOVER EDITION AS FOLLOWS:
Sisman, Adam.
Boswell's presumptuous task / Adam Sisman. — 1st American ed.
        p.   cm.
Originally published: London : Penguin, 2000.
Includes bibliographical references and index.
ISBN 0-374-11561-3 (hc.)
ISBN 0 14 20.0175 9 (pbk.)
1. Boswell, James, 1740–1795. Life of Samuel Johnson.
2. Authors, English—Biography—History and criticism.
3. Johnson, Samuel, 1709–1784.   4. Biography as a literary form.
I. Title.
PR3533.B7 S57   2001
828'.609—dc21
[B]   00-067699

Printed in the United States of America
Designed by Jonathan D. Lippincott

To my mother

CONTENTS

LIST OF ILLUSTRATIONS

Facing Introduction (page xiv): proof of the first page of the *Life of Johnson*, with Boswell's handwritten note to the printer requesting that a revised proof be sent to him at Sir Joshua Reynolds's house

Part One (page 1): "The Biographer in Meditation," an engraving by W. T. Green, from a sketch by George Langton, son of Boswell's friend Bennet Langton

Part Two (page 69): "Bozzy," an engraving by F. Holl, from a pen-and-ink caricature by Sir Thomas Lawrence, *c.* 1790–95

Part Three (page 257): engraving by William Daniell, from a pencil portrait by George Dance, 1793, with Boswell's signature below

At the end of Parts One and Two are versions of the Boswell crest, a hawk hooded for hunting with bells attached to its talons, the Boswell family motto Vraye Foi ("true faith") above, and James Boswell's initials below. At the end of Part Three is Boswell's seal or bookplate, illustrated with the same devices and the misleading title "Boswell of Auchinleck."

ACKNOWLEDGEMENTS

Anyone who has written anything about James Boswell in the last half-century owes a huge debt of gratitude to Frederick A. Pottle and the team of scholars who have worked under his direction (and who continue to work) on the superb Yale edition of the Boswell papers. They broke the ground. I have drawn particularly on Marshall Waingrow's *Correspondence and Other Papers of James Boswell Relating to the Making of the Life of Johnson;* my copy of the first edition has been used so much and so often that the binding is coming away. Fortunately I now have a copy of the smart new second edition.

I am particularly grateful to those friends who kindly agreed to read my book in draft: Rupert Christiansen, Hugh Griffith, Andrew O'Hagan, George and Marjorie Misiewicz, Nick Phillipson, and Henry Woudhuysen. I have benefited much from their comments. On the other hand, I have not always taken the advice on offer, and the flaws and errors that remain in this book are entirely my own responsibility.

I am grateful too to Nicolas Barker for specific bibliographical advice.

I should like to thank Yale University and Edinburgh University Press for permission to quote from the Boswell editions listed in the bibliography. In particular, I should like to thank Gordon Turnbull, chief editor of the Yale Boswell editions, and his assistant, Michele Martinez, for their courtesy and hospitality.

I am grateful to the staff of the Beinecke Library at Yale University for allowing me to examine Boswell's journals and the manuscript of the *Life of Johnson;* and to the staff of the Pierpont Morgan Library in New York for allowing me to read Boswell's letters to his friend William Temple.

The London Library has been most helpful and efficient in finding and supplying books; I am grateful to its staff, and to the Librarian, Alan Bell, who gave me some useful pointers at an early stage. I must also thank the Librarian of Bristol University Library, Geoffrey Ford, for generously allowing me access to the facilities during the vacation, and the staff of the Frome Public Library for general assistance. I also want to pay tribute to the excellent Inter-Library Loans system.

I am particularly grateful to Mrs Drue Heinz and the Trustees of the Hawthornden International Writers' Retreat for providing valuable breathing-space; and to George Amiss for the same.

Many years ago one of my school-teachers, Patrick Hutton, encouraged me to try to write clearly and accurately. I wish to thank him for this, and for steadying me on a path that would lead eventually to this book.

I have been lucky to have had several excellent editors: Kate Jones, who took the book on, and then later saw it through to publication; Simon Prosser, who looked after the book while Kate was away on maternity leave; and my American editors, Jonathan Galassi and Lorin Stein. I am extremely grateful to them all for their patience, help, and encouragement. I am indebted, too, to Sonia Greenbaum for her professional help in preparing the typescript for publication. My agent, Bruce Hunter, has been wonderfully tactful and supportive and I am deeply grateful to him also. Last but certainly not least is my wife, Robyn, who has helped, encouraged, and supported me throughout. Only she knows how much I owe her.

AUTHOR'S NOTE

Spelling and capitalization have been modernized throughout.

THE

LIFE

OF

SAMUEL JOHNSON, LL.D.

TO write the life of him who excelled all mankind in writing the lives of others, and who, whether we confider his extraordinary endowments, or his various works, has been equalled by few in any age, is an arduous, and may be reckoned in me a prefumptuous tafk.

Had Dr. Johnfon written his own life, in conformity with the opinion which he has given[1], that every man's life may be beft written by himfelf; had he employed in the prefervation of his own hiftory, that clearnefs of narration and elegance of language in which he has embalmed fo many eminent perfons, the world would probably have had the moft perfect example of biography that was ever exhibited. But although he at different times, in a defultory manner, committed to writing many particulars of the progrefs of his mind and fortunes, he never had perfevering diligence enough to form them into a regular compofition. Of thefe memorials a few have been preferved; but the greater part was configned by him to the flames, a few days before his death.

As I had the honour and happinefs of enjoying his friendfhip for upwards of twenty years; as I had the fcheme of writing his life conftantly in view; as he was well apprifed of this circumftance, and from time to time obligingly fatisfied my inquiries, by communicating to me the incidents of his early years; as I acquired a facility in recollecting, and was very affiduous in

[1] *Idler*, No. 84.

B

recording

INTRODUCTION

*To write the life of him who excelled all mankind in writing the lives of others . . .
may be reckoned in me a presumptuous task.*[1]

THIS IS THE STORY of a book. Boswell's "presumptuous task" was
to write the life of his friend and mentor, Samuel Johnson; in the pages
that follow I have tried to show how he set about his task, and eventually, after almost seven years of effort and agony, fulfilled it.

Anyone with an interest in biography soon becomes interested in
Boswell's *Life of Johnson*. It stands next to other biographies as Shakespeare stands beside other playwrights: towering above them all. For
more than two centuries it has been continuously in print, and in that
time it has won innumerable admirers. No other biography has given
so much pleasure; no other biographer has created such a vivid central
character. It has become a truism that, as a result of Boswell's extraordinary book, Samuel Johnson is better known to us than any other man
in history.

As well as being a famous and much-loved book, the *Life of Johnson*
is a work that raises fundamental questions about the nature of biography itself. Is it possible for a biographer to understand fully what it is
like to be another human being? However careful and diligent the
writer, can biography be accurate, that is, faithful to life? Everybody

knows "Dr Johnson," or so we think; but is the man we know from the pages of Boswell's book the same Johnson that strode the streets of London 250 years ago? Is biography science, or art? History or fiction?

In his book James Boswell made a heroic attempt to display his friend "as he really was." He did not conceal his partiality; his reverence, affection, and even love for Johnson are obvious throughout, and an endearing feature of his biography. But neither did he conceal Johnson's faults: his rudeness, his prejudices, and his temper. Boswell was the first biographer to attempt to tell the whole truth about his subject, to portray his lapses, his blemishes, and his weaknesses as well as his great qualities: an aim we take for granted today, but in Boswell's time a startling innovation.

Boswell reconstructed Johnson's conversations from fragmentary records. He collected memorabilia of Johnson from every possible source, and then went to unprecedented lengths to verify the accuracy of the material he used. He insisted that "everything relevant to so great a man is worth observing," and though much ridiculed for it, he described the minute details of the way Johnson dressed, what he ate, and how he behaved. The result is that Johnson, a remote, venerable figure to most of his contemporaries, appears to us a warm, living human being.

Boswell's ambition was nothing less than to resuscitate his dead friend in print. Indeed (so Boswell claimed), had Johnson's other friends been as thorough in recording what he said and did, "he might have been almost entirely preserved." As it was, Boswell boasted that in his biography Johnson might be seen "more completely than any man who ever lived."

However, despite Boswell's determination to gather up every remaining scrap of information about his subject, aspects of Johnson's life were forever hidden from him. On a practical level, the two men did not meet until Johnson was fifty-three; and though Boswell came to know Johnson very well indeed afterwards, his knowledge was inevitably circumscribed. Boswell was also limited by his own limitations: he could not imagine what he could not comprehend. Like all biographers, he could show only what he could see. The man we come to know in the pages of Boswell's book is, so far as we can tell, faithful to life, but only to the life that Boswell witnessed and understood.

One way of reading the *Life of Johnson* is as a hybrid: a memoir concealed within a life. Boswell pays much less attention to the period of Johnson's life before they met: his subject's first fifty-three years take up less than one-fifth of his book, the remaining twenty-one more than four-fifths. From this point on, the reader is almost constantly aware of Boswell at Johnson's side; the narrative is much more lively once he appears. The special flavour of the *Life of Johnson* derives from the fact that the biographer is a character in his own book.[2] Readers see Boswell coming to London in the hope of meeting Johnson; writing him letters that he did not send; contemplating writing his life; and proposing the idea to him, very tentatively. It is like watching a play when you can see the stage-hands, the actors waiting to come on, and indeed the playwright scribbling in the wings. Apparently everything is on view; but the more that can be seen, the less obvious it becomes where the true drama is taking place.

Though the Samuel Johnson evoked in Boswell's biography is one of the most powerful personalities in literature, as real as any character in fiction, he never quite escapes from his disciple, James Boswell: they remain as much a pair as Don Quixote and Sancho Panza, or Holmes and Watson. Indeed, much of the pleasure in reading the *Life of Johnson* comes from the presence of Boswell as narrator, just as the presence of Watson (whom Holmes compared to Boswell) supplies much of the pleasure in the Sherlock Holmes stories. There are passages where Johnson appears to be sharing a confidence with the reader, while Boswell struggles to keep up, as if the writer was the last one to be let in on the joke. Johnson's amusement shines through the surface of Boswell's prose.

On the other hand, there are many occasions when Boswell seems almost like a ventriloquist, putting words into Johnson's mouth. He became adept at steering the conversation in directions which would stimulate Johnson to say something memorable; he was proud of this ability, though often it required him to play the straight man alongside Johnson, the butt of Johnson's wit. In this sense Boswell was creating his own copy, the reporter making news for himself.

Johnsonian scholars complain that Boswell has monopolized Johnson: that his gigantic biography dwarfs anything else written about his subject, or even by him. Edmund Burke, who knew them both, remarked that Johnson appears greater in Boswell's books than in his own. Today, people are much more likely to read Boswell's book about Johnson than they are to read Johnson himself. But that is not to say that Boswell was the greater man. Johnson's greatness lay in his mind, the art of thinking, that process which Boswell found so difficult; and it found its most lasting expression in his conversation—more lasting than his writing, which even in his own lifetime was beginning to seem dated. Johnson's particular genius was to express in trenchant form eternal truths; like Oscar Wilde, he is perennially quotable.

Boswell kept a record of Johnson's talk in brief memoranda, noted down as soon as possible afterwards, later written up into a journal, which eventually became a principal source for his biography. This method of recording was flawed; even if the notes were scribbled down the same evening, there was plenty of opportunity for error. Though Boswell had a remarkable memory, it was not infallible; and to recon-struct Johnson's conversation Boswell had to call on his own imagination as well. In this sense the Johnson of the *Life* is Boswell's creation. But Boswell spent so much time in the company of his subject that Johnson's forms of speech, even the patterns of his thought, were deeply imprinted on the younger man's mind. Thus Boswell was to some extent Johnson's creation also, and thus he was able to recapture a version of what Johnson had said many years afterwards, and hand it on to us.

The *Life of Johnson* can be read as an unending contest between author and subject for posterity. Johnson and Boswell are locked together for all time, in part-struggle, part-embrace. Boswell will for-ever be known as Johnson's sidekick, remembered principally because he wrote the life of a greater man; Johnson is immortalized but also imprisoned by the *Life,* known best as Boswell portrayed him. Each is a creation of the other.

For the first hundred years or so after the *Life of Johnson* was pub-lished, critics tended to take the line that it was a great book written by a simpleton who just happened to be in the right place at the right time. The set-piece conversations seemed no more than a naïve record. Then a succession of astonishing finds—the literary equivalent of the discovery of Tutankhamen's tomb—revealed a "colossal hoard"[3] of Boswell manuscripts, including the manuscripts of the *Life of Johnson* and its precursor *The Journal of a Tour to the Hebrides,* and his journals, among the most revealing ever written. We now have much more information about the biographer than we do about his subject. From being regarded as a little man who wrote a great book, Boswell came to be seen as an important literary figure, a pioneer of modern biography—and of autobiography, for the focus of academic interest has shifted from subject to author, from Boswell's books to his journals and manuscripts. It has become clear that many of the best-loved passages in the *Life of Johnson* originated in Boswell's autobiographical journal, and that Boswell was a much more careful and ambitious writer than anybody had supposed. No longer is Boswell regarded as a mere "stenographer," a secretary taking down Johnson's dictation, but as a writer of consummate skill, even genius. But just as these discoveries have led to a greater appreciation of Boswell as a writer, so they have prompted fresh questions about the fidelity of his book. The publication of Boswell's letters and journals started a scholarly debate about the accuracy of the *Life of Johnson:* was it really what it appeared to be, or was it a disguised piece of fiction? Was Boswell's insistence on authenticity a cover? To what extent had Boswell "invented" Dr Johnson, as George Bernard Shaw suggested?[4] And, indeed, himself?

When I became interested in the subject, I first thought of writing a full biography of Boswell, but I soon changed my mind. For one thing, there are several good biographies of Boswell already.[5] I also found that my attention tended to flag when Boswell was not in Johnson's company; it was not Boswell the man that interested me (though he was a very interesting man), so much as Boswell the biographer. As someone who had worked in publishing, I had witnessed the scramble to memorialize an important literary figure after his death; and as a writer, I had experienced the pressures of writing a biography in competition with rivals. I became absorbed in trying to answer questions such as: What drew Boswell to Johnson in the first place? Why did he want to write about Johnson, and why did he persist, in the face of so much adversity? How did he set about his task? Did his ideas change as his writing progressed? Many of the biographical issues Boswell faced are commonplace nowadays, but were quite new when he tackled them. How did he evaluate the varied and sometimes contradictory material he gathered? Why did he put so much stress on verification? How did he deal with "delicate" topics: for example, Johnson's sexual dalliance with a young widow, while his wife was asleep in the next room? Boswell's journals and manuscripts provide a cornucopia of fresh information for anyone seeking the answer to such questions.

My book traces Boswell's erratic course during the years after Johnson's death as he wrote the *Life of Johnson* and *The Journal of a Tour to the Hebrides*. It is rare—possibly unique—to be able to follow the route of an author so closely as he researches and writes his book. Such an approach is, I think, full of fascination, and makes intelligible many aspects of Boswell's book that have previously been a mystery. I have attempted to deconstruct the *Life of Johnson,* through careful study of the published sources and through cautious speculation when these give out: to show how Boswell arrived at decisions about his biography as they arose, how he overcame the manifold difficulties that lay in his path, and how he adjusted the facts to fit his own heroic conception of his subject: how life became translated into art.

The book begins with a biographical sketch of Boswell, leading into his meeting with Johnson and their burgeoning friendship. In this opening part, I outline some of the ideas which are later explored in more detail. I show how Boswell's admiration for Johnson, culminating in his book, originated in his own desperate need for a figure to admire, a mentor, an idol whom he could put onto a pedestal. For Boswell, Johnson represented a pinnacle of sanity, of common sense; he dreaded Johnson's death, though it would free him to write the work that would eventually bring him fame.

The story of Boswell's life as he wrote the epic *Life of Johnson* is itself an epic: in the process Boswell experienced an extraordinary degree of exhilaration and depression, pride, humiliation, confidence, doubt, satisfaction, hurt, loneliness, disillusionment, and grief. As soon as Johnson died, several biographers entered a race to cash in on his memory, a race that Boswell seemed to have lost when their books appeared before his. He was warned that interest in Johnson was waning, but he continued to miss deadline after deadline. Newspapers gloated at his distress; rivals belittled his role in Johnson's life; friends berated him for being so dilatory. To many, the Great Work seemed a Great Folly. His persistence, his desire to verify even the smallest detail, were ridiculed in the press. It seemed as if he would never finish; he almost abandoned the book in despair. He sank into glooms which rendered him incapable of work for weeks on end. Meanwhile, lack of money caused him constant anxiety. He kept abandoning his book to pursue his career, often for months at a time. At various points he lapsed into heavy drinking, which left him hung over and unable to write. Often he worked while eating, concentrating despite the domestic distractions around him. He neglected his wife, who was terminally ill with tuberculosis; when she died he was tormented by remorse. As he accumulated more and more source-material, the book swelled; he was warned that nobody would buy such a huge biography at the high price that it would inevitably command. In the wreckage of his disordered mind, he clung to the memory of Johnson as a shipwrecked sailor clings to a rock. In the midst of his disappointment and despair, Boswell immortalized the life of the man he revered above all others.

By the time the book was finished, his life was in chaos. Boswell had reached fifty without winning any of the glittering prizes he had once confidently anticipated. He had abandoned the Edinburgh bar, but his career at the English bar was at a standstill. His hopes of a seat in Parliament had come to nothing. No other official post that he considered suitable to his talents had come his way, something he found difficult to explain. An arrogant and insulting patron humiliated him. He had disgraced himself repeatedly by drinking and whoring, to the distress of his family and the detriment of his health. His outrageous behaviour made him a laughing-stock. He was embarrassed by debt. As his ambitions withered, one by one, he became desperate; increasingly, his monumental biography of his friend Samuel Johnson was his last hope of achieving anything worthwhile. The book became an apologia—not just for Johnson, but for Boswell, too. In making Johnson a hero, Boswell made sense of his own life.

The final part of my book shows what happened after the *Life of Johnson* was published. Several of Johnson's friends objected to the way they had been depicted in his biography, and shunned Boswell; he acquired the reputation of a man who could not be trusted. The effort had left him exhausted. Sozzled with drink, riddled by venereal infection, despairing of all his hopes, he simply faded away.

After Boswell's death the reputation of his book grew steadily, while his own shrank in proportion. The biography's fame promoted the image of its author as Johnson's stooge. Even in his own lifetime Boswell had been mocked as Johnson's lackey; the book made him seem no more than a cipher. While the *Life of Johnson* came to be recognized as one of the greatest works written in the English language, the name Boswell became a byword for a fool.

This is a story about literature: about the genesis of one of the most famous books ever written. But it is also a story about life: about an unlikely friendship between two very different but both, in their own ways, delightful men. They made such a contrast: the one stern, the other frivolous; one heavy, the other skittish; one sceptical, the other proto-Romantic. And just as Johnson was quintessentially an Englishman, so Boswell was very conscious of being a Scot. Yet their mutual devotion transcended all their differences, to the greater glory of both.

PART ONE

LIFE LIVED

ONE

IMMATURITY

He has a method of treating me, which makes me feel myself like a timid boy.[1]

JAMES BOSWELL WAS BORN in 1740, into a family of Scots landed gentry. He was the eldest of three sons; a daughter had been born earlier, but she died when he was only three months old. Boswell's father, Alexander, an Edinburgh lawyer, was himself the eldest son and heir of another James Boswell, Laird of Auchinleck, a substantial Ayrshire estate about seventy miles south-west of Edinburgh and thirty miles south of Glasgow. This extended to some twenty thousand acres; it was said that the Master of Auchinleck could walk more than ten straight miles on his own land. Young Jamie was always keen to extend the estate, and even before he came into his inheritance he had already encumbered himself with sizeable debts in buying up adjacent property.

There had been Boswells at Auchinleck since 1504, living first in an old castle set on a crag high above a glen, and later in a more modern but still defensible house nearby. It was a romantic setting for the impressionable Jamie, who spent many of his holidays roaming the estate. In his imagination the Boswell family had lived there for ever; he conjured up images of classical scenes among the woods and groves of his ancestors.

As a boy, Boswell absorbed the family pride that made them (so his wife later said) appear ridiculous in the eyes of other people. He characterized himself as "a gentleman of ancient blood, the pride of which was his predominant passion."[2] The Boswells could trace their ancestry back to the Scots kings, and Boswell once informed a startled George III that they were cousins. He styled himself "Mr Boswell of Auchinleck" or, when abroad, "Boswell D'Auchinleck." He affected a gravitas which he felt becoming to one who would some day inherit responsibility for an estate of six hundred tenants. But at the same time he found it hard to settle there.

Boswell's grandfather had been a successful lawyer, whose earnings had enabled him to enlarge the estate and pass it on to his son free of debts. That son, Boswell's father, also became a lawyer, and rose to become a judge in the Court of Session, the supreme court for civil cases in Scotland. The bench of the Court of Session consisted of fifteen judges, and the appointment entitled the bearer to the style of a lord, Alexander Boswell taking the title Lord Auchinleck in 1754. This title did not allow the bearer to sit in the House of Lords, nor did it devolve onto his descendants. The following year Lord Auchinleck was appointed a judge in the Court of Justiciary, the supreme criminal court in Scotland.

Diligent and forceful, and noted for his dry, sarcastic wit, Lord Auchinleck resembled the archetypal Scots judge, speaking from the bench in a harsh Scottish brogue. He was a learned classical scholar, with no interest in modern literature, which he regarded with disdain. Strict and stern, he was intolerant of anything fanciful. He shared the general Presbyterian abhorrence of the theatre. As a father, he was domineering; Jamie barely dared open his mouth in his presence. Like most practical men in Hanoverian Britain, Alexander Boswell was a Whig; his eldest son fancied himself a Tory, even a Jacobite. When Edinburgh was overrun by a Jacobite army in 1745, the five-year-old James had declared himself for the Pretender—until his great-uncle General Cochrane offered him a shilling to pray for King George instead.

Boswell's father succeeded to the family estate in 1749, upon the death of the elder James Boswell. His work required him to live most of the year in Edinburgh, though he took a keen interest in practical estate matters (particularly tree-planting) and tried to instil a similar enthusiasm in his son.

Boswell's mother, Euphemia Erskine, was a gentle, pious, mystical woman, who brought up her children very tenderly, rewarding any small ailment with excessive attention. Young Jamie learned early that he could escape the slavery of school by pretending to be ill.

He was a sensitive child: self-indulgent, physically delicate, timid, terrified of ghosts, frightened of the dark, and tormented by morbid ideas of eternal punishment, on which he dwelt perhaps excessively. He was educated partly at an Edinburgh private school and partly by tutors at home, who taught him the Latin poets and encouraged him to read *The Spectator* as a model of English prose. At thirteen (then not an unusual age) he was sent to Edinburgh University, where he was a promising but not an exceptional student. There he made two life-long friends: the melancholic John Johnston, already Laird of Grange, a heavily mortgaged Dumfriesshire estate; and William Temple, a merchant's son from Berwick-upon-Tweed. Johnston would become a lawyer, Temple a clergyman. These three sat up into the night discussing philosophical issues and sharing their innermost thoughts; at the top of Arthur's Seat they chanted in solemn reverence the "immortal names" of Rousseau and Voltaire. Also at the university was a boy eighteen months younger than Jamie, Henry Dundas, whom Boswell and his friends looked down upon as a "coarse, unlettered dog"—though professionally he would eclipse them all.

At the age of sixteen, Boswell suffered a breakdown; "a terrible hypochondria seized me."[3] Nobody knows exactly what happened or why: only that the young man became very depressed. One possible trigger was the course in logic and metaphysics he was taking at the university: this forced him to confront questions he was unable to reconcile with the Calvinist faith in which he had been raised. In particular, he agonized over the apparent contradiction between God's foreknowledge and Man's free will. Whatever the cause, the breakdown was serious enough for him to quit the university for a while. To recuperate he was sent to the border village of Moffat, known then as the "Spa of Scotland." It was his second visit: at the age of twelve, he had been sent there to recover from an earlier illness, almost certainly another nervous complaint. Young Jamie recovered, and developed into a robust and lively young man; but for the remainder of his life he would suffer from spells of black depression—which he called "melancholy" or "hypochondria"—each lasting up to two or three weeks. In trying to describe what he felt at such times, he would often say that the "enamel" of philosophy protecting his mind had cracked, or was wearing thin. During these depressions existence seemed to him futile; he sank into a lethargy; his mind became "clouded." In his worst moments, he feared that he would go mad and do "some dreadful extravagant thing."

There was madness in the family. Boswell's grandfather, James Boswell the elder, was melancholic; and one of Boswell's uncles, also called James, ended his life in a strait-jacket. Boswell's father may have accentuated this family trait by marrying a cousin, both being descended from a common feeble-minded ancestor. Boswell's younger brother, John, became increasingly eccentric, and by the age of nineteen was no longer responsible for his actions; eventually, he would be confined to an institution. Lord Auchinleck, on the other hand, never felt one moment of low spirits without a real cause, as he pointedly informed his eldest son.

The idea that madness might be hereditary was prevalent in eighteenth-century Scotland. The landed classes were so intermarried that inherited qualities were all too evident. But it was also clear that madness took several distinct forms. There were those, like Boswell's younger brother, whose condition steadily deteriorated until they were permanently insane; and others, like Boswell himself, who suffered episodic attacks of gloom punctuated by long periods of normality. The origin of these attacks was not obvious; they did not appear related to any change in his circumstances. Boswell was certainly capable of bearing adversity without sinking into melancholia. He often ascribed his depressions to physical causes: inadequate circulation of the blood or incorrect functioning of the spleen. When feeling out of sorts he would sometimes refer to his mood as "splenetic." He would become listless, unable to concentrate or to exhibit interest in anything. Activity, particularly physical activity, provided relief. So did almost any form of distraction. The sulphur springs of Moffat would have been no use to a disordered mind, though perhaps the change of scene and long walks in the surrounding hills helped.

Boswell was not depressive by nature. On the contrary, most of the time he was high-spirited and boisterous: leaping up onto the back of coaches to hitch a ride, making romantic pledges on the hilt of his sword, writing extravagant letters, telling absurd stories, and roaring through the streets in search of adventure. Boswell himself had no doubt that the two sides of his character were connected, that the high spirits counterbalanced the low. "I have a flow of imagination that must not be altogether restrained," he wrote, "and spirits that must be fed with amusement, otherwise they will prey upon myself."[4] He scorned those dullards, like Henry Dundas, whose minds were always in a state of unruffled tranquillity.

His depression seemed to become less intense as he matured. It remained a debilitating condition nonetheless. And though he did not sink so deep, neither did he fly so high. By the time he reached thirty, he no longer felt those "grand ebullitions and bright sparkles" that had lit up his youth. "I *must* submit to life losing its vividness," he complained on one occasion.[5]

There is no doubt that Boswell's depression was real, but no doubt too that he felt a perverse satisfaction and pride in his gloom. A "cast of melancholy" was, he believed, a mark of a distinguished mind, or even of genius in the family.[6] Melancholy was a fashionable pose; there was a general perception that it was an affliction of superior intellects.

All this was so much nonsense to Lord Auchinleck. "I was much hurt at being good for nothing in life," Boswell wrote later of his first breakdown—which sounds like an echo of his father's words. He appeared to prolong his convalescence in Moffat deliberately; this would have been very irritating to his father, who had little sympathy for his son's condition. Forever after, he treated Jamie as a fool, checked him in conversation, and spoke of him disparagingly to others. Many years later, when Lord Auchinleck was dying, Boswell berated him for his lack of compassion towards his youngest son, John, by this time hopelessly insane. "If my sons are idiots," Lord Auchinleck cried out in exasperation, "can I help it?"[7]

As Boswell grew into a young man, the differences between him and his father became obvious. Indeed, the two could hardly have been more unalike: the son flighty, the father down-to-earth; the boy romantic and impulsive, the man prudent and restrained. Inevitably they came into conflict, Jamie see-sawing between rebellion and resentful compliance.

At the age of seventeen, young Boswell began to study law, under his father's direction. But perhaps sensing that he could never become the kind of son Lord Auchinleck hoped for, he began to search for an identity of his own, trying out roles until he found one that suited. One moment he was the Spectator, the detached and philosophic observer; the next, Tom Jones, the lusty innocent. He sought out older men who might serve as models for different ways of living, whose strength of character would help him to resist being crushed by his powerful father. One such was Sir David Dalrymple (later elevated to the bench as Lord Hailes), a man fourteen years older than Boswell: though a lawyer like Lord Auchinleck, he had been educated at Eton, which had smoothed away the rough Scottish edges to his speech and his prose; he corresponded with English literati and contributed to London papers such as the *Gentleman's Magazine*. Boswell admired him as "a man of great ingenuity, a fine scholar, an accurate critic, and a worthy member of society. From my early years I used to regard him with admiration and awe, and look upon him as a representative of Mr Addison."[8] Under Sir David's influence Boswell began to write verse (often of a ludicrous kind); a poem of his was published in the *Scots Magazine* while he was still only seventeen. Dalrymple became Boswell's first mentor, in whom he confided his schemes and from whom he sought advice; who also interceded for the young man when relations with his father became particularly strained.

It was not that Boswell rejected Lord Auchinleck: on the contrary, he respected him greatly and was careful never to voice the slightest criticism of him in public, even when they were in bitter dispute and Boswell felt sorely provoked. Once, he prepared to fight a duel to defend his father's honour against an imagined insult (typically, Lord Auchinleck dismissed the incident as trivial). But to achieve a sense of self-worth, of manly dignity, he needed an alternative to the standard set by his father, to whom he would be always a boy.

Lord Auchinleck's contempt undermined his son's confidence. Though he developed into an outgoing youth, Boswell remained unsure of himself, the child concealed within the man. He reacted stubbornly or even sulkily to criticism. He tended to avoid adult responsibilities; even in mid-life, he would ask others to determine his future for him—though if the advice provided was not to his liking, he ignored it and sought another opinion elsewhere, or tried to persuade the adviser to change his mind. His father's scorn might also explain Boswell's absurd vanity, so transparent as hardly to be objectionable. Boswell longed for approval; he was delighted by praise from any quarter—even from himself. But it was insecurity rather than conceit that fed his egotism.

By his late teens Boswell had grown into a swarthy young man, a little shorter and plumper than most, with a prominent, curving nose, dark eyes, a hungry appetite for experience, and an engaging cheerfulness, qualities which men found endearing and women attractive. For his part, Boswell became an enthusiastic participant in the game of love; melancholy temperaments, he once observed, are amorous temperaments. He became a shameless flirt. He was perpetually falling in love: falling out again just as readily, as one of his early poems suggests:

> Boswell does women adore,
> And never once means to deceive;
> He's in love with at least half a score,
> If they're serious he smiles in his sleeve.

Throughout his life Boswell could never quite free himself of the delusion that he had a talent for verse.

For all his philandering, Boswell was an innocent. Eager, inquisitive, and naïve, he was apt to repeat what other people had said without considering the consequences. He was not malicious, though his complete lack of tact sometimes made him seem so. "He had rather too little, than too much prudence," he wrote of himself many years later, "and his imagination being lively, he often said things of which the effect was very different from the intention." Irony was alien to him. He could be very lively company, often acting the buffoon; he admitted that he would sacrifice almost anything for a laugh, "even myself." Boswell tried to curb his tendencies to talk too much and too freely, to laugh immoderately, and to imitate other people "in a manner that might be hurtful if they discovered it. But he was an entertaining mimic, capable of impersonating several individuals in conversation, and the temptation to do so was often irresistible.

Boswell adored acting, when he could be anyone he wanted to be. He liked to cut a figure. He played the part of the gallant highwayman Macheath at a country-house gathering, and fancied himself in the role ever after. He frequented the theatre, then illegal (but tolerated) in Edinburgh, and he began to socialize with some of the actors, particularly West Digges, very much a man of fashion, reputedly the best Macheath of his generation. The young Boswell became infatuated with an actress, Mrs Cowper, a widow. He ran up debts. Gossip about his activities began to circulate. "You are continually in the Playhouse, I am told," Temple wrote enviously from Berwick. "I heard an odd story here of you and one Mrs Cooper."9

Lord Auchinleck decided to put a stop to this frivolity, and in September 1759 he informed his son of a change: Boswell would not be returning to Edinburgh for the autumn term. He was sent to continue his studies at the University of Glasgow, where there were fewer distractions (and no theatre). Among his tutors there was the Professor of Moral Philosophy, Adam Smith. Boswell attended Smith's lectures on Rhetoric and Belles-Lettres, and he was particularly struck by Smith's advocacy of a pure English style. It was a period when many educated Scotsmen struggled to eliminate Scots pronunciation from their speech and Scotticisms from their prose. David Hume, for example, was said to have died in 1776 confessing not his sins but his Scotticisms. Boswell was by no means the only Scotsman who felt proud of his blood but self-conscious about his accent. Here was another difference from his father, whose broad Scots diction was all of a piece with his blunt, caustic character.

Boswell's success as a mimic was founded on careful observation of those around him: particularly of their mannerisms and the cadences of their speech. Perhaps his sensitivity to Scots accents made him attentive to the way people spoke.

After six months in Glasgow, Boswell ran away. Perhaps influenced by Mrs Cowper, he had become interested in Catholicism; deciding that his love for her was hopeless, he announced in a letter to his father his plan to become a monk. Lord Auchinleck summoned him home; instead, Boswell mounted a horse and rode the three hundred miles to London in two and a half days. There he found dingy lodgings and launched himself upon the town. His religious interests soon surrendered to more worldly distractions, as he experienced for the first time "the melting and transporting rites of love" with a Miss Sally Forrester at the Blue Periwig, Southampton Street. He haunted the London theatre, and through his Edinburgh connections contrived to arrange an interview with David Garrick, the leading actor of the day, "the man whom from a boy I used to adore and look upon as a heathen god."[10] Garrick was quite a scalp for a nineteen-year-old—perhaps the most famous man in England, after the King.

Lord Auchinleck appealed to his Ayrshire neighbour, the urbane Earl of Eglinton, then living in London, to take the wayward boy in hand. Eglinton duly called at the unsavoury address he had been given, lent Boswell some money, and offered to act as his host. Soon Boswell was staying at Eglinton's elegant Mayfair house. His rebellion had lasted less than three weeks.

The Earl of Eglinton was a man of nearly forty, unmarried, with a reputation as a rake. He was very well connected, and soon introduced the young Boswell "into the circles of the great, the gay and the ingenious." He escorted Boswell to the spring races at Newmarket, and secured his admission to the Jockey Club. Among Eglinton's friends was another young man about Boswell's age, Edward, Duke of York, brother to Prince George (who would become King in a matter of months) and next in line to the throne. This was Boswell's first brush with royalty, and he found it exhilarating; he was astonished to find "simple Ned" a lad much like himself. An encounter with Laurence Sterne, then being lionized by London society on account of the recently published novel *Tristram Shandy,* renewed his enthusiasm for literature, especially when Sterne, accosted in the street by the young poet, commented favourably on Boswell's verse.

Boswell was intoxicated by the *beau monde:* the parties, the fine clothes, the fashionable society with its opportunities for gallantry with fine women, the glamour of Court, the excitement of the theatres and their beautiful painted ladies. Boswell decided that his future had to be here in London, and he wrote home suggesting that his father should purchase for him a commission in the Guards. This was the most glamorous of regiments, stationed in London or Windsor, with a splendid uniform.

"What have *I* done to deserve this?" asked Lord Auchinleck plaintively, when he received his son's letter. Not only would it be prohibitively expensive to purchase a commission in such a sought-after regiment; the life of an idle officer would surely prove ruinous to a young man like Jamie. The estate needed a man of business, not a man of pleasure; based in Edinburgh, not in London. Lord Auchinleck journeyed down to London to retrieve his feckless heir. After three months of freedom, Boswell returned home to resume his law studies, working under his father's strict supervision. If he worked hard, Lord Auchinleck promised that afterwards he might return to London, where he could try to obtain a commission through the favour of Eglinton, or some other influential person. Boswell reluctantly complied, though he felt like a "Newmarket courser" yoked to a dung-cart. He was perhaps less inclined to resist because he had contracted the first of many venereal infections and was suffering from its effects. In any case, he had little choice but to obey his father; he had no money of his own and Lord Auchinleck controlled the purse-strings.

> But my mind, once put in ferment, could never apply itself again to solid learning. I had no inclination whatever for the Civil Law. I learned it very superficially. My principles became more and more confused. I ended a complete sceptic. I held all things in contempt, and I had no idea except to get through the passing day agreeably . . . My fine feelings were absolutely effaced.[11]

Boswell did not hide his resentment at being brought home in chains and compelled to "conform to every Scots custom." He had tasted the delights of London; by comparison, Edinburgh provided poor fare. The broad Scots brogue of Robert Hunter, Professor of Greek at the University, made him groan: *"Will you hae some jeel**? o fie! o fie!"*[12]

*Jelly.

The young Boswell longed to be accepted as one of the fashionable upper classes, elegant in diction and demeanour, which meant suppressing Scots pronunciation, purging his speech of Scots expressions, and eliminating the informal "vulgarity" of manner prevalent in much Scots society. The Scots aristocracy looked south towards London, increasingly the capital of all Britain and not just England. Lord Auchinleck was a very respectable Scots gentleman, but he spoke with an accent and in an idiom that would have grated in London's politest drawing-rooms, had he ever chosen to visit them.

In 1761, Boswell attended the popular lectures on English language and public speaking given by Thomas Sheridan, the Irish actor-manager who had made himself something of an expert on "correct" English usage. Sheridan had come to Edinburgh at the invitation of the Select Society, a body of Scotland's most distinguished literary men. Boswell had been invited to join the Society, almost certainly at the suggestion of Sir David Dalrymple. The Society cannot have been *too* select, if young Boswell became a member; his literary output at this time was confined to the publication of some mediocre poems. Perhaps Sir David thought that membership of the Society might encourage the lad into better behaviour.

Between lectures Boswell sought out Sheridan, a man twice his age, and confided in him all his hopes, dreams, and ambitions. Sheridan no doubt enjoyed the attention of this earnest young man. He advised that Boswell's genius could flourish only in the fertile soil of London, and recommended that Boswell should prepare for the English bar, to enable him to live there permanently. He even registered Boswell's name at the Inner Temple. Boswell himself was certain that a glittering future awaited him in the nation's capital. "I am thinking of returning to England," he wrote to a like-minded Scots friend, "of getting into the House of Commons, of speaking still better than Mr Pitt, and of being made principal Secretary of State."[13]

Boswell continued to write poems and pamphlets, under a variety of pseudonyms: one that he would often use in later life being "A Gentleman of Scotland," another simply "A Genius." He dedicated his pseudonymous *Ode to Tragedy* to "James Boswell Esq." In 1762, he produced at his own expense *The Cub at Newmarket*, a semi-autobiographical piece of Shandean whimsy. He had written this while in London with Eglinton, and read it aloud to Prince Edward. He now issued it with a Dedication to his royal chum—a monumental gaffe, a piece of *lèse-majesté* which annoyed the Prince (now trying to live down his playboy image) and mortified Eglinton. It was the first of many such.

Another of Boswell's (unfinished) productions during this period was a dramatized "song" (a sort of opera) entitled *Give Your Son His Will*. A young man is wishing to enter the Guards; his father prefers him to go into trade. It was not hard to identify the individuals involved.

Matters between Boswell and his father now came to a crisis. Lord Auchinleck threatened to sell off the estate; better, he said, to snuff out a candle than leave it stinking in its socket. He was dissuaded (perhaps by his wife) from taking such an irrevocable step, but he compelled Boswell to sign a deed surrendering his hereditary rights; it empowered his father, if he so chose, to leave the estate in the hands of trustees after his death. This was a public acknowledgement that Lord Auchinleck thought his heir incompetent to manage the property, a humiliation for them both. In return he settled Boswell's debts, and guaranteed him an allowance of £100 a year—£10 more than he would have earned as a Guards officer. When Boswell left for London, his father increased this allowance to £200. Even this was not enough to prevent Boswell from sinking further into debt. Though a contemporary essayist had written that £50 per annum "was undoubtedly more than the necessities of life require," Boswell found it impossible to live on four times that amount. In London he budgeted £50 for lodgings alone, and the same sum for clothes, not to mention such extravagances as wax candles, having his hair dressed and sheets cleaned every day, and "sundries"—by which he meant prostitutes.

Around this time Lord Auchinleck abandoned the old family house and began building a neo-classical mansion in the Adam style, surrounded by parkland. It was an appropriate home for a prosperous landowner, in a Scotland domesticated by the Union. Above the doorway was a frieze with symbols denoting the occupations of Lord Auchinleck, his brother, and his sons. Carved into the stone was a Latin inscription from Horace, *Quod petis hic est, est Ulubris, animus si te non deficit aequus*—"What you are looking for is here, at Ulubrae, if only balance of mind doesn't desert you." Ulubrae was a town renowned for its remoteness from Rome, and it is difficult to read this as anything but a heavy hint to Lord Auchinleck's eldest son.

But Boswell lacked the *animus aequus*. He was repeatedly drawn to the bright lights of London, where his status as a Scots landed gentleman attracted as much derision as respect.

In the autumn of 1762, after scraping through his law examinations, Boswell was at last allowed to return to London to pursue his scheme of obtaining a commission in the Guards. He was taken by Eglinton to dine at the Beefsteak Club, where he attempted to convince the Earl that he was no longer the "raw, curious, volatile, credulous" youth he had been two years earlier. "My Lord," said Boswell, "I am now a little wiser." "Not so much as you think," replied Eglinton.[14]

As if to confirm Eglinton's observation, Boswell soon received a sharp rebuke from David Hume. Boswell had been introduced to Hume, the most luminous of all the Edinburgh philosophers, when he was only seventeen; Hume was at that time nearly fifty. Boswell had confessed that he was not clear whether it was right for him to keep company with an unrepentant atheist; but then, the young man declared, "How much better are you than your books!" Hume had taken Boswell's observation bravely. But now, five years on, he was annoyed to discover that Boswell, together with his friends Andrew Erskine and George Dempster, had published a pamphlet in which they quoted remarks and opinions Hume had expressed in private:

> You must know, Mr James Boswell, or James Boswell Esquire, that I am very much out of humour with you and your two companions or co-partners. How the devil came it into your heads . . . to publish in a book to all the world what you pretend I told you in private conversation?

In reply Boswell rather feebly protested that the David Hume quoted in the pamphlet was not him but another David Hume, a bookseller in Glasgow.[15]

After two venereal infections, Boswell was determined to avoid "houses of recreation." Instead, he began to lay siege to an actress two years older than him, Mrs Lewis (identified in his journal as "Louisa").

The campaign culminated in a successful seduction at the Black Lion Inn, off Fleet Street, where he had registered under the name of Digges. "Five times was I lost in supreme rapture." Afterwards he proudly noted, "I surely may be styled a Man of Pleasure." Alas, ardour cooled, and a week later an examination confirmed his suspicions: "Too, too plain was Signor Gonorrhoea." Louisa was a woman "hackneyed in the ways of gallantry." On medical advice he confined himself to lodgings in Fleet Street, busying himself with a programme of systematic reading, beginning with the six volumes of Hume's recently completed *History of England*. Far from being downcast, he was delighted by this enforced break:

> How easily and cleverly do I write just now! I am really pleased with myself; words come skipping to me like lambs upon Moffat Hill . . . There's fancy! There's simile! In short, I am at present a genius.[16]

He was still searching for an identity he could make his own: "I felt strong dispositions to be Mr Addison," he wrote, soon after arriving in London: "Mr Addison's character in sentiment, mixed with a little of the gaiety of Sir Richard Steele and the manners of Mr Digges, were the ideas which I aimed to realize."[17] Jocular, garrulous, and noisy, Boswell longed to be grave, dignified, and reserved. He strove to acquire a more polished manner, "a composed genteel character" very different from the "rattling uncultivated one" of his youth. He practised reserve, and was vexed when friends arrived from Edinburgh and teased him about becoming dull.[18]

Boswell tried to regulate his behaviour with daily memoranda, in which he set out the programme for the day ahead. He addressed himself in the second person, as if holding a conversation with himself. The injunction "Be retenu" appears in these memoranda frequently—hold yourself back.

The young Scot could scarcely have chosen a less favourable moment to come to London. Englishmen—Londoners in particular—felt swamped by a flood of Scotsmen spreading south in search of fame and fortune. The young King George—grandson of the previous King,

George II, and only a couple of years older than Boswell—had made a Scotsman, Lord Bute, his Prime Minister, at the expense of William Pitt, the English "patriot" who had led his country to a succession of thrilling victories over the French and Spanish in what had become known as the Seven Years War. It seemed inconceivable that Pitt, the Churchill of his day, could be superseded; but he was. Bute had been Prince George's counsellor for some years before his accession, and Bute's secretary, the Scots playwright John Home, his tutor. Writing of the new King to Joseph Baretti in Milan, the Englishman Samuel Johnson expressed his doubts about expecting too much from a young man who had been "long in the hands of the Scots."[19]

Bute, as First Lord of the Treasury and the King's principal adviser, controlled the extensive patronage dispensed by the Crown. He was suspected of favouring his fellow-countrymen; the arrival of so many Scots in town seemed to indicate that they were being preferred. Scotsmen were seen as freeloaders, enjoying all the benefits of the Union without contributing their share of revenue to the public purse (taxes raised in the whole of Scotland were said to be less than half the amount raised in Yorkshire alone). Concomitant with this jealousy of the Scots was a more general anxiety that Scotsmen (Bute in particular) would encourage the reassertion of royal power to crush hard-won English liberties. Had not the Stuart kings repeatedly called on Scots armies to suppress the people? The forty-five Scots MPs were thought to be willing instruments of royal oppression; and, as well as these, a disproportionate number of Scotsmen sat for English constituencies. When he met Boswell for the first time, Johnson was sensitive on the subject of patronage, not least because he had recently accepted a Crown pension from the hand of Lord Bute: a welcome but somewhat embarrassing gift to the man who had defined the word "pension" in his *Dictionary* as "pay given to a state hireling for treason to his country."

As Boswell arrived in London, English resentment of Scots influence was seething. Bute's government had just signed the preliminaries of an unpopular peace, returning many of the fruits of victory (Cuba and the Philippines, for example) to defeated opponents. Boswell had been in the capital barely a fortnight when he witnessed an unpleasant outbreak of English xenophobia at the Covent Garden Theatre. Just before the overture began, two Highland officers came into the pit, where Boswell was standing. The mob in the upper gallery hissed, "No Scots! No Scots!" and pelted them with apples. Boswell's Scottish blood boiled with indignation. He leaped up onto the benches and roared out, "Damn you, you rascals!" At that moment, he "hated the English; I wished from my soul that the Union was broken and that we might give them another Bannockburn."[20]

Afterwards Boswell spoke to the two officers: they explained that they had just returned from the West Indies, where they had been on active service in the army of Great Britain. "And this is the thanks we get," they complained bitterly, "to be hissed when we come home." Had the mob been French, could they have done worse?

Indeed, the Highland regiments had served the nation well during the war that was coming to an end. But Scots soldiers were still associated in English minds with Jacobite rebellion; less than twenty years earlier, an invading Scots army led by Prince Charles Edward Stuart had reached as far south as Derby, causing panic in London. Londoners had only to look up to be reminded of these events; the heads of two Jacobite officers were still to be seen rotting on pikes over Temple Bar.[21]

Since the Act of Union in 1707, the two countries had been united by treaty, but not yet by sentiment. The very name "Britain" was disliked by the English. When George III told Parliament that "I glory in the name of Britain," suspicious Englishmen wondered why he did not glory in the name of England.

Anti-Scottish feeling was inflamed by the satirical publication the *North Briton*—meaning Scot—edited by the pungent poet Charles Churchill and the libertine MP John Wilkes, who himself had been passed over for a lucrative job (Governor of Quebec) in favour of a Scotsman. The *North Briton* (the *Private Eye* of its day) relentlessly attacked the Government, Bute in particular, who, it suggested (almost certainly wrongly), was the lover of the young King's mother. Bute was abused, insulted, and threatened with violence by the mob, so much so that he took to travelling around town with a group of heavies to protect him. While the *North Briton* heated the resentment felt towards the Scots, Churchill's poem *A Prophecy of Famine* (1763) encouraged the erroneous impression that famine in Scotland was driving Scotsmen south. There was a strong sexual undercurrent to this Scottophobia: just as Bute was supposed to be preying on the Dowager Queen, so Scotsmen in general were thought to be rapacious in their pursuit of English wives and daughters.[22] The *North Briton* and other scurrilous publications seethed with references to ballooning kilts; implicit was the fear of what lay beneath them. The lewd behaviour of young men like Boswell and his fellow-Scot James Macpherson seemed to match the stereotype. When asked why he stayed in England if he disliked the English so much, Macpherson replied, "Sir, I hate John Bull, but I love his daughters."[23]

The most notorious issue of the *North Briton* was number 45, published towards the end of April 1763. (The numeral was in itself significant, referring as it did not only to the '45 rebellion, but also to the number of Scots MPs.) In it Wilkes suggested that the King's speech to Parliament on the peace just concluded had been a pack of lies. Everyone knew that such speeches were written by ministers, just as they are today, and that was how Wilkes had treated it; but a panicky Government took the view that Wilkes had libelled the King. It was decided that Wilkes should be prosecuted; in the haste to silence such a damaging propagandist, he was seized and taken to the Tower before a warrant could be obtained. Such a clumsy exercise of arbitrary power played into Wilkes's hands, and within a matter of days he had to be discharged, on the grounds of parliamentary privilege. Bute resigned. An immense crowd gathered outside Wilkes's house in Great George Street and cheered as he stood bowing from the window.

This scene took place only ten days before Boswell's first meeting with Samuel Johnson. It was the climax to the English resentment of the Scots, which abated once Bute's influence was seen to have diminished. Johnson was no supporter of Wilkes: quite the contrary. Wilkes was "a vile Whig"; Johnson a Tory. Wilkes championed liberty; Johnson preached subordination. In politics they were at opposite poles. But they were both Englishmen, with English fears and prejudices. No less than Wilkes, Johnson was ready to defend England against the Scots "invasion." So when an importunate young Scotsman appeared before him, Johnson was inclined to be scathing.

FORWARDNESS

I do indeed come from Scotland, but I cannot help it.

BOSWELL FIRST ENCOUNTERED Samuel Johnson in his books. Lord Auchinleck possessed one of the best libraries in Scotland, and there the impressionable young Jamie, in revolt against his upbringing but unsure which way to go, found the essays that Johnson called *The Rambler.* They were just what he needed. Johnson's writing is reassuring: he shows his readers how to live. "The observations of a strong mind operating on life" (to quote Johnson's own words about Bacon's essays), delivered in authoritative, aphoristic prose laced with tenderness and wit, comforted the confused and frightened boy. He read Johnson's works "with delight and instruction, and had the highest reverence for their author, which had grown up in my fancy into a kind of mysterious veneration, by figuring to myself a state of solemn elevated abstraction, in which I supposed him to live in the immense metropolis of London."[1] Many Scotsmen, including Lord Auchinleck, regarded Johnson as a heavy, pompous pedant; bolstered by his reading, Boswell felt able to reject his father's view. "In my opinion," wrote the young Boswell, "Mr Johnson is a man of much Philosophy, extensive reading, and real knowledge of human life."[2] He liked to read aloud Johnson's

Rambler essays in the evening. It was not just what Johnson wrote, but how he wrote, that was so impressive. As Boswell later put it, "Johnson writes like a teacher. He dictates to his readers as if from an academical chair. They attend with awe and admiration; and his precepts are impressed upon them by his commanding eloquence."[3]

Johnson bulked large in the public imagination. He brought a keen intellect and a fresh approach to each of the areas he touched. He hacked away mightily at tired literary conventions; under his blows the rotten trees of the past came crashing down, one after another. Johnson was beholden to no one; his only loyalty was to the reader; he spoke directly to the heart. Though his politics were conservative, his instincts were democratic. He measured the subjects he examined by the yardstick of everyday experience, and brought common sense to bear in areas choked by pedantry and obfuscation. Johnson came to prominence when books and periodicals were being published in greater numbers than ever before, as writers and publishers experimented with new forms to meet a seemingly insatiable demand for literature of all kinds. By the middle of the century, literacy had spread to a majority of the population; the reading public was not much smaller than it is today. This rapidly expanding market sustained an industry of writers, publishers, booksellers, and printers. Authors were no longer gentlemen-amateurs, content to circulate their works to like-minded friends in manuscript, nor were they courtiers beholden to an aristocratic patron—they could subsist, and though a majority lived in poverty, a few of them could become rich, as Pope or Richardson had done, solely on the income from their books. Johnson personified the professional author as none other. Though his sales were not enormous, his influence was pervasive. His powerful personality, his manifest integrity, his distinctive style, his penetrating intellect, his original ideas, his prodigious learning, his extraordinary versatility, and his imposing figure combined to make him a dominant literary presence.[4]

In Edinburgh Boswell had frequently heard Thomas Sheridan expatiate on Johnson's extraordinary knowledge, talents, and virtues, repeat his pointed sayings, and boast of being his guest, sometimes until two or three in the morning. He therefore looked forward confidently to meeting Johnson at Sheridan's house in London—though he was apprehensive, because he had "heard much" of Johnson's supposed prejudice against the Scots. Every Scotsman was familiar with the infamous definition of oats in Johnson's *Dictionary:* "A grain, which in England is generally given to horses, but in Scotland supports the people." What made this jibe so provocative was that it encapsulated the English vision of Scotland as a backward, primitive country.

On his arrival in London, Boswell was disappointed to find that Sheridan had quarrelled with Johnson, so badly that they were no longer on speaking terms. Moreover, Boswell quickly became disillusioned with Sheridan, who rejected a Prologue the young man had written for Mrs Sheridan's play *Elvira*. Once, Sheridan had been Boswell's "Socrates"; now, his "bad taste, his insolence, his falsehood, his malevolence" and his "Irish wrongheadedness" became apparent.[5]

Boswell's disappointment at finding Sheridan estranged from Johnson was relieved when he made the acquaintance of Tom Davies, an actor-bookseller who kept a shop in Russell Street, off Covent Garden market. Davies told Boswell that Johnson was very much his friend, and offered to introduce them. He arranged several meetings, which for one reason or another fell through. But at last, on 16 May 1763, Boswell happened to be sitting in Davies's back-parlour at about seven in the evening, when Johnson unexpectedly came into the shop. Davies spotted a formidable figure advancing towards the glass door: a huge man, shabbily dressed, whose powerful strides were punctuated by convulsive jerks. Assuming a portentous manner, Davies quoted Horatio's line to Hamlet on the appearance of his father's ghost: "Look, my Lord, it comes." This was the waggish atmosphere that Johnson entered; whereupon Davies, knowing Johnson's prejudice against the Scots, mischievously introduced Boswell as "the gentleman from Scotland"—despite Boswell's plea not to say where he was from. "I do indeed come from Scotland, but I cannot help it," protested Boswell. "That, Sir," replied Johnson disdainfully, "I find, is what a very great many of your countrymen cannot help."[6]

Johnson's crushing retort was a play on words. That Scotsmen come from Scotland was self-evident, and pointing it out made Boswell's apology seem absurd. This was a response to Boswell's abjectness, a quality Johnson despised. But Johnson also meant that a very great many Scotsmen—too many—were coming from Scotland to England.

Boswell was floored by Johnson's first words to him, but he was soon back on his feet. When Johnson began grumbling that Garrick—Johnson's former pupil, and one of the richest men in England—had refused him a theatre ticket worth three shillings, Boswell chirped up, "O, Sir, I cannot think Mr Garrick would grudge such a trifle to you." Once again he was knocked down. "Sir, I have known David Garrick longer than you have done: and I know no right you have to talk to me on the subject." Boswell felt "much mortified," but despite this rough reception he "remained upon the field," and when they were left alone together for a while Boswell "ventured to make an observation now and then," which Johnson "received very civilly." By the time Boswell rose to leave, they had been talking together for three hours. Davies saw him out; at the door Boswell complained a little at some of the hard blows the Great Man had dealt him, but his host told him not to be uneasy: "I can see he likes you very well."

Some days later Boswell called on Johnson at his lodgings in Inner Temple Lane. He felt some trepidation at visiting "the Giant in his den," but was pleased to find himself received very courteously. When the other gentlemen present got up to leave, Boswell rose too, but Johnson pressed him to stay. After they had chatted *tête-à-tête* for a while, Boswell again rose to leave, and Johnson again pressed him to stay. Eventually Boswell was permitted to go, with the promise that Johnson would call on him one evening; as he left, Johnson shook him cordially by the hand.

Boswell called on Johnson a second time three weeks later. Again Johnson shook the young man's hand on parting, and asked him why he did not call more often. Boswell shyly reminded his host of their first conversation. "Poh, poh!" said Johnson, with a smile. "Never mind these things. Come to me as often as you can. I shall be glad to see you."[7]

Johnson was then fifty-three, renowned as the author of the poems *London* and *The Vanity of Human Wishes,* the novel *Rasselas,* his biography of his friend Richard Savage, the *Rambler* and the *Idler* essays, and, of course, his *Dictionary.* He was known to be working on an edition of Shakespeare, which, it was confidently expected, would prove superior to any previously published. Johnson was unquestionably the most famous scholar in the land. If Garrick was Prince of the Stage, Johnson was Ruler of Literature—a tyrant, some complained. Boswell, by contrast, was a naïve twenty-two-year-old. His only publications at that time were some mediocre poems and reviews, and a silly, self-important volume of letters. But he was an attractive companion, and Johnson liked young people, as he told Boswell:

> because, in the first place, I don't like to think myself growing old. In the next place, young acquaintances must last longest, if they do last; and then, Sir, young men have more virtue than old men; they have more generous sentiments in every respect. I love the young dogs of this age; they have more wit and humour and knowledge of life than we had . . .[8]

Two of Johnson's closest friends were of Boswell's generation: Bennet Langton, who was three years older, and Topham Beauclerk, only one year older than Boswell. It was this pair—perhaps while they were still Oxford undergraduates—who had roused Johnson at three o'clock one morning and lured him out on a "frisk" that lasted well into the following day. Some years before, Langton, like Boswell, had come to town hoping to meet the author of *The Rambler,* and had been lucky enough to win his friendship at an even younger age, while Langton was still in his mid-teens. At this stage of his life, Johnson, a widower without any children of his own, was often lonely, and he welcomed lively company.

On Saturday, 25 June 1763, after a chance encounter at a chop-house, Boswell and Johnson arranged to have supper together at the Mitre Tavern on Fleet Street, just around the corner from where Johnson was living. Boswell, who was very gratified to find himself eating in such company, "opened my mind to him ingenuously, and gave him a little sketch of my life." He explained the difficulties he had been experiencing with Lord Auchinleck. "Your father has been wanting to make the man of you at twenty which you will be at thirty," opined Johnson. "Sir, a father and a son should part at a certain time of life," he continued. "I never believed what my father said. I thought he spoke *ex officio,* like a priest." The young man confessed to unorthodoxy in religion, and Johnson smiled. "Give me your hand," he said. "I have taken a liking to you." Boswell complained that he had not yet acquired much knowledge, and asked Johnson's advice; Johnson agreed to provide him with a plan of study. Boswell could scarcely believe his luck: "Will you really take a charge of me?" They sat talking until the early hours of the morning, over a couple of bottles of port. When the time came to go, Boswell exclaimed, "It is very good in you to allow me to be with you thus. Had it been foretold to me some years ago that I should pass an evening with the author of *The Rambler,* how should I have exulted!" Johnson replied cordially that he was glad that they had met. "I hope we shall pass many evenings and mornings too, together."

"I am now upon a very good footing with Mr Johnson," Boswell wrote proudly to Sir David Dalrymple. "When I am in his company, I am rationally happy. I am attentive, and eager to learn, and I would hope that I may receive advantage from such society. You will smile to think of the association of so enormous a genius with one so slender."[9]

A couple of weeks later, on the evening of 6 July, Boswell entertained Johnson and some others to supper at the Mitre. He had intended them to come to his lodgings, but only that morning he had quarrelled with his landlord (who believed, falsely but not implausibly, that he was concealing a girl in his rooms) and resolved not to spend another night in the house. In some distress, Boswell called on Johnson in the morning and explained his embarrassment. Johnson laughed: "Consider, Sir, how insignificant this will appear a twelvemonth hence." Boswell was relieved, and impressed by this reminder of his friend's good sense. "Were this consideration to be applied to most of the little vexatious incidents of life, by which our quiet is too often disturbed, it would prevent many painful sensations. I have tried it frequently, with good effect."

The guests included Johnson; Davies; the novelist, playwright, and biographer Oliver Goldsmith; and the Reverend Mr John Ogilvie, a Scots poet who, as Boswell noted, "was desirous of being in company with my illustrious friend, while I, in my turn, was proud to have the honour of showing one of my countrymen upon what easy terms Johnson permitted me to live with him." Johnson enjoyed baiting his friend Goldsmith, an awkward, improvident, and slightly ridiculous Irishman, whose genius he nevertheless acknowledged and championed. The conversation ranged over a number of topics: Goldsmith "disputed very warmly," and Johnson retaliated "with great fervour." It was into this animated discussion that the unlucky Ogilvie plunged with the seemingly irrelevant observation that "Scotland had a great many noble wild prospects." Johnson's sally produced a roar of applause: "I believe, Sir, you have a great many. Norway, too, has noble wild prospects; and Lapland is remarkable for prodigious noble wild prospects. But, Sir, let me tell you, the noblest prospect which a Scotchman ever sees, is the high road that leads him to England!"[10]

Johnson liked to tease the Scots whenever an opportunity presented itself. He disliked various aspects of Scottish society, particularly Presbyterianism, which he saw as narrow and intolerant. But there were many individual Scotsmen whom he liked, not least Boswell himself. "There are few people to whom I take so much to [sic] as you," Johnson had assured him, within only a few weeks of their first meeting. "Boswell, I believe I am easier with you than almost anybody," he would later say. Indeed, Johnson's mockery was often affectionate. Joshing was in his nature.

English resentment of the Scots, even at its most virulent, was never strong enough to prevent friendly relations between Englishmen and Scotsmen. Boswell was introduced to both Wilkes and Churchill only a few days after Wilkes's release from prison; they were "very civil to me, and Wilkes said he would be glad to see me in George Street." Boswell enjoyed the *North Briton,* which he tried to obtain on the day it was issued, and he sent on each number to a friend in Edinburgh once he had read it; he even submitted his own essay, which was not published. "There is a poignant acrimony in it that is very relishing," Boswell noted of the *North Briton;* he did not seem to resent its attacks on Scotland and the Scots.[11] In fact, he prevailed on Wilkes to "frank" a few of his letters—members of Parliament could post letters free of charge by franking them, and the system was widely abused—"to astonish a few North Britons."

Eight days after the supper-party at which Ogilvie had been trounced by Johnson, Boswell and Johnson met again at the Mitre, this time by themselves. The young man wondered how the two of them should be such very good companions, unlike Boswell and his father, even though Johnson was almost exactly the same age and certainly as learned as Lord Auchinleck. (Indeed, there were other similarities between these two: both formidable personalities, and both classical scholars with practical interests.) Johnson thought the difference might be that he was a man of the world, whereas Lord Auchinleck was a judge in a remote part of the country. "Besides, there must always be a struggle between father and son, while the one aims at power and the other at independency." After they had drunk two bottles of port between them, Johnson took Boswell by the hand, exclaiming, "My dear Boswell! I do love you very much."

Johnson recommended Boswell to keep a journal of his life, "full and unreserved" (he gave others the same advice). "He said it would be a very good exercise, and would yield me great satisfaction when the particulars were faded from my remembrance." His young friend was delighted to reveal that he was already doing so.

Boswell had decided to mark his stay in London by keeping a daily journal. This was a practice advocated by Addison, as a means of cultivating refinement. To keep a journal, and to peruse it frequently, was to be a spectator of oneself. It helped the writer to lead a better, fuller life.[12]

He began keeping his journal a couple of months before leaving Scotland, so as to be fluent when the moment of departure arrived. During this probationary period, he developed "an excellent method of taking down conversations," noting at the time the essence of what was being said so that later he was able to reconstruct the whole from memory. He also learned the technique of introducing ("starting") subjects, to stimulate his companions into saying something worthy of record.[13] Once he arrived in London, his journal became fuller, in response to the great variety of new sensations and impressions he was experiencing. As he settled into the journal, Boswell carried out various narrative experiments: recording fragments of conversations overheard in a coffeehouse, for example, or dramatizing dialogue:

BOSWELL. You must know, Madam, I run up and down this town just like a wild colt.

LADY MIRABEL. Why, Sir, then, don't you stray into my stable, amongst others?[14]

One of Boswell's motives in beginning a journal was to develop his style. "I have an ardent desire for literary fame," he would confess a few years later, in the Preface to his first book. He craved recognition as a writer, and he knew that there was no better way to improve his prose than by practice, always taking pains to express himself as clearly and accurately as possible. "Style is to sentiment what dress is to the person," he noted in his journal. "The effects of both are very great, and both are acquired and improved by habit. When once we are used to it, it is as easy to dress neatly as like a sloven; in the same way, custom makes us write in a correct style as easily as in a careless, inaccurate one."*[15] By "correct style" Boswell was not referring to some abstract standard, but using the term in the sense of precise, accurate prose. Johnson had counselled his young friend that his journal should be a history of his own mind, and Boswell strove to develop a style capable of transmitting directly to paper his thoughts and perceptions. Sometimes he failed in the attempt; "I cannot portray Commissioner Cochrane as he exists in my mind," he wrote in his journal, many years later. In describing his method, Boswell often used the metaphor of engraving to describe the degree of fidelity he strove for; "I find it almost impossible to *take off an exact impression* of the state of my mind at this time," he lamented on another occasion.[16] Reading Boswell's journal would be like reading his mind; reviewing his journal at a later date would enable Boswell to relive the events he had recorded. The effect was spontaneous and natural, even artless; but it resulted from conscious effort.

Boswell felt that the act of writing regularly was beneficial in itself, both as a discipline which would encourage the habit of application and as a means of staving off the depression which often resulted from inactivity. Moreover, he hoped that "knowing that I am to record my transactions will make me more careful to do well. Or if I should go wrong, it will assist me in resolutions of doing better . . ." This may

---

*Asked by Sir Joshua Reynolds how he had attained such extraordinary accuracy and flow of language, Johnson replied that "he had early laid it down as a fixed rule to do his best on every occasion, and in every company; to impart whatever he knew in the most forcible language he could put it in; and that by constant practice, and never suffering any careless expressions to escape him, or attempting to deliver his thoughts without arranging them in the clearest manner, it became habitual to him."

have been one reason why Johnson encouraged him to keep a journal, as a means by which the young man might police his own behaviour. Boswell's friend Temple warned him that his journal did him harm, as it made him hunt for adventures with which to adorn it. Indeed, Boswell confessed that one of his motives for keeping a journal was to lay up "a store of entertainment for my after life." But he persisted in the belief, despite copious evidence to the contrary, that his journal helped him to improve. "As a lady adjusts her dress before a mirror," he observed many years later, "a man adjusts his character by looking at his journal."[17]

Boswell's London journal was written partly for his own edification and partly for his Edinburgh friend Johnston and his former tutor, Wilham McQuhae, to whom he sent it in weekly parcels. At this stage Boswell still saw himself as the romantic rake, the dashing man of the world who was also a poet and a philosopher. But his journal often showed its hero to disadvantage: foolish, weak, drunken, remorseful, ridiculous. Anyone with the slightest sense of discretion would have omitted some of the episodes he recorded; anyone with the least sense of guile would have put a more self-serving gloss upon them. Even his erotic adventures could appear as sordid transactions when experienced at second hand. It was dangerous to entrust such revealing narratives to others, even close friends; it could be only a matter of time before these stories became more widely known. Sure enough, McQuhae's host, the Reverend George Reid, somehow gained access to one of Boswell's early journals, and communicated part of its damaging content to Lord Auchinleck, including Boswell's rude remarks about people who had extended their hospitality to him. Embarrassed and annoyed, Lord Auchinleck reported Reid's remarks as a reproof to his son:

> He made these reflections, that he was surprised a lad of sense and come to age should be so childish as to keep a register of his follies and communicate it to others as if proud of them. He added that if the thing were known, no man would choose to keep company with you, for who would incline to have his character traduced in such a manner, and this frequently after your receiving the greatest civilities and marks of friendship?[18]

As if "these strange journals" were not enough, Lord Auchinleck was further mortified to hear of the publication of a volume of impudent letters between his son and another young Scotsman, the Honourable Andrew Erskine, full of gossip about their friends, families, and acquaintances: he had seen a sample reprinted in one of the newspapers, "and found that though it might pass between two intimate young lads in the same way that people over a bottle will be vastly entertained with one another's rant, it was extremely odd to send such a piece to the press, to be perused by all and sundry." The work had been reviewed in the *London Chronicle* as "a book of true genius, from the authors of which we may expect many future agreeable productions." The reviewer was Boswell himself. In fact, his father was right to be apprehensive; the letters gave widespread offence, particularly in Scotland. Eglinton, already nettled by Boswell's tactlessness in dedicating his poem *The Cub at Newmarket* to Prince Edward, urged Boswell to "give over that damned publishing"; nobody, he said, wanted an author in their house. "By the Lord, it's a thing [even] Dean Swift would not do — to publish a collection of letters upon nothing."[19] He accused the young man of having no sense of shame. Lord Auchinleck remonstrated with his son, and again threatened to disinherit him. Boswell's attempt to obtain a commission in the Guards had come to nothing, and in truth he was no longer sure that he wanted to be a soldier. A compromise was reached, whereby Boswell agreed to study law in the Dutch city of Utrecht, as his father and grandfather had done before. Afterwards he might travel a little in Europe, with Lord Auchinleck's blessing, before returning to Edinburgh to commence the serious business of life.

When Boswell mentioned his imminent departure, Johnson exclaimed affectionately, "My dear Boswell, I should be very unhappy at parting, did I think we were not to meet again." Boswell felt encouraged to share with his new friend the secret of his depressive illness:

> I complained to Mr Johnson that I was much afflicted with melancholy, which was hereditary in our family. He said that he himself had been greatly distressed with it, and for that reason had been obliged to fly from study and meditation to the dissipating variety of life. He advised me to have constant occupation of mind, to take a great deal of exercise, and to live moderately; especially to shun drinking at night.[20]

He found it "a great relief" to confide thus in Johnson. For some years Boswell had found that Johnson's writings alleviated mental and spiritual distress. Now he could draw solace from the man himself. Johnson counselled that melancholy should be resisted rather than endured, and showed him how. Simple mental exercises could keep depression at bay. Boswell had the type of mind that was easily distressed by moral or philosophical problems, particularly those which challenged his religious beliefs. Johnson's common-sense approach to these was immensely comforting to this flighty young man. When Boswell raised the question that had troubled him since his teens, the difficulty of reconciling free will with divinely ordained destiny, Johnson replied, "Sir, we *know* our will is free, and *there's* an end on't."[21] Responding to the philosopher Bishop Berkeley's belief in the non-existence of matter, Johnson kicked a large stone: "I refute it *thus*." And when Boswell described how his friend James Macpherson "railed at all established systems," Johnson observed that there was nothing surprising in this: "He wants to make himself conspicuous." Boswell had been perplexed by Macpherson's insistence that there was no distinction between virtue and vice; Johnson commented, "Why, Sir, when he leaves our houses, let us count our spoons."[22]

Boswell admired the manner in which Johnson applied his intellectual powers to practical, everyday problems. Johnson loved business, for example; he "loved to have his wisdom actually operate on real life."[23]

> His superiority over other men consisted chiefly in what may be called the art of thinking, the art of using his mind; a certain continual power of seizing the useful substance of all that he knew, and exhibiting it in a clear and forceful manner; so that knowledge, which we often see to be no better than lumber in men of dull understanding, was, in him, true, evident, and actual wisdom.[24]

Johnson was a man of reason who believed in God, a philosopher who applied his mind to moral questions, a pious Prometheus. Boswell, by contrast, was imaginative rather than analytical: romantic rather than rational. Johnson was valuable to Boswell *because* they were so unlike: Boswell submissive, Johnson domineering, Boswell a quivering jelly of sensibility, Johnson a solid mass of sense. Boswell was only too pleased to enrol in the Johnsonian school, to abandon any claim to intellectual independence.

During Boswell's last month in London before leaving to study law in Holland, the two men met every other day. Their friendship was now so well established that Johnson offered to accompany Boswell to Harwich to see him off. "I hope, Sir, you will not forget me in my absence," said Boswell, as they embraced on the beach. "Nay, Sir, it is more likely that you should forget me," replied Johnson.[25] He waited as Boswell's ship put out to sea. Boswell kept his eyes on the figure of his friend standing on the shore for a considerable time, "rolling his majestic frame in his usual manner," until at last "I perceived him walk back into the town, and he disappeared."[26]

As soon as Boswell arrived in Utrecht, he sank into a deep depression. He feared that his mind was "destroyed":

> I thought that at length the time was come that I should grow mad. I actually believed myself so. I went out into the streets, and even in public could not refrain from groaning and weeping bitterly.[27]

His only remedy against the black thoughts that invaded his mind was the thought of Johnson, "the ablest mental physician that I have ever applied to." Boswell's memoranda from this period are full of exhortations to "Think of Johnson," "Remember Johnson," "Be Johnson." Occasionally he mentions other examples to emulate, such as Lord Chesterfield (or even "Be Rock of Gibraltar"), but Johnson is predominant. "Mr Johnson is ever in my thoughts," he wrote to Temple, "when I can think with any manliness"[28] — by which he means moral courage. "O Johnson! how much do I owe to thee!" he wrote in his journal as he began to recover. He resolved "to pursue a rational plan of life," and drew up an "Inviolable Plan," to be read over frequently:

> For some years you have been idle, dissipated, absurd, and unhappy . . . all your resolutions were overturned by a fit of spleen. Your friend Temple showed you that idleness was your sole disease. The Rambler showed you that vacuity, gloom and fretfulness were the causes of your woe, and that you were only afflicted as others are . . . You studied with diligence. You grew quite well . . .[29]

Encouraged by a letter from Johnson, Boswell continued with his journal in Holland. By this time he was no longer writing for others, though he would occasionally allow friends to read passages from his journal; he was writing principally for himself, for his own entertainment and instruction, as Johnson recommended. From being a diversion, or an exercise, the journal quickly became central to his existence, an activity surpassing all others in importance. Even when the rest of his life was in turmoil, when a multitude of concerns demanded his attention, Boswell's first loyalty was to his journal: "Bring that up, and all will then be well."

The journal became a lifelong habit; within its pages Boswell amassed a vast hoard of memory which he raided for all his books. It made burdensome demands on his time; as a young man he would often work through the night to bring it up to date. Sometimes writing his journal kept him from activities he would otherwise have relished. It exposed him to the danger of discovery—a danger especially acute because of his commitment to record actions that most people would want to forget, and thoughts that few would admit even to themselves—and it was written in direct defiance of his father. So why did he do it? The compulsive nature of his journal-keeping suggests a powerful personal need.

Boswell once wrote that he wanted nothing about himself to be secret. In his journal he described behaviour that would be damaging if revealed, but left the journal about so that it could easily be read. Was this exhibitionism? Or confession? Sometimes he wrote in code, but at other times he provided explanatory details which strongly suggested that he was writing (perhaps subconsciously) for readers other than himself. His attitude to the possibility that others might read his journal remained equivocal throughout his life. After the journal he wrote in Holland was lost, Boswell was anxious that it should not be discovered and used against him, particularly as it revealed him in a pitiful mental state. More than ten years later, he came across some old boxes containing journals written by different persons. He was depressed to see "what had been written with care, and preserved as valuable, treated as lumber; and I could not but moralize on what might become of my own journals. However, they serve to entertain and instruct myself . . ." Later still, he read a revealing journal kept by a man who had died of "intemperance and dissolute conduct of every kind."

Reading this journal made me uneasy to think of my own. It is preserving evidence against oneself; it is filling a mine which may be sprung by accident or intention. Were my journal to be discovered and made public in my own lifetime, how shocking would it be to me! And after my death, would it not hurt my children? I must not be so plain. I will write to Dr Johnson on the subject.[30]

But despite such warnings, Boswell continued with his dangerous journal. He had a sense that his life had not been lived until it had been recorded—or perhaps that experience was meaningless unless a record had been preserved. "I should live no more than I can record," he once wrote, "as one should not have more corn growing than one can get in. There is a waste of good if it be not preserved."[31] At another point he wrote that he would go through almost anything with a degree of satisfaction if he could only put an account of it in writing. It was almost as if Boswell needed to reassure himself that he was real by committing his thoughts to paper. It is not unusual for a young man or woman to begin keeping a diary of some kind. The impulse is usually something like this: look at me: my life means something. What is more unusual is to continue such a diary into adulthood, when a man's sense of self is normally founded on his status within society and the respect he receives accordingly. "You are longer a boy than others," remarked Johnson later, when Boswell was in his mid-thirties.[32]

Boswell had a terror of oblivion. The notion that one day he would not exist, that nothing would remain of him but dust and bones, filled him with horror. The journal provided a comforting sense that not everything of James Boswell would be lost. In preserving the journal for posterity, he was preserving himself, "leaving myself embalmed," as he put it. He often referred to his "archive" at Auchinleck, and deliberately solicited letters from famous men to store there. He speculated about his journal being discovered and read two thousand years after his death.

Boswell had an almost mystical faith in his journal. He was always drawing up reviews of his life and trying to plan out his future on paper. He seriously considered tabulating his progress in various accomplishments. He appended his accounts to his journal, reassuring himself that his finances were in good order by balancing hypothetical credits against his debts. Even though the creditors would never pay, the books balanced; he could relax. He filled the journal with resolutions. Most of these were never kept; but the mere fact of writing them down comforted him.

> I have often determined to be strictly sober, and have often fixed an era for the commencement of my proper conduct. I have a curious inclination to have an era for almost everything. The era for my being sober has been advanced from one time to another.[33]

Boswell spent the winter of 1763–64 studying law in Utrecht. He began a long flirtation with the beauty Belle de Zuylen ("Zélide"), "a young lady free from all the faults of her sex." Her intelligence both attracted and repelled him; her directness he found disconcerting. He did not know how to respond to a woman his intellectual equal, if not superior—especially one who advocated free love. She rejected his proposal of marriage, but teasingly encouraged his correspondence: "It will not matter if the end of your letters contradicts the beginning."

Lord Auchinleck rewarded his son with a tour of the German princedoms. Then, instead of returning to Scotland as instructed by his father, Boswell travelled south. He displayed an undisguised enthusiasm for the famous, presenting himself at their doors and demanding an audience. Frederick II of Prussia, known already as "Frederick the Great," brushed off his approach, but in Switzerland the philosophers Rousseau and Voltaire both succumbed to Boswell's naïve charm. "Gods: Am I now then really the friend of Rousseau?" exulted Boswell. He was still only twenty-four.

Boswell pressed on Rousseau a theory that he was later to outline to Johnson, that like the Hebrew Ancients, a man might reasonably enjoy perhaps thirty virgins before marrying them off to grateful peasant husbands. Neither of his two masters felt able to endorse this code of conduct. Like Johnson, Rousseau had a reputation as a moralist, a man of unusual probity—a reputation that would be shattered only months after Boswell's visit by revelations in an anonymous pamphlet, penned by Voltaire, that Rousseau had fathered five illegitimate children, who had been abandoned in a foundling hospital. The public outrage at this apparently hypocritical behaviour by the author of such improving works as *Émile* would make it impossible for Rousseau to remain in Switzerland. In September 1765, his house was stoned by an angry mob.

Meanwhile, Boswell continued his Grand Tour to Italy, where for a while he fell in once more with Wilkes, in exile after his scandalous *Essay on Woman* had made London too hot for him. They became friends; Wilkes praised Boswell as "the agreeable scatterbrain, the gay drinking-companion, the quaint Scots chatter-box, the admirable and untiring listener." Then Boswell decided to pay a visit to the remote and inaccessible island of Corsica. His trip was opportune. Corsica was beginning to excite the public imagination, as a small nation which had thrown off the shackles of autocratic rule by the corrupt Genoese in favour of a supposed democracy. Rousseau himself had been invited to draft the new Corsican constitution. The Corsican cause was popular, and in the next few years would become even more so in Britain when the French annexed the island, eventually driving its ruler, General Pasquale Paoli, into exile. Paoli was a man of many admirable qualities, more of a statesman than a soldier, justly seen as the Father of his country. Rousseau championed Corsica as a little country of noble savages, which would one day astonish the world. (It did, by producing a tyrant.)

Boswell was one of the first foreigners to go there, and he made the most of his visit. He petitioned Paoli for an interview. At first Boswell was reluctantly received; Paoli feared that he might be a spy, especially when he found Boswell writing down everything he said. But Paoli's suspicions dissolved in Boswell's charm. Soon Boswell was dining and supping constantly with the general, receiving visits from all the Corsican nobility, and being accompanied by an escort of armed guards whenever he made an excursion. He remained seven weeks in Corsica. At last he began the long journey back to Britain, returning at the insistence of his father. Lord Auchinleck urged his son not to tarry. "There is nothing to be learned by travelling in France," he wrote. "I can say this from my own experience."[34]

The Corsican adventure enabled Boswell to indulge his propensity for self-dramatization to the full. As he made his way back through Europe, he sent a series of unsigned letters to an English newspaper. These anonymous reports, a skilful blend of fact and fantasy purporting

to come from a correspondent with insider intelligence, suggested that
Boswell's visit to Corsica might have profound consequences. Corsica
was described as being of strategic importance to Great Britain; Boswell,
they hinted, was more than a tourist; he was in fact on a secret mission.
The letters alluded to clandestine negotiations, concealed papers, and
diplomatic intrigue. The Genoese were said to be seriously alarmed by
Boswell's activities. One letter even suggested that he had gone to the
island to explore the romantic possibility of establishing the Stuart line
on the throne of Corsica (a rumour which rendered Lord Auchinleck
apoplectic). This was all nonsense, of course, but it was effective in
whipping up public sympathy for the cause of Corsican independence.
It also served to publicize the book about his travels which Boswell
planned to write. Boswell was pleased to portray himself as a man of
both mystery and importance.

On the journey back north through Europe, Boswell stopped in
Paris, where he was shocked to read in an English newspaper the
announcement of his mother's death. There was nothing he could do;
his mother's body was already lying in the family crypt. Characteristically he spent that evening in a brothel. The next day he received a fond
letter from his father, urging him to return home "with all speed."
Rousseau's mistress, Thérèse Le Vasseur, was also in Paris preparing to
follow the philosopher to England, where he had sought exile as the
guest of Hume after being hounded out of Switzerland. It was agreed
that Boswell should be Thérèse's escort. To pass the time during the
trip, the forty-five-year-old Thérèse offered the young man a "lesson in
the art of love"; by the time they reached Dover, Boswell boasted, they
had "done it" thirteen times.

In a witty letter written to the Comtesse de Boufflers, another
friend of Rousseau's, Hume speculated on the likely consequences of
these two travelling together: he recalled the young Roman who married the elderly widow of Cicero and Sallust, imagining that she must
possess some secret which would convey to him eloquence and genius.
Such was Boswell's "rage for literature," he explained, "that I dread
some event fatal to our friend's honour." For the benefit of his correspondent, Hume described Thérèse's travelling companion: "a young
gentleman, very good-humoured, very agreeable, and very mad."[35]

Depositing Thérèse with Rousseau in Chiswick, Boswell hurried off to see Johnson. The sage was crushingly sarcastic. "It seems you have kept good company abroad—Wilkes and Rousseau!" Boswell was crestfallen. "My dear Sir, you don't call Rousseau bad company? Do you really think him a bad man?" Johnson replied that Rousseau was "a rascal who ought to be hunted out of society." Warming to his theme, Johnson declared that Rousseau should "work in the plantations" like a convicted felon. "Do you think him as bad a man as Voltaire?" asked Boswell, back-pedalling furiously. "Why," Johnson replied, "it is difficult to settle the proportion of iniquity between 'em." Boswell's two prize scalps were now in tatters.

Boswell decided he should share his Corsican expertise. He sought an interview with Pitt, still an influential figure in Parliament though he had been out of office since 1761. Pitt replied to Boswell's request by suggesting that a meeting with the current Secretary of State might be more effective. But Boswell would not be denied: the opportunity to appeal personally to the Friend of Liberty was irresistible. He was ushered into the statesman's presence dressed as a native Corsican chief, armed with stiletto and Paoli's pistols in his belt, and wearing a cap complete with a tuft of cock's feathers.[36] It was a ludicrous display— though perhaps no more ludicrous than Byron dressing in Greek costume half a century later. Pitt received Boswell politely enough. Later Boswell appeared at Garrick's spectacular Shakespeare Jubilee in Stratford-upon-Avon wearing the same outfit.

His first literary success was his *Account of Corsica* (1768), a book which combined a general introduction to the country with a journal of his tour. It was an immediate success, rapidly selling through three editions in English, as well as being translated into Dutch, German, Italian, and French. Boswell became a celebrity, known as "Corsica Boswell." Strangers would approach him, wanting to shake the hand of one who had shaken the hand of the great Paoli. Many years later, Boswell remarked to Paoli that "it was wonderful how much Corsica had done for me, how far I had got in the world by having been there. I had got upon a rock in Corsica and jumped into the middle of life."[37]

THREE

SUBORDINATION

—◁◁◁∫∩▷▷▷—

I thought of his death with dreadful gloom. It appeared to me that if he were gone, I should find life quite vapid, and myself at a loss what to do, or how to think.[1]

BOSWELL HAD BEEN AWAY from home four years. On his return to Scotland he settled down to the law, as Lord Auchinleck had always wanted—though typically he did so only under protest, announcing to his new colleagues that he had been "pressed into service" by his father. It was not the ideal beginning to a legal career. At the age of twenty-seven, he passed advocate and began to practise in the Edinburgh courts. In his black robes, surrounded by his peers at the annual meeting of the Faculty of Advocates, "I felt myself *Mr James Boswell,* comfortable and secure."[2] But this feeling was only temporary; he remained unsure of himself. Even after he had been practising at the Edinburgh bar for the best part of a decade, Boswell still felt "a kind of wonder" in observing other men defer to his opinion.[3]

He attracted a fair number of clients, though his earnings never seemed enough to pay his outgoings. It was no disadvantage to be the son of a judge: quite a few clients came to him in the naïve hope that they would be favoured if their cause came up before his father. In fact,

Lord Auchinleck seemed to relish deciding against causes pleaded by his son.

After a promising start, there seemed no reason why James should not follow his father onto the bench in due course. But early on, he acquired a reputation for defending the hopeless and the helpless: drunken soldiers, forgers, horse-thieves and sheep-stealers, rioters, brawlers, arsonists, the poor and the needy, clients that other, more prudent advocates avoided. Boswell's zeal in the defence of such people damaged him in the eyes of those who might have advanced his career. He showed little sign of the cool detachment expected from one who hoped to become a judge.

His first criminal client was John Reid, a man accused of stealing sheep from a farm on the borders. It was a serious offence: if found guilty, the defendant would be hanged. In his first year of practice, Boswell managed to procure Reid's acquittal, but eight years later Reid was again tried on a similar charge. Despite Boswell's advocacy being conducted "in a very masterly and pathetic manner"—so much so that he was applauded by several members of the jury when they convened at a tavern afterwards—Reid was this time found guilty. Boswell appealed for a stay of execution: the judges, one of whom was his father, refused. Further appeals, including one for a royal pardon, proved fruitless.

Boswell was by now emotionally involved. He spent hours with the condemned man in his cell, and eventually accompanied him to the gallows. Desperate to save Reid's life, he planned to have the body cut down, carried into a stable, and there resuscitated with the aid of a surgeon. But when the moment came, Reid was beyond recall. This failure, and the pity Boswell felt for his hapless client, affected him deeply—though it must be admitted that he relished the drama of the occasion. "God has blessed you with one of the best hearts that ever man had," exclaimed Charles Hay, one of his fellow-advocates, afterwards.[4]

Hay's good opinion of Boswell was not shared by those pilloried by him in print; on the contrary, he was acquiring a reputation for malice. Following his return from the Grand Tour, he had issued a stream of plays, poems, and pamphlets, all of them ephemeral and many of them provocative. He bombarded the periodicals with letters, often abusive of individuals with whom he mixed, socially and professionally. The Lord Justice-Clerk, for example, President of the Court which condemned John Reid, was dismayed to see an anonymous letter maligning his integrity published in the *London Chronicle;* his son challenged Boswell to admit what was in fact the case, that he had written it; and the affair nearly led to a duel. The chancellor of the jury that had sat in judgement on Reid proposed that Boswell should be prosecuted for publishing an account of the trial in the newspapers. In the wider circles of London, such indiscretions might not prove so significant; but in the narrower world of Edinburgh, he made more enemies than was prudent for an ambitious young barrister.

In 1769, after courting a succession of potential brides, Boswell married his cousin Margaret Montgomerie, who was to bear him five children, two boys and three girls. Though an excellent wife in most ways, sensible, tolerant, and understanding, she had no money. Lord Auchinleck, who had been hoping for a wealthy daughter-in-law to secure the future of the estate, bitterly opposed the match. Henry Dundas, he pointed out, was now earning £700 a year and had just married a very genteel girl with £10,000 (who later left him). To Boswell's indignation, Lord Auchinleck took a second wife, marrying on the very same day as his son—perhaps a coincidence, but more likely a deliberate demonstration of his disapproval. For Boswell, his father's action was a breach of the compact between them: he had complied with his father's wish that he practise at the bar, on the understanding that he would inherit the estate in due course. Now he feared that he might be supplanted as heir if his father had any more children. These fears were probably groundless; under the terms of his original marriage contract, Lord Auchinleck could not have disinherited his eldest son even if he had wanted to. But Boswell felt cheated; he ranted that his father's new bride was a "prostitute," encouraging carnal desires in a man too old to fulfil them (Lord Auchinleck was sixty-two). There followed a seven-year struggle between father and son over the entail. Froideur characterized the relations between Boswell and his stepmother; neither Margaret nor the children were welcome at Auchinleck. Boswell was torn between feelings of filial loyalty and rejection. In 1775, for example, "I called at my father's, willing to talk with him, but as usual felt myself chilled."[5] Lord Auchinleck continued to treat his heir as a youth devoid of understanding, encouraging even his clerk to speak to him impudently. Boswell was in a difficult position while he remained dependent on his father, who had increased his allowance to £300 after his marriage; despite this, and periodic top-up loans from his father, Boswell's debts accumulated. As a result, his independence was compromised; even at the age of thirty-six, he felt it necessary to seek his father's permission to go to London. At one stage Lord Auchinleck threatened to call in the money he had lent his son; if carried out, the threat might have forced Boswell to go to jail for debt. The chill persisted to the grave. Boswell attended his father at his death-bed, but "alas! there was not affection between us."[6]

Boswell himself was a loving father and an affectionate husband, though neither loyal nor steady. After the first few years of marriage he started to rove, flirting with fashionable ladies and fondling servant-girls. He began visiting prostitutes again, with the inevitable consequence of repeated venereal infections. Following these lapses he was usually remorseful, often confessing to his wife where he had been and what he had done. Almost as distressing to her were his bouts of very heavy drinking, which led him into dangerous scrapes and which often left him hung over the next day. "It gave me much concern to be informed by my dear wife that I had been quite outrageous in my drunkenness the night before," he confided to his journal in 1774, "that I had cursed her in a shocking manner and even thrown a candlestick with a lighted candle at her."[7] But he was not an alcoholic; these drunken binges were punctuated by periods of sobriety lasting six months or more.

Margaret Boswell exerted a steadying influence on her husband. She consoled him when he woke after nightmares, provided him with practical advice, and overlooked his transgressions. "She is my best friend, and the most generous heart," he wrote after one such episode. More than once, Margaret discovered his misdemeanours by reading his journal, though ironically she disapproved of his habit of "journalizing," which she believed left him "embowelled to posterity."[8] But in general, she acknowledged his authority. She conformed to his preference that she call him "Mr Boswell," rather than Jamie. "She is in a proper degree inferior to her husband," Johnson wrote, on meeting her for the first time: "she cannot rival him, nor can he ever be ashamed of her."[9]

They had been married only a few years when Margaret began to spit blood, and soon it was clear that she, like so many others in her family, was consumptive. All her siblings had already died of tuberculosis; sooner or later, Boswell realized, he would be left alone.

Apart from his wife, Boswell had only one truly intimate friend in Edinburgh, his fellow-student from the university, John Johnston of Grange. Johnston, a mild, withdrawn, melancholic character, had qualified as a "writer" (a solicitor), but never prospered, perhaps due to indolence. Unmarried, he moved into the flat below the Boswells, and became virtually a member of their household. Boswell took comfort from his company and relied on his (somewhat eccentric) advice. His other close university friend, the Englishman William Temple, had taken holy orders, and through family connections obtained the living of Mamhead, near Exeter. (Later he was given the more profitable living of St Gluvias, in Cornwall.) He shared many of Boswell's literary interests and ambitions, and his interest in sex. In 1767, he married a shrewish, ill-tempered woman, who presented him with what seemed like an endless succession of children. Disappointed of his hopes in life, and embarrassed by financial difficulties, Temple became increasingly querulous, nervy, and prematurely middle-aged. Nevertheless, he and Boswell remained close; though their paths diverged, their mutual affection was constant. They wrote to each other regularly, exchanging confidences they would admit to no one else. In his letters Boswell described his sexual conquests and his conversations with the Great; it was a kind of innocent boasting. "My life is one of the most romantic you or I really know of," Boswell wrote to Temple in 1767, "and yet I am a very sensible, good sort of man."[10]

He remained in Scotland for the first three years of his marriage. Then, in 1772, he travelled down to London once more, ostensibly to plead a cause which had been referred on appeal from the Court of Session to the House of Lords. He was due to speak on behalf of a schoolmaster dismissed for "undue severity" towards his pupils; one of his arguments was ingeniously autobiographical. Had he not been beaten very severely at school himself, Boswell maintained, he would not have been able to make the defence he was now putting forward. The Lord Chancellor smiled at this line of argument, and some of the other lords cried out "Bravo!" But the House decided against Boswell's client.

A few days before setting out for London, Boswell had written to Johnson:

> I fairly own that after an absence from you for any length of time I feel that I require a renewal of that spirit which your presence always gives me, and which makes me a better and a happier man than I imagined I could be before I was introduced to your acquaintance.[11]

On the day of his arrival, Boswell hurried round to call on his friend. Johnson greeted him with an affectionate embrace—so unlike the receptions Boswell was accustomed to receive from his undemonstrative father! Their friendship was speedily re-established. During his stay in London of eight weeks, Boswell saw Johnson almost every other day, sometimes more than once on the same day.

Through Johnson, Boswell gained access to the heart of literary London. Johnson was a pivotal figure in English intellectual life, in regular contact with most of the learned men and women of his day. In particular, he had been a member of the Literary Club since it was founded in 1764. Other founder-members included the brilliant Whig intellectual and orator Edmund Burke; Goldsmith; Langton; Beauclerk; and the fashionable portrait painter and President of the Royal Academy Sir Joshua Reynolds. Boswell had been introduced to Reynolds by Goldsmith in 1769, and the two men soon became close friends, though Reynolds (like Johnson) was old enough to be Boswell's father. As well as being an outstanding painter, Reynolds was a man of letters, interested particularly in aesthetic theory. Successful and wealthy (with an annual income estimated at £6,000), invariably polite and even-tempered, Reynolds was a generous host and a solicitous friend, though not perhaps an energetic one. It was his idea to form a Literary Club, at least partly to occupy Johnson during a period when he was often lonely and miserable—or, as Reynolds put it, to give his friend "an unlimited opportunity of talking." In 1773, Johnson would propose Boswell as a member, and though some reservations about him were expressed, Johnson's authority carried the day.

Garrick was admitted to the Club that same year. Subsequent members included the witty and wealthy Whig politician Charles James Fox; the historian Edward Gibbon; the political economist Adam Smith; the playwright Richard Brinsley Sheridan (son of Thomas Sheridan); the botanist Joseph (later Sir Joseph) Banks; the literary scholars George Steevens and Edmond Malone; the brothers Joseph and Thomas Warton, both poets and scholars; the music historian Charles Burney; and the collector Sir William Hamilton. Much earlier the antiquarian divine Thomas Percy had been admitted to the Club; indeed, many of the cleverest men in England (women were not eligible) were members.

Boswell could hardly express his delight at being in town again. One evening soon after his arrival

> Mr Johnson and Dr Goldsmith and nobody else were the company. I felt a completion of happiness. I just sat and hugged myself in my own mind. Here I am in London . . . and here is Mr Johnson, whose character is so vast; here is Dr Goldsmith, so distinguished in literature. Words cannot describe our feelings.

While in London, Boswell was taken by Edward Dilly, publisher (with his brother Charles) of his Corsica book, to the Lord Mayor's ball and banquet, held at the Mansion House. Boswell showed a Pooterish pleasure in being introduced to the Lord Mayor. There was a scramble to get into the dining-hall, everyone jostling for the best places. Afterwards Boswell encountered his old friend Wilkes, now, somewhat incongruously, Sheriff of London, soon indeed to be elected Lord Mayor. On his two previous visits to London, Boswell had avoided Wilkes, who had spent a term in prison on the old charge of seditious libel; he would maintain an element of reserve towards his former friend for another three years, until Wilkes, by then back in Parliament as well as being installed as Lord Mayor, had become almost respectable. On this occasion the outlaw-turned-Sheriff greeted Boswell cordially, before gently chiding him for his neglect. Boswell pompously assured Wilkes that he was pleased to see him, but he could not visit him at home. "I am a Scotch laird and a Scotch lawyer and a Scotch married man. It would not be decent."[12]

• • •

Despite scoffing at Scotland, Johnson had long planned to go there, as he had told Boswell within weeks of their first meeting back in 1763. He suggested then that they might one day explore the Hebrides together. After nine years Boswell had begun to despair of this ever happening; but following Boswell's return to Scotland in 1772, Johnson wrote to reaffirm his sincere intent "to pay the visit and take the ramble";[13] and when Boswell saw him in London again the following spring, he "talked of coming to Scotland later that year with so much firmness that I hoped he was at last in earnest." Boswell renewed his siege. "I knew that if he were once launched from the metropolis, he would go forward very well; and I got our common friends there to assist in setting him afloat." He secured invitations from the Highland chiefs Macdonald and Macleod, and wrote to some of the most learned men in Scotland enlisting their support, "so that every power of attraction may be employed to secure our having so valuable an acquisition." In reply, the historian William Robertson, Principal of Edinburgh University, welcomed the prospect; he acknowledged that Johnson "sometimes cracks his jokes upon us," but argued that Scotsmen could distinguish between good-humoured teasing and "stabs of malevolence."

At last, Johnson agreed to come to Scotland during the summer of 1773, arriving in Edinburgh on 14 August. He stayed a few days at the Boswell family home—long enough to annoy Margaret Boswell by his habits of endlessly drinking tea and spilling candle wax as he read late into the night—where he received visits from many of the city's literati. Then he and Boswell set out for the Highlands together, accompanied by Boswell's servant, Joseph. It was tough going, especially for Johnson, by this time in his mid-sixties. In the Lowlands they could travel by coach, but in the Highlands there were no roads, and they were compelled to ride or walk. Neither were there any inns; but the credit attaching to the family name of Boswell, and the fame of his illustrious companion, ensured that they seldom lacked somewhere to stay. They travelled up the east coast to Inverness—passing over the very heath where Macbeth met the witches, which delighted Boswell so much that he immediately wrote to Garrick ("Here I am, and Mr Samuel Johnson actually with me") — and then followed the shores of Loch Ness, before ascending into the Highlands. On the west coast, they took ship to Skye, and subsequently called at several other Hebridean islands, including Mull and Iona, before returning to the mainland and then descending the west coast via Oban, Inverary, and Glasgow, with a diversion to Auchinleck. The whole tour lasted a little over three months.

The route Boswell and Johnson undertook through the Highlands and the Hebrides followed that of the rebel Prince after Culloden, and there are many indications that this was deliberate.[14] Like Boswell, Johnson had a strong affection for the "old interest." Though he grudgingly accepted the authority of the Hanoverian kings, he regretted the usurpation of the Stuart line, and admired the courage of the Jacobite attempts to bring about a restoration of the Stuart kings.

Boswell was delighted to have Johnson with him in Scotland. He likened himself to a dog, which, having got hold of a bone, retreats to the corner to devour it. In London there were always others to claim Johnson's attention; in Scotland he had Johnson mostly to himself. There was further pleasure in presenting Johnson to his countrymen, and his countrymen to Johnson — though the meetings were sometimes stormy. Johnson created a fuss the moment he arrived in Edinburgh, hurling his drink out of the window when a waiter used his greasy fingers to drop a lump of sugar into Johnson's lemonade. But Boswell enjoyed the intrinsic tension of having Johnson in Scotland. He relished their skirmishes, as Johnson launched into the Scots, and Boswell did his best to defend them. In Boswell's book about the tour, he would play up the combative, defiant image of the man, showing him as if spoiling for a fight. He would describe Johnson as a "John Bull," a "true-born Englishman," and depict him striding into the barbaric, hostile Highlands carrying an enormous club, carved from English oak.

The joshing between the two men continued throughout the tour. Johnson got in plenty of digs: Scotland was backward, primitive, treeless, and so on. Visiting Leith, he remarked that "I see a number of people barefooted here; I suppose you all went so before the Union. Boswell, your ancestors went so when they had as much land as your family has now." This was a smart blow against a man so puffed up with genealogical pride, and Boswell relished any opportunity to retaliate.

When another waiter, this time in Montrose, handled a sugar-lump, Boswell gleefully pointed out that the keeper of this uncouth inn was an Englishman. In response to Johnson's crack about oats in his *Dictionary,* Boswell "insisted on scottifying his palate"—a scene that was to be the subject of one of Rowlandson's most famous cartoons—but the food was dried fish, not oats. (Had it been the latter, this would have been a rare example of a lexicographer forced to eat his words.)[15]

The most dramatic of these exchanges occurred in the Parliament House in Edinburgh, in front of the Treaty of Union itself. Boswell began to express regrets that Scotland had lost her independence, and the Keeper of the Records chipped in that the Scottish Parliament had been bribed with English money to sign the Treaty. "Sir, that is no defence," said Johnson: "that makes you worse." The Keeper of the Advocates' Library, alarmed by the warmth of the conversation, suggested that they had better say no more on the subject. Boswell burst out that the English had been glad to have the Scots in the last war, to fight their battles. Johnson rebuffed him. "We should have had you for the same price, though there had been no Union, as we might have had Swiss, or other troops. No, no, I shall agree to a separation. You have only to *go home.*"[16]

Johnson was of course referring to the familiar English complaint against the number of Scotsmen coming to England, but this was an outrageous remark to make in the circumstances and cannot have been intended seriously. It was banter, not animosity. And it occurred very soon after Johnson's arrival in Scotland. After the tour he returned to England "in great good humour, with his prejudices much lessened"; he later described the time he spent in Scotland as "the pleasantest part of his life."

One of Johnson's motives in undertaking the journey to the Highlands had been to investigate the claims made by James Macpherson, who until the early 1760s had been an impoverished tutor with an interest in old Gaelic manuscripts. Then Macpherson had published *Fingal,* an epic poem in six books, ostensibly a translation from a Gaelic original written by the warrior-bard Ossian in the ancient past, perhaps as many as 1,500 years before. Another epic, *Temora,* this time in eight books, followed a year later. Their impact was extraordinary, eventually spreading all over Europe, and beyond. Ossian was compared to Homer; his work rated alongside the masterpieces of world literature. Indeed, Thomas Sheridan told the young Boswell that Ossian "excelled Homer in the Sublime and Virgil in the Pathetic."[17] Boswell himself raved about *Fingal* to his friend Andrew Erskine. All the Romantic poets would be influenced by Ossian—as were novelists, playwrights, painters, musicians, soldiers, and statesmen. Ossian became a favourite of Goethe's, and an inspiration to Napoleon, who carried an Italian edition of his works with him on all his campaigns. Thomas Jefferson considered Ossian "the greatest poet that has ever existed."[18]

The time was ripe for such a find. In the decade before *Fingal* was published, Rousseau had outlined a theory of the Noble Savage, extolling the virtues of the "natural" state and deploring the effects of commerce and civilization. In the 1760s and 1770s, his ideas seemed confirmed in the discoveries of South Sea Island utopias by voyagers such as Captain Cook and Sir Joseph Banks. Natives brought back from Tahiti or North America were lionized in elegant society. There was a cult of the Primitive, one which flourished in the increasingly safe and comfortable conditions of the late eighteenth century. The past was put on a pedestal; antique qualities sentimentalized. Writers began to celebrate the grandeur of nature, unsullied by cultivation; mountains and wild places, previously regarded as desolate, were now described as sublime. Ossian hit all the right notes. Here was an authentic Celtic genius free from the taint of Anglo-Saxon domination, a pre-Christian poet to set alongside, or even above, Shakespeare.

Over the decade that followed, the authenticity of the Ossian poems was hotly debated in both England and Scotland. The Scottish literati were enthusiastic about Macpherson's "discoveries," almost to a man: among them John Home, Adam Ferguson, Hugh Blair, David Hume, Adam Smith, and Lords Elibank, Kames, Hailes, and Monboddo, virtually a roll-call of the principal figures of the Scottish Enlightenment. Home ensured that Bute became Macpherson's principal patron. Ferguson and Blair organized a recital of ancient Gaelic poetry for Thomas Percy, author of the seminal *Reliques of Ancient English Poetry;* Percy proclaimed himself satisfied (though he later retracted) that what he had heard bore a convincing resemblance to a passage in *Fingal.*

Johnson was sceptical about Ossian's verse. Both his experience as a scholar and his innate intellectual rigour made him reluctant to accept claims unsupported by evidence. Moreover, he had been wary of fraud since being taken in by another Scottish schoolmaster, William Lauder, in 1750. Lauder persuaded Johnson to write a preface and a postscript to a pamphlet alleging that much of Milton's *Paradise Lost* had been plagiarized, an allegation Lauder supported with a series of elaborate fabrications. When Johnson discovered that he had been deceived, he was indignant; chastened, he was much more careful thereafter.

Johnson had formed a low opinion of the Ossian poems early on; he found them primitive and chaotic. Short-sighted from birth, he was un-moved by the grandeur of Nature; born into poverty, he was unsenti-mental about primitive living. "Don't cant about savages," he snapped at Boswell. He was suspicious of "sensibility." In 1763, Boswell's friend the Reverend Dr Hugh Blair, who had written a *Dissertation on the Poems of Ossian,* in which he had pronounced the poems authentic from internal evidence, asked Johnson whether he thought any modern man could have written such poems: expecting the answer no. "Yes, Sir," replied Johnson: "many men, many women, and many children."

Anyone could have written the poems, and Johnson was sure that they were fakes. On the tour of Scotland, Johnson time and again encountered Scotsmen who professed themselves able to authenticate the Ossian poems; but when confronted by Johnson to produce the evidence, their claims invariably collapsed. Johnson concluded that "a Scotchman must be a very sturdy moralist, who does not love Scotland better than truth."[19] Repeatedly he posed the key question: where are the manuscripts? Without these, the evidence for Ossian amounted to no more than testimony from biased witnesses. So far as Johnson could discover, there were no Gaelic manuscripts of any antiquity; there was no indigenous written culture in Scotland. "A nation that cannot write, or a language that was never written, has no manuscripts."[20]

In this inquiry Johnson was inspired by more than just a desire to humiliate the Scots. He was passionately concerned about language: not just in a dry, academic sense, but as a means of ordering and putting form on a chaotic universe. For him, the *Dictionary* was a weapon to beat back the uncertainty that perpetually threatens mankind. Precision sharpened the blade; provenance tempered the steel. It was therefore essential to expose literary fraud, which might undermine the entire enterprise. The Ossian poems were an affront to taste; worse, they were a virus that might infect the entire body.

Johnson understood that the Scots believed in Ossian because they were hungry for a literature they could call their own; Macpherson, like many a forger since, fed this appetite. What made his deception much easier was the fact that so few educated Scotsmen spoke Gaelic. Even David Hume, blinded by his loathing for the English, was convinced initially by Macpherson, though he quickly realized his embarrassing mistake, and later told Boswell that he would not believe *Fingal* an ancient poem "though fifty bare-arsed Highlanders should swear it."[21]

On his return to England, Johnson expressed his views about the Ossian poems in print for the first time. Macpherson's failure to produce the original manuscripts from which he claimed to have copied the poems led Johnson to the conclusion that he must have written them himself; and the vigorous support Macpherson received from his fellow Scotsmen only showed their fondness for their supposed ancestors: "Credulity on one part is a strong temptation to deceit on the other." Johnson's remarks were doubly inflammatory to Scotsmen: first, he denied the existence of an ancient written culture in Scotland; second, he accused the Scots of deceit in pretending that one existed. The more they protested, the more they proved his point.

Macpherson tried to force Johnson to retract, and, when this attempt failed, to intimidate him with threats. Johnson's response was robust: he wrote Macpherson a defiant reply. Then he armed himself with an oak stick (a replacement for the one he had taken to Scotland, which he lost in the Hebrides) as a means of defence in case he should be attacked. His courage was not in doubt: Macpherson was a man even taller than himself, and twenty-seven years younger. As it was, no attack was forthcoming; Macpherson went to ground.

Boswell was not overly dismayed at Johnson's unpopularity with his compatriots. He had lost interest in Ossian, and in truth his feelings about his homeland were ambiguous. When Johnson told him that he was "the most unscottified" of his countrymen, Boswell was flattered. When Johnson informed him that his pronunciation was not offensive,

Boswell understood him to mean that it had little trace of the Scots accent; and when Johnson praised him as a Scotchman without the faults of a Scotchman, Boswell was delighted.[22] He felt distaste for Scots manners and Scots accents. Encountering a Scotsman in London, the chemist Dr George Fordyce, at a meeting of the Literary Club, Boswell was disgusted that Fordyce should be so coarse and noisy; "and, as he had the accent strong, he shocked me as a kind of representative of myself."[23]

But at the same time, Boswell had a strong sentimental attachment to Scotland, which he conceived of as a small nation oppressed by its larger and wealthier neighbour. It was for this reason that he identified with the Corsican revolutionaries in their struggle for independence, and rejoiced at the victory of the American colonists. Scotland's proud past; its independent traditions; the "shameful" Union; the slaughter at Culloden; the fierce loyalty of the Highlanders to the fugitive young Prince—these were all subjects which aroused powerful emotions in him. And though he wished to avoid Scotticisms himself, he was by no means contemptuous of the Scots dialect; for many years he planned to compile a Scots dictionary, a project which Johnson encouraged.

Boswell and Johnson had arrived in the Hebrides by taking a boat from Glenelg on the mainland to Skye, where they had arranged to stay with Sir Alexander Macdonald, one of the two principal landowners on the island. Boswell looked upon the Macdonalds as family; Sir Alexander's wife, Elizabeth, was the daughter of Godfrey Bosville, a Yorkshire squire whom Boswell (though nobody else) acknowledged as chief of the Boswell clan. She was a beauty; Boswell had considered marrying her himself. The previous spring, when Sir Alexander was in London, Boswell had taken him to meet Johnson, and afterwards Johnson and Boswell had been guests at the Macdonalds' London house. Sir Alexander had sent his coach to collect Johnson before dinner, and had ordered it to take him home afterwards. Both men felt grateful towards their attentive host. "I really like the Knight," Boswell noted in his journal afterwards.[24] So when they arrived on Skye a year later, following a difficult and dangerous journey across the Highlands, they expected to be entertained in some comfort by the head of the Macdonald clan in his ancestral castle.

They were rudely disappointed. Sir Alexander and his wife had already left Monkstadt, the Macdonald family seat, on their way to Edinburgh; they received their guests in the modest house of one of Sir Alexander's tenants. Dinner was meagre, the Macdonalds travelling without a cook. No claret appeared. Boswell and Johnson were expected to share a room, until Boswell protested. It was like living in a London lodging-house, Johnson commented. The conditions were no worse than those they had endured elsewhere—but to be treated thus by Sir Alexander Macdonald was more than disappointing; it was offensive. The two guests suspected that their hosts had left the Macdonald seat on the far side of the island early, in order to avoid the expense and trouble of entertaining them in style. Johnson was particularly upset at tea, when the sugar was served without tongs or spoons. It was insanitary, it was insulting. He had not come all the way from London to be treated like this.

Boswell was embarrassed. He was Johnson's host in Scotland, where he hoped to display himself to his friend as a man of consequence. Sir Alexander's invitation had been part of the bait with which Johnson had been enticed to the Hebrides. Boswell had expected traditional Highland hospitality. As it was, their reception seemed so mean that Boswell contemplated leaving the very next day. He suggested as much to Johnson before they went to bed that Thursday night; but Johnson decided that they should stick it out until the Monday.

On Friday Boswell confronted Sir Alexander, and they had a violent quarrel. Boswell complained of the meanness of the Macdonalds' appearance here; of his wife's travelling without a maid, for example, and being dressed no better than one. The guests from the South, Tories both, had a romantic notion of a Highland chieftain; Sir Alexander did not fit the bill. He had composed some Latin verses in honour of Johnson's visit; he should have roasted oxen whole, and hung out a flag as a signal to his fellow Macdonalds to come round for beef and whisky. Sir Alexander was a modern man, an old Etonian with little sense of the rights and responsibilities of a Highland patriarch. He spent much of his time in London and had no compunction about running his estates as a business, raising his rents and clearing off the land men whose ancestors had lived there for generations. The results were immediately apparent: the erosion of tradition, the loosening of family ties, and mass emigration.

Perhaps Boswell and Johnson were a little unfair in singling out Sir Alexander for condemnation. They had come to the Western Isles in search of a system of life different from that found in the rest of Britain: a feudal society based on subordination, hereditary jurisdiction, and clan loyalty. This was their first glimpse of the Hebrides, and they were not to know then what they discovered later, that such a way of life was fast disappearing everywhere as a result of both economic and political pressures, particularly since the defeat of the Jacobites in 1745–46 and the subsequent suppression of the clan system. The regulations then introduced abolished the rights of chieftains to raise armies and exercise justice, and forbade the Highlander from carrying a dirk or wrapping himself in plaid. The two visitors were aware of these laws, but not of their effects. As a Lowland Scot, Boswell was almost as much a stranger in the Highlands as Johnson: he too had an archaic vision of how life was lived there.

The argument with Macdonald rumbled on through the weekend. On Saturday Johnson told Sir Alexander that if he were in his place he'd keep a magazine of arms. Sir Alexander remarked drily that they would rust. "Let there be men to keep them clean," Johnson cried. "Your ancestors did not use to let their arms rust."

It was no good trying to inspire in Macdonald the manly, gallant values of the clansmen. "He has no more ideas of a chief than an attorney," commented Johnson in disgust. They quitted his house on Monday morning, on horses provided by their host: but even in this the guests considered him ungenerous, as Sir Alexander asked that the horses be returned once they reached the other side of the island. In the event, Boswell decided they should keep the horses as long as they could, since others might be difficult to find there. For the remainder of their tour, Sir Alexander's parsimony, and the lamentable effects of greedy landlords without a sense of loyalty to their tenants were themes that recurred frequently in the conversation between the two men, recorded in Boswell's journal.

On the far side of Skye, they stayed with Allan Macdonald (known as "Kingsburgh"), whose father had sheltered the Young Pretender, Prince Charles Edward Stuart, under the very same roof. Kingsburgh was "quite the figure of a gallant Highlander," a large man with jet-black hair tied back and screwed ringlets on each side, dressed boldly in tartan plaid. He received them "most courteously"; his hospitality, his demeanour, and his appearance contrasted with those of his clan chieftain, that "wretch," the "insect" Sir Alexander Macdonald, whose company they had quitted only six days earlier. In the evening they were joined by their hostess, Kingsburgh's wife, "a little woman, of a mild and genteel appearance": the same Flora Macdonald who at the tender age of twenty-four had helped the Prince to escape the manhunt after Culloden. Boswell was entranced: "To see Mr Samuel Johnson salute Miss Flora Macdonald was a wonderful romantic scene to me." That night Johnson slept in the very bed where "the Wanderer" had lain.

"My heart was sore to recollect that Kingsburgh had fallen sorely back in his affairs, was under a load of debt, and intended to go to America," lamented Boswell in his journal. Pressed by the rapacious Sir Alexander, with whom he had quarrelled, Kingsburgh could no longer continue to live in the home of his ancestors. This was a melancholy conclusion for the two visitors. The next morning Boswell found a slip of paper on which Johnson had scribbled a line of Latin: *Quantum cedat virtutibus aurum* ("With virtue weighed, what worthless trash is gold!"). He affected not to understand what Johnson meant by this, but surely the meaning is clear: Johnson was praising the loyalty of the Highlanders, not one of whom had betrayed the Prince, despite a bounty of £30,000 on his head.

At breakfast they were again joined by Flora Macdonald, who gave them an account of her adventures with the Prince. She had agreed to escort him away from the island of Lewis when it was discovered he was there, though the country was full of troops and the sea full of ships searching for him. In a small open boat, they escaped from Lewis, and reached Skye after being shot at from the shore. Once on land again, Flora Macdonald had ridden on horseback while the Prince walked beside her, disguised as her maid. They made for Monkstadt, where she sought help from Sir Alexander's mother, only to find the castle occupied by troops looking for the Prince. He concealed himself on a nearby hill, while Flora entered the castle and was forced to dine in company with one of the officers to avoid suspicion. Afterwards she escorted the Prince to Kingsburgh, and then helped him to complete his escape. Johnson listened to her story attentively, and declared: "All this should be written down." The meeting with Flora Macdonald became one of the highlights, arguably the climax to Boswell's account of their tour.

The brave story of the Jacobite rebellion and its sad aftermath stirred Boswell deeply. Though he was always flattered by any attention from the Hanoverian King George, Boswell could bring himself to tears by thinking of the Stuart Prince Charles. He admired the noble and chivalric values supposedly personified by the Prince. And he identified with the Prince himself. Boswell craved approval from his father, though almost everything he did increased Lord Auchinleck's disapprobation. It is often forgotten that in 1745 the Old Pretender was still alive, and had the rebellion succeeded, James III was due to become King, not Prince Charles. Here was a son who had embarked on a dangerous adventure for his father's sake. Boswell indulged in the fantasy that by some similar dramatic act he too might prove himself a worthy son.

Johnson remained in Scotland until 22 November 1773. When the time came for him to leave, Boswell escorted him for the first few miles from Edinburgh; they paused to admire Hawthornden Castle by moonlight, where a century before Ben Jonson had quarrelled with his host, the Cavalier poet William Drummond. A couple of days later, they parted at Blackshiels, where Johnson boarded the coach for London.

Though they were able to meet only intermittently over the years that followed, Johnson always remained Boswell's mentor—his "Guide, Philosopher, and Friend," as Boswell (quoting Pope) would write in the closing pages of his *Life of Johnson*. Boswell had a lively imagination which would prey upon his undisciplined mind if not kept under control; Johnson's powerful intellect provided the necessary tether. For Boswell, Johnson's writings were "the food of my soul"; when he did not hear from Johnson for a while, "my mind wanted its great SUN"; and on his way to see Johnson after a period of melancholy, "sunshine broke in upon my mind."[25] He contemplated the thought of Johnson's death with dread. While they were staying with Sir Alexander Macdonald on Skye, Boswell had felt an onset of "spleen": had he not been with Johnson, "I should have sunk into dejection; but his firmness supported me. I looked at him, as a man whose head is turning giddy at sea looks at a rock, or any fixed object."[26]

On a trip together to Oxford in 1776, they put up at the Angel Inn, and that evening they discussed Boswell's melancholy. Johnson commented that Boswell had "a very ticklish mind," and advised him to divert distressing thoughts rather than combat them. "He said that to have the management of one's mind was a great art, and that it might be attained in a considerable degree by experience and habitual exercise." Boswell treasured "his sage counsel." On this occasion he was comforted to be sharing a twin-bedded room with Johnson. "I fancied tonight that I was prepared by my revered friend for conducting myself through any future gloom."[27]

For all his failings, Boswell was a sincere Christian, though troubled by religious anxieties. Johnson's presence soothed these, and whenever they were together, Boswell found satisfaction in attending church services alongside him. Johnson's companionship always relieved Boswell when he was in distress. While the two men spent a fortnight together in Derbyshire, Boswell complained "of a wretched changefulness—that I could not preserve for any long continuance the same views of anything."

> It was most comfortable to me to experience in Dr Johnson's company a relief from this uneasiness. His steady, vigorous mind held firm before me those objects which my feeble and tremulous imagination presented, for the most part, in such a wavering state that my reason could not judge well of them.[28]

But when Boswell was alone in Scotland, his melancholy quickly returned. Time after time, he wrote self-pityingly to Johnson, and Johnson wrote back reproving him for indulging in melancholy. In February 1781, for example, Boswell sent Johnson an anxious letter, agonizing about the same metaphysical issues that had disturbed him since his boyhood breakdown. Johnson's reply was robust: "I hoped you had got rid of all this hypocrisy of misery. What have you to do with Liberty or Necessity? Or what more than to hold your tongue about it? Do not doubt but I shall be most heartily glad to see you here again, for I love every part about you but your affectation of distress . . . Come to me, my dear Bozzy, and let us be happy as we are. We will go again to the Mitre, and talk old times over."[29]

It was by no means a friendship of equals: the differences in age, temperament, and intellect made a vast gulf between the two men. Boswell was unquestionably the pupil, and Johnson the master. Johnson had no hesitation in providing his younger friend with pedagogic advice. "My dear Sir," he wrote to Boswell a couple of years later, "mind your studies, mind your business, make your lady happy, and be a good Christian."[30] As one keen-eyed observer remarked, Johnson "generally treated Mr Boswell as a schoolboy."[31]

When they were together, Boswell was not ashamed to act as Johnson's disciple. It was enough for him that he could stimulate Johnson to talk. He put forward whimsical ideas to see how Johnson might react; and pitted him against formidable opponents, to watch the sparks fly. In 1776, Boswell was delighted to have brought Johnson together with Wilkes—"two men more different could perhaps not be selected out of all mankind"[32]—though the two of them took the opportunity to tease him. He began to write essays under the pseudonym "The Hypochondriack," a self-conscious imitation of *The Rambler.* He fancied that he had learned to think like Johnson, and he even found himself unconsciously adopting some of Johnson's expressions.[33] In a contest to see who could most accurately imitate Johnson's manner, Garrick—the greatest actor of his time, who had known Johnson since his schooldays—was the victor in reciting poetry, but Boswell was judged to be better at imitating Johnson's conversation.[34] "He had an odd, mock solemnity of tone and manner, that he had acquired imperceptibly from constantly thinking of and imitating Dr Johnson," noted Fanny Burney in her diary: "every look and movement displayed either intentional or involuntary imitation."[35]

Boswell hardly ever questioned Johnson's authority. At a dinner in 1778, at the painter Allan Ramsay's house, the guests discussed Johnson before he arrived; Boswell frankly admitted that he "worshipped" him. "I cannot help worshipping him; he is so much superior to other men."[36] Boswell's reverence for Johnson had irritated Goldsmith, who complained that Boswell was "making a monarchy of what ought to be a republic."[37]

The younger man's respect for Johnson was unwavering, and his manner deferential. London society soon began to mock Boswell's devotion to his master: he was unkindly portrayed as a sycophant, a whipping boy, a spaniel. Fanny Burney left a cruel description of a dinner party in Streatham, when Boswell actually moved his chair from the table and placed it behind Johnson's as the booming began:

> His eyes goggled with eagerness; he leant his ear almost on the shoulder of the Doctor; and his mouth dropped open to catch every syllable that might be uttered; nay, he seemed not only to dread losing a word, but to be anxious not to miss a breathing. And there he remained until Johnson happened to turn and see him and shouted an ill-pleased "What do you do there, Sir? Go to the table, Sir!"[38]

Johnson's friends were amused by Boswell's sycophancy—though most of them deferred to him to a greater or lesser extent. If Johnson was the schoolmaster, they were a pack of unruly schoolboys, defiant behind his back but respectful in his presence—and Boswell was the teacher's pet. All were used to rough treatment from the irascible Socrates; few endured it so uncomplainingly as Boswell. Langton, for example, though mild-mannered and not easily roused, disapproved of Johnson's "roughness," which Boswell excused as an "indication of the vigour of his genius." Indeed, he usually delighted in Johnson's "grand explosions," even when they were directed at himself. Perhaps he had become hardened to such treatment at the hands of his father. Sometimes, however, his feelings were hurt: after Johnson had spoken to him rudely during a dinner at Sir Joshua Reynolds's, Boswell was "vexed and angry," so much so that he stayed away from Johnson for nearly a week to show his displeasure, and might have gone back to Scotland without being reconciled had they not been brought together by Langton. He was particularly upset because there had been "enemies" present—possibly other Scotsmen, who delighted to see Boswell "tossed and gored" by Johnson. Boswell felt that Johnson's ill-treatment of him had exposed them both.[39]

On several occasions Boswell tested the older man's affection for him. In 1779, for example, he sulkily refused to write to Johnson for several months. Johnson was exasperated by such puerile behaviour.

He found it necessary to reassure Boswell of his affection time and again. When Boswell speculated that they might quarrel at some future date, Johnson assured him that his regard for him was greater than he had words to express, "but I do not choose to be always repeating it; write it down in the first leaf of your pocket-book, and never doubt of it again."[40] Boswell was delighted to have secured this documentary evidence. It was important for Boswell to feel that Johnson thought well of him, and to record the fact. In general, he was liked but not respected by those whose company he sought—and not entirely trusted either, because he was known to keep an entertaining and indiscreet journal, some portions of which had been read by intimate friends. Wilkes observed, only half-jokingly, that Boswell was a dangerous man, because he wrote down conversations.[41] But for Boswell, the fact that Johnson himself had repeatedly encouraged him to keep up his journal was justification enough. Johnson's continuing friendship vindicated Boswell (at least in his own eyes) against criticism from others.

"Mr Boswell was never in anybody's company who did not wish to see him again," pronounced Johnson, and it was true that Boswell was lively and good-natured; but some could wish him more discreet, less loud, less bumptious. One of his less lovable traits was to tiresomely insist on his status as "an ancient Baron"; he remained both proud and insecure, always nervous of being slighted.

Since 1772, Boswell had made a visit to London almost every year, usually in the spring, while the Edinburgh courts were in recess. His habit was to stay a period of two or three months, lodging with his Corsican friend, General Paoli, now in exile. Indeed, he referred to Paoli's comfortable London house as "home." Lord Auchinleck disapproved of these jaunts, which were an expensive* distraction from the serious business of building a career at the Edinburgh bar. On several occasions he threatened to cut off his son's allowance to prevent them. Boswell bitterly recorded how his father sneered at him, "as if I thought myself

---

*Boswell's six-month stay in London in 1785 cost £150, even though he was living rent-free as Paoli's guest.

a very wise man, and was the reverse, and how I went to London among the *geniuses,* who despised me."[42]

The death of Boswell's father in 1782 meant a change to this routine: not only were the restrictions imposed by his father lifted, but Boswell became Master of Auchinleck. His peregrinations became triangular. Something had to give: he could not keep shuttling between Edinburgh, London, and Auchinleck. Boswell's family allegiance was not to Edinburgh, but to Auchinleck, where moreover the estate provided essential income. In Edinburgh, on the other hand, there was nothing but drudgery and humiliation, or so it seemed to Boswell. In 1783, he skipped one of the sittings of the Court of Session, for the first time since passing advocate in 1766.

For Boswell, Scotland represented the world of his father: there he felt himself oppressed by gloomy, narrow-minded, and disapproving Presbyterians, coerced into tedious grind with little hope of reprieve. London represented an escape, freedom, fun, fashion, and fortune, and the lively company he enjoyed most of all. In Edinburgh he was dull; in London he could shine. Coming to London quickened his spirits, and returning to Edinburgh dampened them. "I know not if you will be at rest in London," his fellow-Scotsman, the royal physician Sir John Pringle, told Boswell, "but you will never be at rest out of it."[43] Pringle himself had retired to Edinburgh after a very successful career in England, but found it so depressing that he returned to live in London.

Boswell wanted to move permanently to London, but could he afford it? He estimated the travelling expenses—assuming that the whole family was to return to Auchinleck at least once each year—at £120 annually, and the extra cost of maintaining a house in London at £600. Even if he could earn as much at the English bar as he was making in Scotland, the figures did not look promising. Moreover, his debts had been accumulating steadily; by the time he came into his inheritance, they totalled £4,000, approximately five years' estate income. If only he could become an MP! Parliament promised rich pickings: the Crown ensured support for its ministries by handing out lucrative jobs—"places"—of all sorts, many of them with only nominal duties.

Boswell failed to understand the eighteenth-century system of patronage, whereby almost everybody was beholden to somebody else.

He never seemed to realize that nobody would ever give him anything unless he offered something in return; whenever he approached one of the powerful for a favour, Boswell always insisted that he could not be bought. As a substantial landowner, Boswell should have had some political influence in his native Ayrshire, but he had no more idea of local than he had of national politicking. Ayrshire politics were controlled by two or three local grandees; only their candidates had any hope of being elected. Not only was Boswell not a player; he did not even understand the rules of the game.

He sought Johnson's approval to join the English bar. Johnson was sympathetic to Boswell's desire to live in London—how could he be otherwise, when he proclaimed London superior to anywhere else in the world?—but he advised Boswell that a laird ought to live contentedly on his own land. "Wrap yourself up in your hereditary possessions, which, though less than you may wish, are more than you can want." This was not what Boswell wished to hear. He remained tortured by "pangs of neglected merit."

Margaret Boswell tried to encourage her husband's career in Scotland, where his practice, initially plentiful, had steadily diminished since his father's retirement in 1775. She told him that they should entertain more often at their Edinburgh home, but Boswell had no heart for this. Margaret was anxious that Boswell might alienate too many influential Scotsmen by thoughtlessly insulting them in print, and failing to cultivate them in private. His incessant talk about moving to England was unlikely to enlarge his practice or to improve his chances of advancing to the bench of the Court of Session in due course. In 1784, Boswell's friend the Honourable Alexander Gordon, himself newly elevated to the bench of the Court of Session as Lord Rockville, told Margaret privately that Boswell's "jocularity" was against him in his claim for a judge's place, also his so openly declaring his antipathy to so many people. "I was discouraged to think that my merits were so coldly considered," a petulant Boswell noted in his journal, "and I indulged a kind of satisfaction in discontent, and earnestly wished for an opportunity to treat the world with disdain."[44]

Margaret wrote to Henry Dundas, who, as the Government's chief power-broker in Scotland, controlled all Crown appointments, including those to the Court of Session, asking him to help her husband.

Dundas had made himself right-hand man to the young Prime Minister, William Pitt, second son of the Pitt whom Boswell had gone to see dressed in Corsican costume; it was Dundas who had persuaded Pitt to accept the King's invitation to form a government twelve months before. The canny Dundas refused to commit his thoughts to paper in response to Margaret's appeal, but he agreed to have a confidential chat with Boswell about his prospects.

Boswell's relationship with Dundas was complicated. The Dundases of Arniston had maintained friendly relations with the Boswells of Auchinleck for at least two generations; they too had a family tradition at the bar. Dundas's father had been Lord President of the Court of Session, a post now occupied by Henry's half-brother, Robert. Dundas had attended the same classes as Boswell and Temple at Edinburgh University. Perhaps because he was two years younger, Boswell and Temple looked down on Dundas and tended to belittle his achievements, even after he had risen far above them both. Dundas had become Solicitor-General of Scotland only three years after qualifying as an advocate. In 1775, when Dundas was appointed Lord Advocate, the highest law officer in Scotland, at the age of only thirty-three, Boswell wrote exasperatedly to Temple, "Why is he so lucky?"[45] As Dundas consolidated his grip on Scottish politics—at the peak of his power, he controlled thirty-two of the forty-five Scottish seats[46]—Boswell opposed him on a number of occasions, prominently but ineffectually. He had to be persuaded out of challenging Dundas to a duel when he felt that Dundas had insulted his father in 1776, even though Lord Auchinleck had made light of Dundas's remark and continued on good terms with Dundas and the rest of his family.

For Boswell to go cap-in-hand to Dundas was therefore awkward. But Dundas was forgiving by nature, and Boswell was hardly a serious opponent. He told Boswell that he approved of his plan of moving to London and trying the English bar, provided that Boswell had enough money to cover the extra expense, which Dundas estimated at £1,000 or £1,200 a year (Johnson too had estimated the sum necessary to maintain Boswell's family in London at £1,000 a year). When Dundas learned that Boswell had only £500 a year to spend, he was much less sure that the move was advisable. He promised to talk to his colleagues, the Prime

Minister, the Attorney-General, and the Lord Chancellor, to see whether they might find Boswell a place bringing with it some hundreds a year. Dundas did not think that Boswell should go to the bench yet, because once he became a judge he would no longer be entitled to any other new office; better to get something first that Boswell could carry to the bench with him. Boswell was encouraged—"I left him quite animated and full of manly hope"—but Margaret was not convinced. She thought that Dundas was encouraging her husband to go to London only because he had more pressing claimants to a seat on the bench.[47] There the matter rested.

Boswell saw Johnson for what would be the last time on 30 June 1784. They met for a "friendly confidential dinner"—in the eighteenth-century sense of a large meal taken in the late afternoon—at the London home of Johnson's intimate friend Sir Joshua Reynolds. Johnson was a dying man, suffering increasingly from breathlessness; the three men discussed the possibility that he might spend the coming winter in Italy, to escape the English damp. During the winter that had just passed, Johnson had been so ill that he had been unable to leave his house for 129 days in succession. Boswell had consulted three Edinburgh doctors on Johnson's condition: the consensus had been that if Johnson were to live through another winter, he should certainly spend it in a milder climate. The problem was the cost. Johnson's friends had discussed among themselves how the money might be raised, and Boswell had come up with the idea of applying to the Lord Chancellor for funds. Lord Thurlow was known to respect Johnson, and vice versa; and as Lord Chancellor he was well placed to press Johnson's claim to support from the state. Johnson already received a Crown pension of £300 a year, granted to him more than twenty years before, in recognition of his achievement as author of the *Dictionary of the English Language*.

   These plans had been kept secret from Johnson until the day before the dinner at Sir Joshua's, when Boswell had hurried round to Johnson's home in Bolt Court, just north of Fleet Street, to read him the Lord Chancellor's encouraging reply. Johnson had listened attentively.

"This is taking prodigious pains about a man," he said, when Boswell finished reading. "O! Sir, your friends would do every thing for you," Boswell replied affectionately. But Johnson grew more and more agitated, until tears started in his eyes, and he exclaimed, "GOD bless you all." For some moments neither man was able to speak. Then Johnson rose abruptly and left the room.

The next day, at Reynolds's house in Leicester Fields (the south side of Leicester Square), the party discussed whether the expected "munificence" might come in the form of one large donation, or as an increase to Johnson's pension. Johnson preferred the latter. The other two began to talk of the prospect of a winter in Italy, a country revered by all men of learning for its classical connotations, and one that Johnson had never seen. (He had planned to go there in 1776 with his friends the Thrales, but the trip had been cancelled after the death of their son.) Johnson did not expect much happiness: "Were I going to Italy to see fine paintings, like Sir Joshua Reynolds, or to run after women, like Boswell, I might be sure to have pleasure in Italy. But when a man goes to Italy merely to feel how he breathes the air, he can enjoy very little."

Nevertheless, Johnson felt sufficiently robust to discuss the relative merits of urban and rural life in characteristically dogmatic style. "Those who are content to live in the country," he pronounced, "are *fit* for the country." This remark must have tantalized Boswell, who was on the point of leaving for Scotland yet again, and who was still hesitating about whether to live in London, Edinburgh, or Auchinleck. Only a few weeks earlier, Johnson had at last succumbed to Boswell's bullying and provided the required advice: he agreed that Boswell might try his luck in London after all. Even then, Boswell had not been satisfied until Johnson had given him this opinion in writing. Boswell planned to frame Johnson's letter and hang it on the wall, so that if anyone asked why he had come to London, he could point to it and say: "*There are my reasons!*"

After the dinner was over, Reynolds offered his guests a ride home in his coach. This was a kindness to Johnson, who could not now walk any distance without discomfort. Outside Johnson's lodgings the coach waited while the two friends made their goodbyes. Then Johnson stepped down onto the pavement. He called out, "Fare you well," and without looking back, sprang away "with a kind of pathetic briskness."[48]

Johnson returned to Bolt Court to find a letter waiting from Hester Thrale. For nearly twenty years, since she was in her early twenties, this lively, quick-witted, and bird-like woman (only four feet eleven inches tall) had been his intimate friend and confidante. Her husband Henry, a wealthy brewer, had also been one of his most trusted friends. The Thrales' large, comfortable houses in Streatham and Southwark had been like second homes to him. He had kept his own room in each of them; he had been accepted there almost as part of the family. But three years before, Henry Thrale had died; since then, for reasons that Johnson may have suspected but could not wholly comprehend, Hester Thrale had begun to withdraw from him. "Do not neglect me, nor relinquish me," he wrote to her: "Nobody will ever love you better, or honour you more." But he had seen her less and less; even when he had been so desperately ill, she would not come to him. Now her letter explained everything: she had fallen in love with her daughter's singing teacher, the Italian Gabriel Piozzi, and planned to marry him. Johnson was shocked and hurt. He sent her an angry letter, and though he subsequently tried to retract, their friendship was at an end. He never saw her again. Boswell had gone back to Scotland; and he had lost Hester Thrale for ever.

Johnson was now nearly seventy-five. His strength had at last begun to fail. He had suffered a stroke the previous year, and his legs and feet swelled, as a result of heart failure. His acute emphysema—which he called "asthma"—made breathing miserable. His wheezing forced him to sit up in bed at night, and increasingly he could sleep only with the help of drugs, which left him exhausted by day. When the plan to send him to Italy came to nothing (the King declined to increase his pension), he set out on a valedictory tour of his old haunts in the English Midlands. He hoped that leaving the polluted air of London for a while might ease his chest, but it was a wretched summer. From Ashbourne in Derbyshire, he wrote to his friend Dr Charles Burney: "I am now reduced to think, and am at last content to talk of the weather."[49]

Boswell's disorder was of a different kind. On his return to Edinburgh, he plunged into one of the periodic glooms that could paralyse him for weeks or even months at a time. "How strange, how weak, how unfortunate is it that this my *native city* and my *countrymen* should affect me with such wretchedness," he wailed to his friend Temple: "What of my love of England, where I am *absolutely certain* that I *enjoy life*, whereas *here* it is *insipid*, nay, *disgusting*."[50]

He longed to return to London and pursue his fortune at the English bar, but his debts and the ill-health of his wife kept him in Scotland. He had almost abandoned his career as an Edinburgh advocate—but he was forty-three; perhaps he had left it too late to start again? Friends and family combined to dissuade him from embarking on such a hazardous venture. He felt at once misery and indecision. In such a dejected and fretful state, he wrote to Johnson, describing a dream which had filled him with anxiety: was his friend ill, perhaps even dying? Johnson, however, was not grateful for such solicitude. Boswell annoyed him by tactlessly harping on death and the afterlife. Johnson knew that death was near; he did not want to be constantly reminded of it. He reproached the younger man for "affecting discontent, and indulging the vanity of complaint . . . Nothing ailed me at the time; let your superstitions at last have an end . . . My dear friend, life is very short and very uncertain; let us spend it as well as we can." Throughout their friendship Johnson had advised Boswell not to indulge in melancholic introspection. Now he urged him, "Write to me often, and write like a man."[51]

But Boswell was not easily roused. After replying that his friend was doing him an injustice, he fell silent for a period of months. The summer passed, and then the autumn. Johnson complained that he had heard nothing from Boswell for months. "I have this summer sometimes amended, and sometimes relapsed, but, upon the whole, have lost ground, very much," he wrote on 3 November. "My legs are extremely weak, and my breath very short, and the water is now increasing upon me. In this uncomfortable state your letters used to relieve; what is the reason that I have them no longer? Are you sick, or are you sullen?"[52]

Boswell's self-pity must have been irritating to such a sick man as Johnson. Even Boswell seemed to recognize this, when on the advice of his sensible wife (who, herself coughing up blood, had good reason to be impatient with her husband's hypochondria) he suppressed a letter written "in a kind of despair" and wrote a milder one instead, merely detailing "my sad illness."[53]

Johnson returned to London, and his health worsened. In early December he began urgently putting his affairs in order. He made a will, and burned some of his papers and diaries. He spent much of the time in prayer. On 13 December 1784, at about seven o'clock in the evening, he died.

PART TWO

LIFE WRITTEN

FOUR

INDEPENDENCE

꧁ ꧂

I am soon to publish the Journal of a Tour to the Hebrides, in company with him, which will exhibit a specimen of that wonderful conversation in which wisdom and wit were equally conspicuous. It will be a prelude to my large work, the Life of Samuel Johnson LL.D. . . .[1]

BOSWELL HEARD THE NEWS of Johnson's death in Edinburgh four days later. He felt "stunned, and in a kind of amaze" at the loss of his friend. He had loved and revered Johnson, clinging to him as a source of spiritual and moral strength. Now he resolved to "honour his memory by doing as much as I could to fulfil his noble precepts of religion and morality."

The very next day, he received a letter from the bookseller-publisher Charles Dilly. "In the true spirit of *the trade*," Dilly urged Boswell to prepare an instant book: four hundred pages on Johnson's conversations, by February. Johnson had been a celebrity, a literary colossus, renowned for the declamatory style of his speech; the public would be hungry for titbits. His friendship with Boswell, which stretched back more than twenty years, was well known; Boswell was rumoured to have kept a record of everything Johnson had said in his presence, and to be collecting anecdotes about him; these could easily be made into a book. His loss was also his opportunity.

Boswell had already received an earlier proposal from Dilly that he should edit Johnson's works and write his biography in a uniform edition. He replied confirming that he did indeed have "a large collection of materials for his life, but would write it deliberately." He did not want to write a rushed book, nor was he capable of doing so, for he was still in a state of torpor, suffering from the depression which had plagued him on and off since the summer. In his journal he confessed to a feeling of unease: "There would be considerable expectations from me of memoirs of my illustrious friend, but . . . habits of indolence and dejection of spirit would probably hinder me from laudable exertion."[2]

Dilly kept up the pressure. Two days after his letter suggesting a volume of Johnson's conversations, another letter arrived from him, this time recommending that Boswell should announce to the press his intention to write Johnson's life, presumably as a deterrent to others. It was already obvious that there *would* be others; within a fortnight of Johnson's death, as many as six biographies were rumoured to be in preparation. The body had barely settled in the earth before the scuffle began to exhume Johnson in print. "The news writers threaten us with many lives of him," chuckled Boswell's friend Temple. "Your long and entire intimacy with him well qualify you to satisfy completely the public curiosity."[3]

A few days later Dilly wrote once more, asserting that the public would respect a life of Johnson written by Boswell more than one written by an executor[4] — a reference to the lawyer and magistrate Sir John Hawkins, who had appointed himself Johnson's official biographer, following an approach from a consortium of London booksellers only hours after Johnson's death. Hawkins was a poor writer and unpopular with many of Johnson's intimate friends. But as executor Hawkins had the advantage of access to Johnson's private papers, his diary in particular; in addition he had known Johnson much longer than had Boswell: since the 1740s, when Johnson was working on his *Dictionary*. In 1749, Hawkins, Johnson, and a few others had formed the Ivy Lane Club, a literary discussion-group; and in 1764, Hawkins had been among the founder-members of the more famous and exclusive Literary Club, to which Boswell was only much later admitted. In view of Hawkins's advantages, therefore, Dilly advised Boswell to prepare for publication as soon as he could.

Another dangerous rival was Johnson's former friend and confidante Hester Thrale, now Mrs Piozzi. She was still honeymooning in Italy with her new husband, but there was strong expectation that she too would produce a memoir of some kind. She had occupied a special place in Johnson's heart, and might know secrets inaccessible to others.

Others besides Dilly recommended Boswell to publish his biography of Johnson sooner rather than later. John Nichols, editor of the *Gentleman's Magazine,* told him he might get "three—nay, ten times as much" money if he were first to publish a life of Johnson.[5] Underlying this urgency was the fear that interest in the subject might rapidly diminish. Though Johnson had been one of the most famous men alive, his reputation was not certain to last after his death. In his lifetime he had been revered as a sage; after his death he might be forgotten.

But Boswell did not want to be rushed. "I wish first to see many other lives of him," he informed Reynolds, "that I may both receive additional information and correct mistakes and misrepresentations."[6] While he waited for these, he planned to publish his account of the tour to the Hebrides that he and Johnson had undertaken eleven years earlier, as a prelude to writing Johnson's biography. His journal of the tour already existed in manuscript, and might form the basis of a book. Meanwhile, he would continue to collect material for the longer work to follow.

Johnson was buried in Westminster Abbey on 20 December, a week after his death. Boswell could not have reached London in time to attend the funeral, even if he had left immediately on hearing the news of Johnson's death. The service was conducted by one of Johnson's oldest friends, the Reverend Dr John Taylor; Edmund Burke delivered the eulogy.

Johnson's will was published a week later. Besides Hawkins, there were two other executors: Sir Joshua Reynolds, and another old friend of Johnson's, the academic-turned-barrister Dr William Scott. Apart from a stepdaughter, Lucy Porter, Johnson had no family living, and the bulk of his estate was left in trust for his black servant, Francis Barber; but there were also bequests for his godchildren and others, and he left £200 to the representatives of the late Mr Innys, a bookseller at St Paul's Churchyard who had helped Johnson's father to continue his bookselling business after he became a bankrupt. Boswell was uneasy to find his name missing from the list of those that Johnson had nominated to receive a book from his library; but then (he reflected) so were those of several other old friends. Boswell was further consoled by a letter from Johnson's physician, Dr Richard Brocklesby, who assured him that Johnson had loved and respected him sincerely, and had spoken of him on his deathbed.[7]

Boswell remained in a state of shock. "His death still made an impression of amazement upon my mind," he noted in his journal on 28 December, eleven days after receiving the news. "I could not fully believe it. My *imagination* was not convinced."[8] But at the end of the year, his depression lifted; and he was further cheered by a series of unsigned letters that appeared in the *St James's Chronicle* in early January. These hailed him as the man most suited to write Johnson's biography, and disparaged other claimants, Hawkins and Mrs Piozzi in particular. "It is evident from the conduct of the late Dr Johnson, that he designed Mr Boswell for the sole writer of his Life," stated the anonymous contributor: "Why else did he furnish him with such materials for it as were withheld from every other friend?" Johnson had intended to destroy such papers as might assist any other biographer, the letter continued; such scraps as had escaped destruction (a reference to the diary) were "trifling." Boswell, on the other hand, had been collecting Johnsoniana for more than twenty years:

> His playful importunities and anxious solicitations were alike prevalent with Johnson. If he failed once in an inquiry, he renewed it at a more lucky hour, and seldom retired without the intelligence he sought. During his long association with the Doctor in England, as well as throughout his Hebridean tour, he may be pronounced to have lost no opportunity of search respecting the past occurrences of our author's life, or his sentiments relevant to men and literature; nor will it be suspected by those who are acquainted with Mr Boswell's active mind that his curiosity permitted one circumstance to escape him that might illustrate the habits or exalt the character of the sage whom he respected almost to adoration.[9]

Boswell was so flattered by this letter of praise that he felt it prudent to write to the *St James's Chronicle* explaining that he had not written it himself. In fact, the author was the scholar George Steevens, who had known Johnson well, having collaborated with him on his edition of Shakespeare and contributed to his *Lives of the Poets*. Steevens may have urged Boswell's claim because he actively disliked Hawkins.

Perhaps encouraged by this attention, Boswell wrote to various informants asking for recollections of Johnson and copies of his letters: to Lucy Porter, Johnson's stepdaughter; to the Reverend Dr William Adams, now Master of Johnson's old college, Pembroke; to Anna Seward, whose novel *Louisa* had made her one of the most prominent literary personalities in Lichfield, Johnson's birthplace; and to Johnson's childhood friend Edmund Hector. He had already sent a similar request to Francis Barber. Soon he began to receive Johnsoniana in response. Boswell was anxious to ensure that no detail, however small, was omitted; to Mary Cobb, a contemporary of Johnson's from Lichfield, he wrote: "You will oblige me much, and will help me to oblige the world, if you will take the trouble to write down and send to me every anecdote concerning him, from his earliest years, and every one of his sayings that you recollect. The utmost minuteness will be desirable."[10]

One of the replies to these inquiries led Boswell to make perhaps the most serious of the very few factual errors in the *Life of Johnson*. Adams had made a search of the college books, and on the evidence of these he informed Boswell that Johnson had been an undergraduate at Pembroke from 1728 until 1731, when a shortage of funds following his father's insolvency had forced him to leave the university without a degree. This last part was true: Johnson had indeed been forced to leave Oxford because of lack of money, but after only thirteen months, not three years—an understandable mistake on Adams's part, because the college records were confusing, showing charges against Johnson's name continuing for almost two years after he had left.[11]

On the night of 5 February 1785, Johnson appeared to Boswell in a dream. "I saw him distinctly, sitting in the chair opposite to me in his usual dress. He talked something which I do not perfectly recollect about his library not being in such order as he could have wished, and gave as a reason his being hurried as death approached." The dream left "a deep and pleasing impression on my mind." To the credulous Boswell, who was frightened of ghosts and who believed in second sight, dreams were significant: not as vehicles for the dreamer's subconscious thoughts, but as literal manifestations of the spirit world. To the modern reader,

Boswell's dreams of Johnson suggest that he (rather than Johnson's spirit) was unsettled: disturbed not to have been mentioned in his friend's will, not even to the extent of being left a book from his library; and perhaps uneasy about the propriety of his plan to write Johnson's life.

The idea that Boswell might write Johnson's biography had taken root many years before; even at their first meeting Boswell resolved to "mark what I remember of his conversation." In the opening paragraphs of the *Life of Johnson*, Boswell would write that he "had the scheme of writing his life constantly in view" throughout their twenty-year friendship. But it seems that for a long time he regarded this as an extremely sensitive subject, one to be approached only very delicately.

Passing through Wittenberg in 1764, Boswell had visited the church where Luther first preached the Reformation, and where he had subsequently been buried, alongside his contemporary and fellow-theologian Philip Melanchthon, their tombs being marked by plates of metal fixed to the floor. Inspired by this sight, the impressionable young Boswell decided to write to his mentor on that very spot, vowing eternal attachment, and promising that "if you die before me, I shall endeavour to do honour to your memory." In keeping with his romantic mood, Boswell lay full-length on the church floor to write the letter, pressing against the tomb. Boswell was too nervous of Johnson's reaction to post the letter to him straight away, for fear "lest I should appear at once too superstitious and too enthusiastic"; he delayed sending it until almost *thirteen years* had passed, when the subject of Boswell's plan to write Johnson's biography had already been raised more than once in conversation between them.[12]

In his *Account of Corsica*, Boswell had offended Johnson by quoting an extract from one of his letters without obtaining his permission beforehand. After apologizing, Boswell asked Johnson tentatively whether it would be improper to publish his letters after his death. "Nay, Sir," came the reply: "when I am dead, you may do as you will."[13]

Boswell and Johnson discussed the topic of biography during Boswell's trip to London in 1772, his first in three years. Encouraged by this conversation, Boswell confessed in his journal that he had "a constant plan to write the life of Mr Johnson. I have not told him of it yet, nor do I know if I should tell him. I said that if it was not troublesome and presuming too much, I would beg of him to tell me all the little circumstances of his life, what schools he attended, when he came to Oxford, when he came to London, etc, etc. He did not disapprove of my curiosity as to these particulars, but said, 'They'll come out by degrees.'"[14]

Johnson continued to talk about biography, and he returned to the subject just before Boswell left London in May, saying that he hoped Boswell would write the lives of all their friends.[15] It is hard to resist the conclusion that Johnson was teasing Boswell, dangling before him the possibility that the young Scot might write his life, without allowing the subject to be discussed openly. In the autumn of the same year, Boswell confided his design to write Johnson's biography in a letter to Garrick, written from Edinburgh. Perhaps he hoped that Garrick might disclose this to his old master, sparing Boswell any confrontation that might ensue.[16]

On his next trip to London the following spring, Boswell again asked Johnson for details of his early life. "You shall have them all for twopence," Johnson replied. "I hope you shall know a great deal more of me before you write my Life."[17] His remark suggests that by now Boswell's scheme was being discussed openly between author and subject, and so it has generally been taken; but perhaps Johnson was still teasing Boswell (just as he would tease Mrs Thrale; within three months of this conversation, shortly before Johnson set out for Scotland, he would suggest that *she* might write his life). During their tour of Scotland in the summer of 1773, Boswell took the opportunity to solicit further details from Johnson:

> The Sunday evening that we sat by ourselves at Aberdeen, I asked him several particulars of his life from his early years, which he readily told me, and I marked down before him. This day I proceeded in my inquiries, also marking before him. I have them on separate leaves of paper. I shall lay up authentic materials for THE LIFE OF SAMUEL JOHNSON, LL.D., and if I survive him, I shall be the one who shall most faithfully do honour to his memory. I have now a vast treasure of his conversation at different times since the year 1762 when I first obtained his acquaintance;* and by assiduous inquiry I can make up for not knowing him sooner.

*This is an error; they did not meet until 1763.

Boswell subsequently added a footnote to this passage in his journal: "It is no small satisfaction to me to reflect that Dr Johnson read this, and, after being apprised of my intention, communicated to me, at subsequent periods, many particulars of his life, which probably could not otherwise have been preserved." Such was the curious manner in which Boswell informed Johnson of his decision to write Johnson's biography. He had nursed this ambition for many years, almost from the first moment the two men met, but he had always been nervous about broaching the subject. And though it had been obvious to Johnson that Boswell was collecting material about him, Boswell had not dared to raise the matter directly. Now he announced his intention in his journal, and showed it to Johnson; when no protest was forthcoming, he took that as Johnson's consent.[18]

By the time Boswell returned to London in 1775, it seems that his plan to write a book about Johnson was no longer secret. On 8 April, Boswell was quietly writing his journal at Dilly's, where he was lodging, when Tom Davies called. "I am quite full of Dr Johnson's sayings," Boswell told him. "I am tapping myself." "Well," said Davies, "it will be good wine to draw off for the public." (This, it should be remembered, was a conversation between a bookseller and an author, in the home of his publisher.)[19] Boswell grew less inhibited about his scheme, and began to collect source-material for the book from friends and colleagues of Johnson's. As he accompanied Johnson on tours of his master's old haunts, Oxford, Birmingham, Lichfield, and Ashbourne, he collected anecdotes (which he recorded in his special notebook) *en route* from many of those who had known Johnson before he came to live in London. In 1778, William Strahan, the publisher of many of Johnson's works, replied to a request for information by saying that he would be glad to contribute to the "Great Life."[20] The year before, Lord Monboddo had warned Boswell that Johnson was not a fit subject for biography, and advised that he should concentrate on Homer instead.

Boswell's status as Johnson's biographer was unofficial but widely acknowledged. The mere fact that Johnson did not discourage Boswell's efforts to collect information about him, and at various times provided such information himself, meant that Boswell could claim to have his subject's blessing. "Dr Johnson knew that I was his Biographer,"

Boswell confirmed to Anna Seward, after Johnson's death: "and gave me a thousand particulars which will be interwoven into my narrative."

If Boswell's plan to write Johnson's biography was so widely known, why then did the London booksellers approach Sir John Hawkins immediately after Johnson's death? Why not Boswell? William Strahan was one of the two-man deputation sent to call on Hawkins; he was certainly aware of Boswell's intention to write a "Great Life."

For commercial reasons, the booksellers were anxious to move quickly. There was a wave of interest in Johnson; they wanted to ride this before it broke. Hawkins was in London, on the spot, and as one of the executors, he had access to Johnson's papers, including his diary, which promised more than it delivered. Boswell was marooned in Edinburgh, far away from the sources of information, and no one knew when he might be in London again.

The booksellers had approached Hawkins, in his capacity as an executor, about the possibility of producing a collected edition of Johnson's works; presumably he would be in a position to license the copyright. It was for this reason that they had clubbed together, to finance such a large project jointly. The proposal for a biography emerged naturally out of this discussion; it was normal practice for a short life to be appended to the works. It quickly became clear that Hawkins planned to write something more ambitious; when he showed himself to be in possession of valuable source-material, eager to write a biography, and in a position to authorize himself to proceed, the booksellers may have decided that this was an offer too tempting to refuse. Hawkins was a dull writer, but he was known to be reliable; he had compiled a huge, five-volume *General History of the Science and Practice of Music*. Anything he produced was likely to be authoritative, in keeping with the eminence of the subject; while Boswell, though a more fluent writer, lacked both judgement and discretion, was prone to disabling bouts of melancholia, and was thought by some to be flighty or even half-mad.

Only Dilly pursued Boswell immediately after Johnson's death. Perhaps the London booksellers decided that they might have the best of both worlds: an "official" biography, to be written and published as soon as possible; and Boswell's *Magnum Opus,* to appear at some unspecified date in the future.

In the first three months after Johnson's death, Boswell made little progress with his book on the Hebridean tour. Part of the problem was the form: should he publish the journal unaltered, or should he write it up into a more conventional narrative? His only previous full-length book, published sixteen years earlier, had been a hybrid, a journal of his tour to Corsica combined with a narrative history of the island. Boswell felt that his journal had been the most valuable part of his Corsican book, and his opinion had been supported by Johnson: "Your History is like other histories, but your Journal is in a very high degree curious and delightful."[21] Now Boswell hesitated; but gradually he persuaded himself, with the help of friends to whom he had read portions of the manuscript, that his Hebridean journal might be printed much as it had been written. "I resolved that I would set myself down quietly in London, and get the Work executed easily."[22]

In deciding to publish his journal of the Hebridean tour without substantial modification, Boswell was taking a risk—perhaps more of a risk than he knew. Inevitably he would be revealing many personal details about Johnson; such intimate biography was extremely controversial. Boswell would cite Joseph Spence's anecdotes of Pope in defence of his method; but Spence had not published these in his lifetime, and his executors had thought them unsuitable for publication afterwards. When Mrs Thrale dipped into Johnson's copy of Spence's manuscript, more than twenty years after Spence's death, she had been shocked to see "how all privacies are thus discover'd"—though not too shocked to prevent her from continuing to read it and copy down extracts.[23] Like Aubrey's *Lives,* Spence's *Anecdotes* would not be thought suitable for publication until the early nineteenth century, a hundred years or so after they were written. Nor were other examples of this style of biography encouraging. Anthony Wood, who had drawn on Aubrey's work for his biographical dictionary *Athenae Oxonienses,* had been expelled from the University of Oxford as a result. This had happened nearly a century before, but the general reluctance to expose private life to public gaze persisted.

On 21 March 1785, Boswell left Scotland to travel to London. At the border-town of Carlisle, he again dreamed of Johnson.[24] The effect was gratifying; obviously Johnson approved of Boswell's intention to publish the journal, and in due course to write his life. "It is a great consolation to me now, that I was so assiduous in collecting the wisdom and wit of that wonderful man."[25]

On the tour of Scotland in 1773, Boswell had taken with him two blank notebooks, later supplemented by a third which Johnson gave him on Skye, and when this ran out he continued on loose sheets of paper that he managed to obtain on the remote island of Col. His technique then was to write rough notes on everything that had happened (in particular, everything that Johnson had said) as soon as possible after the event, writing these up into journal form afterwards. It was important to do so promptly because, as he asserted more than once, no man's memory could preserve facts or sayings with such fidelity as could be done by writing them down at the time. For the most part, Boswell was a diligent journal-writer, but inevitably he was almost always a few days behind. Ironically the work of writing up the journal restricted the amount of time he and Johnson spent together on the tour. ". . . It is curious that although I will run from one end of London to another to have an hour with him, I should omit to seize any spare time to be in his company when I am in the house with him. But my Journal is really a task of much time and labour, and Mr Johnson forbids me to contract it."[26]

Within the pages of Boswell's journal one can discern a struggle for control between author and subject. Johnson, at sixty-four then exactly double Boswell's age, was senior to Boswell in every way, as the younger man would have been the first to concede. He possessed enormous authority throughout the literary world, probably more than any other man living; consequently while he was alive Johnson could to a large extent dictate what was said about him by his friends, and repel attacks by his enemies. Yet Johnson knew that he was nearing the end of his life; his authority was waning; and he had already opened discussions with prospective biographers, including Boswell. He recognized, perhaps from the start, that he could not prevent Boswell from publishing a revealing book about him after his death, but he could perhaps postpone it until then, and meanwhile he could try to influence what Boswell might write.

Johnson was aware that Boswell was keeping a record of their tour; he read it as they went along, correcting and helping to fill blanks which Boswell had left when he was unsure what had been said. Boswell also recorded Johnson's comments while he was reading: "It is a very pretty journal"; "I take great delight in reading it"; "the more I read of this, I think the more highly of you"; "it grows better and better"; "it might be printed, were the subject fit for printing."[27]

Was this last remark a hint to Boswell not to publish? Later in the tour Johnson pronounced: "This will be a great treasure to us some years hence"[28] — perhaps another hint. The descriptions of Johnson were generally respectful, but by no means always flattering: Boswell did not shrink from describing Johnson's peculiar habits, such as talking to himself. He considered it remarkable (and was slightly disappointed) that Johnson should have read such passages without comment. On one occasion Johnson remarked that the journal painted "a very exact picture of his life":[29] perhaps too exact to be wholly welcome to its subject. Moreover, Boswell's journal was full of indiscretions; some of Johnson's comments, his slighting comments about friends in particular, were not ones that he could have wanted broadcast in his lifetime.

There was strong public demand for an account of their experiences; travel writing was then in vogue, and everything Johnson did and said excited interest. For most Britons, the Hebrides was still a wild and exotic region, one of the least explored in Europe. The Grand Tour was very much the fashion in the mid-eighteenth century, but the route directed the sons of the aristocracy to the sites of classical European civilization. Johnson and Boswell, by heading for the barbarian North, were going in the opposite direction. While the pioneers were away, there was much speculation in London and elsewhere about their adventures. Johnson, for example, was reported to have been obliged to swim from Skye to the mainland clutching the tail of a cow. In particular, the public was keen to learn what Johnson made of the Scots, and vice versa.

Boswell had hoped to capitalize on this interest by publishing a book about the tour after their return, but his ambition was soon

squashed. On 21 October 1773, when they were on the brink of departure from the Hebrides, Boswell overheard Johnson casually asking
their host, MacLeod, whether he might make use of a manuscript a
local schoolmaster had written, "in case I publish anything."[30] This was
the first indication Johnson had given to Boswell that he too planned a
book about their experiences.[31] "I rejoiced at the thought," wrote
Boswell; but it must have been a blow, for he abruptly abandoned his
journal, though it was by then almost complete. It would be six years
before he took it up once again.

The senior man had pulled rank. Boswell was in no position to discourage Johnson from proceeding, while he was unable to publish his
own book without Johnson's authorization. To have done so would
have been to put at risk the most important friendship of his life. He
was snookered.

As they proceeded on the tour, Johnson had been writing long letters describing what he was seeing to Mrs Thrale. These would form
the basis of a book when Johnson returned to London in the winter of
1773–74 and began writing. He borrowed Boswell's journal for reference. Over the next few months, he sent a series of letters to Boswell in
Edinburgh inquiring about various Scottish topics, and Boswell duti-
fully obliged by trying to provide answers. Johnson was normally a
dilatory writer, but for once he wrote quickly, and by midsummer his
Journey to the Western Islands of Scotland was finished. "I wish you could
have looked over my book before the printer, but it could not easily
be," he wrote to Boswell, who afterwards was sorry that Johnson had
not allowed him the opportunity to read the manuscript before it was
printed. "I should have changed very little; but I should have suggested
an alteration in a few places where he has laid himself open to be
attacked."[32] Later in the year, Johnson again wrote to Boswell that "I
wish you could have read the book before it was printed, but our distance does not easily permit it." In late November Johnson presented
printed copies of his book to Mrs Thrale and to the King; he regretted
that he could not send Boswell a copy before it was published: "trade is
as diligent as courtesy."[33]

Boswell received his copy of Johnson's book on 18 January 1775.
It was nothing like Boswell's journal; there was no gossip in it; instead, there was a thoughtful and sympathetic portrait of a decaying

Highland culture. Boswell was pleased to find himself mentioned in the opening paragraphs as "a companion, whose acuteness would help my inquiry, and whose gaiety of conversation, and civility of manners, are sufficient to counteract the inconveniences of travel." In fact, he was so pleased that he would quote Johnson's remark in his own book when it was finally published, ten years later.[34]

Now that Johnson's book was available, Boswell hoped that he might be permitted to publish his journal; but the omens were not encouraging. He tested Johnson's attitude by writing to ask if Johnson preferred the devotional Latin verses he had written on the sacred island of Inchkenneth to be kept private. Back came the rebuke: "Your love of publication is offensive and disgusting, and will end, if it be not reformed, in a general distrust among all your friends."[35]

For another opinion, Boswell lent the three volumes of his journal to his friend and banker Sir William Forbes. In due course Forbes returned the journal, which, he said, "has both instructed and delighted me to a very high degree." Indicating that he, like Johnson, thought it unsuitable for publication, Forbes added: "I am perfectly of opinion with your learned companion that it will be a treasure to you in all time to come."[36]

But Boswell still hoped his journal might be published, especially when Dilly urged him to bring it to London. In the spring of 1775, Boswell arrived in town to find Johnson's recently published *Journey to the Western Islands of Scotland* the common topic of conversation there. "We have all been reading your travels, Mr Boswell," remarked Lord Mansfield, the Lord Chief Justice, at one of his Sunday-evening get-togethers; "I was but the humble attendant of Dr Johnson," replied Boswell. In the public mind, Boswell was now identified as Johnson's companion.

The next day he drove with Johnson to Sir Joshua Reynolds's house, and while Johnson sat for Reynolds's sister, who was painting his portrait, Boswell read passages from his journal to their host. Reynolds observed confidentially, "It is more entertaining than his." In the hackney-coach home, Boswell told Johnson that he had been approached about the possibility of publishing his journal; Johnson advised him not to show it to anybody, "but bid me draw out of it what I thought might be published, and he would look it over."[37] Boswell expressed his frustration in a letter to Temple: "Between ourselves, he is not apt to encourage one to *share* reputation with himself."[38] Still seeking support for publication, he lent his journal to Mrs Thrale; she returned it to him a couple of days later with "a thousand thanks for your entertaining manuscript." Though, as Boswell later discovered, she had not read it thoroughly, she complimented him by suggesting that she had read it so avidly as to strain her eyes: "Your Journal has almost blinded me."[39]

Johnson's equivocal feelings about the journal can be judged by his letters to Mrs Thrale. "I am not sorry that you read Boswell's journal," he wrote, while she had it in her possession: "Is it not a merry piece? There is much in it about poor me." Three weeks later he asked her about it again: "You never told me . . . how you were entertained by Boswell's journal. One would think the man had been hired to be a spy upon me"; and a week afterwards, he returned to the subject once more: "Do you read Boswell's journals? He moralized, and found my faults, and laid them up to reproach me. Boswell's narrative is very natural, and therefore very entertaining; he never made any scruple of showing it to me. He is a very fine fellow."[40]

Discouraged by Johnson's reaction, Boswell put aside his journal, although he brought it out from time to time to show friends. When he took it up again, years afterwards, to write up the remaining month he and Johnson had spent on the Scottish mainland, he regretted that "my Journal cannot have the same fullness and freshness when written now as when written recently after the scenes recorded."[41] He castigated himself for not having completed the journal earlier, while the events were still fresh in his memory: "much has thus been irretrievably lost." He still had his original notes to draw on, though these were not as full as he would have wished. He wrote very slowly, perhaps because any hope of publishing the book in Johnson's lifetime was now extinguished. As he had done on the tour itself, he continued to show what he had written to Johnson from time to time, and in the early summer of 1784, when they were together in Oxford, Johnson added a note on a blank page in the journal.

Boswell was stunned and saddened by his friend's death later that year, but in one sense it liberated him. At long last, more than a decade after the tour it described, he was free to publish his own account.

FIVE

COLLABORATION

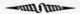

Your kind attention to my book is wonderful.[1]

HE HAD RESOLVED to settle himself down quietly in London to finish his book. But the pleasures of the capital proved irresistible. His host, General Paoli, allowed him to come and go as he pleased, and on his first Saturday in London he did not return home until seven in the morning. During his first few weeks in London, he did little work, hurling himself into a giddy round of dining, drinking, and whoring. On 19 April 1785, for example, he began the day with a brandy and a talk with Sir Joseph Banks, now President of the Royal Society. He breakfasted at a coffee-house in Shepherd Market, then called on William Almack, a barrister, son of the founder of the club later known as Brooks's. By the time he left Almack's, he was "quite intoxicated." He next encountered an acquaintance from Scotland, Sir Charles Preston, before meeting one Polly Wilson for what he described in his diaries as "a double." Another brandy gave him "a wild glow." He saw Miss Palmer, niece to Sir Joshua Reynolds, and met Edmund Burke with his son, before dining in a party that included his old friend John Wilkes. Afterwards he listened to music at the home of Mrs Cosway, the beautiful wife of the Court miniaturist Richard Cosway, before a supper with an Ayrshire friend, washed down with two bottles of claret. Though he claimed to be "quite sober" when he went to bed, he felt ill the next day, and did not rise until the afternoon.

In these circumstances Boswell's writing progressed slowly. On 30 April, after yet another dinner, Boswell called at his publisher, Dilly's, where he and the printer Henry Baldwin fixed how the book would be printed. They agreed that Baldwin's compositor should set the text as he received it, and print the sheets, afterwards redistributing the type. Baldwin stressed the importance of a regular supply of text: "You must *feed* the press." Alas, lamented Boswell, "Dinners, etc. I *feed myself.*"

On 7 May, Boswell dined with Bennet Langton, one of Johnson's closest friends, who had been with him when he died. Among the other guests was the bluestocking poet and dramatist Hannah More, founder of the Sunday School movement. When the subject of Boswell's planned biography of Johnson arose in conversation, she entreated him to be tender towards their "virtuous and most revered departed friend," begging Boswell to "mitigate some of his asperities"; Boswell answered roughly that "he would not cut off his claws, nor make a tiger a cat, to please anybody." Hannah More's concern reflected a widely felt anxiety about how Johnson would appear under the scrutiny of biographers. As a Christian moralist, Johnson had been a national figure; those who admired him most feared that personal weaknesses might undermine the standing of their hero. Hannah More was only too aware of his irascibility, having been lashed by his tongue herself. Nobody was quite sure what might emerge about Johnson's relationship with Mrs Piozzi. As the first biographies of Johnson—all of them feeble stuff by comparison with what was to come—began to roll off the presses, they were read with keen anticipation. In general, the early biographers of Johnson took one of two approaches: straight-forward eulogy; or (the approach which Boswell himself would take) the triumph of character over flaws.[2] There was much speculation about Boswell's book. The Queen herself discussed the subject with one of her ladies-in-waiting. "I can't tell what he will do," the Queen remarked. "He is so extraordinary a man that perhaps he will devise something extraordinary."[3]

Despite the level of public expectation, Boswell found plenty to distract him from writing. Friday the thirteenth of May 1785, for example, began with Betsy Smith, a favourite prostitute, "twice." Then Boswell called round briefly to Dilly's, before breakfasting with Molly Knowles, a witty Quaker who had not been too intimidated to spar with Johnson himself. Together they went on to the annual gathering of the Society of Friends, where a man rebuked Boswell for reading the *St James's Chronicle* at Quaker Meeting. At Batson's Coffee-House in Cornhill, Boswell met William James, a banker ruined when one of his partners had speculated unwisely in East India Company stock. Everyone was then talking about the new hot-air balloons, and James took him to the gardens of the Bethlehem Royal Hospital for the Insane (also known as Bethlem or Bedlam), where they were amongst a crowd estimated at up to one hundred thousand watching the Italian Vincenzo Lunardi ascend in his balloon, only the second time he had done so in England. Boswell was "shocked and pleased" at the sight, and by the "pleasing ladies" gathered to watch it. Afterwards he looked in at the wards where the lunatics lived, a common diversion at the time, and sang part of a song, "Maid of Bedlam," with a pretty inmate. He dined with Dr William Scott, to whom he outlined the argument of a pamphlet he was preparing; his host told him "there was a great deal of phlogiston" (hot air) in it. He drank heavily, and was "intoxicated much." Afterwards he found himself singing ballads with two women in red coats, probably prostitutes, in St Paul's Churchyard. His pocket was picked, he fell down in the street, and had to be helped home by two strangers.

Three days later "something not quite right" appeared, and Boswell hurried over to see Betsy Smith. She "thought not," but a week later she consented to seek treatment at St Thomas's Hospital, where Boswell paid her medical bills, entering them in his meticulous accounts under "sundries." He treated himself with mercury pills, under the supervision of a doctor who had twice before cured him of venereal infections, and within a few weeks the problem cleared.

Another distraction came from public executions, which Boswell had viewed with a horrid fascination ever since, as an Edinburgh schoolboy, he had witnessed the grim processions towards the gallows in the Grassmarket. These were popular public spectacles, held in the early morning; a small group of prisoners would be hanged on each occasion. Large crowds gathered to watch, including the diseased, who believed that being touched by the sweaty hands of the dying could cure them. But Boswell's interest in everything to do with dying was unusual, even in an era when execution was a popular entertainment. He cultivated Richard Akerman, the Keeper of Newgate Prison, who fed him stories of the inmates and gave him special access to the prisoners. On the morning of the executions, Boswell would rise early and slip into the prison so that he could mingle with the men and women about to die. He talked to them, and tried to imagine their thoughts. He watched as their chains were struck off, a brief moment of release before they were taken outside to the waiting crowd. During the executions themselves, he tried to secure a position nearby where he could watch uninterrupted as life departed from the victim's body, even mounting the scaffold to do so. On at least one occasion, he spoke to the prisoner as he waited to die. He wondered at those who met their fate calmly, and speculated how he might behave in such circumstances. The knowledge that the prisoners had been sentenced by a judge like his father, and vainly defended by a barrister such as himself, played on his mind.

Afterwards he liked to see the bodies cut down, and to examine the faces of the men and women with whom he had so recently been chatting. Sometimes the experience unnerved him. On one occasion he rushed to find a prostitute while the bodies were still dangling. "I have got a shocking sight in my head," he told her. "Take it out." His reaction is indicative. To banish the image of death, Boswell sought to affirm his vitality.

As if Boswell had not distractions enough already, he had decided to write a pamphlet opposing a bill just introduced into the House of Commons, to reduce the number of the judges in the Court of Session from fifteen to ten. Boswell spent much of May writing his *Letter to the People of Scotland on . . . Diminishing the Number of the Lords of Session,* which was published towards the end of the month. It is hard to know quite why he should have chosen to write this, unless he felt that reducing the number of Lords of Session might lessen his own chances of a seat on the bench later on. Whatever his motives, he managed to work up a fine patriotic fervour, portraying himself as the defender of Scottish liberty. "My friends and countrymen, be not afraid," proclaimed a letter sent to the *Edinburgh Advertiser* and the *St James's Chronicle* in the middle of May. "I am *upon the spot*. I am *upon the watch*. The bill shall not pass without a spirited appeal to the justice and honour of the laws of Great Britain. Collect your minds. Be calm; but be firm. You shall hear from me at large a few days hence."

The pamphlet argued that the proposed measure was a pernicious and alarming innovation which threatened to undermine the guarantees given to Scotland at the Union. In particular, it attacked Henry Dundas, the bill's progenitor. As political ruler of Scotland in Pitt's government, Dundas exercised such total control north of the border that Boswell was able to brand him "Harry the Ninth." Disarmingly, Boswell sent Dundas a signed copy.

Even Boswell realized that what he had done was provocative, and he nervously anticipated a challenge from Dundas, or from one of his supporters, such as Sir Adam Fergusson, the Ayrshire MP against whom Boswell had campaigned ineffectively in the last parliamentary election. He became so concerned about this imaginary threat to his safety that he hastily drew up his will. In reality the danger was more to Boswell's political prospects, to his dreams of being "a spoke in the great wheel" and becoming "Baron Boswell of Auchinleck," than to his person—as the MP Jack Lee warned him. Though a friend of Boswell's, Lee himself had been lampooned by him in print. "You're a very odd fellow," commented Lee.[4]

One amusing feature of Boswell's pamphlet was the admission of much extraneous material, including "sketches" of many named individuals, among them Thurlow, Burke, Wilkes, Pitt, Fox, and "a Great Personage" (George III). There was plenty too about the author himself: for example, three pages of genealogical information "showing my consanguinity to Royalty past and present." He was able to demonstrate that he was a distant cousin to both the Stuart Pretender and the reigning monarch, information that would be useful in a future encounter with King George. Interested readers could find an account of Boswell's friendships and differences with men such as Dundas and Fergusson; and a frank revelation of his feelings of honour and happiness in being married to a kinswoman of the Earls of Eglinton. Referring to his wife's maiden name, Boswell praised her in his pamphlet as a "true Montgomerie"—a phrase ridiculed by Wilkes, which became something of a running joke in the literary pages for years to come. Overall, the *Letter to the People of Scotland* was an extraordinary performance, written in such an exuberant style as to lead one scholar to suggest that he must have been drunk as he wrote it.

On 20 May, Boswell attended a levee* at Court. Dressed in a scarlet suit, he felt confident that he "looked like a baron," and he conversed with the titled grandees present "with a perfect possession of myself and serene gaiety." When the King approached and began talking to his companions, Boswell was "a little in a flutter," as he was not quite sure that King George would remember him. (They had last met at a levee almost a year earlier, when Boswell had entertained the King with an account of his scheme to practise at the English bar. On an earlier occasion, he had been so awed by the royal presence that he had answered the King's questions "Yes, my Lord.")[5] So he was relieved when the King turned to him and flatteringly inquired how the biography was progressing. Boswell explained that he first planned to publish his "logbook" of the "curious journey" he had made with Johnson "through a remote part of Your Majesty's dominions, the Highlands and Islands." He revealed his intention to present the finished work to the King. "But when are we to have your other work?" asked King George. "Sir, Your Majesty a little ago remarked that people were sometimes in too great a hurry before they had collected facts. I mean to avoid that fault, and shall take time, as I intend to give a very full account." The King then observed that "there will be many foolish lives first. Do you make the best."

"I believe you knew him more intimately than any man," he continued, adding the name "Dr Johnson" to the others present so that they might know who was being talked of. The two men discussed Johnson's sincere Christian principles and his extraordinarily retentive memory. Nearly twenty years earlier, the King had met Johnson in the

---

*Literally, a reception held on rising, now usually held in the early afternoon, attended by men only. The King circulated around those in attendance, chatting to them informally.

Royal Library at Buckingham House, and they had held a private conversation together which had been the subject of much subsequent comment and speculation.

Boswell was immensely gratified: "The King's gracious benignity refreshed the loyal flame in my bosom." His mind was now "amazingly firm." He decided to take advantage of this valuable interview with the King to raise with him a delicate question. In his forthcoming book, Boswell planned to include the anecdotes he had gathered on the tour of Scotland "concerning that person who in 1745–1746 attempted to recover the throne upon which his ancestors sat"—i.e. Charles Stuart, popularly known as Bonnie Prince Charlie, who had attempted to unseat King George's grandfather, George II. Boswell felt himself at a loss to know how to designate "that person." He wondered whether it might not be insulting to refer to him as "the Pretender," but would it be going too far to refer to him as "Prince Charles"? In a subsequent letter to the King, Boswell stated his confidence that "the only Person who is entitled to take it amiss will liberally excuse my tenderness for what *has been* blood royal."

It was not a tactful subject to raise with the King. The Pretender was still alive, albeit living in increasingly pathetic exile in Rome; and while the threat of Jacobite rebellion had receded, many Englishmen and particularly Scotsmen still harboured an affection for "the King across the water," if not a preference for the House of Stuart over the House of Hanover. Had the army of Highlanders led by "Prince Charles" not turned back when it reached Derby, it might have been he and not King George sitting on the throne.

"Perhaps I am too presumptuous," concluded Boswell, but nevertheless he attended another levee a few days later to press the point with his sovereign. When the King acknowledged his presence, Boswell asked if his letter had been received: "I am come to receive Your Majesty's commands." The King appeared puzzled, and confessed that he had never before been asked his opinion on this point. "What do you think?" he asked. "How do you feel yourself?" Boswell was temporarily at a loss. He bowed low and answered: "That, Sir, I have already stated in writing to Your Majesty." The King smiled benignly. "I think and feel as you do," he said. Boswell asked if he might then do as he had proposed. "But what designation do you mean to give?"

asked the King. Boswell replied that he thought "Prince Charles" was the common expression. His Majesty appeared to hesitate—perhaps anxious to put an end to this embarrassing conversation.* "Or shall it be 'the grandson of King James the Second?'" tried Boswell. The King assented. Boswell agreed with the King that it was not a question of right; his difficulty was simply one of sentiment: "pretender" might be a *parliamentary* expression, but it was not a *gentlemanly* expression: "and, Sir," continued Boswell to the now no doubt astonished King, "allow me to inform you that I am his cousin in the seventh degree."

It was important to clarify this royal nomenclature, because the subject was a selling-point. By the mid-1780s, the Jacobite uprising, its brutal suppression, and the escape of the handsome young Prince had become a legend, bound up with the nostalgia for the Stuarts and the passing of an ancient Highland culture. The danger of a Stuart restoration was in the past; otherwise the Whigs would not have felt so free to attack a Hanoverian King. Jacobite passions had cooled into sentimentality. Boswell's book exploited this. The stories that Boswell had gathered in the Hebrides would be advertised prominently, on the title-page: "WITH AN AUTHENTICK ACCOUNT OF the distresses and escape of the GRANDSON OF KING JAMES II, in the year 1746."

One sign of the way things were changing was the fact that by the time Boswell and Johnson arrived in Scotland in the mid-1770s it was becoming more acceptable to wear Highland costume. After the defeat of the '45 rebellion, the right to bear arms or to wear "plaid, philibeg, trews, shoulder-belts or tartans" had been forbidden to all except the Highland regiments serving in the British Army.[6] But thirty years later, these regulations were no longer enforced (and would soon be abolished): so much so that even the anglicized Sir Alexander Macdonald chose to have his portrait painted in tartan, with kilt, sporran, and bonnet. Within a generation the Hanoverian George IV would be portrayed in Highland dress by Sir David Wilkie. Barbarian garb had become fashion. Revolt had decayed into style.

---

*According to one eye-witness, the King attempted to end the conversation and turned away, but Boswell took his sovereign by the elbow and brought him back round. Henry Dundas was near at hand, no doubt smirking.

•   •   •

Once Boswell had settled this matter of royal protocol, the way was clear for him to publish his book. He had only to finish it. Fortunately, he had found a collaborator, the Irish scholar Edmond Malone, who was everything Boswell was not: consistent, reliable, and methodical. One year older than Boswell, he was a slight, fastidious man, with thin lips and piercing eyes. Shy and awkward in company (especially female company), Malone was confident, even aggressive, in literary matters. Where Boswell vacillated, Malone was decisive. Publication of the journal raised issues of taste, of style, and of tact; all these were too much for Boswell to cope with unaided. Eighteenth-century publishers did not employ editors; Boswell needed advice from a man who knew his own mind, even if only to reject it.

Vicious to his enemies (at least in print), Malone was generous to his friends. A fellow-member of the Literary Club, Malone was also, like Boswell, a lawyer; though a private income of £1,000 a year allowed him the luxury of literary work without thought of return. A bachelor, he lacked domestic distractions. Like Boswell, Malone was a Johnsonian, a fervent admirer of their late friend, whom he had known almost as long. And like Johnson, he was a Shakespearian; his edition of Shakespeare's works would become the natural successor to Johnson's. As a scholar, he recognized Johnson's importance in the history of literature; and as a friend, he was anxious that Johnson's memory should not be traduced by inept or malignant biographers. He recognized the importance of Boswell's work on Johnson, which is why he was prepared to act as his editor, selflessly sacrificing innumerable hours of his time to the preparation of Boswell's books when his own edition of Shakespeare demanded his attention.

Boswell had been in London a month when he met Malone at a dinner on 29 April; and though the two men had not known each other particularly well before, that night they sat up talking until two in the morning. It seems that Boswell may have been dithering about the form his book should take; though he had decided in Scotland that it should be printed much as it had been written, he was still seeking advice on this issue after he arrived in London. Malone added his

weight to the views already given by Reynolds and Banks, that it should
be published in its original form, as Johnson himself had read it. There
was therefore no need for Boswell to continue transcribing it, as he had
been doing; he could make the necessary changes on the manuscript,
adding extra text on "papers apart" and using the combination as setting copy. This made life easier for Boswell, if not for the compositor.
He felt encouraged, and it was perhaps no coincidence that the next
morning he worked seriously on his book for the first time since arriving in town. Unfortunately, he was occupied for the following few
weeks writing his *Letter to the People of Scotland*. This was published
towards the end of May, when Boswell immediately resumed work on
his book, spending all day on it at home in his night-gown on 28 May.

Until early June Malone was preoccupied with other tasks, but on
the third he was free to help Boswell, and from this date until it was finished, Boswell rarely, if ever, worked alone on his book. The two men
met several times each week to collaborate on the text, often labouring
into the night. On 11 August, for example, the two of them devoted the
whole day to the book, breakfasting, dining, taking tea, and supping
together, working until the small hours of the morning: "Yet we did not
get a great deal winnowed, there was so very much chaff in that portion
of it."[7] By this time Boswell had discovered that he had to excise as much
as possible, because the printed book threatened to be far too long;
about one-third of the whole manuscript was eventually discarded.

Few writers have been edited so thoroughly; the manuscript of
Boswell's book shows far more revision in Malone's hand than in
Boswell's. Many of his suggestions concerned minute details: the choice
of individual words or phrases, for example, or the correction of errors
of fact or grammar. But Malone's editing extended much further than
this. He rephrased much of what Boswell had written, even his record
of what Johnson had said. He ruthlessly deleted most of Boswell's
reflective or descriptive passages. He also added long footnotes ampli-
fying or qualifying the main text.

One reason why Boswell needed an editor was to eliminate Scotticisms, about which he was particularly sensitive. Scots usage was
frowned upon as "not English." During the tour Boswell had asked
Johnson to "translate" his journal into good English, and he had proudly

recorded Johnson's response: "Sir, it is very good English."[8] But in writing about Johnson, codifier of the English language and arbiter of English prose style, Boswell knew that he was sailing into dangerous waters. The irony was that he should have found an Irishman to correct his English.

Boswell's journal displayed an informal Johnson: eating voraciously, taking tea at all hours, talking to himself, flying into rages, laughing at the lack of privies in Scotland, anxiously calling out after Boswell in a storm, addressing him as "Bozzy," grumbling at poor hospitality they received, or strutting around the bedroom dressed as a Highlander. To the public, Johnson was a venerable figure, a pious philosopher who commanded respect, even reverence: moreover one only recently dead. The issue arose of whether it was not better to draw a veil over the less dignified episodes which showed Johnson's humanity rather than his majesty. To some extent, this was a matter of eighteenth-century taste. Contemporary biography was supposed to be edifying and instructive; the lives of the great were depicted as examples of how to live. Some readers would be horrified to learn of Dr Johnson's "total inattention to established manners."[9] Inevitably too, Boswell's journal had recorded Johnson's uninhibited comments on those they encountered on their travels, as well as reflections on their acquaintances in London, not all of them complimentary. It was bad enough for the Reverend Kenneth Macaulay (a great-uncle of the historian) to find himself described as a "coarse man" in the published version; but at least this was better than the description Johnson had actually given him: "the most ignorant booby and grossest bastard." Malone's editing concentrated on deleting or moderating material which might be offensive to the living or which might, in retrospect, reflect poorly on Johnson's memory.

Boswell himself balked at describing the most bellicose confrontation of the tour, which had occurred when he took Johnson to Auchinleck. He had warned Johnson beforehand to avoid controversial subjects in the presence of Lord Auchinleck, but they had been there only a few days before the inevitable clash occurred. When the subject of Charles I's execution—a touchstone for Tories—arose in passing, the conversation became "exceedingly warm and violent"; though Boswell was distressed to see this argument between the two men he revered most, he dared not interfere. "In the course of their altercation, Whiggism and Presbyterianism, Toryism and Episcopacy, were terribly buffeted."

This clash between two such well-matched opponents — champions of their respective parties, nations, and religions, as well as competitors for Boswell's soul — should have provided the climax to the book. (Sir Walter Scott attempted to fill the gap by providing his own account of the quarrel more than half a century later, ostensibly drawn from oral records.) This is such a rare example of Boswell's discretion that it is worth pausing to consider why he should have felt unable to provide readers with more than the briefest description of what happened. It would have been hard to do so without showing at least one of the two "intellectual gladiators" to disadvantage — but both were dead by then, and nobody remained to be hurt by the story (except, perhaps, Boswell's stepmother, Lady Auchinleck). It may be relevant that at the very moment when Boswell came to write this part of the book, he was particularly sensitive to the charge of disloyalty to his father's memory. A letter to the *Public Advertiser* signed "An Ayrshireman" had accused him of "insinuations" against Lord Auchinleck in his *Letter to the People of Scotland*; Boswell hotly denied the accusation.[10]

There were passages which could have harmed Boswell's prospects, too; in the manuscript journal he confessed to "a kind of liking for Jacobitism," not a very prudent sentiment to express in a volume that the author planned to present to a Hanoverian king: out it went.

In his editing Malone followed the conventions of the period. Sir Joshua Reynolds's *Discourses* had pronounced that art consisted of rising above singular forms, local customs, peculiarities, and details of every kind; in eliminating these Malone aimed at elegance, refinement, and generality. He wanted Boswell to cut the account of Johnson playing with Boswell's infant daughter, Veronica, for example, and later lamented that she had not been "left quietly in her nursery." But Boswell had sentimental motives for keeping the passage: "Veronica is so fond of her appearance that she would be much mortified if I should now delete her."[11]

Malone favoured the sonorous, Latinate style, of which Johnson himself had been such an exponent. Indeed, Malone said that Johnson had "made an era in the English language"; everybody wrote a higher style now, even in advertisements.[12] Boswell was not so sure. That kind of prose was increasingly unfashionable; one of Boswell's oldest friends, now Professor of Rhetoric and Belles-Lettres at the University of Edinburgh, had criticized Johnson's style as "turgid, unnecessarily crowded with words of Latinate derivation and too full of antithesis."[13] In any case, such a formal style was inappropriate to this type of book. "Are you not too desirous of perfection?" Boswell asked Malone at one point. "We must make *some* allowance for the book being a *Journal*."[14]

Typical is Malone's proposal to change Boswell's "violent quarrel" to the more tepid "warm altercation." Sometimes—as in this case— Boswell rebelled against such suggestions. He had his own ideas about the language; when, years earlier, Johnson had declared that "civilization" was not a word, Boswell had respectfully suggested that the great lexicographer might be wrong. In general, Boswell's instincts seem right to modern readers. His book is fresher, franker, less bland, and more indiscreet than Malone would have liked it to be. On the other hand, Malone had a surer sense than Boswell of what the reviewers might say.

Though Boswell did not accept all his suggestions, Malone's calm authority, his decisiveness, and his careful scrutiny of the text gave Boswell confidence, at a moment when he felt understandably nervous about some of the material he was planning to publish. Malone's persistence ensured that Boswell was not distracted from the task. Boswell acknowledged the vital part Malone had played in the genesis of the book by dedicating it to him, referring to Malone as "one of the best critics of the age." The acknowledgement was not entirely selfless; by advertising that a scholar and a Johnsonian of Malone's stature had scrutinized his manuscript, Boswell reinforced his claim that the journal had been published as it had been written—albeit abbreviated. "You have obligingly taken the trouble to peruse the original manuscript of this tour, and can vouch for the strict fidelity of the present publication."

In the opening pages of the journal, Boswell inserted a character-sketch of Johnson. This was a superb summary, brief, beautifully written, and carefully observed, conveying to the reader a vivid sense of the man in all his aspects. Boswell made much of the physical appearance of his subject: his size, his scars, his convulsions, his voice, even his clothes and his hair. "Let me not be censured for mentioning such minute particulars," he wrote. "Everything relative to so great a man is worth observing."[15]

At last, on 8 September, the work was finished. Malone was with Boswell at the printer's as he wrote the last lines; afterwards they returned to Malone's house and passed the rest of the day together. Two days later Boswell breakfasted with Reynolds, who finished painting his portrait. Boswell had commissioned this picture on an unusual basis: he proposed to pay for it out of the first fees he received at the English bar. In fact, though Reynolds halved his usual price of one hundred guineas, the debt was never paid.

On Wednesday, 21 September 1785, Boswell again attended a levee at Court. The King—perhaps a little wary of Boswell by now—asked him when he planned to return home to Scotland. Boswell explained that he would be leaving on Saturday: his book had detained him in London longer than expected, but now it was finished. Referring to the anniversary of the King's coronation on 22 September, Boswell informed his sovereign that "tomorrow is *coronation* day with me too." He promised that the King should have a copy of the book the next evening.

Boswell dined at Malone's house on the following day, together with Reynolds, Brocklesby, Langton, and a friend from Scotland, the Perth MP George Dempster. These four, "the jury," had all been sent copies of the newly printed book some hours earlier. The jury gave its verdict: Boswell was not merely acquitted, but "applauded." Two days later he left London for Scotland; by the time he reached Auchinleck on 3 October, *The Journal of a Tour to the Hebrides with Samuel Johnson, LL.D.* was published.

SIX

ANGER

————◆————

Damn me if with a heavier weapon I do not tickle your ass's head . . .[1]

THE JOURNAL OF A TOUR TO THE HEBRIDES was an immediate success: the first edition sold out in just over two weeks, and a second edition appeared before Christmas. For the next year, the book dominated the review pages. There was of course intense interest in Johnson, whom readers recognized as the true subject of the book. "The success of our book," wrote Boswell to Malone (acknowledging the extent of Malone's contribution by his choice of pronoun), "is very flattering indeed."[2]

The publication of the *Tour* sharpened the impression, already established by Johnson's *Journey to the Western Islands of Scotland*, of Boswell as Johnson's companion. Unfortunately, Boswell's *Letter to the People of Scotland* was still fresh in the public memory, and this coloured the response to the book. Boswell had not been able to resist reminding readers once again of his "relation to the Royal Personage." Even Boswell's friend Temple teased him about his genealogical enthusiasm: "I never knew before that you were allied to the Royal family. No wonder you write to your cousin George."[3] Many reviewers dismissed the *Tour*, coming only three months after Boswell's vainglorious pamphlet,

as more boasting: having advertised his connection to the Houses of
Stuart and Hanover, Boswell now appeared eager to place himself
alongside the Monarch of Letters. "You cannot imagine how much
mischief your own pamphlet has done you," Malone chided Boswell a
month or so after the publication of the *Tour*, "and how slow people are
to allow the praise of good thinking and good writing to one whom
they think guilty of such indiscretion." As Malone pointed out, had
Boswell's admirable character-sketch of Johnson been the work of a
writer with a more sober reputation, everyone would have instantly
recognized its merit.[4]

But nothing could disguise the fact that the *Tour* was, as one correspondent described it, "exquisitely entertaining. I have hardly ate,
drank, or slept since I got it."[5] Unlike Johnson's *Journey*, which was a
serious topographical, sociological, even anthropological work, Boswell's *Tour* was full of gossip and humour, enjoyable most of all because
of the interplay between writer and his companion. Indeed, much of
the fun in Boswell's journal arose from his own presence in the story.
Boswell did not spare himself when it came to describing incidents
which showed him in a poor light. "As I have been scrupulously exact
in relating anecdotes concerning other persons, I shall not withhold
any part of this story, however ludicrous."[6]

The reviewers deplored Boswell's egotism and lack of taste, while
conceding that the book was entertaining. A satirical poem showed
Boswell catching scraps from Johnson's mouth, and urged him now to
search the sage's privy for further remains. The *Public Advertiser* could
not resist comparing Boswell to one of Lunardi's balloons, propelled
upwards by "the learned Doctor's gas, to give himself a short-lived ele-
vation above his natural element, but as this gradually evaporates and
loses its force, the dead weight attached to the literary car must speedily
fall into its native obscurity."

Wilkes feigned to see the book as an attack on Johnson. "If it were
possible, you would kill his reputation," he wrote facetiously to Boswell.
Referring to Boswell's forthcoming *Life* and the anticipated volume from
Mrs Piozzi, he continued: "The pocket pistol of your octavo has severely
wounded him. Your blunderbuss quarto will be his coup de grace, but
should he linger, the stiletto of Piozzi should give the finishing stroke."

He admonished Boswell about his supposed Scotticisms (*"Please send* is not English. *Please to send"*), and affected indignation at the "horrid deal of trash you have made the press groan under."[7]

The MP and former Attorney-General Jack Lee, a man with a reputation for speaking his mind frankly, even crudely, cautioned Boswell that his book could undermine his prospects at the bar. "I cannot conceive of anything more injurious to a man's success as a lawyer," Lee warned, "than that it should be thought that he has such a copiousness of communication that he must reveal everything he knows . . . there is hardly any quality more essential to success in our profession, than that sort of prudence, which knows, what is fit to be said, and what ought to [be] concealed." He deplored the practice of publishing private conversations with the sovereign. "There are many reasons, why the conversations of Princes . . . should be held secret."[8]

The banker Sir William Forbes was startled to find a private letter he had written to Boswell nearly nine years earlier printed in the book. Forbes's letter had praised the manuscript of the journal; in the text of the book, Forbes himself was eulogized. Although the panegyric to Forbes was added after he had returned the manuscript to Boswell, readers could not know this. His letter of praise looked like a response to flattery. Embarrassed, and alarmed by Boswell's indiscretions, Forbes urged him to pay "particular attention in your Life of Dr Johnson to insert nothing that can give either pain or offence to any mortal."[9]

A letter to Thomas Percy provides a representative reaction to the book. "I have been amused at it, but should be very sorry either to have been the author or the hero of it."[10]

The Journal of a Tour to the Hebrides strikes the modern reader as such a natural, informal book that it is hard for us to appreciate how different and disturbing it seemed two hundred years ago. One aspect of the book that many of Boswell's contemporaries found particularly difficult to accept was its record of private conversations. To them, Boswell's behaviour in publishing these amounted to an abuse of Johnson's trust and a betrayal of his friendship. It was not respectable; it was undignified. Furthermore, what had been tried once could be done again. If this new style of biography caught on, nobody would be safe, perhaps not even the King; everybody would be anxious that their remarks might be recorded and then published.

Even those who frankly admitted to having enjoyed the book doubted the propriety of revealing so much about Johnson: Dr Adams, for example, the Master of Pembroke, who qualified a letter of appreciation with the wish that "some few gross expressions had been softened, and a few of our hero's foibles had been a little more shaded; but it is useful to see the weaknesses incident to great minds, and you have given us Dr Johnson's authority that in history all ought to be told."[11] Adams was referring to a conversation about the ethics of biography in the *Tour*, when Johnson had been asked whether it was not wrong of the biographer of Swift to "expose the defects of a man with whom he lived in intimacy." Johnson's reply, according to Boswell, was: "Why no, Sir, after the man is dead, and it is done historically."[12]

Assuming that Boswell's design was "to hold up Dr Johnson in the most respectable light," argued the *English Review*, "was it meritorious, was it right or justifiable in Mr Boswell to record and publish his prejudices, his follies and whims, his weaknesses, his vices?"[13] The same reviewer speculated on how damaging it would have been to the reputation of Socrates if Xenophon had pursued the same approach as Boswell, haunting the great moral teacher in his retreats, gaping at everything he did, and publishing his infirmities.

Boswell was not altogether unaware of the disquiet his journal would cause. In an addition to the text made only two weeks before publication, almost certainly in response to a comment of Malone's, he scornfully defended himself against the anticipated criticism:

> It may be objected by some persons, as it has been by one of my friends, that he who has the power of thus exhibiting an exact transcript of conversations is not a desirable member of society. I repeat the answer which I made to that friend: "Few, very few, need be afraid that their sayings will be recorded. Can it be imagined that I would take the trouble to gather what grows on every hedge, because I have collected such fruits as the *nonpareil* and the *bon chretien**?"[14]

---

*Particularly delicious fruit, an apple and a pear respectively.

On the other hand, argued Boswell, how useful such a faculty of recording conversations could be!

> How delighted should we have been if thus introduced in to the company of Shakespeare and Dryden, of whom we know scarcely anything but their admirable writings! What pleasure would it have given us to have known their petty habits, their characteristic manners, their modes of composition and their genuine opinion of preceding writers and their contemporaries! All these are now irrevocably lost.

In his postscript Boswell defended his record not just of Johnson's conversations, but also of the personal detail which many of his contemporaries found so distasteful. To understand a man fully, he argued, one needed to know not just what he said, but what he did, how he looked, even what he ate. If this meant exposing his weaknesses and his personal idiosyncrasies, his involuntary nervous tics, for example, then the eventual portrait would appear all the more natural, the more accurate. Many years before, while still an undergraduate, Boswell had been delighted by Adam Smith's remark that we are pleased to know even the minutest details about a great man, such as that Milton's shoes were secured with laces rather than buckles. And in stressing the importance of characteristic detail, Boswell took his cue from Johnson himself, who had written a *Rambler* essay on this very subject.

For Boswell, the fact that Johnson had read his journal exonerated him from any blame. If he could demonstrate that his book had been authorized by Johnson, then he could shelter in His Master's Shadow. Hence the importance of authenticity. The journal that Johnson had approved in manuscript ought not to differ from the printed version. "I have resolved that the very journal which Dr Johnson read shall be presented to the public."

But Boswell was equating Johnson's approval of the journal with his permission to publish. Though Johnson might have chuckled over the manuscript in private, he certainly had not sanctioned its publication. Nor was the text of the published book identical to that of the manuscript Johnson had read; if it had been, Boswell could simply have handed his journal to Baldwin's compositor when he arrived in London, without the need for months of rewriting or help from

Malone. What Boswell meant by his use of the phrase "the very journal which Dr Johnson read" was that the printed book was as faithful to the memory of his friend as he could make it, within the constraints of what he considered to be acceptable.

"Authenticity is my chief boast," declared Boswell.[15] This argument cut both ways. It was the very authenticity of his book which made so many of his contemporaries feel so uncomfortable. Boswell was prepared to expose himself in print, and he always found it difficult to understand why others might be less ready to see what they had said or what had been said about them published. Boswell believed that he had suppressed everything which "could *really* hurt any one now living." He had naïvely convinced himself that the victims of "the lighter strokes of Johnson's satire" would have "the good sense and good temper not to be displeased."[16] He was wrong, as he would soon discover.

On 12 January 1786, at the Advocates' Library in Edinburgh, Boswell spotted James Burnett, one of his father's colleagues in the Court of Session, who had taken the title Lord Monboddo. He bowed, but Monboddo made no acknowledgement. Boswell realized afterwards that Monboddo had cut him deliberately.

This should have come as no surprise. Monboddo, a scholar and a writer as well as a judge, had been cruelly lampooned in the *Tour*. In particular, Boswell had ridiculed Monboddo's belief in men with tails, quoting Johnson's remark that Monboddo was as jealous of his tail as a squirrel. The subject forms a running joke throughout the book, as when Monboddo is described as a judge *a posteriori*, to Johnson's amusement.

Monboddo had reason to feel aggrieved, or even betrayed. He had known Boswell for more than twenty years, and had given him kind and disinterested advice on numerous occasions. In the late 1760s, he had urged Boswell to marry Margaret Montgomerie, counsel Boswell eventually took, one of the most sensible decisions of his life; and Monboddo had mediated between Boswell and his father, when it seemed as though Lord Auchinleck might disinherit his wayward son. In 1772, Boswell had represented Monboddo in the Court of Session in his suit against a farrier for violation of instructions: the farrier had added treacle to the mixture prescribed for Monboddo's horse, which subsequently died. His peers decided against Monboddo, and he sulked, refusing to share the bench with his fellow judges from then on. But he remained friendly towards Boswell, and when Boswell brought Johnson to Scotland, he had entertained the two men to a hearty dinner.

Monboddo was notoriously eccentric, which made him an easy target for mockery. Though a gentleman by rank, he dressed like a rustic farmer, and at night anointed himself, dribbling scented oil over his head like one of the Ancients. Monboddo was interested in primitive societies, and like many anthropologists since, he had a naïve trust in the primitive idyll. But his thinking was not so simple as Boswell depicted. He grasped the important idea that men shared a common ancestry with apes, a concept so revolutionary that it still provoked derision when advanced by Huxley a century later. And he argued that language was the key distinction between men and animals, a notion that did not become current until the twentieth century. Posthumously, Monboddo could be said to have had the last laugh.

Boswell did not seem much concerned to have been the cause of distress to an old friend. On the contrary, he judged that the rift would allow him to make Monboddo "fair game" in his forthcoming *Life of Johnson*—as if he had not done so sufficiently already.[17] Boswell seemed to think that because the jibes at Monboddo he quoted came mainly from others, particularly Johnson, this absolved him of any responsibility for them.

Monboddo eventually forgave Boswell, but afterwards he was more guarded in Boswell's company. So too was Edmund Burke. During the tour of Scotland, Boswell had discussed Burke's qualities with Johnson, and he printed a record of their conversation in his book, including Johnson's comment that Burke "never once made a good joke." This was bad enough, though perhaps forgivable on the grounds of candour. But Boswell compounded his tactlessness by adding a very long footnote (made even longer by subsequent additions from Malone), dissenting from Johnson's opinion and supporting this view with some rather feeble examples of Burke's wit.

Boswell esteemed Burke, whom he had counted as a friend since the mid-1770s. He had cultivated Burke as an influential politician, one who might some day be willing to secure him a valuable post, despite their political divergence. He had been delighted to hear from Reynolds in 1782 that Burke thought him "the pleasantest man he ever saw." A founder-member of the Literary Club, Burke, more than any of his contemporaries, spanned the two worlds of politics and literature, a position that Boswell himself aspired to but never achieved. In short, Burke's was a friendship that Boswell valued.

It was for this reason that Boswell wrote to Burke, enclosing a copy of his book and highlighting the footnote that he and Malone had compiled "in defence of your wit": an action which rendered it impossible for Burke not to respond. His reply thanked Boswell and Malone for their "friendly solicitude":

> I should be well content to pass down to a long posterity in Doctor Johnsons authentic judgement, and in your own permanent record, as a dull fellow and a tiresome companion, when it shall be known through the same long period, that I have had such men as Mr Boswell and Mr Malone as my friendly counsel in the cause which I have lost.

Later in the letter, Burke's anger almost broke through the ironic façade of his prose:

> I am sure there are very few, (let them be qualified as they will) [who] shall be indiscreet enough to interrupt, by the intrusion of their ideas, the strong flow of your real wit . . .

It was a letter such as would cause even the most obtuse recipient to feel uneasy. Boswell called on Burke, hoping to put matters right, but his visit had the opposite effect. During the conversation he "imprudently touched on a calumny against Mr Burke, in order to be enabled to refute it." The calumny has never been explained, but at the time Burke was suffering continual attacks in the press from his political opponents, who alleged that he was secretly a Roman Catholic, that he was a sodomite, that his financial dealings were dishonest, and so on. No doubt Boswell made some reference to one of these. It would have been tactless at any time, but especially so at a moment when Burke had good reason to fear that Boswell might relay anything he said to others, or even publish his remarks. They "parted on sad terms." Later that same day, Boswell sent Burke an apologetic letter, assuring him *inter alia* that he "never wrote or intended to put in writing one word upon the subject." Burke replied soothingly, observing that "one of the most known and most successful ways of circulating slander is by stating charges and anticipating defences, where nothing can come to proof, where there is no judge, and where every man credits and carries away what he pleases, and according to the measure of his malice."[18] Burke was referring to the unnamed calumny, but he might just as well have been referring to his reputation for wit.

The damage was papered over, but cracks in the friendship remained. Thereafter, Boswell noticed a coldness from Burke and his family, which he attributed to political differences. But Malone perceived its true cause: "He thinks your habit of recording throws a restraint on convivial ease and negligence."[19] Burke had expressed misgivings about Boswell's suitability to be a member of the Club when his name was first put forward in the early 1770s, only to be overruled by Johnson; now those misgivings appeared to have been justified.

Others felt the same, especially since Boswell had a habit of "stirring," to create good copy for his journal. In 1776, the generally tolerant and good-natured Bennet Langton had to caution him against what Boswell frankly admitted was "my usual fault of repeating to people what was said of them." Later, Langton presented Boswell with a book entitled *The Government of the Tongue;* Boswell recognized this as "a delicate admonition." A few weeks afterwards, Garrick warned Boswell not to repeat to people anything said of them which they might dislike. "You had once like to have made sad mischief by that. I will not tell you between whom, as I have it in confidence."

As a celebrity, one who was constantly being written about, Garrick was understandably sensitive about maintaining the distinction between public and private. The Club existed to promote uninhibited conversation; members might not wish to speak so freely once they knew their words were being recorded. Gradually it became known—Boswell may well have broadcast the fact himself—that he was keeping a detailed journal, and as this awareness spread, so too did the concern. At a dinner in 1778, the anxiety caused by Boswell's habit of recording surfaced when Garrick baited Boswell about his temporary abstemiousness: if Boswell wouldn't drink at meetings of the Club, Garrick argued, he should be searched and his notebook removed. The exchange showed Garrick's ignorance of Boswell's technique. "Nonsense," Boswell noted in his journal. "As if I had book and wrote in company and could not carry in my *head*."[20]

It was one thing to record private remarks in a journal: quite another to publish them in a book. Self-interest if not discretion should have led Boswell to eliminate from the *Tour* passages likely to offend influential and powerful friends. Arguably it was justifiable to print Johnson's comments about Burke; there was a permanent value in knowing what one great writer thought of another. But to publish Johnson's aside about Lord Douglas had no justification, except that it was funny.

The Douglas Cause was the most famous Scottish legal case of the era. In 1761, the Duke of Douglas, one of the wealthiest landowners in Scotland, had died without an obvious heir. Archibald Douglas, his supposed nephew, was next in line. But other members of the family, in particular those representing another near relation, the young Duke of Hamilton, contested his claim. They argued that Archibald Douglas was not really the son of the Duke's sister, who had married in secret at the age of forty-eight and supposedly given birth to twins (one of whom died in infancy) in Paris at the age of fifty; but a French foundling. The enormous inheritance involved, and the prurient interest in the circumstances of Douglas's birth, turned this into a *cause célèbre*. As advocate for Douglas, James Burnett had made his name in the case, which led to his being appointed to the Court of Session. Boswell too had been an early enthusiast for the Douglas Cause, composing ballads, publishing a sequence of effective pamphlets, and even writing a fictionalized account of the cause, *Dorando,* all of which contributed to his eventually being appointed counsel to Douglas. After five years of litigation, the Court of Session found in favour of Hamilton by a majority of only one; this decision was overturned on appeal by the House of Lords two years later. Boswell was in the vanguard of an Edinburgh mob that took to the streets to celebrate Douglas's victory;

judges (Lord Auchinleck included) who refused to show their approval of this verdict by illuminating their windows had them smashed.

Boswell had identified himself in the most public way possible with the Douglas camp. Now he risked all the credit he had earned by publishing a sly aside of Johnson's during their tour. They had been discussing the fact that Holyrood Chapel was in a state of disrepair; Boswell lamented that "my friend Douglas," the owner of a great house and proprietor of a vast estate, should allow the sacred spot where his mother lay interred to remain unroofed and exposed to the weather. "Sir, Sir, don't be too severe on the gentleman," Johnson replied, "don't accuse him of want of filial piety! Lady Jane Douglas was not *his* mother." Boswell attempted to disassociate himself from Johnson's quip; but the damage was done. No subject could have been more sensitive to Douglas; from this point on he shunned Boswell. By championing Douglas's cause, Boswell had estranged himself from one of the most powerful landed families in Scotland; and for the sake of a joke, he had lost the favour of another. It was difficult to imagine a course of action more destructive to his prospects.

The *Tour* was a literary success, but a professional disaster. By publishing so many indiscretions Boswell jeopardized some of his most valuable friendships, and won himself a reputation as an untrustworthy companion. Worse still, he risked the prospect of a duel.

Soon after the book appeared, Boswell received an angry letter of complaint from Alexander Tytler, one of his fellow advocates at the Scottish bar. Tytler had met Johnson over dinner at Boswell's home in Edinburgh on 10 November 1773; in his journal Boswell had recorded their conversation, which made Tytler appear somewhat foolish. Tytler had expressed his certainty that the epic poem *Fingal* had been written in Gaelic, because he had heard a great part of it recited in the original; though when challenged by Johnson, he had been forced to admit that he did not understand the language. More recently Boswell had discussed the exchange with Tytler, and believed that Tytler had agreed to its publication, provided that as a *quid pro quo* Boswell printed an anecdote about his having once ludicrously entertained the audience at

Drury Lane Theatre by lowing like a cow; but it seems that this was a misunderstanding. Tytler insisted that his name be removed from the second and subsequent editions of the book. This Boswell was willing to do, but he asked Tytler in return to apologize for the "hasty" expressions in his letter. Tytler refused, on the grounds that he had already suffered injury by publication of the passage; and Boswell, stirred up by Malone and his fellow-Irishman, the poet and impoverished MP John Courtenay, demanded a formal apology. At this point, there was a possibility that the dispute might lead to a duel. Fortunately, however, Tytler backed down; he wrote to say that he sincerely regretted the harsh terms of his letter and requested Boswell to excuse them. He had consigned his copy of the letter to the flames, "as a monument to the intemperance of passion which ought not to exist."[21]

That Boswell should contemplate killing or being killed just because he had received an abusive letter may now seem foolish. But a willingness to fight to defend one's honour was still, at the end of the eighteenth century, the mark of a gentleman; to refuse a challenge was to risk public obloquy, and to leave oneself open to further insults.[22] Boswell despised Sir John Dalrymple, for example, who had refused a challenge from Lord Barrington after publishing a scurrilous pamphlet attacking him. These matters of honour were essentially public rather than private: what mattered was not what your enemy had done, but what he was seen to have done. Failure to reply to an insulting letter was regarded as cowardice; a copy of the letter could then be displayed to increase the recipient's discomfort. On the other hand, honour was satisfied if an insult was withdrawn; a libel was perceived as harmless if subsequently corrected. Boswell's pride in his lineage and in his social position made him particularly susceptible to such feelings; while his naïveté left him liable to give offence where none was intended.

Although Boswell suppressed some of the passages in his journal most critical of Sir Alexander Macdonald, various references to "the rapacious Highland chief" remained, as did Johnson's remark that Sir Alexander (who had since become Lord Macdonald) was "utterly unfit for his situation." After his book was published, Boswell began to fret about how Macdonald might react. Margaret told him that he had been wrong to allow Johnson's remark to stand, and feared that

Macdonald might challenge him to a duel. "I have no great fear of *that*," bragged Boswell to Malone, affecting bravado. "But why be in any degree a public executioner?" He suggested that changes could be made to the second edition to reduce the risk of giving offence; but he was anxious not to be seen to be wavering. "If you could have an opportunity to know for *certain* that Lord M——d does not take it *hot,* a few lines to Mrs Boswell James's Court Edinburgh would relieve an excellent woman."[23]

But Macdonald did take it hot. Within a month of publication, Boswell received a "most shocking, abusive letter from Lord M. which I thought made it indispensable for me to fight him."[24] The disagreeable business with Tytler had left Boswell depressed and confused. Now Lord Macdonald's violent letter appeared to confirm Mrs Boswell's fears. He felt "quite dismal. Such a dreary force upon me in my gloomy state was terrible. I thought of my dear wife and children with anxious affection. Could not rest. Had a thousand thoughts." Poor Boswell faced a dilemma. At his wife's prompting, he had already decided to make certain changes to the second edition of the *Tour* which would lessen the offence to Macdonald, but he did not want it to be thought that he had done so under threat. Courtenay, who seems to have enjoyed the situation, goaded him with the suggestion that Macdonald might brandish in public a copy of the letter he had sent to Boswell, or even publish it; if so, "I would be obliged to call him out." Boswell was badly rattled, torn between the threat to his honour and the danger to his person. While complicated and delicate negotiations were conducted with Macdonald, Courtenay obligingly showed Boswell how to stand and fire a pistol.

Macdonald spun out the discussions for two weeks, while Boswell suffered sleepless nights of torment. Eventually Macdonald agreed to delete passages from his already-sent letter—Boswell was especially anxious that Macdonald should retract the suggestion that he had fathered "a few rude sayings upon" Johnson—in exchange for the revisions Boswell had already decided to make to the book. Honour was satisfied. The second edition of *The Journal of a Tour to the Hebrides* would be matched by a "second edition" of Macdonald's letter. Macdonald crossed out the remarks which had particularly upset Boswell; but the originals were still legible underneath.

The second edition of the *Tour*, with the revisions insisted upon by Lord Macdonald, appeared towards the end of December 1785. Included in an appendix were the Latin verses which Sir Alexander had presented to Johnson on Skye. Boswell also added a note qualifying his original remark that he had "suppressed every thing which I thought could *really* hurt any one now living."

> Having found, on a revision of the first edition of this work, that, notwithstanding my best care, a few observations had escaped me, which arose from the instant impression, the publication of which might perhaps be considered as passing the bounds of a strict decorum, I immediately ordered that they should be omitted in subsequent editions. I was pleased to find that they did not amount in the whole to a page. If any of the same kind are yet left, it is owing to inadvertence alone, no man being more unwilling to give pain to others than I am.

If he thought that would be the end of the matter, he was wrong. Macdonald may or may not have shown his letter to others, but somehow the story got out. In February 1786, a satirical poem, *A Poetical & Congratulatory Epistle to James Boswell, Esq*, was published under the name "Peter Pindar" (a pseudonym of the Reverend John Wolcot, MD): it depicted a trembling Boswell threatened with a beating by an angry Lord Macdonald, and referred to the "letter of severe remonstrance" which Macdonald had sent, as a result of which, it claimed, Boswell had cut various "scandalous passages" from his book. Though Boswell issued a firm denial, the subject quickly recurred in another Pindar poem. In the summer two sets of caricatures appeared, drawn by Samuel Collings and engraved by Thomas Rowlandson: one of which, entitled "Revising for the Second Edition," fixed the scene imagined by Peter Pindar forever in the public memory. Privately, Boswell had stood up to Macdonald; but to the public, it looked as though he had surrendered.

The controversy helped to prolong the interest in Boswell's book, as the author himself recognized.[25] Indeed, William Mason, the poet and biographer of Gray, claimed tongue-in-cheek to be "very angry" that he had not been attacked by Johnson in the *Tour*: "It looks," he said, "as if one was nobody."[26] Continuing aftershocks from the Macdonald eruption ensured that *The Journal of a Tour to the Hebrides* remained newsworthy, and a third edition was published in August 1786.

• • •

As an appendix to the second edition of the *Tour*, Boswell printed a letter from the poet Dr Thomas Blacklock, politely questioning the accuracy of Boswell's description of a conversation held twelve years earlier. Blacklock had been introduced to Johnson at Boswell's Edinburgh home on 17 August 1773, soon after Johnson's arrival in Scotland; he and Sir William Forbes had come to breakfast. A discussion had followed of whether it was easier to compose a poem or a dictionary. Blacklock's good-humoured letter suggested that Boswell might like to revise the account of the conversation printed in the book, to reflect Blacklock's memory of what had occurred, which was "a little different."

Though Boswell was happy to print Blacklock's letter, he firmly rejected the suggestion that his own account might have been faulty. "I am slow to believe," he wrote, "that any man's memory, at the distance of several years, can preserve facts or sayings with such fidelity as may be done by writing them down when they are recent: and I beg it may be remembered, that it is not upon *memory*, but upon what was *written at the time*, that the authenticity of my Journal rests."[27]

This subject—the superiority of contemporary record—recurs throughout the *Tour*. Boswell frequently cites Johnson's authority to reinforce the point. "How seldom descriptions correspond with realities," remarks Johnson, and goes on to draw the moral: the reason was that "people write them some time after, and then their imagination has added circumstances." "It was but of late that historians bestowed pain and attention in consulting records, to attain to accuracy," Johnson comments; and again: "All history, so far as it is not supported by contemporary evidence, is romance." For Johnson, these arguments were consistent with his general insistence on scholarly rigour, but for Boswell, they were a vindication of his method.

A letter to the *St James's Chronicle* praised the *Tour* as a work of biography: "Mr Boswell has made me personally acquainted with a man to whom I was before a stranger; he has drawn his picture better than Sir Joshua could have drawn it." Boswell had already admitted the biographical nature of his book during his interview with the King: "It will be more a journal of Dr Johnson than of what I saw." In a sense the *Tour* is part of the *Life of Johnson;* the *Life* breaks off at the point where the *Tour* begins, and picks up again where it finishes. The standard edition of the *Life of Johnson* implicitly acknowledges this by including the *Tour* as the fifth of its six volumes.

The *Tour* is also a precursor of the *Life* in another sense, in that it attempts to establish Boswell's claim to be Johnson's authorized biographer. The writing of the journal is itself described, as is Johnson's reading and approving it. Thus the reader is witness to the biographical process; and Boswell is able to award himself retrospective authorization. Now as then, biography is a delicate matter; the negotiations beforehand are sometimes described (sometimes bitterly described) in the preliminary pages, but rarely are they related in the main text, as they are in the *Tour.*

An announcement at the end of the book reinforced Boswell's claim to be Johnson's authorized biographer:

> Preparing for the press, in one volume quarto, the Life of Samuel Johnson, LL.D. . . . Mr Boswell has been collecting materials for this work for more than twenty years, during which he was honoured with the intimate friendship of Dr Johnson . . . Dr Johnson was well informed of his design, and obligingly communicated to him several curious particulars. With these will be interwoven the most authentic accounts that can be obtained from those who knew him best; many sketches of his conversation on a multiplicity of subjects, with various persons, some of them the most eminent of the age; a great number of letters from him at different periods; and several original pieces dictated by him to Mr Boswell, distinguished by that particular energy, which marked every emanation of his mind.

Readers and reviewers were not slow to take the hint. "It would be not only uncandid but ungrateful to dwell on a few minor blemishes after the pleasure and profit we have received in the perusal of this work," concluded a review in the *Gentleman's Magazine:* "Mr Boswell announces a Life of Dr Johnson, for which we shall wait, not without impatience."

• • •

A few days after the resolution of the quarrel with Lord Macdonald, Boswell attended another levee at St James's Palace. The King spoke to him only briefly, and Boswell felt a little disappointed that his book was not mentioned. Boswell was anxious to know what his sovereign thought of the *Tour*, and had written to Malone from Scotland asking him to make inquiries of Bennet Langton, who often discussed literary topics with the King. Malone reported that the two men had indeed discussed Boswell's *Tour*, and although the King seldom gave his opinion of any book, "George Rex" confirmed that he had read it, and laughed heartily on recalling one of Johnson's *bons mots* recorded therein.[28]

The day following the levee, Boswell met Johnson's servant, Francis Barber, in the street. Unlike his rival biographer, Sir John Hawkins, Boswell had always cultivated Barber, and he now extracted Frank's promise to "search for every scrap of his master's handwriting, and give all to me. It vexed me to be told that he had burnt some letters from Dr Johnson to Mrs Johnson."[29]

Earlier in the week, Boswell had received a visit from his younger brother, Thomas David Boswell, known as "T.D.," who urged on him his duty to live at Auchinleck. Since the death of their father, Boswell, as the eldest son, had been head of the family; but over the intervening three years, he had spent as many months in London as at the family seat.

Boswell was still in a state of indecision about whether to move to London permanently and practise at the English bar. He talked about it to anyone who would listen. His host in London, General Paoli, was against the idea; Langton, on the other hand, was for it. Advice was free. Boswell recognized that there were plenty of good reasons to stay in Scotland: he could concentrate on his estate and build up his practice there, as his father had done. He could, indeed he should, become a judge. His wife's health might suffer if the family moved to London, and his children might become estranged from Auchinleck. And there was the considerable extra expense of maintaining a house and family in London. Johnson had given Boswell permission to move to London only if he could afford it, and he was not at all sure that he could.

Though moved by T.D.'s entreaties, and aware of all the strong arguments against coming to London, Boswell remained undecided.

He longed to settle in London. And he wondered whether all these difficulties might evaporate once he was there.

Lord Auchinleck had always opposed the idea, but he was no longer an obstacle. Boswell decided that he should lay the problem before the Lord Chancellor, Lord Thurlow. This was a characteristic (if preposterous) device. Faced with a dilemma, Boswell would turn to another, usually an older, wiser man: not for advice, but for approval of what he wanted to do. Since applying to Thurlow on behalf of Johnson in the summer of 1784, Boswell had continued to pay court to him, and a couple of months before had presented him with a copy of the *Tour*. Like Boswell, Thurlow had represented Douglas in the great Douglas Cause; his comments on the methods employed by one of his opponents, Andrew Stuart, had led Stuart to call him out, and they had fought a (bloodless) duel. Clearly, Thurlow was a man of some spirit, who would surely understand Boswell's yearning to revolve in a "wider sphere."

On the same day as his talk with his brother, Boswell wrote a short letter to Thurlow, as if seeking his advice on a legal issue. He begged that his Lordship would take a few minutes "in considering and deciding upon my Case," which he enclosed sealed: "Should your Lordship reckon me of consequence to merit enough such attention, you will open the seal. If not, you will be pleased to return the enclosure."

Having broken the seal, Thurlow would find Boswell's "Case," couched in the third person. After eighteen years' practice at the bar in Scotland, "Mr Boswell" admitted to a strong inclination to try his fortune in the metropolis; but the difficulties that his father had always warned him of pressed upon his mind.

> He is now five-and-forty, and he fears that the acquisition of new technical knowledge and new modes of practice will be more difficult than he imagined. He has a wife and five children, and the state of his affairs is such that he cannot maintain his family in London with a suitable decency without an addition to his income either by an office or by practice. Yet if neither can be had, how can he retreat without being exposed to ridicule and some disgrace?

If he could but obtain the rank of King's Counsel and become one of the Benchers of the Honourable Society of the Inner Temple, he would be satisfied. He might then return to Scotland to take up office as a judge, for which his experience, assiduity, and principles (and his services to the King's cause) surely entitled him?

Just at the moment it would be embarrassing to return to practise in Scotland. Having thwarted Mr Dundas in his plans to diminish the number of Lords of Session, he had drawn upon himself the displeasure of "that provincial despot," and (he was going to go on to write, but thought better of it and crossed this out), his candour on the subject of Scotland in his recently published book "has given very general offence to an irritable people." He did not suppose that adding some knowledge of the law of England to that of Scotland could be any reasonable objection to his being promoted to the office of judge in Scotland some years hence?

What did the Lord Chancellor think?

SEVEN

DISCRETION

It may be objected by some persons, as it has been by one of my friends, that he who has the power of thus exhibiting an exact transcript of conversations is not a desirable member of society . . .[1]

LORD THURLOW'S REPLY, when it arrived in Edinburgh in early January, was not encouraging. How could it be? Boswell wanted to obtain the ranks of Bencher of the Inner Temple and King's Counsel, if not at once, then very soon. Thurlow explained that the thing was impossible, morally speaking; there were fewer than twenty KCs among the hundreds of English barristers, and they were drawn from the most experienced in the profession. Scots law was completely different from English law; Boswell would have to start afresh, at the bottom of the ladder. As for Boswell's eventual "approach to the Scottish bench," Thurlow feared that coming to practise in England might not be the best route. "But, as I shall not be consulted on that subject, my thoughts . . . will be of little use."

This reply, confided Boswell to his journal, "sunk me a good deal. But my excellent wife suggested that I could not take it as a *decision*, but only as an able evasion of taking any charge of me."[2] Margaret Boswell had few illusions about her husband's chances of success at the English bar, nor was she enthusiastic about moving to London. But, like Sir

John Pringle, she had come to realize that Boswell could not rest until he had given it a try. He had become increasingly obsessed by the subject, talking about it to everyone. The agony of indecision left him exhausted and depressed. At last, after further hesitation, he decided to make the move. It was an experiment, he told himself; if it failed he could always fall back on the Edinburgh bench.

Boswell arrived back in London on 1 February 1786. His plan was to establish himself in practice, staying as usual with General Paoli while he looked around for a suitable house of his own, where his wife and family could join him later in the year. On 9 February, he was called to the bar, and on the following Monday, he invited ten guests — his brother T.D., Wilkes, Reynolds, Malone, Courtenay, Dilly, Baldwin, Brocklesby, the young barrister Thomas Strange, and the Honourable Daines Barrington, a former friend of Johnson's who was Master of the Bench of the Inner Temple — to an extravagant inaugural dinner at the Inner Temple Hall. There were two other new barristers, and three more guests, making sixteen diners in all; between them these accounted for twenty-six bottles of fine claret, eight bottles of port, and four of Madeira. It was a lavish affair, and Boswell insisted that the lustre be lit, apparently the first time this had been done for thirty years. He was extravagantly happy, for once at ease with himself. "I was quite the *Laird of Auchinleck in the Inner Temple,* free from any *imaginary distance.*"

He had done only a little reading of Blackstone's *Commentaries* to prepare himself for the English bar. He planned to master English law by attending the law courts and taking notes on the cases. It could not be too difficult, he reasoned; after all, other Scotsmen had done the same. Lord Mansfield had become Lord Chief Justice and Alexander Wedderburn, now ennobled as Lord Loughborough, Solicitor-General; another Scot, Boswell's distant cousin Thomas Erskine, was forging a brilliant career at the bar that would lead him, like Wedderburn, to become Lord Chancellor in due course. In fact, all these comparisons were false ones, because each man proposed as a model by Boswell had better cause to expect success in England. Erskine, for example, had been educated in England and had always practised there; he was seventeen years younger than Boswell when called to the bar; after being called he had continued to study with a special pleader, the only way to master the complexities of English law; and he was a brilliant advocate: the greatest, according to one legal historian, ever to practise at the English bar.[3]

The day after the inaugural dinner, Boswell began to attend the sittings of Lord Mansfield's court at Westminster Hall. Soon his enthusiasm dulled. English law was far too technical to absorb in this way; moreover, it was incomprehensible without a grounding in the general principles, and Boswell had none. His attendances became less frequent, and after eight days he stopped going altogether.

Boswell was delighted to be in London once again. He immediately resumed his affair with the celebrated *femme fatale* Margaret Caroline Rudd, whom he had known since 1776, soon after her appearance in the Old Bailey, charged with forgery, had made her for a while the most notorious woman in England. Johnson himself had talked of visiting her then, but had been deterred by the fear that it might get into the papers. But Boswell had gone to see her, supposedly incognito, curious to meet a woman credited with an irresistible power of fascination. Mrs Rudd had not disappointed; during their interview he had been so moved as to seize her "silken hand," and later to press it to his lips. She had spoken of all the troubles she had been through; Boswell pointedly advised her that love would be the best remedy, but she must now be very cautious in her choice. He said that he should be much obliged if she would give him leave to call on her sometimes; she answered that she was always at home. Hypnotized, Boswell wished her goodnight with another kiss. He returned to Paoli's feeling "a little confused." That same night, before going to bed, he sat down to describe their encounter in a letter to his wife, which he prudently decided afterwards not to send.

Mrs Rudd could well have been a model for Becky Sharp. She possessed many qualities in common with Thackeray's heroine (including a relation and protector called Rawdon). Born in Ireland, she married at seventeen a Lieutenant Valentine Rudd, whom she soon abandoned. Under a series of pseudonyms—among them Miss de la Rochette, Miss Malfaisons, Mrs Potter, Mrs Gore, and Miss (later Countess) de Grosberg—she pursued a career as a teacher or governess, using her position to ensnare a succession of rich men, from whom she extorted money. She acquired a number of valuable skills, among them the ability to forge handwriting accurately. In 1770, she began to live with one Daniel Perreau in the guise of his wife, and rapidly bore him three children. Perreau was a speculator on the Exchange who lived above his means, already a bankrupt three times over. He was therefore complaisant when Mrs Rudd became the mistress of James Adair, a relative of the wealthy army agent William Adair. She began to forge bonds or promissory notes in Adair's name, and against these Daniel Perreau and his twin brother Robert borrowed money to fund Daniel's speculation. As more and more cash was required, so too were more promissory notes. The Perreaus hoped for a windfall, which would enable them to clear their debts and regain the forged notes, but of course it never came; instead, they sank deeper and deeper in debt. When one of the forgeries was uncovered, the Perreau brothers claimed to have supposed Mrs Rudd's promissory notes genuine. She turned King's evidence; as a result of her testimony, both brothers were convicted and sentenced to death. It was decided that she too should stand trial, and she conducted her own defence, presenting herself as a helpless, modest victim. Her ordeal lasted only half an hour; the jury, and the watching public, were bewitched; her acquittal was greeted in court with loud cheering. Six weeks later the Perreaus were hanged at Tyburn.[4]

While he was in London working on the *Tour,* Boswell had renewed his connection with Mrs Rudd, and they had begun an affair. An accomplished courtesan, Mrs Rudd was familiar with the arts of love. With her, Boswell experienced the sweetest sexual pleasure he had ever known. Her notoriety excited him almost as much as her beauty; he could not resist telling people of his involvement with this "enchantress." Rumours of his affair with her spread as far as Scotland; on a visit to London later in 1786, Sir William and Lady Forbes confronted him with the story, which he was forced to deny. Sir Joshua Reynolds warned Boswell that it would ruin him if he were generally known to have such a connection. For her part, Mrs Rudd wanted Boswell to procure for her an introduction to the Lord Chancellor, whom she hoped to enlist in support of her claim against a former lover. On 26 February 1786, after spending part of the day with her and drinking "rather too liberally," Boswell called on Lord Thurlow, at half past nine in the evening. He was shown up to the drawing-room. Thurlow's other guests had gone home, and his servant informed the unexpected visitor that his Lordship had retired, but after a little while Thurlow appeared and greeted him courteously. Boswell wanted to explain why he had disregarded the Lord Chancellor's advice against moving to London, but Thurlow did not seem at all disturbed on this count; he was more inclined to discuss Dr Johnson. He had read Boswell's book, and he could not understand why he had found it so absorbing: "Why should one wish to go on and read how Dr Johnson went from one place to another?" He was mystified. Boswell boldly asked him why the King had not been prepared to increase Johnson's pension. Thurlow could give no definite answer, but thought that perhaps Johnson's application had been overlooked. Though he had not mentioned Mrs Rudd's claim, Boswell felt sure that she would be pleased to hear of the good reception he had received, and he hurried straight from the Lord Chancellor's house to her lodgings. The servant told him she was not at home, and when he expressed surprise, she appeared, very angry, in her nightclothes, and sent him on his way.[5]

Boswell was now steadily gathering material for his *Life of Johnson*. His *Journal of a Tour to the Hebrides* had not required any research, of course; all he had to do then was to polish the manuscript journal already in his possession. But the *Life* would require him to tap a very wide variety of sources.

He had begun this process some years before Johnson's death. As well as quizzing Johnson himself about his own past, Boswell also collected information from others, particularly old friends who had known Johnson before Boswell did. Often he would take down what they told him in their presence. He kept a special notebook for this purpose.

Boswell was especially keen to obtain letters from Johnson, not just for the information they contained (likely to be more accurate than the memories of the recipients), but also because he had decided to reproduce many of them in the text. Immediately after Johnson's death, Boswell wrote off to several of Johnson's oldest acquaintances asking them for packets of Johnsonian material. He collected more while in London working on the *Tour*. On 6 May 1785, for example, Boswell had dined with Dr John Taylor, a lifelong friend of Johnson's who had been at school with him in Lichfield. Boswell had twice accompanied Johnson on visits to Taylor's home in Derbyshire. Now Taylor was living in London, as Rector of St Margaret's Church, Westminster. Boswell took notes on their conversation.

During a dinner-party at Langton's the following day, Boswell found himself in a corner with Sir John Hawkins. In a circumspect manner, the rival biographers discussed Johnson's fear of death. Had he been afraid that his sins might damn him? Hawkins hinted that he had found evidence of "strong amorous passions" in Johnson's diaries. "But he did not indulge them?" inquired Boswell. "I have said enough," replied Hawkins, having whetted Boswell's curiosity, no doubt deliberately, without giving anything away.

But if Hawkins thought that he had set his rival on the wrong track, he was mistaken. Boswell knew much more about Johnson's "amorous inclinations" than he revealed. Two years earlier, Boswell had dined with Johnson at Bolt Court, and while his host was napping had interrogated Elizabeth Desmoulins, the widowed daughter of Johnson's godfather and one of several women in Johnson's household. As a young woman Mrs Desmoulins had lived in Hampstead with Johnson's wife, Elizabeth Porter. "Tetty" was more than twenty years older than her husband and, it seemed, had repelled his advances. Elizabeth Desmoulins revealed how she would join the spurned husband in his bedroom, laying her head on his pillow and allowing him to kiss and fondle her until he was obviously excited. Then he would cry, "Get you gone."

Boswell thought this story too delicate to include in his *Life of Johnson*. He kept his notes on his conversation with Mrs Desmoulins in a separate file of papers, marked "Extraordinary Johnsoniana—Tacenda," to be kept silent. In fact, Boswell soon related what she had told him to Burke; but to have *published* such details in an eighteenth-century biography would have been difficult. Those who admired Johnson for his moral qualities would have been shocked to read of his toying with a young woman while his wife lay in a nearby room; while those who did not share Johnson's moral standards might have despised him for not making the most of his opportunity. Anyone who published such a story was likely to have been thought odious, and Boswell was particularly sensitive to any criticism that he had abused Johnson's confidence. It seems too that Boswell felt sympathy for his friend, and was reluctant to expose him, even to posterity, in this way. "What a curious account," Boswell noted in his diary after the interview with Mrs Desmoulins: "That he should bring himself to the very verge of what he thought was a crime."

A few weeks after his guarded conversation with Hawkins, Boswell breakfasted with William Strahan, an old and constant friend of Johnson's who had known him since the mid-1750s. Strahan gave Boswell some anecdotes, and promised to hunt for his letters from Johnson, at least some of which he gave to Boswell before he died, only a month later. Boswell was briefly able to see the bookseller Tom Davies before he too died on 5 May; Davies had been mentioned in the press as a potential biographer of Johnson's. Boswell also had several productive sessions with Tom Tyers, who had been first to publish a biographical sketch of Johnson after his death. He endured a dull evening with Brocklesby, rendered worthwhile when the Doctor produced sixteen letters from Johnson; and, most important of all, he secured a copy of Johnson's celebrated letter to Lord Chesterfield. For more than thirty years this letter had been talked of, and speculated about; Boswell was determined that the original should be reproduced in his book.

In 1747, Johnson had published his *Plan of a Dictionary of the English Language,* a prospectus designed to attract advance subscriptions. His publisher, Dodsley, had persuaded him that this prospectus should be dedicated to the Earl of Chesterfield, a distinguished statesman and diplomat, and a nobleman then much admired for his wit, his elegant manners, and his refined tastes: qualities which thirty years later would be characterized as sneering, affectation, and snobbery. It was hoped that Chesterfield might accept the role of Johnson's patron in this important project. Chesterfield did indeed encourage Johnson initially, and presented him with ten pounds, but subsequently neglected him.

In particular, Johnson felt affronted when he called on Chesterfield at his splendid London home, only to be kept waiting intolerably long. There was no further contact between them until seven years later, when the *Dictionary* was nearing publication. Then Chesterfield's interest revived, and he published two flattering essays recommending the work. Johnson was indignant; after the best part of a decade of toil and hardship, he was certainly not prepared to accept Chesterfield's patronage at this late stage. Far from dedicating his *Dictionary* to Chesterfield, as the Earl had hoped, Johnson wrote him a contemptuous letter, repudiating any obligation to acknowledge his help:

> Seven years, My Lord, have now past, since I waited in your outward rooms, or was repulsed from your door; during which time I have been pushing on my work through difficulties, of which it is useless to complain, and have brought it, at last, to the verge of publication, without one act of assistance, one word of encouragement, or one smile of favour. Such treatment I did not expect, for I never had a Patron before . . .
>
> Is not a Patron, my Lord, one who looks with unconcern on a man struggling for life in the water, and, when he has reached ground, encumbers him with help? The notice which you have been pleased to take of my labours, had it been early, had it been kind; but it has been delayed until I am indifferent, and cannot enjoy it; till I am solitary, and cannot impart it; till I am known, and do not want it . . .[6]

This letter quickly became part of the Johnson legend. That a shabby, hard-up* scholar of humble birth should write dismissively to an aristocratic patron was remarkable. And the posthumous publication of Chesterfield's *Letters* (against the wishes of the Earl's executors) raised the quarrel to the level of a *Kulturkampf*. These letters, addressed to his natural son, Philip Stanhope, outlined a programme of behaviour for a young man of fashion: stressing the importance of etiquette, the avoidance of low company, and the need for deceit and dissimulation in relations between the sexes. The cynical amorality permeating the letters outraged a public increasingly intolerant of aristocratic vice; Chesterfield's emphasis on artifice ran counter to the tide of sentiment.[7] Johnson himself declared that the letters "teach the morals of a

---

*A year after the publication of his *Dictionary,* Johnson was arrested for debt.

whore, and the manners of a dancing master."[8] In retrospect, Johnson's defiance of Chesterfield seemed all the more admirable.

The story of Johnson's letter to Lord Chesterfield was passed from mouth to mouth. Chesterfield himself, feigning indifference to Johnson's scorn, had encouraged its spread by leaving Johnson's letter where it could be seen, even pointing out striking passages. Garbled versions had found their way into print. Boswell tried several times to obtain a copy, and in 1781, finally persuaded Johnson to dictate it to him. But this was a copy dictated from memory of a letter written twenty-six years earlier; it turned out that there was an earlier, more authentic copy which Johnson had dictated soon after sending the original to Lord Chesterfield. Johnson gave this copy to Bennet Langton shortly before his death, and Langton gave it to Boswell for inclusion in his biography. At last this famous letter was available to be published, as Boswell triumphantly announced in a footnote to *The Journal of a Tour to the Hebrides.*

On 20 February 1786, Boswell dined with Reynolds, and after the meal he took down some Johnsonian anecdotes dictated by Sir Joshua. This was one of several such meetings with Reynolds; Boswell also received reminiscences from Johnson's Shakespearian collaborator, George Steevens, and from the Italian translator Francesco Sastres, who provided him with a delightful snippet—that in the last year of his life, while discussing who should be a member of a new club, Johnson had coined a previously unknown word: "Boswell," he had said, "is a very *clubable* man." Boswell could not resist quoting this remark in a footnote to his *Life of Johnson.*

On 1 March, Boswell obtained another crucial document, Johnson's own minute of his conversation with George III in the King's Library in 1767. This was to be the basis of one of the most powerful scenes in the *Life of Johnson,* showing the Prince of Literature conversing with the King of England, as it were on equal terms, "with profound respect, but still in his firm manly manner, with a sonorous voice, and never in that subdued tone which is commonly used at the levee and in the drawing room." Boswell had realized the dramatic possibilities inherent in this encounter when he first heard about it from Johnson himself, and he took much trouble to gather every scrap of information which might enable him to reconstruct it. As well as his own record of what Johnson had told him, Boswell also procured several other versions: Johnson's account of what had passed to Dr Joseph Warton, as related by Langton, who was present during the conversation; another account from the King's Librarian, Frederick Barnard; a copy of a letter written by Strahan to Bishop Warburton, which referred to the meeting; and Johnson's minute, written down shortly after the interview itself and sent to Sir James Caldwell. Caldwell was no longer alive, but Boswell was able to secure the minute from his son through the help of Sir Francis Lumm, who obtained the King's permission before delivering it to Boswell for use in his book.[9]

Boswell subtly edited this material to emphasize both Johnson's dignity in the presence of his sovereign and the young King's deference. He explained how the King, on being told that Johnson was working in the Library, had sought out Johnson's company, rather than Johnson seeking his: an important distinction in the eighteenth century, when rank customarily dictated who should make the first move. This was indeed what had happened, but Boswell omitted details, such as the presence of other people whom the King also acknowledged, to magnify Johnson's importance. Boswell described the King complimenting Johnson on his work, questioning him respectfully, and then withdrawing to leave Johnson in sole possession of his Library. Again Boswell manipulated the details, implying that the King had withdrawn to allow Johnson to continue reading uninterrupted, rather than (as had really been the case) in response to a request by the Queen. No reader of Boswell's book could doubt that the King acknowledged Johnson's authority in literary matters. Afterwards Johnson "showed himself highly pleased with His Majesty's considerate and gracious behaviour"—as if it were for Johnson to bestow approval on the monarch, rather than vice versa. Boswell's account stressed Johnson's independence of the King, from whom he had recently accepted a pension. It seemed that Johnson could be cowed by nobody, not even his sovereign.[10]

·   ·   ·

Mrs Piozzi's *Anecdotes of the Late Samuel Johnson LL.D.* was published later in March. The appetite for Johnsoniana had been whetted by Boswell's book, and Mrs Piozzi was in a perfect position to provide more: everyone knew what a significant part she, as Mrs Thrale, had played in Johnson's life. For more than fifteen years, she and her husband Henry Thrale had accepted Johnson into their household; they had taken him with them to France and into Wales; her friendship with him had widened and deepened into one of trust, affection, and regard. Hester Thrale had become the most important person in Johnson's life; scurrilous paragraphs had appeared in the newspapers suggesting an illicit "connection" between them. When Henry Thrale died in 1781, there was speculation that she and Johnson might marry. Her subsequent neglect of and eventual quarrel with Johnson were also public knowledge; a version of his angry letter to her in the summer of 1784, reacting to the news of her second marriage, appeared in the press after his death. All this added spice to the expected feast. The first edition of her book sold out on the day of publication. A copy had to be bought back for the King, who stayed up all night reading it.[11] Three further editions were published that same year.

Mrs Piozzi announced in her Preface that she had "described his [Johnson's] manners as they were"—rather than as perhaps they should have been. In revealing the faults as well as the virtues of her subject she was following Boswell's example. But Mrs Piozzi's portrait of Johnson was much less sympathetic than Boswell's; it depicted him as a bully and a boor. She labelled his presence in her home as a "yoke" put upon her by her late husband; such "confinement" was "terrifying in the first years of our friendship, and irksome in the last." This may have been how she felt in retrospect, but otherwise it was a travesty: in fact, she had been stimulated by Johnson's company, and flattered by his attention; they had become intimate friends; in many ways she had been closer to him than to her own husband. It was only after Thrale's death that the balance of their relationship was upset; and it was her growing attraction to Piozzi which had led her to withdraw from Johnson, not any change on his side. Her initial attempts to begin a new life with Piozzi were frustrated; and though Johnson was not responsible for her misery, her guilty feelings towards him had mutated into resentment. Mrs Thrale had doted on Johnson; Mrs Piozzi shrank from him. Her motives now in showing Johnson in such an unsympathetic light were self-serving; she needed exoneration for her behaviour. If she could show Johnson to have been cantankerous and demanding in his final years, her abandonment of him would appear more understandable.

Her marriage to Piozzi had left her vulnerable. Her elder daughters, and many of her influential friends—the much-admired young novelist Fanny Burney, for example—had ostracized her because of it. Eighteenth-century society found something faintly ridiculous about a woman in her forties marrying for love. She was a rich widow; Piozzi was a foreigner, a Catholic, and a singing teacher, a subordinate. Moreover, he was from Italy, the land of Romeos, gigolos, and stilettos. It was assumed, wrongly, that he was younger than she.

Boswell's relations with Mrs Thrale had been based on their mutual regard for Johnson. "There are many who admire and respect Mr Johnson," she whispered to Boswell, as the three of them breakfasted together at her Southwark home, "but you and I *love* him."[12] They had much in common: they were the same age, and they had come to know Johnson around the same time, in the mid-1760s. At their first meeting, Boswell had been keen to impress on Mrs Thrale that he was "as Johnsonian as herself"; he wrote to her describing the two of them as "rivals for that great man," and referred to her as his "generous rival." She had politely resisted his attempts to secure the collection of Johnson's sayings which she kept in her commonplace book. But their rivalry was cordial; there was no reason for it to be otherwise. Boswell often visited Johnson at the Thrales' Southwark home, next to the brewery, or at their grand country house, Streatham Park; and he was frequently a guest of the Thrales in his own right. He stayed with them on several occasions.

While he was in Scotland, Boswell needed frequent reassurance of Johnson's affection for him; and being the man he was, he could not but be envious of the constant access Mrs Thrale had to Johnson, while he was limited to seeing his friend for only a few weeks each year. Johnson tried to ensure that any jealousy between the two rivals was confined. He often wrote to assure Boswell of Mrs Thrale's goodwill: "Mrs Thrale loves you much"; "She has a great regard for you"; "You continue to stand very high in the favour of Mrs Thrale." Johnson's assurances were undoubtedly exaggerated, but her private correspondence with him betrays no hostility to Boswell, though she did tease him about Boswell's habit of recording his conversation. "I am glad Mr Boswell is with you," she wrote to him in Ashbourne: "nothing that you say for this week at least will be lost to posterity."[13] She encouraged Johnson to go to the Hebrides with Boswell. A discordant note crept in when she sneered at the notion that Johnson might entertain the Boswells at his house. "I was obliged to tell her," Johnson told Boswell, "that you would be in as respectable a situation in my house as in hers. Sir, the insolence of wealth will creep out."[14]

Boswell did not perceive Mrs Thrale as a threat to his friendship with Johnson, or to his status as Johnson's eventual biographer. He suspected that she might write a life of Johnson herself, but this possibility seems not to have concerned him unduly. After the death of Henry Thrale in 1781, he expressed the hope that she and Johnson might marry. As late as the summer of 1784, Boswell seems to have been prepared to defend her against Johnson's grumbling. "He talked of Mrs Thrale, and seemed much concerned. I could not imagine what disturbed him, for I had heard nothing to her disadvantage."[15]

Boswell's reaction to her second marriage is not recorded, but it is likely that he shared in the general disapproval. He was, even by the standards of the day, a bit of a snob; he had forbidden his wife from associating with her own sister after she had made a "low" marriage. The Boswells thought very highly of themselves. Lord Auchinleck had taken elaborate precautions to ensure that an unfortunate cousin who had descended to the status of a "dancing-master" could never under any circumstance succeed to the Auchinleck estate; Boswell could not therefore have been expected to approve of an alliance with a music-master. And he surely deplored Mrs Thrale's neglect of Johnson in his final illness.

However, he was in Scotland when he heard the news of her marriage, and she was in Italy when he returned to London. There was no contact between them. But soon after Johnson's death, their dormant rivalry ignited. When Mrs Piozzi, still in Italy, read Steevens's anonymous letters in the St James's Chronicle, hostile to her and praising

Boswell as the ideal person to write Johnson's biography, she suspected that he had written them himself. And when a letter from Boswell was printed, denying that he had written them, her suspicions hardened into conviction. It was just like Boswell to puff himself and denigrate her, and then to cover up his action with a denial.

So when Boswell's *Journal of a Tour to the Hebrides* appeared, later that same year, Mrs Piozzi's correspondents were quick to inform her of its contents (and its reception). Most of the references to Mrs Piozzi herself were unobjectionable, but there was one damaging aside about Mrs Montagu's* *Essay on Shakespeare:* Johnson had remarked that neither he nor Mrs Thrale nor their literary friend Topham Beauclerk could get through it. This was not untypical; there were hundreds of such asides in the book. Readers (except, of course, the mortified Mrs Montagu herself) delighted in this flick at the Queen of the Blue Stocking ladies: that the great Shakespeare expert could not get through her *Essay* was delicious news. But Mrs Thrale had courted Mrs Montagu, and she had frequented her evening "conversation parties," where card-playing was banned and discussion of literary topics predominated. As Mrs Piozzi, she relied on Mrs Montagu for readmission into female intellectual society (a narrow world) when she returned to England. She wrote to Mrs Montagu protesting that the passage was inaccurate, while she plotted revenge against Boswell in her own book, now in manuscript, *en route* to England.

Boswell had realized that printing Johnson's remark might upset Mrs Piozzi. He had struck out her name in the manuscript, but then, at Courtenay's urging, reinstated it in the proof.

Mrs Piozzi's book contained several sly attacks on Boswell, though he was only once mentioned by name, and then merely in passing. That fact in itself was intended to wound: Boswell was omitted from her list of Johnson's best friends. But most readers would recognize "Mr B——," shown as the victim of one of Johnson's rebukes: the implication of the story being that Mr B—— was so often in his cups as not to be able to distinguish truth from fiction. Boswell read this as an attempt to placate Mrs Montagu. "She is a little artful impudent malig-

---

*Elizabeth Montagu, celebrated for her learning and wit, and dubbed by Johnson "Queen of the Blues," a reference to the Blue Stocking Circle of educated, intelligent, and witty women.

nant Devil," he fumed to Malone.[16] The latter was, if anything, even more hostile to Mrs Piozzi, whom he referred to as "this abandoned woman."

It could have been worse. Mrs Piozzi's friends in London, who were seeing the book through the press in her absence, had saved her from an embarrassing gaffe. Assuming Boswell to have been the author of the St James's Chronicle letters, she had castigated him for his ingratitude in writing these. Fortunately, one of her friends, discovering that she had been mistaken, had deleted Mrs Piozzi's remonstrances, much to her subsequent relief.

Unfortunately for Mrs Piozzi, her friends had left her open to attack on another flank, by adding a postscript cannibalized from one of her letters. This explicitly contradicted the passage in Boswell's book, and announced in public what she had maintained in private, namely that she had "*always* commended" Mrs Montagu's *Essay,* and "heard it commended by *every one* else."

Boswell pounced. He caused a note to be placed in the press, coolly stating that the remark had been Johnson's, not his; that Johnson's low opinion of Mrs Montagu's *Essay* was well established; and that back in 1775, both Johnson and Mrs Thrale had read his journal in manuscript without objecting to the passage—indeed, he had received a letter from Mrs Thrale complimenting him on it. In fact, she had either not read or not noticed the embarrassing passage, but her letter to Boswell had implied that she had scrutinized the whole journal avidly, and she could not now retract without making matters worse. She was trapped.

The note was reprinted in many of the periodicals, and inspired a succession of squibs on the subject, some of them written by Boswell under a pseudonym. It was all grist to the mill, the row stimulating demand for both Boswell's and Piozzi's books, and even Mrs Montagu's *Essay,* which was reprinted. Another "Peter Pindar" poem appeared, *Bozzy and Piozzi, or the British Biographers,* describing a mock contest between the two rivals, presided over by a magisterial Sir John Hawkins.

A postscript to Peter Pindar's earlier *Poetical and Congratulatory Epistle* had purported to reveal the contents of a conversation with Johnson, in which he was imagined to speak contemptuously of Boswell's merit as a biographer. "BOSWELL write my life! why the fellow possesses not abilities for writing the life of an *ephemeron.*" It was only knockabout stuff, but Boswell contemplated suing Peter Pindar's publisher, which he thought might provide an opportunity to announce his *Life* "in the most splendid manner. Erskine would expatiate upon it as not only to be the Life and Conversation of the first Genius etc. etc. etc. but the History of Literature and Literary men during a considerable period." He suggested to Malone that a letter or two from Johnson might be read out in court, to make it clear that Johnson knew about and approved of Boswell's intention to write his biography.[17] Perhaps Malone was not encouraging, because Boswell does not seem to have proceeded with this action.

Another satirical poem, Courtenay's *A Poetical Review of the Literary and Moral Character of the Late Dr Samuel Johnson,* reviewed the qualifications of the rival biographers, but was more friendly to Boswell:

> Amid these names, can BOSWELL be forgot,
> Scarce by North Britons now esteemed a Scot?
> Who to the Sage devoted from his youth,
> Imbibed from him the sacred love of truth;
> The keen research, the exercise of mind
> And that best art, the art to know mankind.

Courtenay's poem appeared on 6 April; it was reprinted twice over the next six weeks. An engraving appeared, entitled: "The Biographers," showing the bust of Johnson looking down on Boswell, Thrale, and Courtenay.

An *Epitaph on Dr Johnson* by the poet Soame Jenyns (who himself had been the victim of one of Johnson's most savage reviews) mocked this new style of biography, in which nothing was withheld from the reader:

> Boswell and Thrale, retailers of his wit,
> Will tell you how he wrote, and talked, and coughed, and spit.

The Reverend Dr Vicesimus Knox, Master of Tunbridge School, an essayist second in popularity only to Johnson himself, took a dim view of publishing Johnson's private conversation, as both Boswell and Mrs Piozzi had now done. "Biography is every day descending from its dignity," he opined. "Instead of an instructive recital, it is becoming an instrument to the mere gratification of an impertinent, not to say a malignant, curiosity." The schoolmaster was apprehensive that "the custom of exposing the nakedness of eminent men of every type will have an unfavourable influence on virtue. It may teach men to fear celebrity."

In her *Anecdotes* Mrs Piozzi had deplored a "trick" which, she said, she had often seen played, "of sitting steadily down at the other end of the room to write at the moment what should be said in company, either *by* Dr Johnson or *to* him." It was obvious that this censure was aimed at Boswell. Such ill-bred and treacherous conduct, she went on, "were it commonly adopted," would exile all confidence from society.[18] Mrs Piozzi could not push this argument too far, because her own common-place book had been her primary source for the *Anecdotes*. She herself had not scrupled to record what Johnson had said; but (she argued) she had selected what was worth recording and what was appropriate to record, and had obtained Johnson's permission before doing so. Boswell had taken down what Johnson said indiscriminately.[19]

Mrs Piozzi's charge has haunted Boswell ever since. The legend of Boswell is of a stenographer, a secretary taking down his master's words as they are spoken. He appears in a subordinate role; and his literary skill seems no more than accurate transcription.

In the *Life of Johnson,* Boswell does not deny Mrs Piozzi's allegation outright, though he records the occasions when Johnson advised him to keep a journal and subsequently encouraged him, more than once, to keep it up. Boswell also points out that if Johnson's conversation is to be recorded accurately, the sooner it is done, the better. He quotes Johnson in support: "You should write down every thing that you remember, for you cannot judge at first what is good or bad, and write immediately while the impression is fresh, for it will not be the same a week afterwards."[20]

Various other passages in the *Life* appear to indicate that Boswell is taking down what Johnson says as he is saying it. For example, Boswell laments that during the second part of his stay in London in 1775, after his return from a visit to the West Country, he "kept very imperfect notes of his [Johnson's] conversation, which had I according to my usual custom written out at large soon after the time, much might have been preserved, which is now irretrievably lost."[21] The inference seems to be that Boswell's notes were made during the conversations themselves.

On 21 March 1783, Boswell visited Johnson at Mrs Thrale's (who, since Henry Thrale's death and the subsequent sale of the Southwark brewery, had given up Streatham Park and was living in central London), where he stayed most of the day. Following an afternoon nap, Johnson joined Boswell and Mrs Thrale at tea; refreshed, he was soon in full flow. "Oh, for shorthand to take this down!" exclaimed Boswell. "You'll carry it all in your head," retorted Mrs Thrale: "A long head is as good as shorthand."

It is hard to know how to interpret this exchange. Mrs Thrale was presumably commenting on Boswell's known ability to preserve the essence of a conversation in his memory. Boswell's exclamation could be understood to mean that he was taking notes, but unable to keep up with Johnson's eloquence; or it could mean that Boswell felt unable to take notes on such an occasion, but wished it were otherwise. In his journal Boswell adds the following comment: "I have the substance, but the felicity of expression, the flavour, is not fully preserved unless taken instantly."[22]

As a lawyer, and as a student of law, Boswell would of course have had frequent need to take notes of what was said in court. It would have been surprising, therefore, if he had not developed his own shorthand technique.

There is another passage in the *Life of Johnson* which appears to support this notion of Boswell as stenographer. On the evening of 10 April 1778, after both men had dined with Johnson's old friend William Scott, Boswell boasted that although he did not write shorthand in the usual sense, he nevertheless had his own method of writing half words and leaving out some altogether so that he could later reconstitute the whole. Johnson challenged him to an experiment: he would read aloud an extract from William Robertson's *History of America,* slowly and distinctly, while Boswell attempted to take it down. The experiment was made, and when Boswell came to read it back, "It was found that I had it very imperfectly."[23]

Geoffrey Scott,[24] the first editor of Boswell's journals, argued that the interpretation commonly given to this passage—i.e. that Boswell took shorthand in public—is unsatisfactory to the point of absurdity. If Boswell had been in the habit of doing so, Johnson, he pointed out, would not need to have been told, as if for the first time, that Boswell had his own method of shorthand, after fifteen years' acquaintance. On the contrary, the story seems to prove that Boswell had not previously used his "shorthand" in Johnson's presence. And given the failure of the experiment, one is tempted to think that he might be reluctant to rely on it again. Indeed, his exclamation at Mrs Thrale's tea-party five years later suggests that he lacked a method of shorthand which could keep up with Johnson's talk.

Scott put several other arguments against the idea that Boswell took down Johnson's conversations as they happened. In the first place, it was out of character: Boswell liked to take part in the conversation, and was proud of his ability to steer it on to fruitful topics that might provoke Johnson into saying something memorable. He could hardly have done so if he were simultaneously taking down what was being said. Second, to have copied down conversation would have been socially unacceptable in the late eighteenth century (as doubtless it would be today). Boswell was a very sociable man; he would never have been welcomed so widely if he were seen to have recorded the conversations of his hosts and fellow-guests. Third, it would have defeated Boswell's purpose to have been writing all the time; to catch the full flavour of each scene, he needed his eyes as well as his ears. Fourth, Boswell often recorded conversations when it would have been impossible for him to have taken shorthand: on a walk, in a boat, in a carriage, or at a levee. The fact that he was able to do so shows that he must have had some other method of recording.

Scott also pointed out that in all Boswell's diaries there is not a single reference to his having followed such a practice. On the contrary, Boswell's journal note after Garrick suggested that he should be searched and his notebook removed if he refused to drink in company* seems to confirm that he did not. Furthermore, Boswell's journals are written *in ink;* before the invention of the fountain-pen, no easily transportable

*See page 109.

means of writing in ink was available. The few references to Boswell scribbling notes upon "a tablet" refer to his using a lead pencil.

A note in Boswell's journal for 25 October 1764 provides an insight into the way he worked:

> My method is to make a memorandum every night of what I have seen during the day. By this means I have my materials always secured. Sometimes I am three, four, five days without journalizing. When I have time and spirits, I bring up this my Journal as well as I can . . .[25]

Some of these memoranda have survived, and they show Boswell using the kind of rapid and abbreviated writing that he boasted of to Johnson after the dinner at William Scott's. He called these condensed notes "portable soup": they were a kind of stock cube from which he could make up a broth, when the time came to feed. He needed only to put down a few words on paper—"the heads" of the conversation—to be able to retrieve the rest later. Then he would expand the notes into a fully written form when he had the leisure to do so. Boswell had a remarkable memory; often only a brief note would be sufficient to prompt his recall of a long conversation, and he was able to write it up into a passage ten or twenty times its length. The practice of keeping a journal over many years had trained him to formulate in advance what he might write. This process was most successful when he knew the individuals whose speech he was recording and was familiar with the way they talked. An exceptionally skilful mimic, he had a keen ear for characteristic habits of speech. When he first came to know Johnson, Boswell was so struck by his "extraordinary colloquial talents" that he found it extremely difficult to recollect afterwards what Johnson had said. Boswell's record of their first meeting, following the dramatic opening exchange, is little more than a string of disconnected quotes. But later, "when my mind was, as it were, *strongly impregnated with the Johnsonian ether,* I could, with much more facility and exactness, carry in my memory and commit to paper the exuberant variety of his wisdom and wit."[26]

This method—of making brief notes as soon as possible after the events described and writing them up into journal form subsequently—was the one Boswell used for most of his life. At the beginning, while he was still a young man in his early twenties, he would often "bring up" his journal without an intermediate stage of notes, sometimes working all night to complete the task. He remembered one week in which he had stayed up all through four nights in order to do so. But this was hardly practical for an older man with a family and a career. Only on a special occasion, such as the evening he was admitted to the Club, would Boswell still sit up late into the night writing his journal, to ensure that he had a full record of such a momentous day.

Boswell's technique for preserving the conversation of Johnson and others was therefore not what it seemed. What appeared as mere verbatim recording was in reality a much more complex process, one at least partly reliant on Boswell's memory. And though his memory was exceptional, it was nevertheless fallible, and susceptible to a variety of distorting influences. What he remembered could never be exactly what he had heard. There would always be gaps in his memory that needed filling, and for that matter non sequiturs in Johnson's conversation that required a link to make sense on the page. Boswell's skill was to sustain the illusion that what he wrote was just what Johnson had said. In this sleight of hand, he was triumphantly successful. His artistry concealed the extent of his invention. The naïveté he betrayed reinforced the sense of authenticity he wished to convey.

Boswell often "brought up" his journal in company, not during a meal or another social occasion, but in a quiet period when Johnson or some other person was present, perhaps reading or working themselves. To see him doing so was very different from seeing him taking down a conversation; it was analogous to Mrs Thrale's writing in her commonplace book.

In exceptional cases Boswell may have scribbled a note or two while the conversation was still in progress, or while those who had been doing the talking were still present. He would have been particularly likely to have done this at the Thrales'; after all, it was open house there. Johnson had his own rooms, where Boswell would often visit him for a large part of the day. Johnson was encouraged to use the Thrales' homes as his own: to work in the library, for example. For Boswell to be writing in such an environment would have been very different from scribbling notes in a more formal setting.

In a private letter to his confidant Malone, Boswell did not deny the truth of what Mrs Piozzi had written. "It *describes* what the Jade has often seen me do," he admitted. But it was done "with Dr Johnson's *approbation;* for he at all times was flattered by my preserving what fell from his mind when shaken by conversation, so there was nothing *like* treachery."[27]

Another passage in Mrs Piozzi's *Anecdotes* described an exchange between her and Johnson on the question of who should write his biography. Johnson had agreed that the multi-talented Oliver Goldsmith, who had already written several biographies, could write his life best (Goldsmith died the following year). "I intend, however, to disappoint the rogues," he told her, "and either make you write the life, with Taylor's intelligence; or, which is better, do it myself, after outliving you all. I am now keeping a diary, in hopes of using it for that purpose some time."[28] Johnson mentioned the possibility of his writing an autobiography to Boswell, too. In an *Idler* essay, he had expressed the view that "every man's life may be best written by himself."

In her own diary, Mrs Thrale recorded another remark from him on the same issue: "Rescue me out of all their hands my dear, and do it yourself."

Who did Johnson think should write his biography? It is impossible to be sure of his intentions, because our record of everything he said on the subject is tainted by the self-interest of the various contenders. He must have known that there would be many lives published, but he seemed to resist the idea. There was a side of Johnson that was deliberately contrary; he disliked being pinned down, by Boswell or anybody else. When two of his friends attempted in his presence to compile a list of his works, Johnson "let them go on as they pleased," without correcting their errors.

Johnson certainly knew that Boswell would be one of his biographers. Towards the end of his life he provided the younger man with many details of his early years, and suggested other sources of information. He took Boswell with him to Oxford, and to his birthplace, Lichfield, where they visited some of the sites of Johnson's youth. He introduced Boswell to his old friends. But he was not unfailingly cooperative; he could be

playfully coy, or even deliberately misleading. He sometimes tired of
Boswell's cross-examination, and rebuked him smartly. "You have but
two topics," Johnson told him on one occasion, "yourself and me, and
I'm sick of both."[29] When Boswell rashly expressed a wish to see Johnson
together with the republican freethinker Mrs Macaulay,* Johnson grew
very angry, and burst out, "Don't you know that it is very uncivil to *pit*
two people against one another?" And when Boswell pressed Johnson on
the sensitive subject of the Cock-Lane ghost,† Johnson became enraged.
"I will not be put to the *question*. Don't you consider, Sir, that these are
not the manners of a gentleman?"[30]

Johnson did not authorize any particular biographer in his will, nor
did he make any special arrangements for the disposal of his papers.
Though he appointed three literary men as executors, he did not spec-
ify a literary executor. Just before his death, so Boswell believed, he had
burned two quarto volumes, "containing a full, fair, and most particular account of his own life, from his earliest recollections." Johnson had
discovered that Hawkins had pocketed one of these volumes,‡ and
indignantly insisted on its return before the burglar could take it away.
Boswell speculated that the agitation into which Johnson had been
thrown by this incident may have caused him to hastily destroy the two
volumes. He regretted that posterity had lost "these two very valuable
articles." Years before, Boswell had secretly read "a great deal in these,"
and had subsequently confessed to Johnson, adding that he had been
tempted to steal them. Johnson told him that had he done so, "I believe
I should have gone mad."[32]

It seems odd that Johnson should have received Boswell's confession "placidly." If the diaries contained secrets that he was anxious to
hide from the world, Boswell was, at least on the face of it, the last man
he could trust to keep silent. (In fact, Boswell had copied down some

---

*Catherine Macaulay, historian and republican.
†Johnson had been part of an inquiry which found this celebrated ghost to have been fraudulent. In
his satirical poem *The Ghost,* Charles Churchill mocked Johnson for taking the imposture seriously.
‡Or so Boswell believed. Hawkins in fact says that he put *two* volumes in his pocket, "a parchment-
covered book . . . of meditations and reflections," together with "a less of the same kind."[31] These
may or may not have been the same as the "two quarto volumes" into which Boswell had dipped
eight years earlier; the differences in the description suggest not (Hawkins would have needed big
pockets to have accommodated two such large volumes). Nor do we know for certain which, if
any, of the diaries Johnson destroyed.

entries from the diaries, an action he seems to have concealed from Johnson.) Another suggestive point is that Johnson took "a pretty full and curious Diary of his Life"—probably one (or perhaps both, though Boswell saw only one) of the volumes referred to above—to Scotland, and left it in a drawer at Boswell's Edinburgh home when the two of them set out on their expedition to the Hebrides. Why should he have done so? If the diary was so private, surely it was risky to have brought it there? If he was still writing it, why did he not take it with him to the Highlands? Did he wish, as Boswell did, that Margaret might arrange to have it copied while they were away, for the benefit of her husband?

Boswell had received his first brief as a barrister only a fortnight after being called to the English bar. The plaintiff was a fellow-Scot, a "writer" (solicitor) who had employed Boswell's services in the past. Erskine was leading counsel; he told Boswell what to do. The case was lost on a technicality, but Boswell had played his part, and he received a fee of two guineas, which he decided to keep as a souvenir rather than spend. A week or so later, another client wanted to give him a brief, but could not find him in time. On 9 March, Boswell set off on a month's tour of the Northern Circuit, during which he hoped to attract some work from local solicitors, while he built up his knowledge of English law by taking notes on the cases he attended. He soon found that most of the work went to local barristers, or to barristers from London with some local connection. He managed to attract two modest briefs, but overall the Circuit was not a success. As the most junior counsel, he was expected to make all the travel arrangements for the gang of barristers who travelled the Circuit together, even though he was twenty years older than the youngest of them. To make matters worse, he was suffering from an uncomfortable venereal infection. What was most upsetting, however, was a faked brief* left at his lodgings. Such japes were

---

*An account left by one of Boswell's fellow barristers on the Circuit, John Scott (William Scott's younger brother), later, as Lord Eldon, Lord Chancellor, suggests that Boswell had been found lying on the pavement the night before, inebriated. His waggish colleagues devised a bogus brief, instructing him to move a writ of "Quare adhaesit pavimento," which Boswell duly attempted in court the following day. This story sadly seems to be a legend, based on a kernel of truth (the faked brief)—typical of the type that attaches to Boswell.

common enough on the Circuit, particularly among the juniors, but he found it a humiliating experience.

Back in London, Boswell tried to resist the temptation to visit Mrs Rudd, but found it impossible. He called on her; they walked together in Bedford Square, and he arranged to dine with her the following Sunday, when they planned to take a hackney-coach to the Magdalen Hospital for penitent prostitutes ("To leave her there?" asked Courtenay pleasantly, when he heard about the excursion). Like the Bethlem Hospital, the Magdalen Hospital was then a fashionable attraction. A neighbour, Mrs Ewen, and her husband's nephew, an officer of the marines from the North of Scotland, made up the party. There was a service at the hospital, and during the sermon Mrs Rudd told him that she had often heard the same preacher at St Martin-in-the-Fields, but that she did not go there now. "You know who is buried there," she said *sotto voce,* referring to Daniel Perreau. "You are an affectionate creature," murmured Boswell; but he was chilled to be reminded of the man Mrs Rudd had sent to the gallows. Afterwards they walked back. "I dislike this *low* association," he grumbled in his journal, and from this time on he avoided her.

In late April Boswell and Malone travelled up to Oxford to gather more Johnsonian material from Dr Adams, Master of Johnson's college, Pembroke; and from Thomas Warton, antiquarian scholar, poet (he was the reigning Poet Laureate) and, like his elder brother Joseph (poet, critic, and Headmaster of Winchester College), a member of the Literary Club. Boswell had already received information from both, and had indeed visited Adams in Oxford with Johnson during the last year of his life, but he was keen to leave no stone unturned. Afterwards he wrote to Adams from London, asking him for copies of Johnson's letters and for any of Johnson's "college exercises," dating from his university days, that might have survived. This was the third time that he had written to Adams asking for copies of Johnson's letters; and, as an insurance against the possibility that Adams might prove insufficiently diligent, he also wrote to Adams's daughter Sarah, requesting her assistance. To the first inquiry Adams had replied that he had no letters that would be of any use; Boswell wrote back to say that any letters, however short, would be of value, but Adams ignored this second request. Adams eventually replied to Boswell's third appeal for letters twelve weeks later, saying that he had looked repeatedly for Johnson's letters but had found "none that will be of the least use to you."[33]

This was frustrating, but Boswell's persistence was reaping rewards elsewhere. He continued to receive parcels of letters and collections of anecdotes; sometimes the information revealed in these would inspire a fresh round of inquiries to those who had already contributed material for the *Life*. Boswell found that specific questions were more fruitful than general ones, and he adopted a technique of approaching his interviewees with a prepared list of topics—which he referred to as a "catechism."

Boswell also received an unsolicited collection of Johnsoniana from the Reverend Daniel Astle of Ashbourne, who had known Johnson for almost twenty years, and who supplemented his own memories of Johnson with anecdotes supplied by others. Most of the information Boswell received was as a result of a direct inquiry, but this collection was sent in response to Boswell's advertisement at the end of the *Tour*.

On 16 May, Boswell took possession of an unfurnished house in Great Queen Street, between Drury Lane and Lincoln's Inn Fields. Margaret Boswell moved out of their home in Edinburgh, from where she sent him twenty-one parcels of furnishings. She and the children planned to spend the summer at Auchinleck before joining him in London in the autumn. Boswell found the solitude of his new house very dreary, as he wrote to his wife only two days after moving in:

> . . . the situation of my affairs is really wretched. I begin to apprehend that it was very ill-judged in me to venture to come to the English bar at my time of life. I see numbers of barristers who I really believe are much better qualified for the profession than I am languishing from want of employment. How then can I reasonably hope to be more successful than they?

He sank into despondency: "I have no expectation now of any continued happiness in this life, as it appears I shall only suffer disappointments."[34] His wife had begun to spit blood again; he knew in his heart that living in London would only worsen her condition. He was supposed to be attending the sittings at Westminster Hall, but he sought any excuse not to go. He had no practice. An unexpected demand for repayment of a £500 loan left him almost desperate, but he managed to have it postponed. Meanwhile, he made himself frantic by worrying whether he should return to Scotland immediately, try a new circuit, or carry on as he had begun. The extra expense of living in London, and the lack of fees, added urgency to his decision. As always when undecided, he sought advice everywhere, imprudently mentioning the possibility of returning to Scotland to those upon whom his prospects in England depended. On one of his worst days, he wandered the streets of London distractedly, and became so depressed that tears ran down his cheeks.

Hanging over him all this time was his book, which he had not yet started, though eighteen months had elapsed since Johnson's death. Several other biographical works had already appeared, albeit most of them slight, in addition to Mrs Piozzi's *Anecdotes:* Thomas Tyers's *A Biographical Sketch of Dr Samuel Johnson; The Life of Samuel Johnson, LL.D.* by William Cook; *Memoirs of the Life and Writings of the Late Dr Samuel Johnson* by the Reverend William Shaw; and *An Essay on the Life, Character, and Writings of the Late Dr Samuel Johnson* by Joseph Towers.[35] Various other compilations of memoirs and anecdotes had appeared in the magazines. A collection of Johnson's letters, to be edited by Mrs Piozzi, was advertised as forthcoming. Sir John Hawkins was said to be making good progress. Others rumoured to be contemplating lives of Johnson included his friend Dr Charles Burney, the scholarly divine Dr Samuel Parr, and the Reverend Dr Andrew Kippis, author of a life of Sir John Pringle and editor of the *Biographia Britannica.* Soon, it seemed, there would be nothing left to say. Pieces began to appear in the newspapers ridiculing Boswell for his tardiness. He received a letter from his old friend the Reverend Dr Hugh Blair, now Regius Professor of Rhetoric and Belles-Lettres in the University of Edinburgh, urging him to give "your great biographical work" to the world "as speedily as you can." Blair warned him not to delay it too long, for fear that the public's appetite for a biography of Johnson might diminish. "For consider that tho' Dr Johnson was, really and truly, *a great man;* yet there was much broad mixture in his character, and if the disagreeable parts of it, should come to strike the public too strongly, according to the common vicissitudes of luck, they might take a disgust, and tire of hearing more about him."

Boswell may have shared this fear. In a letter to the antiquarian Thomas Percy, Bishop of Dromore, in Ireland—who had known Johnson since the mid-1750s and who at one time had been rumoured to be contemplating a life of Johnson himself—Boswell reminded the Bishop of his promise to supply material for Johnson's biography, and begged him to do so "as soon as you can," because of the danger that "if the publication of his life be delayed too long, curiosity may be fainter."[36]

It was high time for Boswell to make a start. On Monday, 5 June 1786, after going to bed early the night before, Boswell spent the morning at home "sorting materials for Dr Johnson's *Life*."[37]

EIGHT

APPLICATION

—◦◦◦◦◦—

My next consideration is Dr Johnson's Life, which it is necessary I should get ready for the press soon, that the public attention may not be directed to some other object.[1]

HE HAD MUCH SORTING to do. Over the years Boswell had hoarded a "great treasure" of Johnsonian material: notebooks, journals, jottings, letters, scraps, and so on. More kept arriving. Now this needed sorting; but it was difficult to know where to start, and how to go on. Malone recommended him to "make a skeleton," arranging the materials in chronological order. This was good advice; indeed, Boswell decided to dispense with chapters altogether and to deal with his subject year by year. A catalogue of Johnson's publications, arranged in date order, provided a framework upon which the other elements of the book might hang; and usually, though not invariably, Boswell would begin each year with a discussion of the works published over the following twelve months.

Bolstered by Malone, Boswell sorted steadily. On 12 June, he sat at home all day sorting, taking neither dinner nor tea; and on 22 June, he "sorted till I was stupefied." By the end of June he was ready to write. He had chosen a method, based on his experience of working on the *Tour*, which would entail the minimum of transcription and allow for later revision and additions. His first draft was written on one side only of a quarto sheet of paper; later corrections which could not be made on the same sheet would be added on the blank verso of the previous page. A separate pile of miscellaneous documents was almost equally high: these "Papers Apart" were keyed into the manuscript by means of a system of symbols and notes to the printer. Once he began, Boswell could write very quickly: years of working to periodical deadlines, plus almost three decades of keeping his journal, had made him fluent.

Boswell was still fretful, however, and found it hard to settle. In early July his melancholy became severe. "My mind has become quite unhinged," he wrote to his wife, who urged him to return to Scotland. His brother reminded him of his duty to live at Auchinleck. T.D. felt strongly that the Boswell children should not become estranged from their ancestral home, and that the family would be of no consequence in London. Boswell himself was torn between his pride as an "old Scottish baron" and his desire to succeed in the wider world. He was anxious about how it might look if he returned to Scotland without succeeding. Malone said that he might be at the English bar, the Scots bar, or no bar at all, and nobody would trouble their heads about what he did. "You are past the age of ambition," General Paoli told him— Boswell was forty-five—"You should determine to be happy with your wife and children."[2] The solitude of the empty house frightened Boswell into "constant dissipation": not vice, but any kind of diversion and a "perpetual succession of company." His chief comfort was "the Gang" of Reynolds, Courtenay, and Malone, the last in particular. But while his future was so uncertain, he found it difficult to concentrate on writing. He described his predicament in a letter to his wife:

> My next consideration is Dr Johnson's *Life,* which it is necessary I should get ready for the press soon, that the public attention may not be directed to some other object; and as I have collected a great variety of materials, it should be a work of considerable value. Mr Malone thinks I can write it nowhere but in London. But I *feel* that it is almost impossible for me to settle to it here on account of the agitation to which I have been used; and, especially in my present state of mind, how can I settle to it, when I am in a kind of fever to think of my absence from *her I love,* and who is *my own,* and with whose illness I was lately so deeply alarmed?[3]

In desperation, Boswell decided to submit a long "Confidential Case" to Henry Dundas, summarizing their dealings over the years and pressing his claims to attention. A few months earlier, Boswell had called on Dundas, and they had talked easily; any rancour caused by Boswell's pamphlet attacking Dundas's plan to diminish the number of Lords of Session seemed to have dispersed. The agitation against the measure had been such that Dundas had withdrawn the bill; "You may be a Lord of Session now if you like it," he had said, smiling. Boswell had taken this as a promise, rather than a pleasantry; what he wanted now from Dundas was a post worth £200 or £300 a year to keep him at the English bar while he waited for a vacancy on the bench of the Court of Session. His "Confidential Case" mixed compliments with hints that it would be unwise for Dundas to ignore his claims. These were empty threats, of course; Boswell had no weapon with which he could hurt Dundas, nor any lever with which he could move him. After waiting four months, he prodded Dundas for a reply. Dundas's response was noncommittal. He promised nothing, though he had shown Boswell's letter to Pitt. He did not regret Boswell's pamphlet attacking his plan to diminish the number of Lords of Session on his own account, but he certainly did on Boswell's.

This was in the future, however, and Boswell, having committed his fate into the hands of another, now relaxed. His spirits revived, and he resolved to work on his book until the end of July, before setting out on the Home Circuit; he would resume writing when he returned to Auchinleck in midsummer, and polish and complete the manuscript when he returned to London in November. Beginning on 9 July, he spent several days confined to the house, eating only dry toast and drinking either tea in the morning or milk at night. He aimed to persevere like this for a week, but on the fourth day Malone and Courtenay called round at the house in mid-afternoon and dragged him out on a ramble to Dulwich. He felt restless the next day, and turned this to good use by going to Malone's, where the two of them trawled through back issues of the *Gentleman's Magazine* for pieces by Johnson.

On the following day, a Friday, Boswell stayed in until mid-afternoon working on the book. He now felt that he should remain in London all summer, and wrote a note to his wife informing her how well he was, "*fixed* by my friend Malone." He asked her to come and join him in town. That night he walked to Richmond Lodge, where he intended to spend the evening with his friends the Stuarts. Colonel

James Stuart was the second son of the Earl of Bute and the younger brother of Boswell's unofficial "patron," Lord Mountstuart (now no longer returning his calls); his wife, Margaret, with whom Boswell indulged in a safe flirtation, was an intimate friend of Margaret Boswell's. Reaching the gate of Richmond Park, Boswell heard the shocking news of the death of the Stuarts' daughter Charlotte, aged only fifteen. After resting for a few minutes, Boswell walked back to London, now "tenderly anxious" to see his own children; and the next day he wrote to his wife telling her that he planned to return to Auchinleck in August after all.

A week later, Boswell returned home after dining at Courtenay's with Wilkes and Malone, and found to his surprise a card from Lord Lonsdale, asking him to dinner the following Monday. The dish was to be a turtle, a special luxury. Boswell "strutted" and said to himself, "Well, it is right to be in this metropolis. Things at last come forward unexpectedly. The great LOWTHER himself has now taken me up. I may be raised to eminence in the state."

"The great LOWTHER" was the tyrant Lord Lonsdale, formerly Sir James Lowther. One of the richest men in England, Lonsdale controlled nine seats in the House of Commons, which in the chaotic politics of the eighteenth century was sufficient to give him considerable leverage. Pitt himself (the reigning Prime Minister, not his father) had been one of Lowther's "ninepins"; and, in return, Pitt had elevated Lowther to the peerage. From his base in the north-west of England, close to the Scots border, Lonsdale exercised power on an almost feudal scale. Brutal and ruthless, he liked to control everything within his fiefdom; and would brook no opposition. He was a bully, who boasted of his prowess at duelling, and who met any serious show of defiance with a challenge.

Ever since he was a young man, Boswell had cherished hopes of a political career: if anyone could get him into Parliament, Lonsdale could. If he would help Pitt, why not Boswell? This was Boswell's reasoning: and for some years he had courted Lonsdale from afar, without obvious success. His *Letter to the People of Scotland* in 1785 had appealed to Lonsdale—"HE whose soul is all great—whose resentment is terrible, but whose liberality is boundless"—to assist "his neighbours" in Scotland, while sending up a balloon to indicate that he was at Lonsdale's disposal. And he had added a respectful footnote about the Lowther family to his *Journal of a Tour to the Hebrides*. Since then he had endeavoured, in various ways, to show himself a partisan for Lonsdale's causes, without apparent effect. At last it seemed that Boswell had been noticed.

Or had he? On second thoughts, this invitation seemed too good to be true. Perhaps it was a hoax. For one man to invite another to dinner without calling on him first was not quite *comme il faut*—though it might be in character for such a potentate, Boswell told himself. He consulted Malone, who also suspected a trick. They agreed that Malone's resourceful servant should call at Lonsdale's house to inquire of the butler whether the invitation was genuine. So it turned out to be, and Boswell then had to decide whether to accept. He already had an invitation to dine that Monday at Malone's, with Reynolds and Wilkes; to refuse this and attend Lonsdale's might look like answering a summons. Boswell was torn between ambition and pride. He hesitated, "as this approach to him might be a great crisis in my fortune." Eventually he decided to use his existing engagement as an excuse to decline Lonsdale's invitation, but to call on him instead: "I would not meet him but as an ancient Baron."

Strolling up The Mall with Malone on Sunday, Boswell ran into Lord Eglinton, successor to the late tenth Earl who had taken Boswell under his wing on his first trip to London in 1760. Boswell had felt peeved at what he saw as Eglinton's neglect of him, and disappointed when Eglinton had evaded his request for an introduction to Lonsdale. Now he inquired triumphantly: "Pray, my Lord, do you by chance dine with Lord Lonsdale tomorrow? I have got a card to a turtle." No, replied Eglinton drily: "I think Lord Lonsdale a great bore." Boswell was incredulous: "What, the great Lowther himself! the potentate!" He stared at Eglinton for a moment, and then broke off—"but I must follow my friend," and hurried after Malone, who had walked on.

•   •   •

A couple of weeks before, on 8 July 1786, Boswell had taken tea at Bennet Langton's house with his rival biographer, Sir John Hawkins. They met to discuss "a delicate question." Langton afterwards assured Boswell that he had weighed and decided upon this as well as it could be done.[4]

What was this "delicate question"? It can only have been an issue which concerned both biographers, and one can infer that it was a question of how much should be revealed about some aspect of Johnson's life. Their discussion the previous May, when Hawkins hinted that evidence of Johnson's "strong amorous passions" was to be found in his diary, suggests that the issue the two men were now addressing was of how much should be revealed of Johnson's sexual behaviour. Both men were aware that Johnson had felt remorse for some offence, though neither man was entirely sure how much more the other knew. In such circumstances both were reluctant to give anything away. Neither biographer wanted to be seen to be muck-raking, but each feared being scooped by the other. Hawkins was in the more vulnerable position, since his book was now certain to be published first.

In his biography of Johnson, Hawkins would hint that Johnson might have succumbed to sexual temptation while living apart from his wife in the late 1730s, when he came under the influence of the buccaneering Richard Savage. Boswell would suggest the same, somewhat more explicitly than Hawkins.[5] The agreement brokered by Langton on this occasion may therefore have been to confine any discussion of Johnson's sexual irregularities to this period in his life.

The evidence for Johnson's feelings of remorse lay in the posthumously published *Prayers and Meditations*. This was a collection of private and personal prayers, compiled in Johnson's last few months. Many of his contemporaries thought that these should not have been published. Some of Johnson's prayers seemed to indicate penance for past transgressions, and Boswell cited a number of these in support of his suggestion that Johnson had been "overcome" by amorous desires during the time when he associated with Savage. Johnson had made no secret of the fact that he used to take women of the town to taverns, to hear them relate their history, and to persuade them to repent. Boswell conjectured that sometimes Johnson had been persuaded to sin.

However, both biographers may have misjudged their subject. Johnson was a man of extreme moral scrupulousness; his notion of depravity was different from most men's. Boswell already knew, from Mrs Desmoulins, how Johnson had struggled to control his inclinations. To Boswell, there was nothing criminal in such behaviour. Mrs Desmoulins herself said that Johnson never did anything that went beyond the limits of decency. But Johnson may have seen it differently. Lust, rather than adultery, may have been the sin for which he felt remorse.

If this speculation is correct, then in attempting to be discreet, both biographers had exaggerated Johnson's sexual peccadilloes. Perhaps Hawkins, detecting that Boswell knew something that he did not, assumed it to be more than it was, and formed his account on this assumption; while Boswell, believing Hawkins to have had access to parts of Johnson's diary that he had not seen, assumed that Hawkins's hints of sexual impropriety were based on evidence he had found there.[6]

Johnson himself had been deeply interested in biography. He had told a gathering at the Mitre that he loved the biographical part of literature most.[7] Isaac Walton's *Lives* was one of his favourite books. "No species of writing is more worthy of cultivation," he wrote, in a *Rambler* essay devoted to the topic. In Johnson's time biography was still an emerging form, though one rapidly gaining in popularity. Many of those in his circle were writing or would write biographies—Tom Davies, Hawkins, Goldsmith, Percy, Reynolds, and Burney, for example, and of course Boswell.[8] But when Johnson first turned his mind to the subject, biographical models were thin on the ground. On their tour of the Hebrides, Johnson remarked to Boswell that "he did not know any literary man's life in England well-written." Literary biographies in Johnson's time tended to be brief, usually consisting of no more than a summary of the external events of the writer's life, often prefixed to an edition of his works. Few biographers attempted to probe the inner life of their subjects, to analyse the writings critically, or to illuminate the work in the light of the life.

"I esteem biography, as giving us what comes near to ourselves, what we can turn to use," Johnson told Boswell and Monboddo during their visit to Monboddo's home, *en route* for the Highlands. He believed in the power of example, the value of learning about other men's lives so that one might live one's own life better. His *Life of Savage* was a morality tale, an account of how a man of talent and even genius could be dragged down by a combination of unlucky circumstance and flaws in his character. This was the book that popularized the myth of the struggling writer, eking out a mean living in Grub Street, where poets starved in squalid garrets. The fact that Savage had been Johnson's friend and even briefly his mentor added a sharp point to the story. There were qualities in Johnson's book that few other writers could exhibit: compassion for Savage's suffering, sympathy for his plight, understanding of his circumstances. Johnson had been there; like Savage, he had touched bottom, but unlike Savage, he had come up again. The writing of a biography could be valuable to the writer as well as to the reader.

If biography was to teach men and women how to live, it followed that it should be realistic. Johnson did not share the general belief that respect for the dead required that their faults should be suppressed or glossed over. On the contrary, "if nothing but the bright side of characters should be shown, we should sit down in despondency, and think it utterly impossible to imitate them in *any thing*." Just as the new fiction of Richardson and Fielding was becoming more realistic, so too should biography. Readers should be presented with "the unvarnished truth"; uniform panegyric made all individuals seem the same. In his famous *Rambler* essay on biography, Johnson challenged the orthodoxy that the biographer should conceal the failings of his subject. "If we owe regard to the memory of the dead, there is yet more respect to be paid to knowledge, to virtue, and to truth."

Boswell followed Johnson's example, quoting Johnson's words in his support: "I profess to write, not his panegyric, but his Life; which, great and good as he was, must not be supposed to be entirely perfect." In every picture, Boswell continued, "there should be shade as well as light." He planned that all of Johnson's faults—his prejudices, his ferocity in conversation, his quick temper, his susceptibility to flattery, his indolence, his slovenly dress, his unpleasant table manners, and even his sexual irregularities—should be shown in his biography, but displayed so that their insignificance beside his great and good qualities would be apparent.

Johnson had urged biographers not to neglect "the minute details of daily life"; he cited the example of Sallust remarking of Catiline "that his walk was now quick, and again slow, as an indication of a mind revolving with violent commotion." One is reminded of Reynolds's account of how Johnson, bored by talk of pictures his poor eyesight prevented him from seeing clearly, stretched out his right leg as far as he could reach, then brought up his left leg, and so on: until startled out of his reverie by his host, who explained that though it was not a new house, the flooring was perfectly safe.

Johnson's *Rambler* essay on biography had deplored the fact that biography had often been allotted to writers

> who seem very little acquainted with the nature of their task, or very negligent about the performance. They rarely afford any other account than might be collected from the public papers, when they exhibit a chronological series of actions or preferments; and have so little regard to the manners or behaviour of their heroes, that more knowledge may be gained of a man's real character, by a short conversation with one of his servants, than from a formal and studied narrative, begun with his pedigree, and ended with his funeral.[9]

Criticizing Goldsmith's life of the Augustan poet Thomas Parnell, Johnson said that "nobody can write the life of a man, but those who have eat and drunk and lived in social intercourse with him."[10] This was going too far, as Johnson would no doubt have acknowledged had the conversation continued; he was himself to write biographies of men he had never met. But what Johnson insisted on was the importance of character. Writers were not anonymous: they were men or women like their readers, with their own idiosyncrasies, their own tragedies, their own struggles. Their works could be fully understood only in the context of their lives. The interaction between character and circumstance was the crucible in which art was made.

Like Johnson, Boswell too was interested in "manners and behaviour." He delighted in those idiosyncrasies which provide clues to a man's character. He planned to fill his biography with such details, trivial in themselves, but characteristic of Johnson. He frequently used the analogy of a Flemish picture: the work of artists such as Rembrandt, Vermeer, or Van Dyck, whose mastery of detail represented a pinnacle of verisimilitude. "With how small speck does a painter give life to an eye!" he exclaimed.[11] As with painting, so with biography: the speck of detail would bring the portrait to life. Mindful of the ridicule that had been heaped on his *Journal of a Tour to the Hebrides,* he nonetheless remained "firm and confident in my opinion, that minute particulars are frequently characteristic, and always amusing, when they relate to a distinguished man." In particular, Boswell would stress the physical appearance of his subject, "a huge uncouth figure, with a little dark wig which scarcely covered his head, and his clothes hanging loose about him." Such descriptions, scattered throughout the *Life of Johnson,* would fix an indelible impression in the reader's mind, so powerful that it could be manipulated to convey an immediate sense of any encounter involving Johnson with the addition of only minimal detail. The image of Johnson would eventually become one of the archetypes of English Literature, known to millions centuries after, so vigorous as to escape altogether its original home and achieve an existence independent of Boswell's book.

Johnson's last major work was his monumental *Lives of the Poets,* comprising short biographies of fifty-two English poets, "exhibiting first each Poet's life, and then subjoining a critical examination of his genius and works." This was something new in the world of letters: the fusion of two previously distinct forms, criticism and biography. Johnson's forceful opinions, expressed in powerful prose, carried an undeniable authority, though they were often highly contentious. Johnson had been known as "the Great Cham* of Literature" as early as 1759, but it was the *Lives of the Poets,* more than any of his other works, which established him as the dogmatic dictator of literary taste.

The *Lives of the Poets,* thought Boswell, was "the richest, most beautiful and indeed most perfect production of Johnson's pen": the work "which of all Dr Johnson's writings will perhaps be read most generally,

*A Tartar ruler.

and with most pleasure." It was, of course, the *Lives of the Poets* to which Boswell was referring in the opening sentence of his *Life of Johnson:* "To write the life of him who excelled all mankind in writing the lives of others . . . may be reckoned in me a presumptuous task."[12]

Some years before Johnson's death, Boswell had decided what sort of book his should be. On 12 October 1780, as they strolled together down Edinburgh's High Street, he told his friend Andrew Erskine that he intended to write Dr Johnson's life "in scenes."[13]

This was a crucial decision. What Boswell meant by a "life in scenes" was that, whenever possible, he would present Johnson as if in a play. The effect would be dramatic, showing his hero to readers as he had appeared to those with him at the time. In particular, it would show Johnson in conversation, in which he was generally reckoned to have excelled above any other man of his age.

Nobody had ever attempted a book of this kind before. Johnson's *bons mots* were legendary; everyone who had known him had their own store of Johnsoniana; indeed an unauthorized anthology of these had been published in Johnson's lifetime. The value of his conversation was widely acknowledged. When Johnson had been in the full flow of his eloquence, those listening to him had frequently exclaimed that his words should be printed in a book. But the most that anybody had contemplated was a string of disconnected (or, at best, loosely con-nected) Johnsonian anecdotes. Mrs Piozzi's book is a good example of the latter: many of the stories recounted there are highly entertaining, but they are brief and wrenched out of context. The connection between them is thematic: there is no sense of the development of a scene in real time, and little interplay between Johnson and those around him.

In Boswell's book, on the other hand, readers would be able to watch the progression of each scene, like fellow-guests at the dinner-table. Johnson's remarks, and those of his companions, would be reported, as if in full; and rather than being given in indirect speech, the most dramatic exchanges would be cued to the speaker's name like an actor's lines, sometimes with stage-directions to indicate manner or inflexion. Boswell had experimented with this technique in his *Journal of a Tour to the Hebrides,* but in his *Life of Johnson* he would develop it much further, and extend it over a much longer period. The result would be a succession of set-pieces, like the progression of scenes in a play.

At the centre of each scene would be Johnson, surrounded by a cast of secondary characters, each of whom would be manipulated to elicit some aspect of the hero. Thus Johnson would be shown in a hot-tempered argument with the fearless aristocrat Topham Beauclerk; shaking his head and smiling complacently down at the antics of his former pupil, the "harum-scarum" David Garrick, who tugged at his lapels; angrily berating the mild-mannered and pious Bennet Langton, who, upon being asked by Johnson to name his faults, mentioned that he sometimes contradicted people in conversation; and crushing the restless Oliver Goldsmith, for sulking when unable to make himself heard above Johnson's overpowering voice.

Boswell took meticulous care in the construction of these scenes, because he knew that they were what made his biography distinct from any other. Moreover, they showed Johnson at his best; in the opening pages, Boswell would proclaim his belief that "the peculiar value" of his book lay in "the quantity it contains of Johnson's conversation; which is universally acknowledged to have been eminently instructive and entertaining." Furthermore, asserted Boswell, it was well established that the conversation of a celebrated man "will best display his character."[14]

To reconstruct scenes in this way would require a detailed record of what had passed, particularly of what Johnson himself had said. It could only be done when Boswell himself had been present and had recorded the scene in his journal, or when he had been able to obtain a detailed account from others, for example of Johnson's meeting with the King in the Royal Library. Since these occasions were few, and since Boswell did not even meet his subject until Johnson was already fifty-three, his method of telling a "life in scenes" would inevitably present a limited and to some extent distorted view of Johnson's life. It would have the effect of suggesting to readers that Boswell was almost always at Johnson's side; or that when he was not present Johnson was less fully alive. On the other hand, it would be extraordinarily vivid. This method would emphasize Johnson's physical presence, by repeatedly describing the impression he made on those in his company, Boswell above all. And it meant that, in his journal, Boswell already had a rough draft for a substantial portion of the book—almost half the eventual total, as it turned out. In preparing his manuscript, therefore, Boswell was able to use his own journals (and other loose notes and memoranda on his meetings with Johnson) as raw material, taking in page after page as "Papers Apart." Many of these were printed almost verbatim; thus Boswell's autobiographical journal became embedded within his biography of Johnson.

Such "scenes" would show Johnson in company. But though Johnson had relished society, and thrived on conversation, his inner life had been at least as significant to him. Johnson was a writer, a philosopher, and a devout and passionate man, with a private as well as a public existence. These facets of his character would also need to be explored in any full biography.

Boswell had another trick up his sleeve, this time one that had been used before. William Mason's life of his friend Thomas Gray, published in 1775, had interspersed Gray's letters in the text (perhaps it would be more accurate to say that he interspersed his text in Gray's letters). Though Mason's was an unsatisfactory book, and though he bowdlerized and even rewrote Gray's letters, his use of these was a milestone in the history of biography. Boswell thought his technique excellent, because the letters "show us the *man*." He acknowledged Mason's book as his model. But Boswell took Mason's technique a step further. He decided to punctuate his narrative not just with Johnson's letters, but with all the outpourings of his mind: his other published and unpublished writings, and his private remarks. Boswell would include extracts from a vast range of documents, including working notes and discarded drafts: letters, prayers and meditations, essays, biographies, pamphlets, definitions, parodies, fables and allegories, decisions on literary disputes, legal opinions, an appeal for votes, poems, a novel, dedications, obituaries and epitaphs.[15] These would be accompanied by Johnson's asides, comments, diatribes, expostulations, greetings, homilies, jokes, observations, sermons, tirades, and personal or private remarks of every kind, including his replies to Boswell's questions about his life. In so far as this was possible, all these would be printed verbatim. Instead of "melting down my materials into one mass, and constantly speaking in my own person," Boswell planned to let Johnson speak for himself.

> I cannot conceive of a more perfect mode of writing any man's life, than not only relating all the most important events of it in their order, but interweaving what he privately wrote, and said, and thought; by which mankind are enabled as it were to see him live, and to "live o'er each scene" with him, as he actually advanced through the several stages of his life.[16]

As much as he could, Boswell would step back from the role of the omniscient biographer, allowing Johnson to reveal himself directly to the reader. The nobility of Johnson's character shines forth from his letters: the letter to Lord Chesterfield, for example, or his letters to the Earl of Bute, which themselves demonstrate that in accepting his pension, Johnson had not compromised his independence.

Boswell's technique was in this respect the absolute antithesis of Johnson's. While Johnson imposed his judgement on the facts he presented, Boswell allowed the facts to speak for themselves. "I am absolutely certain," he declared to his friend Temple, "that *my* mode of biography, which gives not only a *history* of Johnson's *visible* progress through the world, and of his publications, but a *view* of his mind, in his letters and conversations, is the most perfect that can be conceived, and will be more of a Life than any work that has ever yet appeared."[17] He wrote in similar terms to Bishop Percy: "It appears to me that mine is the best plan of biography that can be conceived; for my readers will as near as may be accompany Johnson in his progress, and as it were see each scene as it happened."[18]

One danger of including so much direct quotation from Johnson's writing—as well as Johnson's conversation—would be that his subject's distinctive, powerful style might overwhelm his own. One advantage of doing so would be to reinforce the sense of dialogue between the two men, an aesthetic analogy to the many scenes which showed Johnson and Boswell in conversation together.

• • •

Most of the "scenes" contained in the *Life of Johnson* would be drawn from Boswell's journal; this could provide a source only when Boswell had been with Johnson, in London, or on one of their jaunts elsewhere. Boswell had already dealt with their Scottish excursion in his *Journal of a Tour to the Hebrides,* and planned to refer to this trip only briefly in his *Life of Johnson.*

Boswell had first met Johnson in London in the summer of 1763, only six weeks before departing to study in Holland. He had seen him again briefly on his return from the Grand Tour in 1766. After he qualified as an advocate later that year, Boswell was generally able to see Johnson only while the courts in Edinburgh were in recess, usually during the spring. He made a journey to London in the spring of 1768, and another in the autumn of 1769; then he came to London in the spring of 1772, 1773, 1775, 1776, 1778, 1779, 1781, 1783, and 1784, and during several of these trips went on forays with Johnson to Lichfield, Oxford, Bath, Bristol, and elsewhere. His London stays lasted an average of about ten weeks, and of course during much of this time he was not with Johnson. He also came to London for a fortnight in the autumn of 1779, and spent eleven days with Johnson at Taylor's home in Ashbourne in 1777. In all, including the hundred-odd days he spent with Johnson in Scotland, it has been calculated that there were about four hundred days on which the two men met, in a period of friendship covering more than twenty-one years.

Boswell planned to include his own correspondence with Johnson in the text of his biography. His letters to and from Johnson would provide links between the scenes he had recorded in his journal. These required some explanation: Boswell would need to indicate when he was in London, where Johnson could communicate with him freely, and when he was away. He would be obliged to explain the breaks and the resumptions in the correspondence. To provide a context for the letters, he would have to outline his own activities. The text of the *Life of Johnson* therefore provided a history of the friendship between the author and his subject. The author would become a character in his own book. The meeting between the two men became a turning-point in the story.

• • •

Of course, Boswell drew on many sources besides his own journals and letters, and Johnson's writings in all their multifarious forms. This other material was by its very nature miscellaneous, provided by many different individuals and supplied in many different forms. It included Boswell's own assorted anecdotes and Johnsoniana collected in note-books; his notes on interviews with friends and colleagues of Johnson's; and material supplied by other hands. Some of it had been gathered years earlier, while Johnson was still alive, and was already written up into a more or less finished form. But much of it remained undigested.

Taken as a whole, this material presented a number of problems to the author. It was very variable in quality: some appeared to be authentic, while other parts seemed unreliable, second-hand, or indeed little more than gossip. It was inconsistent, or contradictory; the same anecdotes were duplicated, often with different details or a different emphasis. Many of the anecdotes were undated. Much of it was unusable, for one reason or another.

Boswell had to exercise discrimination in the use of what remained if he was to produce a satisfactory book. The many different styles had to be dissolved into his own narrative to enable this to flow. He therefore subjected it to every type of revision: summary, paraphrase, expansion, contraction, conflation, interpolation, and so forth.[19] Long, rambling stories became more pointed, anecdotes from one source were grafted onto another; notes were expanded into fully written form, and then polished; Johnsonian reminiscences were rewritten to better effect, the emphasis often changed to fulfil a narrative purpose. Circumstantial detail was added to provide verisimilitude.

Boswell went to extraordinary lengths to gather Johnsonian material from every possible source, and he encouraged his informants not to hold back anything, however slight. He frequently referred to his book as a "compilation." He presented it to the world as if it were an anthology of Johnsoniana. He deliberately downplayed his own role in selecting and shaping; he stressed the effort of collection, rather than the art of composition. But the material he used was carefully reworked, so that every detail contributed to the portrait he was painting. Those that did not were altered or discarded.

In organizing and shaping his material, Boswell aimed to create a unified and coherent narrative. Underlying this was his vision of the "real Johnson," Johnson "as he really was."[20] Very early on—beginning before the two had met, when Boswell stumbled across the *Rambler* essays in his father's library—Boswell had formed a vivid picture of Johnson's character: solemn, dignified, combative, incorruptible, pious, rational, endowed with unrivalled intellectual powers, "a King of men." After they met, and as Johnson became familiar to him, this picture became clearer still. His biography of Johnson was intended to communicate this vision. He rejected Johnsonian anecdotes which seemed to him uncharacteristic—even if they were true. In his analysis of Mrs Piozzi's *Anecdotes*, he showed how various stories which seemed to reflect badly on Johnson appeared quite different when placed in context. True authenticity, argued Boswell, came from providing a representative picture.

Of course, Boswell's vision was limited to what he could see. He failed to understand Johnson's politics, for example. Both men were Tories, but of a very different kind. While Boswell had a kind heart, he assumed the superiority of the privileged. *Un gentilhomme est toujours un gentilhomme,* he would write complacently. Johnson too believed that society could not function without order and rank—a belief encapsulated by the term he frequently used, "subordination"—but his conservatism was moderated by his own experience of poverty and neglect. "A decent provision for the poor is the true test of civilization," he told a friend—not a thought that would ever have occurred to the Laird of Auchinleck. Boswell had a romantic notion of "freedom"; slavery did not trouble him. He fancied himself more progressive than Johnson because he favoured American independence;* Johnson, by contrast, was repelled to hear slave-owners mouthing about liberty. "How is it that we hear the loudest *yelps* for liberty among the drivers of negroes?"

---

*This was one of the few questions upon which Boswell dared to argue with Johnson, usually resulting in an outburst from the latter. "I am prepared to love any man," a riled Johnson declared on one occasion: *"except an American."* In contrast, Boswell secretly celebrated news of American victories.

he asked, in his pamphlet *Taxation no Tyranny*. Boswell ascribed John-son's violent dislike of slavery to ignorance.

Boswell's biography stressed Johnson's superiority. He tinkered with anecdotes of Johnson's early life to emphasize his intellectual pre-dominance, even as a child. Johnson's schoolfriend Edmund Hector had told Boswell how he and the other schoolboys had flattered John-son to obtain his assistance with their schoolwork; Boswell attributed to them feelings of deference and submission towards the boy John-son, and illustrated his hypothesis with the anecdote of their carrying him triumphant to school. Thus Boswell's vivid conception of Johnson infused colour and meaning into the facts at his disposal. To some extent he was forced to rely on his imagination to elaborate stories of Johnson's early years, because the resources he could draw on from that period were scant. There were few people living who could remember Johnson in his youth, and their memories were inevitably clouded by the intervening years. Boswell exercised considerable licence in shaping the anecdotes they gave him, projecting the qualities of the man he had known in late middle age back into the past, even as far as childhood. "The boy is the man in miniature," he wrote; he portrayed Johnson's character as unchanging over the years, and adjusted the facts to fit.

Fundamental to Boswell's idea of Johnson was the power and pene-tration of his mind: probing into profound philosophical issues, but untangling also everyday problems. Boswell cherished Johnson's prac-tical wisdom. He quoted Mrs Porter's remark on first meeting the young Johnson: "This is the most sensible man I ever saw in my life," and the words of Dr Alexander McLean, a physician they dined with on Mull: "This man is just a *hogshead* of sense."[21] To Boswell, Johnson was "the apotheosis of sanity."[22] Conceding that at certain times John-son had suffered from a "morbid melancholy," a "horrible hypochon-dria," Boswell nevertheless utterly repudiated the notion that Johnson might at any point have succumbed to madness. "The powers of his mind might be troubled, and their full exercise suspended at times; but the mind itself was ever entire." Melancholia was not the same as mad-ness; Johnson's sanity was never in doubt. To suggest otherwise was anathema to Boswell. Johnson had been his mentor, showing him how the mind might be managed, how mental infirmity could be conquered, keeping him steady and sane. The suggestion that Johnson's mind might ever have tottered on the edge of chaos threatened to upset the equilibrium that Boswell had achieved with so much difficulty. If Johnson had been afraid of losing his wits, how could Boswell hang on to his?

Johnson's dread of madness had been bound up with religious anxiety. He was a devout Christian, with a literal belief in the possibility of eternal damnation. He feared that he might lose his mind and thus his soul. He feared too that he had not lived a good enough life to earn him a place in heaven. Boswell noticed that Johnson became extremely agitated whenever the subject of death arose in the conversation. On one such occasion, Johnson became so provoked by Boswell's repeated questioning on the subject as to break off the conversation—something he almost never did otherwise—and when Boswell was leaving, to call out, "Don't let us meet tomorrow." At a supper-party in Oxford in the last year of his life, while he and Boswell were staying as guests of his old friend Dr Adams, Johnson surprised the company by acknowledging, "with a look of horror," that he was "much oppressed" by the fear of death. He was afraid that he might be one of those who would be damned. Adams, who did not believe in the doctrine of eternal punishment, asked him what he meant by "damned." Johnson replied passionately and loudly: "Sent to Hell, Sir, and punished everlastingly."

Garrick told Boswell that he believed Johnson to be harassed by doubts. If this was true, then Boswell was convinced that he overcame them:

> His mind resembled the vast amphitheatre, the Coliseum at Rome. In the centre stood his judgement, which, like a mighty gladiator, combated those apprehensions that, like the wild beasts of the *Arena*, were all around in cells, ready to be let out upon him. After a conflict, he drove them back into their dens; but not killing them, they were still assailing him.[23]

Boswell could not admit the possibility that Johnson might not have conquered his doubts, because his own faith was shaky. Johnson's firmness on the thorny doctrinal issues was massively reassuring to him. To question the solidity of Johnson's faith was to open a box that Boswell preferred to keep closed. He repeatedly stressed Johnson's authority, and certainty, on religious subjects as on every other. Johnson's conviction, which often seemed to others mere dogmatism, was always a comfort to Boswell. The picture he painted of Johnson was of a hero, a spiritual gladiator, who dared to confront the fiends of hell and vanquish them, his only weapons the muscle of his mind and the purity of his soul.

Boswell was forced to break off from writing on 26 July 1786, when he set out for Chelmsford on the Home Circuit. Once again he found himself the junior barrister, responsible for organizing the meals and the bills on behalf of the others. But since the towns on this Circuit were close to London, he could return at weekends, and did so after only two nights, to attend a splendid dinner at Wilkes's: turtle, venison, ices, fruits, Burgundy, champagne, claret, coffee, tea, and liqueur. Such toing and froing involved extra expense, especially as Boswell considered it *infra dig* for counsel to travel by the public stage-coach, so that he was forced to hire a private post-chaise instead.

In mid-August Boswell returned to his wife and children at Auchinleck, and a month later the whole Boswell family moved to London. It was a busy time: Boswell was particularly anxious to find suitable schools for his children. For Sandy, the eldest, he hesitated between Westminster and Charterhouse, finally deciding on the latter "as by much the safest for his morals": only to find that no place was available there for some time, so Sandy joined his younger brother, James, at Dr Barrow's academy in Soho Square. (The two older girls went to Miss Roubell's in Lincoln's Inn Fields.)

Now that he had achieved what he had long desired, his family in London, Boswell became depressed again. "I shrunk from the practice of the law of England; I read almost nothing and went on very slowly with Dr Johnson's *Life*." The death in Edinburgh of one of his oldest and most precious friends, John Johnston, saddened him. He was disappointed that none of his family seemed so struck by London as he had been when he first came there. He sank into a familiar state, "a dismal apprehension that I should never again be well or have any relish of anything." He suffered a succession of debilitating nervous headaches. Dining at home seemed to him dull. On Sunday, 5 November, Boswell came down to dinner only after being entreated to do so by his wife, but was so peevish and gloomy that he would not sit at table; he went into the drawing-room, shut out the light, and brooded, until Margaret came in to comfort him.

Gradually Boswell began to recover. He attended the sittings of the new term at the King's Bench assiduously. One day Malone surprised him by producing a specimen page with two different types, for Boswell to choose between. This was astute; nothing could be more encouraging to an author than to see his words in type. Malone was tirelessly supportive, stimulating Boswell and sustaining him through his glooms. "I drank tea with Mr Malone, with whom I am always happy," reads a typical entry in his journal; "his conversation never fails to cheer and encourage me," another. In response to one of a string of invitations from Malone, Boswell replied: "I cannot dine with you forever. I had better board with you." But he went anyway.

On 23 November 1786, Boswell was drinking tea with his publisher Charles Dilly when his servant brought news that Lord Lonsdale's representative, Mr John Baynes Garforth MP, wanted to call on him and was in a great hurry. Boswell hastened home to receive Garforth. It was as he conjectured: Lonsdale wanted him to serve as counsel to the Mayor in the Carlisle election, which was to come on next week. Would it be convenient for him to take a jaunt into the North? Boswell told Garforth that he was proud to have it in his power to serve Lord Lonsdale. He admitted that he was not particularly busy; that in fact he had attracted only one brief since being called to the bar the previous February. "When can you set out?" asked Garforth. "Tonight, if you please," replied Boswell obligingly.

Boswell was excited. After Lonsdale's invitation to a turtle, back in the summer, there had been little opportunity to develop this promising connection. Earlier in November Boswell had written to Lonsdale, soliciting the post of Recorder of Carlisle, which, though worth only £20 a year, was generally understood to be a stepping-stone to obtaining a seat in Parliament (the previous incumbent was indeed now an MP). The summons to Carlisle was an indication that his suit had not gone unheard. Here was Boswell's chance to prove his worth.

He arrived in Carlisle early in the morning of 28 November. His task would be to rule on the admissibility of so-called "mushroom" voters: non-residents admitted as "honorary freemen" to boost the support for Lonsdale's chosen candidate. It was the most blatant election-rigging, of course, but not unusual in eighteenth-century politics. Boswell's duty was to consider the evidence and then decide in Lonsdale's favour.

Lonsdale received Boswell courteously, and after admitting forty new voters they dined with half a dozen others in a local public house. Lonsdale did all the talking. Three of his MPs were present, all of whom were utterly quiet. Boswell remembered a couplet from Pope:

> Like Cato, gives his little Senate laws,
> And sits attentive to his own applause.

Boswell dined with Lonsdale every day, and every day the pattern was the same. Lonsdale harangued, and when anyone ventured to speak, even to express agreement, Lonsdale silenced him, ordering "You shall hear." One of Lonsdale's cronies whistled like a bird when Lonsdale treated him with contempt. No private conversation was tolerated. He snapped at a servant who made a noise. He declaimed forcefully on subjects of his own choosing, and recited his favourite poetry at inordinate length. Boswell was struck by the force of Lonsdale's physiognomy, his utterance, his memory. He perceived that several of his fellow-diners took refuge in sleep. Lonsdale himself sometimes appeared to doze off, though Boswell was warned not to relax his guard, as this could be a pretence.

It gradually became apparent to Boswell that it was better not to argue with Lonsdale, even on legal matters. Though Boswell was being paid for his advice, Lonsdale was not interested in his opinion. Lonsdale surrounded himself with hangers-on, all dependent on him, united in fear and greed. Boswell was amazed when Lonsdale ate a whole plate of fresh oysters without offering anybody else one. Most insulting of all, Lonsdale denied his guests wine, while drinking it himself. When a new guest naïvely asked for some white wine, Lonsdale replied: "No. That has never been asked for here." In a private moment, one of the hangers-on explained that while Lonsdale would spend thousands of pounds at elections, he was a miser who begrudged sixpence, let alone the six shillings a bottle of claret cost. Lonsdale was notorious for refusing to pay tradesmen's bills, meeting all protests with an invitation to sue.

One evening two of the MPs stole away to dine comfortably at another public house and to drink good wine, only to be rebuked in front of the others when Lonsdale discovered what they had done.

Eventually, after enduring such treatment for a week and a half, Boswell got up the nerve to ask for some wine himself. At first Lonsdale tried to fend off his request by saying that the wine in public houses was often laced with arsenic, but, perhaps realizing that he could not maintain this argument and drink himself, he eventually acquiesced. "Mister Boswell of Auchinleck, shall you and I drink a glass of wine together?"

An earlier dinner had provided a clue to Lonsdale's character. He explained that as the youngest pupil at a school in Hertfordshire, he had acted as fag for twenty older boys with whom he shared a room. At half past five every morning he was obliged to go and fetch water for the others, which involved pumping until his fingers were numb. There was a fire at one end of the room which the big boys kept to themselves, not allowing the little boys to come near. The older boys would take the blankets from the little boys' beds. The "pissing place" was at the far end of the room from the fire, and the big boys would not take the trouble to go to it, but piss by the little boys' beds. Lonsdale approved of this system, and described how he in turn imposed the same conditions on the next youngest boy to arrive. Boswell was shocked. He could not help thinking it curious that such a domineering figure as Lonsdale had been thus kept in subjection. "It makes a very pernicious succession of slavery and tyranny. The big boys, recollecting what they have suffered, are barbarously severe upon the little boys; and perhaps his own *domination* has been inflamed by that education."

The election business proceeded tediously, until at last the election was held. The poll showed 554 votes for Lonsdale's candidate, 407 of which had been cast by "honorary freemen": two more than the number of votes cast for the rival candidate, who promptly petitioned the House of Commons against the outcome. After the election Boswell felt obliged to accompany Lonsdale to his home, Lowther Castle. He escaped just before Christmas, with a more than useful fee of 150 guineas. Back in London, he attended the Committee of the House of Commons considering the result of the Carlisle election, which gave its decision against Lonsdale's candidate on 26 February 1787.

Boswell resumed work on his book. It had been apparent for some time that Hawkins's biography would be published first. Now it was finished and printed, due to be published, together with a twelve-volume edition of Johnson's works, in the spring. Langton, whom Hawkins had allowed to read it, refused to tell Boswell any details, but said that on the whole it was very entertaining. A steady stream of notices appeared in the newspapers, chiding Boswell for being so slow. Making a virtue out of necessity, Boswell placed his own paragraph in the *Public Advertiser,* claiming that his delay was deliberate.

> The *etiquette* of *precedency* between *Hawkins* and *Boswell,* for both of whom the public have been so long waiting, is not a little curious. The truth is, that the competition between them is not who shall be *first,* but who shall be *last;* in short which shall *see the other's back,* so as to hold the lash of animadversion.[24]

The longer that Boswell's book was postponed, the more he stressed its function as a corrective to earlier "injurious misrepresentations."

"My great Volume will not be finished for some time," he admitted in a letter to his friend Thomas Barnard, Bishop of Killaloe, in Ireland. "I have waited till I should first see Hawkins's compilation. But my friends urge me to dispatch, that the ardour of curiosity may not be allowed to cool."[25]

NINE

RIVALRY

He trusts that in the mean time the public will not permit unfavourable impressions to be made on their minds, whether by the light effusions of carelessness and pique, or the ponderous labours of solemn inaccuracy and dark, uncharitable conjecture.[1]

HAWKINS'S *The Life of Samuel Johnson, LL.D.* was published in March 1787. Unlike many of the works that had gone before, this was a full-scale biography of more than six hundred pages, described as "official" by the London book trade, and dedicated to the King. It was a formidable competitor to Boswell's book, one that threatened to render his efforts superfluous. Hawkins had known Johnson forty or more years, twice as long as had Boswell. As an executor of Johnson's will, Hawkins had exclusive access to Johnson's private papers (a fact made much of in the booksellers' advertisements). Boswell had only a limited idea of what these amounted to; for all he knew, Hawkins had a rich store of material to draw on, which he had been denied. He was anxiously waiting for the moment when he could read what Hawkins had written himself.

Fortunately, Hawkins's book was a disappointment. Its tone was sour and judgemental, its style turgid and ponderous. (One reviewer joked that it was to be *"translated into English."*) It was written in legalese—"whereof, whereon, wherein, hereby, thereby, and wherein before"—and bloated with both long quotations and wearisome digressions.[2] It was inaccurate. Worst of all, the critics agreed, was the way in which Hawkins had treated his subject. Boswell summed up the general view when he wrote that Hawkins had put a "dark uncharitable cast" upon "almost every circumstance in the character and conduct of my illustrious friend."[3] In fact, such criticism was unfair: Hawkins's portrayal of Johnson, though clumsy, was by no means wholly unsympathetic. The problem facing the first biographers of Johnson was the reverence attaching to their subject; any realistic treatment was sure to attract opprobrium. Many of the descriptions in Hawkins's book which so dismayed readers—for example, of Johnson's disgusting eating habits or his slovenly style of dress—would find their equivalents in Boswell's *Life of Johnson*. But by then their sting had been drawn.

Now nearly seventy, Hawkins did not share Johnson's *joie de vivre*, nor his generosity of spirit. He could not be expected to relish Johnson's frolics, nor his bounty to beggars. As a magistrate, he could not understand Johnson's compassion for the condemned. Hawkins's rigid, formal manner, his pomposity, his censoriousness—none of these was endearing. His antiquarianism could easily be made to appear ridiculous. Hawkins had never been popular with Johnson's friends (the good-natured Langton being an exception). He had withdrawn from the Club many years before, after rudely attacking Burke one evening. This would work against him; members of the Club had enormous influence in literary London. Hawkins had not been so assiduous as Boswell in collecting their anecdotes and seeking their opinions. Now several of them professed themselves indignant at the way Johnson had been portrayed. Malone proposed that a solemn protest, to go down to posterity, be drawn up and signed by Johnson's friends, arguing that Hawkins's was a "false and injurious account." Most of the Club members present were in favour of Malone's proposal. Hawkins escaped censure when Reynolds demurred, but his book was mercilessly pilloried in the press.

Hawkins's book had been billed as "official," Boswell's as a respectable also-ran. Their roles were now reversed. In the sense that the Club was the arbiter of literary taste, Boswell's became the authorized biography. He would receive Johnsoniana from most of the Club members who had known Johnson—with the apparent exception of Burke. Others too now threw their weight behind Boswell: Johnson's oldest living friend, Edmund Hector, for example. He was incensed by Hawkins's suggestion that Johnson's benevolence could be ascribed to "ostentatious bounty." Hector knew that Johnson, though often irascible, had helped countless individuals in private acts of charity. He offered Boswell evidence with which to contradict Hawkins; and he invited Boswell to visit him in Birmingham "to chat over some of these fine things."[4]

Hawkins's book had expressed outrage that Johnson should have left the bulk of his estate to his black servant, Francis Barber. It contained unpleasant (possibly libellous) hints about Barber himself, and about his wife. Boswell enlisted Barber's support. He drafted a letter for Barber to send to each of the executors, demanding the return of all Johnson's papers. Barber was only too pleased to help. He had received Boswell's sympathetic letter with "unspeakable satisfaction"; he agreed to Boswell's request "with a heart full of joy and gratitude":

> . . . I am happy to find there is still remaining a friend who has the memory of my late good master at heart that will endeavour to vindicate his cause in opposition to the unfriendly proceedings of his enemies . . . assure yourself Dear Sir it will be to me a subject of the greatest happiness to render abortive the unworthy and false proceedings of the above mention'd gentleman [Hawkins] . . . that basest of mortals . . .[5]

Hawkins had mentioned Boswell only once, as "Mr Boswell, a native of Scotland." Boswell was certainly stung by this. "Observe how he talks of me as if quite unknown," he complained to Temple.[6] There is a story, perhaps apocryphal, told by Hawkins's daughter, that Boswell called on him to protest at being referred to thus: "Surely, surely, Mr *James Boswell*." Hawkins is said to have replied, "I know what you mean, Mr Boswell: you would have had me say, that Johnson undertook this tour with *The* Boswell?" In his *Life of Johnson,* Boswell introduced his fellow-biographer as "Mr John Hawkins, an attorney"—a double hit against the self-important magistrate, because of Johnson's quip also quoted in the book, that "he did not care to speak ill of any man behind his back, but he believed the gentleman was an *attorney*."[7] Of course, Boswell was an attorney, too—of a sort.

He was now working on his *Life of Johnson* almost every day. Friends continued to urge him not to delay: the public appetite for Johnsoniana would surely soon be sated. It seems that Boswell was becoming anxious not to be seen as a Johnson bore; even at a meeting of the Club he was careful not to introduce the subject of his hero. To speed up his rate of work, he tried to cut down on his drinking, taking only water for up to a week at a time. But he was distracted by renewed concern about his wife. She was spitting blood again, and wanting to return to the "air and comfort of Auchinleck." Sometimes it seemed as if she would be too ill even to do that. Boswell feared that she had not much longer to live. He was full of grief and self-reproach. After one dinner at home in early April when she had seemed especially ill, he was so upset that he broke down crying. His eleven-year-old son Sandy comforted him: "O Papa, this is not like yourself."

Boswell was torn between Margaret's desire to return to Scotland and his own need for London. All the familiar arguments revolved around his head, as he decided on first one course of action, then another. Malone told him that if he quit now and returned to Scotland he would hang himself within five weeks.

Meanwhile, he continued to receive a stream of Johnsonian material from various sources. Among his suppliers were Bishop Thomas Percy, who sent him some useful details of Johnson's early life; and the musician, teacher, and historian Dr Charles Burney, another member of the Club, who had overcome his original scepticism about Boswell's fitness for the role of Johnson's biographer. Burney had contemplated writing Johnson's biography himself; now he handed over to Boswell the material he had gathered, including copies of the letters he had received from Johnson.

Malone too supplied Boswell with Johnsoniana. For the last few years of Johnson's life, Malone had kept memoranda of their meetings, which he now made available to Boswell. On Boswell's behalf he obtained Johnson's diary of his visit to France with the Thrales in 1775, and solicited Johnson's letters to various correspondents, including other members of the Club, such as the MP William Windham. Boswell and Malone instigated a regular breakfast on the first of each month, when they met to review the monthly publications and discuss any topics relating to Johnson arising from these.

Another of Johnson's friends, the Reverend Dr William Maxwell, had collected many of Johnson's sayings in his notebooks. Like Percy, Maxwell was now living in Ireland, and he had lost some of his papers, including some letters from Johnson, when a ship carrying them from London to Dublin had been raided by the audacious American privateer John Paul Jones during the recent war. However, Maxwell was subsequently able to retrieve several packets of Johnsoniana, which he sent to Boswell. Boswell was grateful, but entreated Maxwell to transcribe from his journals *"the very words of Johnson taken down at the time"*; and when Maxwell tried to comply with his request, Boswell was obliged to point out that he had made at least one mistake:

> I ought to apologize for having given you so much trouble; but I had *understood* that you had *minutes* of his conversation and I was anxious to have transcripts of them because however strong the faculty of memory may some times be I am persuaded that no recollection can be so authentic as a relation committed to writing *at the time*. We are so apt to imagine that we have *heard* what has been conveyed to us through some other medium. I am sure you will forgive my frankness when I give you as an instance of this what you communicate in the belief of its being a saying of his as to Scottish education which is indeed a sentence in his *Journey to the Western Islands*.[8]

Boswell had to overcome a series of petty obstacles in accumulating Johnsoniana. Several of those who supplied anecdotes were extremely shy of having their names mentioned and often asked for them to be withheld, thereby devaluing their contributions. Some correspondents held back letters or other valuable material, pleading scruples of one sort or another. Moreover, help could become a handicap. Frequently Boswell found that he was being told what he already knew, sometimes what he already knew to be false.

On 11 May, Boswell attended another levee, dressed in a full suit of black clothes, the court garb of a barrister. "How does the writing go on?" asked the King. "Pretty well, Sir." The King then asked when he hoped to finish. "It will be some time yet. I have a good deal to do to correct Sir John Hawkins," replied Boswell. "I believe he has made many mistakes," observed the King. "A great many, Sir, and very injurious to my good friend."[9]

A few days earlier, Boswell had written one of his regular progress reports to his banker, Sir William Forbes, explaining that he now expected to finish in July or August, and to publish at the end of 1787 or the beginning of 1788. He placed another advertisement in the papers, assuring the public that his book was "in great forwardness":

> The reason of its having been long delayed is, that some other publications on the subject were promised, from which he expected to obtain much information, in addition to the large store of materials which he had already accumulated. These works have now made their appearance; and, though disappointed in that expectation, he does not regret that deliberation with which he has proceeded, as very few circumstances relative to the history of Dr Johnson's private life, writings, or conversation, have been told with that authentic precision which alone can render biography valuable. To correct these erroneous accounts will be one of his principal objects; and on reviewing his materials, he is happy to find that he has documents in his possession, which will enable him to do justice to the character of his illustrious friend.[10]

In June, Boswell's brother T.D. again pressed him to return to Scotland. It was discreditable, he said, to stay in London while being neither in Parliament nor in practice. T.D. warned his elder brother that many people kept aloof from him, supposing him to be heading for ruin.

Boswell disliked the thought of returning to Scotland without having obtained honour or profit in England. He feared that if he did so he would be oppressed by the same dreary ideas which had made him miserable in the past. On 13 June 1787, he wrote to Lord Lonsdale, reiterating his wish to be made Recorder of Carlisle. Lonsdale's reply was gracious but non-committal. He wrote that he wished to talk it over with Boswell, and issued a polite but vague invitation to "pass some time with him."

Boswell had been instructed in another case the previous month. His client had been procured for him by Paoli's servant, Giuseppe. Unfortunately, the attorney who briefed Boswell failed to inform him when the case was due to come to court. Boswell called at his house to inquire, and found that it had come to court that same day. By the time he arrived there, the case was over. "I was obliged to you for your assistance this morning," the leading counsel thanked Boswell sarcastically.

Two days later Boswell dreamed of his wife and Mrs Rudd "contending for me." He had stayed away from his "Circe" for some time, but clearly he was finding this a strain. The next evening, heated by the wine he had drunk at dinner, he called at her house. Fortunately, she was not there, having been arrested and imprisoned for debt. Two old women, one of them Mrs Rudd's landlady, told him what had happened to her. One of them asked if his name was Rawdon, Mrs Rudd's sometime "protector." Boswell said no, and asked them to mention to her that "Mr Parr" had called. Why he chose this pseudonym is unclear: it may have been a private joke. Boswell knew the Reverend Dr Samuel Parr, a celebrated Greek scholar.

In July Boswell set out once more on the Home Circuit. Then, in mid-August, the Boswell family returned to Auchinleck for a month. Boswell's presence was required to settle urgent estate business and to collect much-needed rents from his tenants. *En route* the Boswells had expected to stay a week as Lonsdale's guests at Lowther Castle, an ugly but imposing neo-medieval pile a few miles outside Penrith; but as they travelled north they heard that their host had already left for London.

While he was at Auchinleck, Boswell received a letter from Malone, scolding him for neglecting his "great work." Malone mentioned that he had received various letters of Johnson's from their recipients which he would keep for Boswell's return. However, one correspondent, William Bowles, who had been promising to send Boswell his Johnsoniana for more than two years, still had not done so. (He eventually sent these to Boswell on 9 November 1787.) "What an insufferable procrastinator!" exclaimed Malone, "almost as great a one as another person of my acquaintance."[11]

Boswell returned to London with his wife and family in late September, and spent his first week back on the Home Circuit. Then, buoyed by Malone, he resumed work on his book. In the last three months of 1787, he worked on it almost every day. The new term of sittings began at Westminster Hall; Malone advised him to attend "laxly, and get on diligently with my *Life*." Sometimes Boswell's confidence faltered, and he turned to Malone, who never failed to provide the support he needed. One morning in late October, for example, he went to Malone's and read him a year's journal of Johnson's conversation, "which I feared was of little value." Malone "cheered me by praising it."[12]

He was under constant financial pressure. Margaret complained

> of the expense of London, of the injury it did her health and that of both
> my sons, and the obscurity in which my daughters must be. I was very sen-
> sible of this. But my aversion to the narrow, ill-bred sphere [of Scotland]
> was very strong.

Boswell was vexed that he could not afford to send his daughters to a
boarding-school which would give them "elegance of manner." He had
managed to pay off one of his pressing debts by borrowing £300 from
his publisher, Dilly, and another £200 from his printer, Baldwin. But
this was only a short-term expedient. He received £44 for his one-sixth
share in the *London Magazine,* which had been forced to close; this was
a poor return for a share valued five years earlier at £250.

On 28 November, Lord Lonsdale invited him to dine. Walking
home with Boswell afterwards, one of Lonsdale's cronies confided that
the Earl meant to make him Recorder of Carlisle. Boswell sent Lonsdale a memorandum on the subject. He had little hope of success; "this
I considered as a ticket in the lottery." But just before Christmas, he
called on Lonsdale, who informed him that, after much consideration,
he had decided Boswell was the right man for the job. He was planning
to leave for the North the next day, and suggested that Boswell should
accompany him.

Boswell was somewhat embarrassed. He told Lonsdale that he was
very much obliged to him, but that he had several engagements, and
Dr Johnson's *Life* to finish. Would he allow him to consider the matter
until the evening? His Lordship graciously consented to wait until
then. Boswell hurried home, and talked it over with his wife and his
brother. Both thought he should go. Boswell returned to Lonsdale's
that same evening, to say that he should be very happy to take up Lonsdale's kind invitation.

The next morning was cold and frosty. Boswell arrived at Lord Lonsdale's house unshaven and in a flutter. He had intended to be there at
nine o'clock "*to the second,*" but somehow he did not manage to reach
Lonsdale's door until twenty-five minutes past. Garforth—one of

Lonsdale's "ninepins"—smiled at his discomposure, and told him that two hours later would have been time enough. Boswell relaxed, and was shaved in the servants' hall. Two more of Lonsdale's MPs arrived during the next couple of hours, but still there was no sign of the Great Man. Boswell took himself off to a coffee-house in Shepherd Market for some breakfast. Soon after his return, between twelve and one, the coach arrived at the door. Another of Lonsdale's cronies arrived, and said he had known Lonsdale keep a coach waiting so long that the horses needed to be changed. Eventually all their baggage was loaded on the coach—but then, apparently at Lonsdale's command, it was unloaded again, and packed some other way. Sometime in the afternoon, Lonsdale appeared, and then held a series of private conferences with members of the waiting entourage. At last Lonsdale was ready to depart. He insisted that the coach should drive on a little, and wait for them around the corner. Apparently he never boarded a coach at his own door. Once it had passed out of sight, Lonsdale led the group of tired attendants on foot, and after a short walk they caught up with the coach and were allowed to board. That night they dined at Stevenage.

It was an ominous start. After keeping them waiting the whole day, Lonsdale was now impatient; he drove the postboys excessively hard, and made his servant ride ahead to have horses ready and waiting by the door at each stage.

They reached Lowther Castle on the evening of 23 December. It was dreadfully cold. Many of the rooms were unheated, and even those that had fires were supplied with green wood, though Lonsdale owned the largest colliery in the kingdom. Boswell's companions warned him about a total want of comfort there; Garforth had resorted to wiping his shoes with the carpet. All the guests were kept waiting to eat, even after the food was put on the table. The wine was poured only when their host allowed it. After dinner on 24 December, Lonsdale read aloud. At breakfast he had honeycomb, which he took all to himself.

Boswell began to feel misgivings. He foresaw many difficulties in being Recorder, as Lonsdale would not allow "even decent attention" to be paid to his opponents on the Corporation. He now realized that if Lonsdale chose to make him a Member of Parliament, he would expect

Boswell to act as he instructed. Boswell reflected that it was unworthy for the Laird of Auchinleck to place himself in such a position; he seemed to hear his father saying, "James, I left you independent."

Meanwhile, Lonsdale talked incessantly, haranguing his sycophantic listeners with long, tedious accounts, while they all sat "in vile, timid restraint"—on the morning of 26 December, he talked for three hours without intermission. When Lonsdale was drowsy, they sat in stupid silence.

By 28 December, Boswell was desperate. He had hardly slept the night before. Now he realized how he had deceived himself with foolish ideas of honour and advantage from the connection with Lonsdale. He resolved to be in bed all morning, pleading a headache, but tedium forced him to rise between ten and eleven. There was nobody downstairs. Boswell walked back and forth between his bedroom and the dining-room and afterwards on the gravel outside until one o'clock, and even then there was no sign of his host or his breakfast. The servants ignored him, taking their orders only from their master. At last he decided to escape. He walked out from the house with his bag in his hand. At the porter's lodge, he was discouraged by the deep snow, and returned for a while to the house; but when he saw a cart leaving, he swung his bag onto the back. He was too proud to be seen riding in such an undignified vehicle, so he walked on ahead until he was out of sight of the house, and then waited for the cart to catch up before climbing aboard and seating himself on a sack. Cold, gloomy, and hungry, Boswell felt disgusted with almost everything: only the thought of his wife provided a gleam of felicity. The cart trudged forward three miles. At a crossroads Boswell jumped down; lugging his heavy bag, he walked another mile and a half to Penrith, where he hoped to find a coach to London.

Intending to write Lonsdale an emollient letter to explain his departure, Boswell bought some paper in a shop. Then, still uncertain what he should do, he went in search of Saul, one of Lonsdale's minions, who had gone into Penrith earlier in the day to see his daughter. He found Saul at the George inn and outlined his quandary. Saul advised him that Lonsdale would certainly take it amiss if he went off in this way. So, after the first comfortable meal he had taken for days, Boswell walked back to Lowther Castle with Saul, still carrying his bag. He arrived tired and sweaty, and changed all his clothes before sending a message to Lonsdale begging leave to speak to him for a few minutes. This time Lonsdale came at once. Boswell, in a fluster, explained that he had lain awake all night considering his position. The upshot was that he had decided not to accept the Recordership. Lonsdale's manner was now quite different: he was friendly and reasonable, and he sweet-talked Boswell into staying. The dinner that evening was pleasant; and when Boswell mentioned having drunk good coffee at Penrith, Lonsdale ordered a pot to be made for him at the house. Saul, who liked coffee, was amazed; he had never before seen it there. That night Boswell went to bed "wonderfully well."

Things returned to normal the next morning. They were due to set off early for Whitehaven, Lonsdale's fiefdom on the Cumbrian coast, but Lonsdale trifled away the time until after eleven. At Whitehaven, where Lonsdale had another castle, there were two other guests staying; neither was offered wine at dinner, despite many hints. Lonsdale put it off with an appearance of heartiness: "There is little enough for ourselves, eh? And you would not have me go to the cellar again tonight." Boswell was shocked at his behaviour. Lonsdale "harangued away" after dinner and would not let his guests go to bed until around one in the morning; he thought it very funny when Boswell could not find his room. The next morning, one of the other guests asked Boswell if he had ever seen anything so savage as Lonsdale's rudeness to him the night before. He explained that he submitted to such lunatic treatment only because Lonsdale paid for three of his sons to attend Eton. Boswell realized that Lonsdale liked those around him to be dependent on him, so that he could humiliate them. "I felt myself very awkward amidst such people."

On the last day of the year, Boswell asked Lonsdale when the election to make him Recorder would take place. He was anxious to be with his family, and impatient to be back in London and to get on with the *Life*. He knew that the Warton brothers would be there, and felt uneasy that he might be missing "many valuable literary meetings." But Boswell's considerations were as nothing to Lonsdale. "I cannot tell," he answered irritably, "I have not thought of it yet."

They lingered on at Whitehaven for nearly a fortnight. Lonsdale's behaviour towards Boswell swung between flattery and boorishness. When Boswell reminded him how inconvenient it was for him to be there, Lonsdale replied, "I am *thinking* of it." When Boswell received a letter from his brother, written without his wife's knowledge, informing him that she was not at all well and that he should return as soon as he conveniently could, Lonsdale's indifference was shocking. Boswell was tormented with anxiety about Margaret, but loath to leave after enduring so much to obtain the promised post. At last, on 10 January, he was allowed to depart for Carlisle. The next day he was elected Recorder; and the same afternoon he took the mail-coach to London.

Boswell arrived in town at about eight o'clock on the morning of 14 January 1788. He was relieved to find Margaret a great deal better, but it was obvious from her appearance that she had been at the gates of death.

Now he was back in London, he found it difficult to get down to work on the book. In February he hardly picked up his pen. He began drinking heavily again, so that he was frequently incapacitated the next morning. The Italian teacher Francesco Sastres, a friend of Johnson's in his last years, who had been ready to accompany him on the aborted trip to Italy, confessed that having called several times at Boswell's house to give him Johnson's letters, without ever finding him in, he had given them to Mrs Piozzi instead. Boswell received frequent inquiries about his progress. He wrote to Percy that he had still seven years of Johnson's life to write—as it turned out, this meant that he was only a little more than halfway through the book—and he did not now expect to publish it before the autumn. He admitted that the sale might suffer because of the delay, but "I mean to do my duty as well as I can."[13]

Meanwhile, Boswell faced a financial crisis. On 20 February he received a letter from the overseer of the Auchinleck estate, James Bruce, informing him that the purchaser of a bank of wood had defaulted, and that he therefore had only £34 left in his hands. Boswell's credit at the Ayr Bank was almost exhausted; totting up all his liabilities, he reckoned that he had only £129 to live on until September. How could he maintain his family on so little? It made matters worse that he had recently taken up gambling again; one day he lost almost £20 playing whist at Dilly's.

Margaret again pressed him to return to Scotland. She argued that they were in a mean, cramped situation in London, whereas they might live comfortably and creditably at Auchinleck. She reminded Boswell of his father's anxious wish that he should reside there. If coming to town had produced any advantage, it might be justified; but he had not applied himself sufficiently to the law, and indeed had been living a life of dissipation and intemperance, so that he did not even make any progress with his *Life of Johnson*, from which he expected both fame and profit—in short, he did nothing. Margaret told him that he was now neglected by those who used to invite him, for people shunned a man who was known to be dependent and "in labouring circumstances." His children's health was suffering in London—where the filthy air and primitive sanitation, and the crush of people, encouraged disease—and they were acquiring inclinations unsuitable to their situation.

Boswell acknowledged the weight of his wife's arguments. "But the ambitious views which I had fondly indulged, and the fondness of English manners which had made a part of my very existence from my earliest years, weighed on the other side, especially when I apprehended that my returning to the Scotch bar would be a wretched sinking and make me appear a disappointed, depressed man . . ." It was the same old dilemma. Margaret suggested that her poor health was a very good excuse for his returning to Scotland; and that by concentrating on the management of his estate, he could soon make himself independent. But Boswell argued that he could not leave London until he had finished Johnson's *Life;* moreover, he would be sorry to deprive his sons of the benefits of an English education; while he felt reluctant to descend to a "narrower situation," in which he had suffered so much melancholy and where he would be excluded from any chance of "figuring in the great circle of Britain."[14]

A few days later, another letter from Bruce arrived, this time containing news which relieved the financial pressure: a payment of £156 had been received. Boswell's spirits revived; he worked so hard on his book that he completed fifty-two pages in the week that followed this "shameful interval of neglect." As usual, his friend Barnard urged him on, in a letter sent from Ireland on the last day of February 1788:

> I am concerned and disappointed to hear that you have still seven years of Johnson's memorabilia to finish; as I flatter'd myself that your work would have been published long since. You forget that the public curiosity will not wait your leisure. It will have some other object to engage its attention in a year or two; and in twice that time, anecdotes of Johnson will be a subject for an antiquarian rather than a biographer. I have no doubt that your work will be immortal let it appear never so late. But I would have it also popular; and you know still better than I do, how much depends on seizing the critical moment in order to ensure success.[15]

Mrs Piozzi's *Letters to and from the Late Samuel Johnson, LL.D.* was published on 8 March 1788. Her two volumes contained 367 letters, including twenty-seven she had written to Johnson. Dilly sent Boswell a set the day before they were published, and he read straight through them. As he did so, he felt increasingly uncomfortable. "This publication *cooled* my warmth of enthusiasm for 'my illustrious friend' a good deal." It was not just that Johnson's letters contained "less able and brilliant writing than I expected," though this was disappointing; nor was it just that so many of the letters seemed trivial. What distressed Boswell most was the evident intimacy between Johnson and Mrs Thrale (as she then was). He had known of Johnson's affection and respect for her, of course; but it was one thing to be aware of this, and another to read repeated demonstrations of it. Johnson had sensed how his devotion to Mrs Thrale had made Boswell feel insecure; he had compensated for this with ostentatious displays of affection towards his young friend, and even occasional criticism of the Thrales. Now Boswell could see the other side of Johnson, pathetically (so it seemed to him) subservient to Mrs Thrale and sometimes disparaging about his other friends, Boswell included. Most painful of all, he discovered that Johnson and Mrs Thrale had often joked about him in their letters.

Boswell never understood Johnson's emotional dependence on Mrs Thrale. The only reason he could find for Johnson's "fawning" on her so was because he enjoyed the luxury that her husband's wealth provided;*[16] and that in order to please her, Johnson had treated Boswell and his other friends "much more lightly than we had reason to expect." He was depressed to discover how insignificant he appeared in Johnson's letters, indeed how rarely he appeared at all. "I felt myself degraded from the consequence of an ancient Baron to the state of an humble attendant on an author; and, what vexed me, thought that my collecting so much of his conversation had made the world shun me as a dangerous companion."

He lent his two volumes to Malone that same afternoon, and was partly cheered when both Malone and Courtenay expressed strong enthusiasm for the letters. Malone thought that, in general, they were "very pleasing" and "exactly what I expected." He told Boswell that he rated them too low: "I would not have [had] one of them omitted." Aware that Boswell's devotion to Johnson had been shaken, Malone continued, "I love him still more than ever. He had a most tender heart; and as much virtue, I believe, as falls to the lot of humanity." Malone then drew attention to the most controversial aspect of the publication—that Mrs Piozzi had omitted altogether both Johnson's angry letter on being informed of her intended second marriage, and her own firm riposte. "I hope heartily *Madam* will be trimm'd well for her suppression . . ."[17]

Over the next few weeks, Boswell struggled to overcome the negative feelings that reading Johnson's letters had aroused in him. Walking home with him after a dinner at Courtenay's, Langton agreed that Johnson appeared to his disadvantage in his letters to Mrs Thrale; in writing to her of his friends whom he valued most, he seemed to want to make her jealous. This, they both agreed, was "a stooping in the high mind of Johnson." Wilkes visited Boswell at home and seemed to take a mischievous pleasure in pointing out how often Johnson had written slightingly of him to Mrs Thrale.[18] On the same day, he received a short visit from Dilly, "very desirous" that Boswell's book should soon go to press.

Boswell's response to the publication of Johnson's letters was not wholly rational. In drafts of the *Life,* later deleted, he expressed strong

---

*Boswell was not alone in this interpretation; one newspaper described "a vain woman forcing a poor man to write fulsome letters for his daily dinner."

feelings of indignation about Mrs Piozzi's selling the correspondence for five hundred guineas[19]—perhaps thinking of his own financial problems. He complained to the Scottish poet and philosopher Dr James Beattie that the collection had been inflated to fill two volumes, and that the letters contained "many passages which should have been left out."[20]

Some passages *had* been left out. In Mrs Piozzi's Preface, she had admitted to deleting passages in Johnson's letters "to avoid paining many individuals." On his first reading, Boswell had not noticed this. But now, several weeks later, he seized on it, deciding that Mrs Piozzi had deliberately, perhaps maliciously, deleted references to him. In fact, Boswell's suspicions were misplaced. Mrs Piozzi had deleted very few references to him, and those cuts she had made were often for his benefit, omitting Mrs Rudd's name, for example, thus sparing him domestic embarrassment. But Boswell could not know this. He persuaded himself that he appeared so insignificant in Johnson's letters only because of her malevolence; and cheered by this thought, he felt a renewed enthusiasm for the *Life*. Samuel Lysons, the scholar who had assisted Mrs Piozzi with the editing of both her books, now helped Boswell to fill some of the blanks in Johnson's letters.

In editing the letters for publication, Mrs Piozzi had not only excised chunks of Johnson's letters, she had also embellished her own letters so that they might better stand alongside Johnson's. This did not escape Boswell, who was scornful of such practice. But despite his zeal for authenticity, he was prepared to bowdlerize both his own and Johnson's letters when circumstances seemed to demand it, though usually he did indicate where deletions had been made and (sometimes) why. He omitted references to his own melancholia from his correspondence with Johnson, for example, and details of Johnson's symptoms when he became seriously ill. He even altered a letter to Mrs Thrale that had already appeared in print, to remove a rude aside of Johnson's—"a fig for Mr Nichols"—about a man to whom Boswell was beholden.[21] To those reluctant to surrender letters of Johnson's which contained discussion of personal matters, he offered to excerpt from the letters and submit these excerpts to the recipients for approval.[22] In such cases he did not seem to feel that it was his duty to indicate where cuts had been made. Even if he had adopted such a policy, he could not have applied it rigorously, because many of those who had supplied him with letters had not given him the originals. They had copied out Johnson's letters to send him, and no doubt in the process many of the letters were altered, either accidentally or deliberately. In at least one case, the letters to Dr Charles Burney, we know that the copies Boswell received had indeed been expurgated, to remove references to facts that Burney was anxious to conceal.[23]

Among the letters Mrs Piozzi had published was one Johnson had written to her from Skye in 1773. "Boswell writes a regular Journal of our travels," Johnson wrote, "which I think contains as much of what I say and do, as of all other occurrences together; *for such a faithful chronicler is Griffith.*" This last phrase was a quotation, slightly misremembered, from Shakespeare's *Henry VIII*:

> After my death I wish no other herald,
> No other speaker of my living actions,
> To keep mine honour from corruption,
> But such an honest chronicler as Griffith.

To Boswell, there was no mistaking Johnson's meaning: only one biographer was worthy to immortalize him, the "honest chronicler" who had been his companion in the Hebrides. He would print these lines, together with the extract from Johnson's letter to Mrs Thrale, prominently, at the beginning of his *Life of Johnson*.

Some weeks after the publication of the letters, Boswell visited Horace Walpole at his celebrated home, Strawberry Hill. Walpole disliked Boswell and found his visits an imposition, but this time he received him pleasantly enough. He said that Johnson's letters were written in a very easy style. They gave him a much better opinion of Johnson, who was shown to have had a great deal of affection. He felt that the sentiment which Johnson evoked was pity, because he was so miserable. Walpole thought it had been cruel to publish "his diary"—by which he meant Johnson's *Prayers and Meditations* (a volume which Johnson himself had initiated, in the last year of his life). Boswell remarked that there was no man whose diary would not have weak or foolish things in it. Walpole agreed: "and therefore I wonder how any man should choose to review his own life."[24] Neither of course could know that, a couple of centuries later, the two of them would be regarded as the great English autobiographers of the eighteenth century, the many volumes of their letters and diaries open to all, on shelves of libraries around the world.

Boswell had been hurt by the publication of Johnson's letters, because they seemed to reveal that he was not so much loved and respected as he had hoped. Now he convinced himself that this conclusion was false, and that readers had been misled by Mrs Piozzi's design. His love for Johnson was renewed, and his hostility towards Mrs Piozzi deepened. He decided to attack.

Years before, in 1781, only days after Henry Thrale's death, Boswell had composed a scurrilous parody of Johnson's style, an "Epithalamium on Dr J and Mrs T." Though undoubtedly in poor taste, it was a piece of fun, not malice. Johnson's friends often indulged in private comedy at his expense; the reverence he inspired and the domination his presence imposed required an occasional outlet. At the time, Boswell had been anxious that neither Johnson nor Mrs Thrale should hear of his *jeu d'esprit*. But now he felt justified in publishing it—anonymously, though ostensibly under Johnson's name. Its new title was to be *An Ode by Dr Samuel Johnson to Mrs Thrale, upon Their Supposed Approaching Nuptials*. The whole runs to a dozen stanzas; the first few are enough to give a sense of the tone:

> If e'er my fingers touch'd the lyre,
> In satire fierce, in pleasure gay,
> Shall not my Thralia's smiles inspire?
> Shall Sam refuse the sporting lay?
>
> My dearest lady! view your slave,
> Behold him as your very Scrub,*
> Eager to write as author grave,
> Or govern well the brewing tub.†

*A character in Farquhar's *The Beaux' Stratagem*.
† Thrale's brewery.

> To rich felicity thus rais'd,
> My bosom glows with amorous fire;
> Porter* no longer shall be prais'd;
> 'Tis I myself am *Thrale's Entire*!†

Boswell's motive in publishing the "Song" was to hurt and humiliate Mrs Piozzi. To rub salt into the wound, he dated it 1784, the year of her break with Johnson, reminding the public once again of the painful letters that she had omitted from her collection. Possibly with the help of Wilkes, he introduced the poem with both a preface and an "Argument" full of lewd innuendo. He tried to stir up interest in the publication by contributing a suggestive paragraph and this "Thralian Epigram" to the *Public Advertiser*:

> If *Hester* had chosen to wed mighty SAM
> Who it seems, drove full at her his BATTERING RAM
> A wonder indeed, then, the world would have found
> A woman who truly prefer'd SENSE to *sound*.

The *Ode* was not a success. Mrs Piozzi appeared not to notice it, and nor did the public. Boswell attempted to puff the dying embers into flame, but they would not catch. He gloomily ascribed the failure of his *Ode* to "a cooling as to Johnson."[25]

Boswell had been surprised to find in Mrs Piozzi's collection Johnson's passionate letters to Miss Hill Boothby. Johnson had known Miss Boothby since meeting her on a visit to his old schoolfriend Taylor at Ashbourne in 1739, and it seems likely that (unknown to any of his biographers) he contemplated marrying her after the death of his wife in 1752. But just as Johnson felt able to begin overtures to Miss Boothby, her dear friend Mary Meynell, wife of Sir William Fitzherbert, died. Miss Boothby had pledged herself to look after Sir William and his six children in the event of her friend's death; as a result, she was no longer free to marry. Two years later she too became seriously ill, and

---

*Johnson's wife, Elizabeth Porter; also a type of beer.
†A malt liquor sold by Thrale's brewery; also an innuendo.

Johnson wrote to her almost daily, letters steeped in tender affection—
he addressed her as "My Sweet Angel" and "My Dearest Dear"—and
anxious solicitude. When she died early in 1756, he was almost overcome by grief.

Most of Johnson's letters to Hill Boothby were lost, but a few
remained from the period of her final illness, and it was these which
Mrs Piozzi had published. Boswell had known of the letters, but he had
not taken much trouble to obtain copies for himself, probably because
he had heard that they were unavailable. Miss Boothby's brother had
deposited the letters with Taylor, and both men felt reluctant to part
with them. However, the Lichfield literary lady Anna Seward had contrived, after some considerable effort, to acquire them on Mrs Piozzi's
behalf. Why had she done this? Boswell had seen her as an ally; it was
she to whom he had turned first after Johnson's death, to obtain on his
behalf anecdotes and letters from people in the Lichfield area. He had
flirted with her, to the extent of soliciting a lock of "that charming
auburn hair I admired so much that delicious morning I was last with
you." In 1784, he had written a flattering review of her romantic novel,
Louisa, comparing her to the two other Lichfield geniuses, Johnson
and Garrick. She had been grateful enough to supply the lock.

In the mid-1780s, Anna Seward's reputation was still growing: already
she was known as "the Swan of Lichfield"; eventually she would be
crowned "Queen Muse of Britain." She was a woman with strong opinions, which she was not reluctant to express.

Mrs Piozzi had paid a visit to Lichfield in the summer of 1787, and
had won over Miss Seward to her side. Perhaps she flattered Miss
Seward, or perhaps these two intelligent women simply enjoyed each
other's company. Perhaps, too, the poignant story of Hill Boothby
seemed to Anna Seward wasted on Boswell, a middle-aged would-be
seducer, unlikely to understand how one woman could sacrifice her
chance of marriage to the memory of another.

Mrs Piozzi's animadversions on Johnson would not have alienated
Miss Seward; on the contrary, she wanted his dark side shown to the
public, and feared that Boswell's portrait of his "idol" would be too
friendly. Under the name "Benvolio" (a misnomer, if ever there was one),
Anna Seward published a series of letters in the *Gentleman's Magazine,*
attacking those whom she saw as Johnson's uncritical admirers. Her

hostility towards Johnson had a number of causes. She disliked his over-bearing manner, and what she saw as his intolerance, for example of religious nonconformity. His preference for London over Lichfield (or anywhere else) ran contrary to her determined provincialism. Most of all, his dismissal of the picturesque, the sublime, and the sentimental offended against her sensibilities. Anna Seward was a literary progressive, enthusiastic for the poetry of Gray and Mason, and enraptured by Ossian. The literary "despot" had trampled all over her favourite authors.[26]

In December 1786, Boswell had received from the Reverend Darniel Astle, amongst other material, an anonymous "Character" of Johnson, written by "a Person of some eminence in the literary world"—Anna Seward. She described him as "at once the most liberal and the most ungenerous; the most dark and most enlightened; the most compassionate and the most merciless; the most friendly and the least sincere; the best temper'd and the most acrimonious; the most soothing and the most abusive of mankind." She was incredulous at Johnson's dislike of Mason's *The English Garden* (1771–81) and Beattie's *The Minstrel* (1771–74), both poems which extolled the wonders of Nature; she dated "the downfall of just poetic taste in this Kingdom" from the publication of the *Lives of the Poets*. She placed herself among "the generous few . . . who dare think for themselves."

Boswell may have guessed the identity of the anonymous author from various clues in this piece. However that may be, he showed no sign of having done so when he wrote to her on 11 April 1788, a month after the publication of Mrs Piozzi's *Letters*. "What a variety of publications have there been concerning Johnson," Boswell remarked. "Never was there a man whose reputation remained so long in such luxuriant freshness, as his does. How very envious of this do the little stars of Literature seem to be, though bright themselves in due proportion." Perhaps Boswell's letter was deliberately provocative; if so, it certainly succeeded. He received in reply from Miss Seward "a long dissertation" inveighing against Johnson.[27]

On 19 April 1788, at exactly eleven o'clock the morning, Boswell called on Sir John Hawkins, armed with a letter of authorization from Francis Barber, to collect those papers of Johnson remaining in his possession. These were not very many; the printer John Nichols had collected most of Johnson's papers from him on Boswell's behalf the previous summer (some other papers may have been lost when Hawkins's house burned down soon after Johnson's death). The "diary," which the booksellers had advertised so prominently, turned out to be no more than a register of everyday transactions, interspersed with reflections and resolutions, collected in "a variety of little books folded and stitched together"[28] — which does not sound at all like the "two quarto volumes containing a full, fair, and most particular account of his life" which Boswell had sampled back in 1776. Had they been the same, then presumably Boswell would have recognized them. Perhaps, therefore, Boswell was correct in his belief that the diaries he had delved into had been destroyed by Johnson.

The meeting between the two rivals was surprisingly cordial. Hawkins congratulated Boswell on his punctuality, and then remarked, "You are Recorder of Carlisle, Sir." Flattered, Boswell replied, "I have that honour, Sir." Hawkins then presented Boswell with his pamphlet *A Charge to the Grand Jury of Middlesex*. Boswell thanked him, and asked him to inscribe it. Hawkins gladly agreed, and took up his pen, pausing to ask if he should address it to "*James* Boswell, Esquire." Boswell smiled: "Or in your own style, 'Mr James Boswell, a native of Scotland.'" Perhaps a little embarrassed, Hawkins replied, "There is no occasion for that." They parted on amicable terms. Boswell reflected how much enmity might be lessened if men who fought with their pens at a distance would meet calmly face to face. He decided that he would spare Hawkins many of the critical strictures he had planned to make in the *Life*.

At about the same date, he received a letter from Temple, who had read Hawkins's book and both of Mrs Piozzi's. The publication of Mrs Piozzi's *Letters* had stimulated a further rash of newspaper paragraphs chiding Boswell for his dilatoriness. "Certainly every thing now has appeared that can be of any use," Temple told Boswell, "and if not interrupted by the business of your profession, you can have no excuse for not going forward with your great work . . ."[29]

TEN

BEREAVEMENT

The sad apprehension of losing my valuable friend, *whose good sense and kindness had so long been my comfort, shocked me sadly.*[1]

EVEN NOW, Boswell found it difficult to concentrate on his book. In the week following the arrival of Temple's letter, for example, he wrote not a single line. He was still dreaming of making a mark in the world, of getting into Parliament, and of becoming a great man. "I own I am desirous that my life should *tell*," he admitted to Temple.[2] Boswell was indignant when Pitt took no notice of him, during a chance encounter with Dundas in a parliamentary ante-room. Dundas was friendly enough, but Pitt, who was by his side, was "cold and stiff and proud." Could it be that the Prime Minister had failed to recognize him? Boswell was consoled by Langton, who reminded him that the two of them were both gentlemen, from ancient families. "Don't we know that he was t'other day Will Pitt at Serle's Coffee-house, and are we to be awed by *him*, who have lived with Johnson?"[3]

On Saturday, 26 April 1788, Boswell attended the annual Exhibition Dinner of the Royal Academy, where he exchanged a few words with the Lord Chancellor. Afterwards he confessed to Malone that he was "tortured" to see those "who had risen to high situation while I was nothing"—particularly those Scotsmen who had prospered at the English bar—"but I trusted that my being so tortured was a sign that I was made for something great and that it would come." Malone humoured his unrealistic hopes, because he believed that Boswell needed to be in London to write his book. But he deplored Boswell's drinking so much: and following a night when Boswell had been unable to remember how he found his way home, Malone "lectured me upon my intemperance and on my delaying Johnson's *Life,* on which I was to rest my fame."[4]

Margaret Boswell was once again very ill: so emaciated, indeed, that she found it difficult to sit up in bed. While Boswell had been away with Lonsdale, she had been attended by Sir George Baker, President of the Royal College of Physicians. His fees (a guinea a day) were alarmingly expensive, and Margaret formed the impression that her husband grudged the expense; anxious to prove her wrong, Boswell was for calling for the doctor even when he was not needed, and had to be dissuaded from doing so. Sir George told Boswell that his wife had an inflammation on her lungs, which would soon have killed a younger person; as it was, her condition might be alleviated, but it was incurable. He prescribed laudanum, and bleeding at regular intervals. "Oh, Mr Boswell, I fear I'm dying," poor Margaret sighed one afternoon. Normally uncomplaining, she confessed her fear of death: "I am terrified for the dark passage." The two of them had been married twenty years; for more than half that time, Boswell had been aware that Margaret was likely to die early, leaving him alone. The thought filled him with dread, but he could not help wondering what might happen afterwards. As early as 1777, Boswell had begun to dream of marrying a rich widow—perhaps Lady Jean Lindsay, who had married the much older Earl of Eglinton while still in her teens (she died in 1778, at the age of only twenty-one).[5] Such unworthy speculation was accompanied by feelings of shame and self-reproach.

Though he felt guilty at leaving his wife at such a time, he found that he could not rest at home, and dined out more often than not, frequently returning late, often the worse for drink. After one lively evening, Boswell and Courtenay decided it was a pity to go to bed, and walked up to Hampstead as dawn was breaking, crossing the Heath to

Highgate where they ate breakfast, so that it was ten or eleven o'clock in the morning when he finally returned home. Margaret had been so anxious about him that she had become feverish, and was spitting blood.

At last, after further hesitation, Boswell decided that she must return to Auchinleck for the sake of her health, and that he and most of the children should accompany her. The house in Great Queen Street was given up. In mid-May the Boswell family left London, leaving behind only their eldest child, Veronica, in a fashionable Queen's Square boarding-school. Because of Margaret's illness they travelled slowly; at various stages it seemed uncertain whether she would be able to continue. They reached Auchinleck on 21 May. There Margaret began to recover, influenced both by the cleaner country air and by the comfort of being at home again, in the county of her childhood, among old and valued friends.

Boswell took with him to Scotland his journals for the years 1783 and 1784, planning to finish the first draft of his book there, before embarking on the Northern Circuit for the summer session. But as soon as he arrived in Auchinleck, a number of distractions intervened to prevent him from making progress. "I have now been here a fortnight and must acknowledge that I have done very little to advance the Life," he admitted to Malone. There were visitors to be entertained, and there was a great variety of estate business to be attended to, particularly since this was the time of year when rents were due. Political canvassing provided a further distraction; Boswell had counted himself as a candidate for Ayrshire ever since the last election, and he nursed the hope that if the "nominal and fictitious votes" were abolished before the next—the same votes that he had done so much, on Lonsdale's behalf, to maintain across the border—he might stand a chance of being elected as an independent. For this reason he was "riding the county," meeting and being civil and agreeable to as many voters as possible. (Not such a daunting task as it might appear; there were only around a hundred "real" voters in Ayrshire.) A month later he was forced to confess to Malone—"You will be very angry"—that he had written not a page of his book since he left London. "Now do not scold me; for, I promise to set apart so much time for the Life, that the rough draft will be all done, and brought with me to town early in October."[6]

This letter was written from York, where Boswell had joined the Northern Circuit. On his first night, the other barristers had tried to make him serve again as junior; Boswell was so offended that he got up and left the table. The next day he was relieved to discover that this proposal had been dropped. Nevertheless, he counted as one of the younger and less experienced barristers, and found himself obliged to dine with them while the seniors dined in more important company. The rude hilarity of the younger barristers grated on him. As a penalty for his absence from the Circuit, he was required to pay a fine of two and a half guineas, and to go through a ceremony of riding backwards on the back of another barrister (representing a ram), reciting a ludicrous poem:

> Here I am
> Riding on a black ram,
> Like a deserter as I am . . .

At Durham, Boswell encountered one of the hazards of literary fame—a fan. Mr Ambler, the Recorder, turned out to be a keen Johnsonian, and he first pleased and then embarrassed Boswell by praising him to the ladies at the local assembly. After two days of such flattery, Boswell began to avoid Ambler, especially once the enthusiastic Recorder began to address him (in broad northern dialect) as "Bozzy."

Boswell continued on the Circuit, passing through Newcastle. At Naworth Castle, about ten miles short of Carlisle, he foolishly offered to drink "a breastplate of ale," followed by some more hard drinking with the other barristers present. Intoxicated, they mounted their horses and rode into town; Boswell could hardly sit straight, and when he tried to dismount, he tumbled off in a heap. One of Lonsdale's hangers-on supported him to his lodgings. The next morning he woke with a headache, and trembled to think that he had made such an entry to the city where he had been elected Recorder. That evening he supped with two or three of the counsel, and was repelled by their "familiarity and petulance and coarseness."

He returned to Auchinleck on 15 August, where he found a long letter from Malone full of news, including gossip about the recent Westminster by-election—a reprise of the celebrated Westminster election of 1784, in which the Society beauty Georgiana, Duchess of Devonshire, was said to have kissed even the most humble voters in order to ensure a victory for the Whig Opposition leader, Charles James Fox. Because Westminster had a very much larger electorate than other constituencies, elections there were regarded as significant indicators of public opinion, and always closely contested. Courtenay had been active in canvassing for the Opposition candidate, who had once again been successful.

Malone had rented a country house near Cobham, in Surrey, while his London home was being redecorated. He invited Boswell to join him there when he returned to London, but warned: "If you do not bring up *the Life* complete, expect no mercy." Boswell replied a month later, admitting that he had done "nothing to Dr Johnson's Life—Literally nothing—not a single line" since arriving in Scotland. He pleaded the excuse that he had been preoccupied with estate business and local politicking. "I see that *the Whole* will be of London Manufacture," he wrote, and promised to "set myself doggedly" (a Johnsonian phrase) to the task when he returned, to the exclusion of all else. He even offered to give up wine until the book was done. This was too much for Courtenay, who replied in staccato style from Cobham Park, urging Boswell not to think of doing such a thing: "if you do—Your life of Johnston [*sic*] will resemble—Sir J. Hawkins." On the same sheet of paper was a brief greeting from Malone's Irish friend Robert Jephson, and a longer letter from Malone. "Your neglect of Johnson's Life is only what I expected," wrote Malone. "Scotland is not the place for it."[7]

On 26 October 1788, Boswell arrived back in London. He brought with him his two sons, whom he planned to place once again in English schools, so that they might have the benefit of an English education, and (more important) acquire English accents. Margaret remained at Auchinleck.

At first Boswell was nervous and gloomy. "This dreary distance is terrible," he wrote to his wife. He continued to be extremely concerned about her health. When, only a fortnight after he had left Scotland, a letter arrived from Auchinleck sealed in black wax, he feared the worst. He was almost afraid to open it, which he did with great agitation. Then he saw Margaret's handwriting inside, and he fervently thanked God. The relief was such that he was able to bear the reproaches the letter contained, as his reply demonstrated:

> Sensible as I am of conduct which I so sincerely blame that I can scarcely believe it to be true, and of which I have repented most seriously and with vexation of mind, I cannot but think it hard that the regard which I express should be doubted, or rather not credited, when I am sure that, notwithstanding many culpable deviations, there was never a more lasting attachment, more true esteem, or more tender love.

He had confessed to his affair with Mrs Rudd months before, while his wife was still with him in London; now that he had returned there without her, she feared that it might resume. "The creature to whom you allude," he insisted, "was totally dismissed from my attention." Despite Boswell's assurances, Margaret remained suspicious, and four months later he found it necessary to reassure her that "what I am truly sensible was very bad indeed" was totally at an end. He affirmed his continuing devotion to her in letter after letter. "One happy circumstance I can mention," he informed Margaret, after they had been apart five months, "which is that I have all this time been free from *any* such *folly* as I look back on with regret."[8]

Boswell had decided that he needed to be in London at least one more year, and after much searching he took a small house in Queen Anne Street West, just off Cavendish Square, the rent £50 per annum. The new address was convenient for Malone, who lived only a short walk distant, in Queen Anne Street East. His younger son James returned to the school he had been attending in Soho Square, while Boswell organized private tuition for his heir, Alexander (Sandy), whom he planned to send to Eton in due course.

Once settled in London, Boswell began to work furiously on his book, hoping to have it done by Christmas. He had now reached almost the end of the first draft. One remaining problem was to decide how to treat undated memorabilia of Johnson supplied by Langton and others. Langton was one of Boswell's most important sources for the *Life*, and many of the *bons mots* and anecdotes of Johnson's that he had given Boswell were now scattered separately through the narrative, in places where they seemed to belong chronologically, or where they served to illustrate a particular point Boswell was making. But there remained more than twenty pages of Langton's Johnsoniana without an obvious place. Boswell decided to use this collection *en bloc,* to fill a gap in his text for the year 1780, when he had been unable to come to London himself and therefore lacked a journal of Johnson's conversations. He placed the mass of anecdotes provided by the Reverend William Maxwell to fill the year 1770, another for which he had no record of his own. Boswell admitted in his *Life of Johnson* that he had rewritten some of these sayings of Johnson's into what he considered the authentic Johnsonian style.[9]

Much of this was guesswork. In trying to decide what Johnson might actually have said, Boswell had to reconcile the texts he had been given with the style of the man he knew. After so many years of recording Johnson's conversation, he was familiar with its peculiarities; he had used this facility time and again to make up blanks in his memory while writing up his journal. Boswell had spent so much time with his subject that the forms of Johnson's speech, perhaps even the patterns of his thought, were deeply imprinted on the younger man's mind. "It is amazing how a mimic can not only give you the gestures and voice of a person whom he represents; but even what a person would say on any particular subject," he had reflected on one occasion to Johnson, who remained sceptical.[10] Though Boswell had known Johnson very well indeed, there were sides to the man that were always hidden from him—Johnson's behaviour when alone with a woman, for example. And knowing Boswell's reverence for him, Johnson presented a more solemn figure to the earnest young man than he sometimes did when Boswell was absent. The way that Johnson spoke when Boswell was present was not the way that he always spoke. Johnson was aware that Boswell was recording what he said, and this knowledge in itself may have influenced the way that he talked when they were together. Boswell was steeped in Johnson's writings, and these were another tool in helping him to recapture what Johnson might have said. But written prose is different from speech: so that in re-creating what Johnson had said, there was a tendency to make it more measured, more sonorous, and more impressive than it had been in reality, and to emphasize its rhetorical aspects: for example, his habit of beginning a sentence with "Sir."

Johnson's manner of speaking eventually became something of a caricature, easily imitated. Boswell noticed that Johnson "seemed to take a pleasure in speaking in his own style." When Johnson caught himself carelessly missing it, he would repeat the thought "translated' into a more rounded, pronounced sentence. Commenting on a play, he first observed, "It has not wit enough to keep it sweet," and then corrected what he had said to "It has not vitality enough to preserve it from putrefaction."[11] There was an element of self-parody in this, of course. As he became famous, Johnson developed an ironic attitude towards his own celebrity. Much of this was lost on Boswell.

While he laboured on his manuscript, Boswell drew on yet another source of Johnsonian material: his own memory. He had astonishing powers of recall; a quarter of a century after an evening when he had walked arm in arm with Johnson in Greenwich Park, he remembered that it had been so cold as to make him shiver; and much else besides, enough to fill four new paragraphs.[12] Throughout the book he was able to add details which he had failed to record in his journal at the time. His journal in Holland—which had begun with his departure from London, together with Johnson, for the coast—had been lost; but with the help of his surviving rough notes, he found that he was able to construct a lively narrative of their journey to Harwich, containing some dramatic scenes and characteristic dialogue. In this case the act of writing his journal had helped to preserve events in his memory, even though the journal itself had gone missing twenty-five years before. Boswell had never written up the part of his journal covering the famous dinner on 15 May 1776, at which he had introduced Johnson to Wilkes. His only record of the occasion was some brief notes, but he drew on these more than a dozen years later to produce an account of approximately four thousand words, a scene as entertaining as any in the *Life of Johnson*.

Back in November, at a dinner at Windsor, the King had risen from his chair, seized the Prince of Wales by the collar, and dashed him against the wall. For some weeks before this, he had exhibited alarming symptoms, both physical and psychological: now it was no longer possible to conceal that he was seriously ill. Rumours began to sweep London that the King was dead, or insane. His doctor, the same Sir George Baker who had attended Margaret Boswell, reported that his patient was rambling, foaming at the mouth, preoccupied by strange delusions, and prone to uncontrollable convulsions. His behaviour was bewildering, distressing, occasionally indecent. More doctors were called, and the King was subjected to a variety of painful and humiliating treatments. Often he needed to be restrained. It was clear that he could take no further part in public life unless his condition improved.

On 10 November, Boswell heard a report that the King was dead, and he spent much of the day anxiously inquiring in various places whether the rumour was true. He learned that the King was alive—"thank GOD"—but delirious, with only a faint hope of recovery. "Some say that the disease is dropsy; some that it is a severe nervous fever. The Queen is in the most miserable distress. You cannot imagine," he wrote to Margaret, "how much real concern there is here amongst all but the Opposition party."[13]

The King's illness opened a period of intense political activity. The prospect of a Regency meant that suddenly everything was up for grabs. The Government would be obliged to resign, and in any new election the influence of the Regent was sure to be decisive. The court-in-waiting surrounding the Prince of Wales prepared to assume power. The Opposition Whigs who clustered around him sensed that their moment had come. They began to negotiate for the offices that would surely soon be theirs. The portly Charles James Fox came panting back from holiday in Italy, leaving his mistress behind in the rush. Pitt was reduced to delaying tactics, postponing the inevitable moment when he would be forced to relinquish power. Many Government supporters hesitated, unsure whether to leave the sinking ship or try to keep her afloat. Some declared openly for the Opposition, and campaigned for an immediate Regency. Others held back, waiting to see if the King would recover. As Lord Chancellor, Lord Thurlow played a crucial role: it was he who shuttled between Westminster and the Royal Palace at Kew, where the King was now confined, to report on the King's condition. At first Thurlow flirted with the Opposition, but he scurried back to the Government when the King seemed to recover.

Like many an ambitious man, Boswell surveyed the possible opportunities that might arise if the Government were overthrown. With any change of administration, hundreds, perhaps thousands of lucrative posts would change hands. Boswell watched Lonsdale nervously, to see which side he would choose. He was excited when his patron, *en route* to the North, asked Boswell to act on his behalf in a confidential matter. "The business alluded to is highly flattering to me," Boswell confided to his wife, "but is a secret, which I might communicate to you, were we together, but would not put in writing."[14]

In Parliament the Whigs' impatience quickly became obvious. During the operating debate on the Regency issue, Fox demanded an end to Pitt's procrastination. He argued that Parliament had no right to stand in the way of an immediate Regency, endowed with the full powers of the monarch. This was a disastrous mistake: in just one speech he betrayed the fact that the Whigs were prepared to abandon one of their most sacred principles—the right of Parliament to limit royal power—in their greed for office. The Whig spokesman, the playwright Richard Brinsley Sheridan, also over-reached himself, threatening reprisals against those members who voted to limit the Regent's powers. The Opposition charge faltered, amid much bickering about who would do what when the moment came.

For a while Boswell had been carried away with the notion of right having devolved onto the Prince, and had drafted a "very warm popular pamphlet" on the subject. The theme of an heir denied his birthright by his father was one still close to Boswell's heart, though Lord Auchinleck had been dead these past six years. But Lonsdale was taken ill with rheumatic fever, and Boswell did not see him for five weeks; while he waited to clarify his patron's sentiments, he prudently refrained from committing himself.

Until this moment George III had not been a popular king. His early attempts to reassert the influence of the Crown had been botched; and he bore some personal responsibility for the humiliating loss of the American colonies. But the Fox–North coalition formed in April 1783 was felt to be a cynical misalliance; and when the King dismissed the coalition eight months later, and asked the twenty-four-year-old William Pitt to form a new administration, this was seen as the beginning of the process of national recovery. Now that he was ill, the King attracted sympathy; the cynical manoeuvres of the politicians evoked repugnance. His homely virtues—his probity, his dedication, his uxoriousness—contrasted with the notorious vices of the Prince of Wales. Perhaps unfairly, the public formed a picture of a greedy Prince grasping at the throne, while his father was laid low. The King had never been loved so much as when he was at his most defenceless, confined within a strait-jacket.

By mid-February the King no longer needed to be restrained; his behaviour was slowly reverting to normal. A Regency bill, allowing the Regent only limited powers, had passed through the Commons, but now it was adjourned in the Lords. Thurlow announced in Parliament that the King, though still nervous, was recovering. The happy news from Kew meant that it would be indecent to proceed further with the Regency bill, when it might become wholly unnecessary. Pitt's Administration had ridden out the storm. Now he and his fellow ministers consolidated their power; the Whigs were routed, their society ladies humiliated. Dundas's mistress, Jane, Duchess of Gordon, triumphed over Georgiana, Duchess of Devonshire.[15] Those who had deserted the Government for the Opposition now tried to scramble back.

Boswell's enthusiasm for a Regency had likewise receded. "I begin now to think," he wrote to Temple, "that whatever Administration should appoint you and me to good places would be the best." Though Pitt was "an insolent fellow," who "has behaved very ill in his neglect of me," still Boswell could not help feeling that Pitt was the "ablest and most useful minister" of any that he knew. That being so, it seemed "utter folly" for Pitt not to reward and attach to his Administration "a man of my popular and pleasant talents." Langton encouraged Boswell in his manly resentment; Pitt's neglect was "disgraceful." Boswell failed to comprehend why the Prime Minister had not found time to answer several letters he had written proposing an interview; finally his patience was exhausted. Such behaviour was not generous, he warned Pitt, in a final demand: "I think it is not just, and (forgive the freedom) I doubt if it be wise. If I do not hear from you in ten days, I shall conclude you are resolved to have no further communication with me; for I assure you, Sir, I am extremely unwilling to give you, or indeed myself, unnecessary trouble."[16] He received no reply.

Boswell reported on his progress to his banker, Sir William Forbes, in mid-December. The book had been interrupted by political, legal, and convivial activities, but he had now reached the last few months of Johnson's life, and he hoped that it would be published by the end of May. He was under increasing financial pressure: summarizing his finances at the beginning of 1789, he found that his accumulated debts amounted to £4,670. The interest alone on this total came to more than £200 each year. He had estate income to offset this, of course, but he also had liabilities; the strain of maintaining two households and his determination to educate his children in England meant that his debt increased inexorably. He no longer had any income from his legal practice in Scotland, which at its peak had earned him £200 or £300 a year; and while he concentrated on the *Life of Johnson,* he had little chance of earning more than the occasional crumb at the English bar. It became more and more important to finish the book.

Early in the New Year, Boswell was able to tell Temple that he had almost concluded a rough draft of the *Life.*[17] He had written both the Introduction and the Dedication (to Reynolds). But he was finding it hard going. By late January he had still not reached the end, as he lamented to Margaret: "O, if this Book of mine were done! Job says, 'O, that mine enemy *had written* a Book!' I shall rejoice when I can speak in the *past* tense. I *do* hope to be at *Finis* in ten days."[18] Ten days later he found that he had done nothing all week. "I cannot *absolutely* see when I shall be done with it," he confessed to his wife on 9 February.[19] He wondered whether to go home to Auchinleck for a fortnight, or perhaps try the spring Northern Circuit. To do so would cost about £50, and take up thirty days, when he ought to be writing. And perhaps there was no point in continuing at the bar. As he admitted to Temple, he was "sadly discouraged by having no practice, nor probable prospect of it; and to confess fairly to you, my friend, I am afraid that were I to be tried, I should be found so deficient in the *forms,* the *quirks* and the *quiddities,* which early habit acquires, that I should expose myself."[20]

Still he pressed on with the book, and by early March 1789, he was able to tell Temple that the first part was ready for the press: "I shall probably begin to print next week."[21] But meanwhile he was pondering

an ominous report on his wife's condition: a severe cough, fever, and
swollen legs. She had already decided to dispense with further medical
advice; such treatment as she had received—mainly bleeding—had been
unpleasant and of dubious efficacy. Alarmed, Boswell wrote to Dr
Campbell, her physician in Scotland, asking him to call in and see her, as
if making a casual visit while in the neighbourhood. On 8 March,
Campbell reported that he had seen Mrs Boswell perhaps six times since
she had returned from London, and on none of those occasions would
he have said that she could live more than a month, "had she been anybody else than my old friend Mrs Boswell." The weather was now
milder and she was somewhat better; Campbell thought that Boswell
might wait and see how she continued before deciding whether or not
to return.[22] Boswell took some comfort from this report, though over
the week that followed he was disturbed by several distressing dreams.
He anxiously awaited the next letter from Auchinleck.

On 10 March, Boswell and his children, after dining with General
Paoli, joined the celebrations for the King's recovery. The whole of London was illuminated, the streets thronged with people. The Boswells
rode in a coach slowly through Grosvenor Square, Berkeley Square,
Bond Street, St James's Street, Pall Mall, the Strand, Fleet Street, up as
far as India House in Leadenhall Street, returning by Newgate, Snow
Hill, and Holborn to Cavendish Square. It was "the most brilliant show
that ever the metropolis exhibited," Boswell wrote to his wife. "The
general blaze of light was very fine, and many particular places were conspicuous by ingenious arrangements of coloured lamps, transparent figures, etc." The Boswell home was illuminated with candles, and Sandy
had placed translucent crowns in each drawing-room window, with "G"
under one and "R" under the other.[23]

Boswell felt guilty at taking pleasure when he knew his wife was in
such distress. But, as he inquired of Temple, "Is it not true philosophy,
my friend, to procure as much happiness, to make as much honey in life
as we can?"[24]

Margaret now pressed her husband to return home; still Boswell
could not tear himself away. He promised that he would not go without
Veronica, then decided that she should not leave her expensive boarding-
school before the end of term. Meanwhile, he enjoyed the carnival-like
atmosphere prevalent in London. On 26 March, the Queen held a

reception to mark the King's recovery; Boswell persuaded himself that it was important for "every gentleman who is at all in the way of going to Court" to show himself at this time. Accordingly, he had a new suit made, of imperial blue, lined with rose-coloured silk, ornamented with rich gold-wrought buttons—the uniform prescribed for those who wished to display their loyalty to the monarch.[25]

He was tempted to stay for the continuing festivities. But on 29 March, he received such an alarming report from Campbell that he decided he could delay his return no longer. On 2 April, he left London with his daughter Veronica; four days later he arrived at Auchinleck. They found Margaret miserably emaciated and weak, unable to receive more than a very little sustenance from either food or drink. Dr Campbell told Boswell frankly that she had no hope of recovery. Boswell poured out his heart in a letter to Temple:

> No man ever had a higher esteem or a warmer love of a wife than I of her. You will recollect, my Temple, how our marriage was the result of an attachment truly romantic. Yet how painful it is to me to recollect a thousand instances of *inconsistent* conduct. I can justify my removing to the great sphere of England, upon a principle of laudable ambition. But the frequent scenes of what I must call *dissolute* conduct are inexcusable. Often and often when she was very ill in London have I been indulging in festivity with Sir Joshua Reynolds, Courtenay, Malone, etc. etc. etc., and have come home late, and disturbed her repose.

Boswell acknowledged that he was in a pathetic state, "full of ambition and projects to obtain wealth and eminence, yet embarrassed in my circumstances, and depressed with family distress."[26] He had returned to Auchinleck meaning to soothe and console his wife. There was no doubt that he loved and valued her. But even now, while she was so ill, he could not rest. Over the following weeks he was repeatedly away from home, politicking and socializing and drinking heavily. At a dinner given by a neighbour, he drank so freely that he fell from his horse while riding home in the dark, and badly bruised his shoulder.

While the King had been ill, numerous adulatory petitions had been submitted to the Prince of Wales from all over Britain, by those hoping for preferment when he came to power, as it had at one time seemed certain that he would. Now their signatories were lying low, hoping to escape retribution from the resurgent ministry. But Boswell failed to realize that the game was up. As chairman of the General Quarter Sessions at Ayr, he proposed and carried a new Address to the Prince of Wales, congratulating him on his "admirable moderation and truly patriotic conduct" during the recent crisis. "This will add something to my *conspicuousness*," he boasted to Temple. In truth, it was a stupid move, which could bring him no credit and could do him only harm. The Prince's behaviour had been at best tactless, at worst callous; angry crowds in London had attacked his coach. His influence was zero; Pitt and Dundas were now picking off those who had sided with him, one by one. Temple rebuked Boswell for his folly: "You show every one how eager you are for office and preferment, and yet by your own rashness throw obstacles in your way."[27]

Boswell was in bed, recovering from his bruised shoulder, when he received word that Lonsdale required his presence. He had known for some months that he might be needed, in his official capacity as Recorder, for a case due to come before the King's Bench in late May, concerning the ability of the Carlisle Corporation to create "honorary freemen" with voting rights. Lonsdale asked him to come to Lowther, so that they might travel down to London together. Boswell hesitated to leave his wife at such a time, but she generously pressed him to go. He left Auchinleck on 19 May, resolving to return as soon as possible. On the road he shed tears of dejection. Lonsdale had seemed so importunate that Boswell feared he might not reach Lowther before his patron set out; but when he arrived he found no hurry for departure. Days passed, while Boswell nursed his shoulder, fretting about his wife, and the time away from his book. "His Lordship's *way* is extremely dilatory," he complained to Temple. At last the party left for London; he had been there only a few days when news came from Auchinleck that Margaret was dying. With the two boys, Boswell began a frantic dash home, reaching Auchinleck in just over sixty-four hours, but as they approached the house, his daughter Euphemia ran out, crying. Margaret was dead.

"O! my Temple! what distress, what tender painful regrets, what unavailing earnest wishes to have but one week, one day, in which I might again hear her admirable conversation and assure her of my fervent attachment," lamented Boswell, "notwithstanding all my irregulari-ties." He had been anticipating Margaret's death for more than a decade, but still it was a heavy blow. "She is the prop and stay of your life," Johnson had told him, in a letter which Boswell would quote in his *Life of Johnson*;[28] now that prop had been kicked away.

His grief was compounded by guilt that he had left her alone at the last; "she would not have left me." He could hardly bear to allow the body to be removed, "for it was still a consolation to me to go and kneel by it, and talk to my dear, dear Peggie." He derived some comfort from her funeral, which was well attended, with nineteen carriages fol-lowing the hearse, and a large body of horsemen; he read the funeral service over the coffin himself, in the presence of his two sons.[29]

Boswell remained at Auchinleck most of the summer. He had put himself forward for a by-election, due on 3 August, caused by the appointment of the local MP to a comfortable sinecure: Baggage-Master and Inspector of the Military Roads of Scotland, stipend £500 per annum. As usual, Boswell was standing against one of Dundas's candi-dates, and though he did not expect to win, he hoped to make a good showing. But he was disappointed even in this; his turn-out was so poor that he decided it was not worth standing in the forthcoming General Election.

One pressing problem was to settle the children's future. While Margaret had been alive, she had taken care of the children; now Boswell needed to be both father and mother to them. He was particu-larly concerned about the girls; it was a great disadvantage for a young lady to be without a mother who could introduce her into Society. One of a mother's prime duties was to help her daughters find husbands, and to steer them past the many snares that lay in wait for unwary young women. The two elder girls, in their mid-teens, were proving quarrelsome; Boswell confessed to Temple that he had scarcely any authority over them. He did not feel that it would be proper for them to live with him in London, nor to remain unsupervised at Auchinleck. Nor could he bear for them to become "Edinburgh-mannered girls." Sandy too, now fourteen, was proving difficult to manage. After a good deal of worry, Boswell decided that his eldest daughter, Veronica, should board with a respectable widow in London; while the second,

Euphemia, should be placed at a boarding-school in Edinburgh, where Boswell's stepmother, Lady Auchinleck, could keep an eye on her. Sandy would start at Eton in the autumn, and his younger brother, James, would continue as a day-boy at Soho Academy, living with his father, as a preparation for going to Westminster the following summer. At first Boswell thought of sending his youngest daughter, Betsy, to a school near Temple in Cornwall, but eventually he placed her at a boarding-school in Chelsea.

Boswell had written to his patron of his loss even before the funeral, and six weeks later he received a reply, inviting him to Lowther Castle: "It may be some satisfaction to open your mind upon family affairs to your friend, Lonsdale." On 10 August, therefore, Boswell left Auchinleck for Lowther. He was in a vulnerable state, unhappy and maudlin, and once again drinking heavily. The Castle was so full that Boswell was obliged to share a room; one morning he was embarrassed not to be able to find his wig. A strict search was made, but all in vain. No gentleman could appear in smart company without some form of covering for his shaven head—Boswell was obliged to spend the day lingering about the house in his night-cap, and to forgo both a party by the lake and a dance—and the next day he rode twenty-five miles into Carlisle to have a new wig fitted. His friend Temple suspected a cruel practical joke, especially as the wig was found on a subsequent visit.

One night during his stay at Lowther Castle, Boswell dreamed that Johnson entered the room suddenly and looked at him with a very angry expression. "My dear Sir, you certainly have nothing to say against me," Boswell said defensively. "Have I nothing to say against you, Sir?" thundered Johnson. Boswell woke feeling uneasy. Perhaps his conscience was troubling him: he had not touched his book since March. *Hoc age,* as Malone was always saying—get to work.

ELEVEN

HUMILIATION

‒‒‒‒‒‒‒‒‒‒‒‒

O! my old and most intimate friend! what a shocking state am I now reduced to.[1]

BOSWELL ARRIVED in London early in October, and almost immediately resumed work on the *Life,* after an interval of seven months.

Now that he had reached the end of the first draft, the process of revision and polishing ("nice correction") began, and for this Boswell needed Malone's help. His method was to read the text aloud to Malone (whose eyesight was fading), and then to mark Malone's comments on the manuscript—unlike their collaboration on *The Journal of a Tour to the Hebrides,* when it had been Malone who had read the text aloud and marked corrections on the manuscript. This process of "nice correction" was painstaking work: eliminating repetition; replacing colloquialisms and Scotticisms; pruning verbose passages; reducing the all-too-frequent references to Boswell himself; providing alternatives for words repeated nearby; ameliorating expressions thought to be gratuitously offensive; converting indirect speech into direct speech and (less often) vice versa; suppressing the identity of various individuals; deleting facts, opinions, or quotations thought to be unsustainable, irrelevant, indelicate, or provocative; refinements for the sake of "elegance," such as changing Anglo-Saxon into Latinate words, or delicacy; deleting material thought not to be authentic; further rewriting of quotations into what Malone—a scholar skilled at recovering authentic texts—believed that Johnson was likely to have said; adding new material acquired since the first draft was written; and elaborating or qualifying passages for the sake of greater precision.[2] Many of these changes required discussion and consideration before they could be implemented, if indeed they were to be implemented; for though Malone was, in Boswell's words, "Johnsonianissimus," his tastes, his instincts, and his judgements were often very different from Boswell's. Even when Malone's suggestions were rejected, however, his advice was still valuable, because it forced Boswell to consider the issue from a different viewpoint. But working this way was grindingly slow, and very laborious. "You cannot imagine how tedious it is to revise and correct a work with the nicety which Mr Malone has taught me to do it," Boswell moaned to Forbes.

Boswell was anxious to spend as much time as possible revising with Malone, who planned to go to Ireland for a while, once his edition of Shakespeare was published. But as before, he found it necessary to dance attendance on Lonsdale, who threw out tantalizing hints about the possibility of getting him into Parliament. Boswell had solicited such a promotion, in a succession of sycophantic letters. "May your steady friends be made to shine around you in their several orbits," hinted Boswell on 26 October. Such fawning belied Boswell's feeble protests of independence; Lonsdale knew that he could command his satellites. It was frustrating to have to pass another tedious evening paying court to his patron when Malone had promised to set time aside to work on the book, but Boswell was warned not to risk breaking an engagement.

When not with Lonsdale or Malone, Boswell dined with Sir Joshua Reynolds, who remained as hospitable as ever, despite the recent loss of sight in one eye—a catastrophe for a painter. In early November, for example, Boswell dined with Reynolds on five consecutive days. He had also begun a brief affair with a woman identified only as "C," a courtesan who turned out to have more than one "friend." He endured much raillery from Lonsdale and his cronies when he confessed to a painful venereal infection. Boswell consoled himself by drinking heavily. After returning tipsy from Lonsdale's in a coach one evening, he staggered out as far as Wimpole Street, planning to visit "C"; his son James followed and brought him back. "Wretched scene," he wrote in his journal. One morning he woke in tears after dreaming of his wife.[3]

Though Boswell had finished the first draft of his *Life of Johnson,* he was still accumulating source-material, and there remained many details—"little Johnsonian particulars"—that he needed to check. He was still trying to establish an authoritative catalogue of Johnson's prose writings, a difficult task since Johnson had been so prolific, and so much of what he had written had been anonymous. (Percy had compiled such a catalogue in Johnson's lifetime, which had been checked by Johnson himself; but Boswell kept finding omissions.) The more he discovered, the more he found there was yet to discover. He continued to collect letters, and it became clear that there was still a large number of people who had known Johnson whom it would be useful to interview. He had gathered information about Johnson from a wide variety of informants; some of these were more reliable than others, and indeed some of the information he had received was contradictory. Wherever possible he wanted to verify his sources.

For example, Boswell had begun to wonder whether the anecdotes provided by Anna Seward might not be tainted by her prejudice against Johnson. She had given him an account of the young Johnson's conversation with his mother, when he was seeking her permission for his proposed marriage to Elizabeth Porter. According to Miss Seward, Johnson had told his mother that Mrs Porter knew "the worst of him," in particular that an uncle of his had been hanged. Boswell wrote to Mary Cobb, an elderly Lichfield widow who had known the Johnson family, asking for information about the uncle who had been hanged. Mrs Cobb replied that neither she, nor any of Johnson's oldest neighbours whom she had been able to consult, knew anything of such a person. She was inclined to think that it had been said in jest. Boswell's doubts about Anna Seward's reliability were confirmed; she had given him this story "as having been *told by Mrs Cobb.* As I find my authority quite erroneous in one remarkable particular, I cannot trust to it for any part."[4] After the publication of the *Life of Johnson,* there was a sharp exchange of letters in the *Gentleman's Magazine* on this point. Writing from Lichfield, Anna Seward defended the account she had given to Boswell:

> The conversation which young Johnson is reported to have held with his mother, when he asked her consent to marry the widow Porter, and which formed one of the anecdotes, I sent to Mr Boswell, and which he suppressed, I have heard frequently and generally mentioned, and credited here. I forget whether or not I quoted to *him* any particular authority for that memoir—yet, to the best of my remembrance, I heard it first from the late Mrs Cobb, of this place. If I were asked who told me that Johnson said of Chesterfield, "he is a wit among lords, and a lord among wits," I should find it difficult to specify an individual from the numbers whom I have heard repeat the sarcasm. Neither can I *now* with *certainty* in this instance— but I never doubted the reality of either story, because there is the Johnsonian spirit in both.

Johnson had been a living legend, famous since the 1740s; people had been telling stories about him ever since, and inevitably many of these had become embellished or confused. Anecdotes about him circulated in conversation and in print; Johnson himself had been known to encourage confusion, by allowing currency to the occasional amusing but inaccurate story. As a lawyer, Boswell was accustomed to weighing evidence; he knew how seldom witnesses provide reliable accounts, even of recent events; and he was aware of the strange human tendency to believe oneself to have been present at a scene that one has only imagined from a description. Malone too was a lawyer, and a scholar with a genius for arranging documentary material and reconciling apparent conflicts; he was expert at rubbing off the tarnish to reveal the original texts gleaming below. These skills would prove invaluable in removing the layers of myth that had accumulated around the figure of Johnson.

One example will serve the place of many. In 1742, Johnson had been hired by the bookseller Thomas Osborne to catalogue the immense library of the late Robert Harley, Earl of Oxford. Osborne had bought the library as a speculative venture for the vast sum of £13,000, and he needed a descriptive catalogue to attract buyers. Johnson worked speedily and under pressure; when Osborne, a brutal, ignorant man, charged

him with inattention and delay, Johnson picked up a large folio volume
and knocked him down. Johnson's pugnacious defiance symbolized the
resentment felt by Grub Street writers against those who exploited them.
It was a good story: so widely known that when, twenty years later, the
Scots lawyer Alexander Wedderburn was asked by the Earl of Bute to
offer Johnson a Crown pension, he had been too nervous to approach
Johnson himself, and had persuaded the playwright Arthur Murphy to
do so on his behalf. More than ten years later, Lord Marchmont too had
hesitated when Boswell proposed that he might revise Johnson's life of
Pope. "So (said his Lordship) you would put me in a dangerous situation. You know he knocked down Osborne the bookseller."

Mrs Thrale had tried to get Johnson to elaborate on the story, without
much success. By the time Boswell came to write his book, several versions had already appeared in print, with different details: Johnson had
placed his foot on the prostrate body of his employer and told him not
to be in a hurry to rise, lest next he be kicked down the stairs; while Johnson stood, his foot on the breast of his victim, he had declaimed, "Lie
there, thou son of dullness, ignorance and obscurity"; he had placed his
foot on Osborne's neck, not his breast; Osborne had alarmed his family
with his cries; and so on. Even the volume wielded by Johnson had been
identified, as a sixteenth-century Greek Bible—and offered for sale as
such. It must have been tempting for Boswell to incorporate some of
these dramatic touches, but he refrained:

> It has been confidently related, with many embellishments, that Johnson
> one day knocked Osborne down in his shop, with a folio, and put his foot
> upon his neck. The simple truth I had from Johnson himself. "Sir, he was
> impertinent to me, and I beat him. But it was not in his shop: it was in my
> own chamber."[5]

Of course, Boswell was keen to draw attention to any errors made
by his rivals. For example, Hawkins's biography asserted that warrants
had been issued for Johnson's arrest in 1739, after Johnson had published a satirical pamphlet attacking the reigning Hanoverian family and
the ruling Whig administration of Sir Robert Walpole. According to
Hawkins, messengers had been sent to apprehend Johnson, and he had
lain concealed in Lambeth marshes until the scent had grown cold. Boswell doubted this story, and made inquiries of the relevant authorities.

The records were searched, and no trace found of any warrant ever having been issued.

His desire to show up errors in his rivals led Boswell into error himself. According to Mrs Piozzi, the young Johnson had written some verses for his friend Edmund Hector to give a girlfriend—just like Cyrano de Bergerac. Anna Seward informed Boswell that on the contrary, Johnson had written the love poem ("Verses on Receiving a Sprig of Myrtle from a Lady") for himself, to give to Lucy Porter, Tetty's daughter. It seemed that Johnson had been sweet on Lucy before transferring his affections to her mother. Boswell printed this story as a corrective to Mrs Piozzi's account, which he believed to be inaccurate. But after the book was published, Hector insisted that there was no truth in Anna Seward's story; Boswell had made an embarrassing mistake. He confessed his error in the second edition of the *Life of Johnson,* which led to another public spat with Miss Seward.*

In his thirst for accuracy, Boswell even tried to check the records that Johnson himself had cited in his life of the poet Richard Savage, in an attempt to prove that Johnson's partiality for Savage had led him into error. Boswell's energy in pursuing such details was unusual, and contrasted strongly with Johnson's customary indolence. When Johnson had been writing his *Lives of the Poets,* for example, Boswell had taken some trouble to arrange for Johnson an interview with Lord Marchmont, Pope's friend and executor, only to be rebuffed. "If it *rained knowledge* I'd hold out my hand," said Johnson irritably, "but I would not give myself the trouble to go in quest of it."

Boswell's persistence, his desire to verify what seemed to others the most trifling detail, his zeal for "scrupulous authenticity," seemed absurd to many of his contemporaries. The Scottish judge Lord Hailes, who had known Boswell all his life, warned him to omit insignificant details—and to remember that Dr Johnson was the principal subject of the book.[6] Boswell was sensitive to such criticism. "Were I to detail the books which I have consulted, and the inquiries which I have found it necessary to make by various channels, I should probably be thought ridiculously ostentatious," he wrote defensively in the "Advertisement" to the first edition of the *Life.* "Let me only observe, as a specimen of

*See pages 278–79.

my trouble, that I have sometimes been obliged to run half over London, in order to fix a date correctly; which, when I had accomplished, I well knew would obtain me no praise, though a failure would have been to my discredit." This was a period when most authors, including Johnson himself, were content to rely on previous authorities, or just on memory as a source. Boswell deplored the habit of introducing anecdotes, facts, and even quotations with phrases such as "I think I have read" or "If I remember right," when the originals were available to be examined. He was determined to paint a "Flemish picture" of his friend, faithful to life and accurate in every detail. The nature of such a work consisted of "innumerable detached particulars," and to ascertain their authenticity Boswell was prepared to go to "a degree of trouble beyond that of any other species of composition." There were moments when he felt that the task might be beyond him. "You cannot imagine," he exclaimed to his friend Temple, "what labour, what perplexity, what vexation, I have endured in arranging a prodigious multiplicity of materials, in supplying omissions, in searching for papers, buried in different masses—and all this besides the exertion of composing and polishing. Many a time have I thought of giving it up."[7]

Only a few days after writing this letter, on 2 December, Boswell woke in poor spirits, "doubting if I *could* get *Life* finished." He spent that evening revising the manuscript with Malone, and felt better. During the remainder of December, the two men worked together on more than a dozen evenings. On 1 January 1790, Boswell delivered the Introduction to his printer, Baldwin, "that I might say my book was *at* if not *in* the press on New Year's day." He proposed to feed the printer copy as it became ready, so that it could be set up in type, while simultaneously correcting proofs as they became available; "the honest friendly Printer was a little gruff about my mode of carrying on the Work, but I made allowances for him." There followed over the next few days much discussion of the size of both the type and the book itself. Baldwin calculated the length of the draft manuscript at 416,000 words— even if printed in the slightly smaller than usual "Pica"* type, it would still make two quarto volumes of about four hundred pages each.

---

*Known nowadays as 12-point. The modern equivalent of the then usual type, known as "English," is 14-point.

Boswell had been hoping that his book could be published in one volume, priced at a guinea; Baldwin advised that it would have to be two volumes, priced at thirty shillings. Boswell wondered whether it might not be better to print the book as one volume in folio, a larger format; Malone told him that he might as well throw it into the Thames. People did not read books in folio nowadays; it had become an antiquated size, reserved for lengthy reference works. Malone felt strongly that the book should be published in one quarto volume, however thick.*

Malone had proposed printing one thousand copies in quarto, running on a further thousand sheets in the smaller octavo size for a subsequent cheaper edition. Both Dilly and Baldwin endorsed this proposal. Boswell consulted John Nichols, editor of the *Gentleman's Magazine* and printer of the *Lives of the Poets,* who convinced him that this was a bad plan. To begin with, the saving was only small; next, there would be no opportunity to make corrections in the second edition; and finally, the knowledge that one thousand octavo sheets were ready to be bound would damage the sale of the quarto edition. Nichols assured Boswell that there would be no risk in printing 1,500 copies in quarto. His confidence restored, Boswell decided to print 1,750.

From this point on, manuscripts and proofs shuttled back and forth regularly between Boswell's and Baldwin's. Boswell was frequently at the printers, delivering copy, collecting new proofs or returning them corrected. Often there would be a need for a revised proof, and sometimes a revise of a revise. Once a sufficient number of pages to fill a sheet of printer's paper (usually eight) had been proofed and passed for press, a run of 1,750 sheets was printed and the type broken up for reuse. The sheets would then be folded into sections and gathered—collated with the other sections—before being sewn and bound. Any changes at this stage, known as "cancels," were expensive; they meant

---

*It may help those readers unfamiliar with eighteenth-century printer's terminology to have a note of book sizes in Boswell's day. These were named according to the number of leaves that resulted from folding a sheet of printer's paper to that size: i.e. folio meant two (four pages), quarto four (eight pages), octavo eight (sixteen pages), and duodecimo twelve (twenty-four pages). The exact dimensions varied according to the size of the sheet, but typically they would be as follows (the vertical dimension given first): folio 18 × 11½ inches (similar to the largest modern atlases), quarto 11¼ × 9 inches, octavo 9 × 5¾ inches (slightly smaller than most modern hardcover books, including this one), and duodecimo 5¾ × 4 inches (considerably smaller than a modern mass-market paperback).

cutting out the offending leaf and substituting one corrected. The book advanced steadily; by early March over a hundred pages had been proofed and printed. Boswell's spirits recovered, now that at least some of what he had written was in print. If it was not the end, or even the beginning of the end, maybe it was the end of the beginning.

Boswell relaxed into the bottle; after a dinner at Sir Joshua Reynolds's, where he had stayed late, he was arrested and taken to the watch-house for calling the hour in the streets after midnight. The next morning he appeared before the magistrate charged with creating a disturbance; Boswell's defence was that "he did it to put the watchmen right, as they never laid the emphasis on the *hour* but on *past* and *o'clock*." The magistrate's reprimand had little effect, because later that same day Boswell was again to be found wandering around London intoxicated.[8]

"I am at present wonderfully well," Boswell wrote to Temple a few weeks later.

> I cannot account for my "healthful mind" at this time. There is no change to the better in my circumstances. I have no better prospect of gratifying my ambition or of increasing my fortune. The irreparable loss of my valuable wife, the helpless state of my daughters, in short all that ever hung heavy upon me is still as it was. But my spirits are vigorous and elastic. I dine in a different company almost every day, at least scarcely ever twice running in the same company, so that I have fresh accessions of ideas. I drink with Lord Lonsdale one day; the next, I am quiet in Malone's elegant study, revising my *life of Johnson,* of which I have high expectations both as to fame and profit. I surely have the art of writing agreeably.[9]

One sign of Boswell's renewed exuberance was his attendance at services at Westminster Abbey dressed "in a scratch wig* and watchman's great coat, as like as he could be to old Sam Johnson." A series of newspaper articles, many of them written by Boswell himself, speculated that Mrs Piozzi was dreading the imminent appearance of his biography. "I think it will be, without exception, the most entertaining book you ever read," he enthused to Temple.[10]

---

*A wig covering only part of the head, not the kind normally worn in public by a man of fashion such as Boswell.

Perhaps too entertaining for some tastes. Boswell had already received a letter from his old friend the Reverend Dr Hugh Blair, who hoped that he would not feature prominently in the *Life of Johnson*. "Your anecdote about the *Cow*, in a former Publication,* tho' harmless in itself, was very unnecessary and exposed me to some laughter." (Poor Boswell had been pressured to include this anecdote by Alexander Tytler.) Langton too had become apprehensive that some of the stories he had given Boswell "might not be what I should choose to have published." He asked Boswell if he might vet the relevant pages, a request to which Boswell agreed. Percy presented a more awkward problem. He had supplied several batches of interesting and seemingly authentic early Johnsoniana; now he wanted his name suppressed as an informant, and offered to pay the cost of any leaves cancelled as a result. "I will do any thing to oblige your Lordship but that very thing," replied Boswell: "I am quite resolute as to this matter." This was not mere obstinacy; Boswell was determined to establish the authenticity of the work, by displaying his sources whenever possible. Percy responded that he felt it an honour to be mentioned in any book of Boswell's. His only anxiety, he wrote, was that the trifling nature of some of the anecdotes might expose him too much to ridicule. He too asked to be allowed to see those passages for which his name was produced in support before publication. "If you do not indulge me in this request, I shall really take it ill."[11] Boswell appears to have ignored this request. He was prepared to go only so far in accommodating the wishes of Johnson's friends. If he were to omit anything which might offend anybody, his book would become bland; moreover, it would falsify Johnson's character. Johnson was notorious for handling his friends roughly in conversation, as Boswell knew only too well. Few wanted to see in print what Johnson had said to them to their faces, still less what he might have said about them behind their backs. Several former friends

---

*See *The Journal of a Tour to the Hebrides,* 11–19 November 1773. Boswell described how, many years before, he had been sitting with Blair in the pit of the Drury Lane Theatre; "in a wild freak of youthful extravagance," he had entertained the audience "prodigiously" by lowing like a cow. Encouraged by the cry of "*Encore* the cow!" from the galleries, he had attempted imitations of some other animals. "My reverend friend, anxious for my *fame*, with the air of utmost gravity and earnestness, addressed me thus: 'My dear sir, I would *confine* myself to the *cow*!'"

of Johnson's appealed to Malone to remove the most offensive of his observations from the manuscript, or at least to tone them down. Malone tried to do so, for the sake of Johnson's memory, as well as for Boswell's sake. "Why raise up against him a host of enemies, by telling a thing that need not be told, and in which perhaps your information may have been inaccurate?"[12] Why make enemies for yourself?

If Boswell had any doubts about the effect that publication of uncensored anecdotes involving named individuals might have, he had only to remember the rows in which he had become embroiled after the publication of the *Tour*. At least one of these was still rumbling on more than three years later. During a dinner on 5 November (auspicious date) 1773, Johnson had become offended by the remarks of their host, the Reverend Mr Dun, Presbyterian minister at Auchinleck. Dun had been very critical of the Church of England, and had spoken of "fat bishops and drowsy deans"; according to Boswell, Johnson had retorted, "Sir, you know no more of our church than a Hottentot." More than fifteen years after this exchange, Dun was still insisting that Johnson had not used the word "Hottentot" to him; he continued to demand its removal, even though, out of deference to the awkward elderly clergyman, Boswell had deleted his name from the second and subsequent editions of his book.

Boswell now began to consider what he might do after the *Life* was finished, and to cast around for any form of employment which might relieve his financial difficulties. "I am resolved to go to any corner of the globe," he declared, "rather than continue in embarrassed circumstances."[13] When there seemed a possibility (later dashed) that one of his friends might be appointed as first British Ambassador to the United States, Boswell was keen to accompany him as Secretary to the Legation. He was still paying court to Lord Lonsdale, though he found himself increasingly disgusted with the company of cringing "dogs" whom he met at Lonsdale's table, hoping for their master to toss them a bone or at least to offer them a glass of wine.

He was also contemplating what he might write next. Briefly, he floated the notion of a history of Carlisle: no rise from Lonsdale. Many

Englishmen welcomed the end of absolutism in France, but Boswell had been appalled by the disturbances there, which he described as "an intellectual earthquake, a whirlwind, a mad insurrection without any immediate cause"; and he now planned a play about the Marquis de Favras, a martyr to the Royalist cause. Favras had been a Scarlet Pimpernel–like figure, who plotted to rescue Louis XVI and his family from the hands of the Parisian mob, and who had been executed as a result. Though the play was announced in the press, it seems never to have been written. Boswell clashed with several of his friends who were sympathetic to the French Revolutionaries, though not with Burke: what was happening in France, Burke told him early in 1790, "would almost make me adopt your Tory principles"—an indication that his own views were changing. Later that year Burke would publish his *Reflections on the Revolution in France,* the book that marked his desertion from the Radical Whigs. General Paoli, on the other hand, who had led an unsuccessful liberation struggle against the French after they had annexed his country, sent a Corsican delegation to the new French National Assembly, which voted to make Corsica a province of France, offering Corsicans the same rights as other French citizens, an offer which Paoli accepted. He prepared to return to his homeland, after twenty years' exile. Though Boswell disapproved of Corsica's accepting French sovereignty, he gave a farewell dinner in honour of his old friend, before Paoli left England on 29 March.

The other great issue of the moment was the trial before the House of Commons of the immensely wealthy nabob Warren Hastings, the former Governor of Bengal. The enormous and ever-increasing power of the East India Company over the Indian people had led to increasing anomalies; Hastings was accused of bribery, corruption, and oppression of the native population. For some years the Whigs had been in disarray; at last they had found an issue on which they could unite, a scandal that they hoped might eventually destabilize the otherwise rock-solid Pitt administration. Hastings's impeachment had begun in February 1788, opened by Burke; it seemed as if it might continue indefinitely, widening in scope and dragging down others in the process. Boswell had first met Hastings and his handsome wife at Reynolds's house in March 1787, when his reputation was already under a cloud. He had called on Hastings the following day, pleased to pay such a compliment

to a man in his situation. Now he used his search for Johnsonian materials as a pretext to renew their acquaintance. When Hastings returned
his call, Boswell greeted him with a prepared speech, mingling compliment with condescension:

> Any temporary difference in your situation I assure you makes no differ-
> ence in my mind . . . I view you, Sir, with the eye of Lord Thurlow as an
> Alexander; and though I am not surly and proud, I flatter myself I am to
> some degree a philosopher. Your visit, therefore, to me may be compared
> to that of Alexander to Diogenes, for indeed my small hut is not much big-
> ger than a tub. Let me add, Sir, that you have saved me the trouble of going
> into the street with a torch at noonday to look for a man.

Boswell was delighted to be in a position to address a man who had
once been "an oriental emperor" *de haut en bas*. Hastings subsequently
sent Boswell several uninteresting letters from Johnson, each of them
seeking favours for persons serving in India; but what Boswell valued
most was the covering letter from Hastings himself, pompous and flatteringly deferential, which he described as "pure gold of Ophir." Naturally he decided to print this in full in the *Life of Johnson*.

Boswell had begun to think about marrying again. Nobody could
replace Margaret, he thought, but he was prepared to contemplate a
union with a sensible, good-tempered woman of fortune. Marriage to
a wealthy woman would ease his financial difficulties. Indeed, remarriage might serve "as an insurance against some very imprudent connection."[14] Boswell began a series of flirtations with possible marriage
partners, some of them simultaneous, none of which led anywhere.
And he began a more serious affair with a married woman, unburden-
ing his heart to Temple in a "Rousseau-like confession." Temple was
amazed—"in love at fifty!"—but alas, this exciting romance proved
short-lived.

Almost two centuries passed before it was discovered that Johnson too,
like Boswell, had planned to marry again, following the death of his
wife Tetty in 1752. No previous biographer had even hinted at this possibility. Most assumed, if they thought about the subject at all, that
Johnson's attitude towards second marriage was encapsulated by his

aphorism: the triumph of hope over experience. But in 1936, a letter to *The Times* announced that a hoard of previously unseen Boswell papers had been found: among them two quarto sheets in Boswell's hand. The context made it clear that they were entries copied from Johnson's diary; it seems likely that these were copied out on the occasion described in the *Life of Johnson,* when Boswell came across Johnson's diary by accident during a visit to Johnson's lodgings in Bolt Court, and surreptitiously started reading. The diary entries showed that Johnson had planned to take a second wife in 1753, a little more than a year after Tetty's death. They provided no clue to her identity.

This was important evidence about Johnson. His strange marriage to a woman twenty years his senior, his ostentatious grief after her death—which Hawkins and many others since have felt to be exaggerated—his apparent remorse for sins unspecified, and his relations with women generally are topics which have exercised biographers from Hawkins onwards; this new clue has caused all of them to be reassessed. But as well as opening up a fresh perspective on Johnson, the discovery of these two quarto pages posed an intriguing question about the man who copied them out. Why is there no mention of Johnson's plan to take a second wife in Boswell's *Life of Johnson*?

There can be no doubt that Boswell regarded these diary entries, and the revelation they contained, as significant. That he chose to copy out these and not some other extracts from the diary in itself suggests that he thought them the most important of any that he was able to read there. He was copying these at Johnson's lodgings, where he might be interrupted at any moment. The fact that he managed to copy down only a few entries suggests that he was hurried; and the fact that he did not tell Johnson what he had done (though he admitted to having read some of the diary) suggests that he was afraid of Johnson's reaction. But he was prepared to risk Johnson's displeasure, because he wanted his own record of this intriguing autobiographical fragment. Boswell was fascinated by every detail of Johnson's life; he must have been particularly excited by this disclosure, so unexpected that no one would even guess at it over the century and a half to follow. As Johnson's biographer, he knew that he was in possession of a scoop, information that perhaps nobody else alive (apart from Johnson himself) knew. So why did he suppress it?

One explanation for this omission can be dismissed: that Boswell had forgotten what he had learned in Johnson's diary when he came to write his biography, ten years later. Apart from being implausible in itself, there is evidence to the contrary: in a letter from Temple to Boswell written on 11 March 1792, after the publication of the *Life of Johnson,* in response to a letter from Boswell, now lost. Temple refers to Boswell's own plans to marry again, and then remarks that "the similar circumstance you mention of Johnson is curious, and as it serves still further to paint the man, and to shew the tender sensibility of his mind, ought to enrich your next edition."[15]

It seems unlikely that Boswell declined to mention the subject simply out of delicacy. For one thing, Boswell's inclination was always to publish facts that he knew to be true, even if others often considered it inappropriate to do so; but anyway, this was not news that most people would have considered inappropriate to publish, as the reaction from Temple (a cautious country clergyman) shows. When Johnson became a widower, he was still in his early forties, seven years younger than Boswell would be when Margaret died. Johnson had no children of his own, and no other dependants, his stepdaughter being a mere six years younger than him. Of his two stepsons, one had become a prosperous merchant, the other a naval officer. There was no reason, moral or legal, why Johnson should not marry again. There was certainly no eighteenth-century bar against doing so. Indeed, because so many wives died young, particularly in childbirth, it was common for widowers to marry for a second or even a third time. Given that Johnson remained a widower for more than thirty years, it would appear natural to ask whether he had ever contemplated remarriage, even if there were no evidence for it. The more one thinks about the subject, the more surprising it seems that the possibility of Johnson's marrying again is never mentioned in Boswell's otherwise exhaustive biography. The fact that Boswell himself was thinking of marrying a second time while he was finishing the *Life of Johnson* makes it more surprising still. And if we consider that Boswell had no need to speculate, that he *knew* Johnson had planned to remarry, his silence on this subject becomes more than merely surprising; one is forced to conclude that he must have had some strong reason for omitting it.

One reason why Boswell might not have wanted to reveal Johnson's plan to take a second wife is that it could have undermined his case against Mrs Piozzi. He had benefited from the revulsion felt by many of Johnson's friends and admirers towards her second marriage. The indignation against Mrs Piozzi would lose some of its force if it became generally known that Johnson too had planned to marry for a second time, at a similar age.

Another explanation for Boswell's reticence on this subject, advanced by the most famous of all Boswell scholars, Frederick A. Pottle, is that Boswell did not mention Johnson's plans to marry again because he could not cite the source of his information. Both Boswell and Hawkins had dipped into Johnson's diaries without his permission; and though both subsequently confessed, each may have felt constrained from using anything to Johnson's detriment they had found there; especially as Johnson had indicated, by the act of burning the diaries, that he wanted them suppressed. Boswell and Hawkins had come to an agreement "upon a delicate question" during their conversation over tea at Langton's house in 1786. Part of that agreement seems to have been to confine any mention of Johnson's suspected sexual irregularities to the period when he was living apart from his wife and associating with Savage. Did they also agree not to use any "delicate" matter from the diaries? To have done so, Pottle argues, would have been an abuse of Johnson's trust. This, then, is the explanation for the otherwise curious omission of Johnson's plans to take a second wife from Boswell's biography, and perhaps from Hawkins's also.[16]

Pottle's argument works better if the diaries each perused were the ones Johnson wanted destroyed at his death. In fact, while this was probably true for Boswell, the evidence for Hawkins points the other way. Another weakness in the argument is that both Boswell and Hawkins describe Johnson's reaction on discovering that each had looked into his diaries: neither description suggests that Johnson was anxious about anything that they might have read there, nor that he made any injunction against mentioning any part of their content. Indeed, he seems to have received the news complacently from both (though he was very anxious in each instance that the diaries should be returned).

But in any case, why should the subject have been thought "delicate"? If Johnson himself had been prepared to marry again, surely there was no reason for his biographers not to mention the fact after his death? If both Boswell and Hawkins felt constrained by loyalty to the memory of their friend, why should they have been willing to speculate about sexual transgressions, for which (so far as we know) no direct evidence existed? Why deal with Johnson's alleged adultery, but stop short of his planned second marriage?

In weighing the importance of any agreement between the rival biographers, it may be significant that Hawkins failed to mention in the first edition of his book that he had pocketed a volume of Johnson's diaries while Johnson was dying, but added a long account of this incident to the second edition, published later that same year. Perhaps Boswell's moves to obtain from him the papers (especially the diaries) remaining in his possession prompted Hawkins to place his own version of the story on record before Boswell could do so. Though Boswell and Hawkins achieved a degree of rapprochement when they met in the spring of 1788 to hand over Johnson's papers, this subsequently deteriorated. It seems that Boswell may have been influenced by Malone to denigrate Hawkins in his *Life of Johnson*.[17] On 5 March 1789, Boswell wrote to Temple, asking his advice on some wording:

> In censuring Sir J. Hawkins's book, I say "there is throughout the whole of it a dark uncharitable cast which puts the most unfavourable construction on every circumstance of my illustrious friend's conduct." Malone maintains *cast* will not do. He will have *malignancy*. Is that not too strong?

In this letter Boswell resurrected his resentment, apparently buried at their meeting a year earlier, at the way he had been described in Hawkins's book. "Hawky is no doubt very malevolent," he observed to Temple. This is a very different attitude from the one displayed in Boswell's journal record of the meeting between the two rival biographers, in which Hawkins is described as behaving "politely" and "serenely," and the business as being conducted "in perfect good humour."

If the concordat between Boswell and Hawkins had broken down by the time Boswell came to revise his manuscript, he would have had less reason to feel bound by any agreement reached between them.

Hawkins had died by this time (though Langton remained as witness to their agreement). Boswell might well have thought it prudent to stick to their decision to place Johnson's possible infidelities within the period when he was associating with Savage. This was undoubtedly "a delicate question." But there was no reason why he should not have mentioned Johnson's intention to marry again unless he had specifically agreed with Hawkins not to do so—and there is no evidence that Hawkins was even aware of it.

Another theory about why Boswell omitted any mention of Johnson's proposed second marriage has been advanced by the Johnsonian collectors Donald and Mary Hyde.[18] They argue that Johnson's plan to remarry did not fit with Boswell's conception of Johnson, in particular with Boswell's conception of Johnson's marriage to Elizabeth Porter. In his *Life of Johnson,* Boswell was critical of the unflattering portrait Hawkins had painted of Johnson's marriage; his own description of the marriage was much more favourable. Hawkins had portrayed Tetty as an embarrassment, drunken and grotesque, and had suggested that Johnson's feelings towards her were "dissembled," hinting that his real motive was to obtain her dowry; in contrast, Boswell emphasized his feelings of loyalty and tenderness towards her. Johnson's love for Tetty was "of the most ardent kind," Boswell insisted: "Why Sir John Hawkins should unwarrantably take upon him even to *suppose* that Johnson's fondness for her was *dissembled* (meaning simulated or assumed), and to assert, that if it was not the case, 'it was a lesson he had learned by rote,' I cannot conceive; unless it proceeded from a want of similar feelings in his own breast."[19] This was a clever strike at Hawkins, the son of a carpenter, who had married a very wealthy woman. But in his attempt to right what he believed to be the wrongs perpetrated by Hawkins, Boswell went to the other extreme. Many of his contemporaries thought that he had sentimentalized the relations between Johnson and Tetty.

Perhaps he had. He could scarcely consider Johnson's feelings for his wife without considering his own; as he sketched his picture of Johnson's marriage, Boswell could hear Margaret coughing up blood in the next room. For more than ten years, Boswell had been aware that Margaret was afflicted with a fatal condition, one that had already carried off most of her family. Watching his own wife wasting away, it was natural for Boswell to identify with Johnson, tenderly caring for Tetty in her final illness. And now that he was a widower himself, his grief led him to idealize his dead wife, to wish that he had been a better husband, and to insist on his enduring love for her. Being the man he was, he naturally projected these feelings onto the man he was writing about.

The passage in which Boswell takes Hawkins to task for suggesting that Johnson's fondness for Tetty was dissembled continues as follows:

> To argue from her being much older than Johnson, or any other circum-
> stances, that he could not really love her, is absurd; for love is not the
> subject of reasoning, but of feeling, and therefore there are no common
> principles upon which one can persuade another concerning it. Every man
> feels for himself, and knows how he is affected by particular qualities in the
> person he admires, the impressions of which are too minute and delicate to
> be substantiated in language.

"Every man feels for himself": who can doubt that Boswell was think-ing of Margaret when he wrote these lines?

Donald and Mary Hyde were the first to identify Hill Boothby as the most likely candidate to become Johnson's second wife. If she was the woman he had contemplated marrying in 1753, then there is no need for any further elaboration: her decision to undertake the care of the orphaned children of her friend Mary Meynell, and her subsequent death, are sufficient to explain why Johnson's plans came to nothing. The evidence in favour of Miss Boothby as the object of Johnson's affection is powerful, if not absolutely conclusive. It is remarkable, however, that none of Johnson's contemporaries suspected his inten-tion to marry Hill Boothby, not even after his fervent letters to her were published in Mrs Piozzi's collection. Boswell himself does not seem to have guessed that she was the one he intended to marry. He must have wondered whom Johnson had in mind. Perhaps he reached a conclu-sion about the mystery woman's identity which he disliked, and which he thought did no credit to the memory of his friend, so that it was better suppressed?

One of the possibilities considered and rejected by the Hydes is that Johnson may have intended to marry Anna Williams, a woman whom

Boswell describes as being "of more than ordinary talents and litera-ture." Miss Williams moved in with Johnson soon after Tetty's death and remained with him (almost uninterrupted) until she died. In John-son's lifetime some of his friends speculated that he had formed a "criminal connection" with her, as an explanation why he tolerated her scolding. Boswell tended to dismiss the idea, maybe because he found it repellent. Her appearance was plain, but Johnson was short-sighted; she was a few years older than Johnson, but much younger than Tetty. Miss Williams had come to London in the hope that an operation on the cataracts in her eyes might lead to a cure; in fact she became totally blind. If Johnson had planned to marry her, this tragedy would have been reason enough to call off the marriage.

Perhaps Boswell thought that Johnson had intended to marry Anna Williams; perhaps not. What is clear is that Johnson's plan to marry for a second time was a minefield for a biographer. For Boswell in particu-lar, it raised all the questions which he would prefer not to have to answer. He had formed his conception of Johnson's character before he chanced upon Johnson's diaries, and he preferred to stick to what he thought he knew.

Though Boswell was energetic in his pursuit of biographical mate-rial, he was capable of ignoring facts that seemed irreconcilable with a wider truth, or even of inventing facts to suit his purpose when his psy-chological need to do so was strong enough. In 1776, for example, he had conducted a long interview with the dying philosopher David Hume, whose biography he was hoping to write. Boswell was dis-tressed by Hume's consistent rejection of the concept of an afterlife, and earnestly tried to persuade him to recant. When Hume died, hav-ing steadfastly refused to do so, Boswell was very disturbed. That such a powerful intellect could contemplate oblivion composedly was upset-ting; for years Boswell read and re-read Hume's works, and practised arguments to refute them. At last, nearly eight years later, he dreamed that he had found Hume's diary, revealing that Hume had indeed been "a Christian and a very pious man." This dream reassured him, and afterwards he was tranquil again.[20]

The Hydes contend that it suited Boswell to show Johnson as a heartbroken widower, so overcome by grief that he devoted himself entirely to his wife's memory. This is consistent with the idealized portrait Boswell gives us of the marriage, and indeed the heroic portrait he paints of Johnson himself. For Boswell, Johnson was a moral giant, capable of human weakness, susceptible to temptation, but triumphing over both by the force of his intellect and still more by the strength of his character. The Johnson that Boswell held up as an exemplar to the world was incapable of ignoble or unworthy action. It was important to Boswell to explain his hero's transgressions, to mitigate his faults, and to conceal behaviour that could not be explained.

"I had now resolved *Life* into my own feelings."[21] This remark, in Boswell's journal for 7 December 1789, remains obscure. The context suggests that Boswell had overcome his fear that he might not be able to finish the book. But another way to read Boswell's meaning is as an expression of a fundamental truth, that in order to understand the experience of another, we must relate it to our own. Boswell's Johnson is an heroic expression of Boswell himself.

On 14 May 1790, Boswell's oldest surviving friend, the Reverend William Temple, arrived in London. He brought with him his daughter Nancy, who was a year older than Boswell's daughter Veronica. Boswell insisted that the two Temples should be his guests.

Boswell and Temple had maintained a most intimate correspondence for well over thirty years, since their mid-teens, when they had been classmates together at Edinburgh University. Each had confided to the other his innermost thoughts, hopes, dreams, and follies; each had comforted the other at moments of misery; each had tried to provide the other with sensible advice. Their friendship was, to some extent, one-sided: Boswell led a much more exciting life than Temple, who seemed to derive vicarious pleasure from reading about Boswell's experiences. For Boswell, there was the pleasure of displaying the contents of his mind to his appreciative friend. "You have told me that I was the most *thinking* man you ever knew," he had written to Temple, a year before this meeting: "I am continually *conscious,* continually *looking back* or *looking forward* and wondering how I shall feel in situations which I anticipate in fancy."[22]

It was strange for two men who had shared so much at long distance to be in close proximity. They had not seen each other for seven years; Boswell was pleased to perceive no alteration in Temple's outward appearance, though he was struck by the feebleness of his manner. But he had little time to reflect on this, for the very next day he was dragged away by Lord Lonsdale to his seat at Laleham in Middlesex, about seventeen miles from town. Boswell had tried to cry off, complaining to Lonsdale that it was hard on him to have to leave his friend who had only just arrived from Cornwall; but his complaints only irritated the tyrant, who "was violent and abusive, talking of what strange company I kept—Sir Joshua, etc, etc, etc." Boswell indignantly protested that he felt honoured to be admitted into such company.

After two nights away with Lonsdale, Boswell returned to London in time to dine with his guest, and over the next few weeks the two friends were often alone together. Boswell took the opportunity to discuss his situation with Temple. He felt degraded by Lonsdale's treatment, and had begun to think of severing their connection. But even so, he found it difficult to let go of the hope that Lonsdale might bring him into Parliament. Temple advised his old friend to wait until the General Election; if Lonsdale did not give Boswell a seat in Parliament then, to gradually withdraw from him.

Unfortunately, Boswell now sank into one of his depressions. Temple said he had never seen anybody so idle; Boswell scarcely seemed able to take the necessary trouble to prepare his book for the press. Though Temple had some reason to be irritated with his host, his accusation of idleness was unfair. It was true that Boswell was slow, easily discouraged, and often disheartened. But in other respects he was far from idle; on the contrary, his diligence, his perseverance, and his almost obsessive desire for accuracy were remarkable by any standard. On 8 June, for example, he went to Sewell's, the Cornhill bookseller, to obtain yet another little piece of information for his book; "hundreds of such pieces of trouble have I been obliged to take in the course of the printing." He formed the habit of calling at Sir Joshua's with a proof-sheet in his pocket; if any of the company there happened to have been present at a conversation recorded on the relevant proof, he would ask them to look it over and to correct any mistakes.[23]

Boswell continued to receive a trickle of letters offering him Johnsoniana, some valuable, some less so. The occasional letter arrived from a crazed individual who felt an affiliation with Johnson even though he had none. Others were self-serving: from people who felt that their own importance had been understated, or who wished to make use of this opportunity to flatter a patron. Boswell's *Life of Johnson* was likely to be widely read; it was it rumoured to be encyclopaedic; its scope suggested that it might become, as Boswell intended, a permanent record of life and letters in the middle years of the century. Those wishing to present themselves to posterity in a flattering light knew that Boswell controlled the illumination.

Even Boswell recognized that he would have to stop revising the manuscript sooner or later if the book was ever to be published. The first draft had been finished more than a year before; much of the manuscript had now been revised and polished, and several hundred pages printed. As the book proceeded, it became increasingly difficult to incorporate fresh material. Hitherto Boswell had accepted anything that he was offered almost indiscriminately, provided that it seemed authentic. Now, perhaps influenced by Malone, he began to adopt a more pragmatic policy. When something special cropped up, Boswell was prepared to find a space for it, even at this late stage. Sometimes the press halted, while Boswell sought the answer to a query. But when the information on offer was of little interest, second-hand, or of doubtful authenticity, or when it seemed likely to duplicate material already obtained from other sources, he turned it away. Of course, in doing so he allowed the occasional nugget to spill over the edge of his pan.

On the morning of 14 June, Boswell's servant James found him at Dilly's; Lonsdale had sent for him, twice. Apparently the Recorder was needed in Carlisle, to determine the Poor Rate, and Lonsdale wanted him to stay on there for the upcoming election, due to take place in four weeks' time. Boswell was reluctant to be away for so long, while Temple was in London, and while Malone was available to help with the *Life of Johnson;* Lonsdale said meanly that this was all he had to do to earn his salary of twenty pounds. Two of Lonsdale's hangers-on hinted to Boswell that he must not hang back *now*. He found himself coerced into agreeing, but felt so agitated that he "rashly went three times in the course of this day to a stranger." In the evening he sought out Malone, whose advice was to do as Lonsdale asked for now, and to ascertain whether he meant to bring Boswell into Parliament; if it proved not, to withdraw from so disagreeable a connection. Boswell groaned. After a restless night, he called again on Lonsdale, offering to go to Carlisle for the election, but asking to be spared for the moment. Lonsdale told Boswell that he must go immediately, unless he wanted to resign the office of Recorder. Boswell then calmly offered to resign. Lonsdale muttered that this would be very inconvenient and reflect badly on him, for having chosen Boswell in the first place. "My Lord," said Boswell, "I'll go directly, do the business handsomely, and then resign with a good grace." Appeased, the Earl told him that he intended to set out at four or five o'clock the following morning, and it was arranged that he should send for Boswell when he was ready to depart. Boswell went to bed "with the stillness of a desperate man," prepared to be called at four. But in the morning there was no word from Lonsdale. Boswell waited at home all day. Malone called on him, and together they arranged for work on the *Life of Johnson* to continue in Boswell's absence. At eleven o'clock that night, Boswell received a note from Lonsdale summoning him to breakfast the *next* morning. He duly arrived at nine; no sign of Lonsdale. He waited almost two hours, before going home for a while and then returning. Lonsdale, now at breakfast with one of his cronies and a servant, was irritable, accusing Boswell of having a "sinister motive" for not wanting to go. "I suppose you think we are fond of your company," Lonsdale said angrily. "You are mistaken. We don't care for it." The tirade continued. "I suppose you thought I was to bring you into Parliament. I never had any such intention."

The rancour persisted throughout the afternoon, until Lonsdale was at last ready to leave. Taking Boswell under his arm, he walked by Grosvenor Square towards Oxford Street, where the coach was wait-ing. Lonsdale expressed the opinion that Boswell, if brought into Par-liament, would "get drunk and make a foolish speech." Boswell was stung into expressing his unwillingness to take up a seat unless special terms were granted, consistent with his liberal and independent views. This show of defiance enraged Lonsdale. In the coach his passion rose "almost to madness"; he uttered some "shocking words" to Boswell, followed by the challenge, "Take it as you will. I am ready to give you satisfaction." He continued with another insult. "What are *you*, Sir?" Boswell, stunned, replied that he was a gentleman, a man of honour, and hoped to show himself such. "You will be settled when you have a bullet in your belly," Lonsdale remarked brutally.

They stopped for the night at Barnet. Boswell remonstrated with Lonsdale that he had been treated very unjustly. "I am ready to give you satisfaction now," raged Lonsdale: "I have pistols here." But Boswell had no pistol, and Lonsdale refused to lend him one. After a cold dinner, Boswell apologized. They drank a glass of wine together. Then Lonsdale held out his hand, saying: "Boswell, forget all that is past." The journey continued the next day; there were no further arguments, but Boswell felt as wretched as a convict heading for captivity. He was inwardly mortified to think that he had deceived himself so woefully, and reflected gloomily that he was "now obliged to submit to what was very disagreeable to me without any reward or hope of any good, but merely to get out of the scrape into which I had brought myself."

Lonsdale stopped at Lancaster for some electioneering, while Boswell travelled on to Carlisle by mail-coach. He arrived dejected and insignificant. The weather was wet; he had very little to do; and he knew virtually nobody in Carlisle except the mayor. He was suffering from yet another venereal infection, which made it painful to walk. One morning he awoke from a nightmare, and thought of his father. "What was I doing here at Carlisle? In what a scattered state was the Family of Auchinleck?"

The next week passed slowly. Boswell remained indoors much of the time, sitting by the fire. Only recently he had boasted to one of Lonsdale's cronies that he was "as proud as Lucifer"; now he begged another of them to be allowed to leave, pleading that his venereal infection required urgent treatment. While he waited, all Boswell's familiar obsessions took hold of him once more: he had achieved nothing, he was despicable, he would be forced to retreat to the country. He felt a dead indifference to the election, now that all prospects of advancement by means of Lonsdale were cut off. He wrote several letters bemoaning his miserable existence. "What galls me and irritates me with impatience," he complained to Malone, "is the thought that I lose those hours which you could now have given me for revising my M.S. and that perhaps you may be gone before I get back to town." There were 350 pages of manuscript yet to be gone over by Malone, Boswell reported to Forbes; only one-third of the book had been printed before he left London for Carlisle. Boswell received a letter from Temple, informing the absent host that his guests were returning to Cornwall. Boswell's reply was distraught: "How unfortunate! to be obliged to leave my friend and interrupt my work! Never was a poor ambitious projector more mortified. I am suffering without any prospect of reward, and only from my own folly."[24]

At last Lonsdale and his retinue arrived in Carlisle. Boswell perceived with amazement that Lonsdale was indifferent to his suffering; "he is certainly the most *cruel* man on earth." A local barber-surgeon carried out a minor operation on his sore, which provided some relief; it being a Sunday, Boswell attended church afterwards.

Lonsdale's behaviour veered between violent abuse and conciliation. Boswell was asked to negotiate on Lonsdale's behalf with the opposing candidates; when he tried to do so, Lonsdale flew into another fury. The next day Boswell spoke in the Town Hall on the issue of honorary freemen, restating Lonsdale's position clearly and forcefully; afterwards Lonsdale was polite, even whispering to Boswell that he might have a glass of Madeira, followed by claret at dinner. He now promised to release Boswell on the following Monday, once the polls closed. It was arranged that Boswell's second daughter, Euphemia, would come down from Edinburgh to join him in Carlisle, so that they might travel on to London together.

That evening Boswell and several other members of Lonsdale's entourage were compelled to sit up late with their master, who slept part of the time, snoring. Boswell felt tired and humiliated. "What sunk me very low," he wrote in his journal afterwards,

> was the sensation that I was precisely as when in wretched spirits thirty years ago, without any addition to my character from having had the friendship of Dr Johnson and many eminent men, made the tour of Europe, and Corsica in particular, and written two very successful books. I

was as a board on which fine figures had been painted, but which some corrosive application had reduced to its original nakedness.[25]

During the last weekend before the election, tension between the rival camps reached boiling-point. Lonsdale's technique of steamrollering all opposition by creating large numbers of "honorary freemen," whose only function was to vote for his candidates, was unpopular and much resented. A large group of armed men, estimated at one thousand strong, proposed to carry the opposing candidates aloft through the town, as the moral if not the actual victors. Lonsdale had gone to the country for the weekend, leaving orders that any such "chairing" should be prevented; if necessary, the militia should be called out to keep order. As one of the magistrates, Boswell found himself responsible for enforcing Lonsdale's commands. He was swearing in constables at the militia's garrison when the mob arrived, chasing the militia-men inside. Stones rattled against the windows. Boswell became scared, fearing that he might be killed. Twice he went outside, signalling to the protesters to desist; but flying stones forced him back into the house. Eventually the mob dispersed, to chair the opposing candidates through the town. About three dozen militia-men had been injured, some of them severely.

On the Monday when Boswell was due to depart, Lonsdale insisted that he should stay a while longer, to prosecute some innkeepers accused of selling ale without a valid licence (their licences having been granted by Lonsdale's sworn rival, the Duke of Norfolk). Boswell was annoyed to be detained further, but he felt that he had no choice. On Wednesday morning Boswell duly convicted the innkeepers, imposing a fine of forty shillings upon each of them. He was urged to seize their licences, but he doubted if he had the power to do this, now that he had tendered his resignation as Recorder. This sparked another outburst from Lonsdale: Boswell was trying to get off, he had sent for his daughter as a pretence, he had assumed Lonsdale would bring him into Parliament, he had done everything wrong since leaving London, he had earnestly asked for the Recordership, then thrown it up in the most unhandsome manner. While Lonsdale raved, Boswell wisely kept silent.

The poll was concluded, and Lonsdale's candidates returned. Afterwards Lonsdale recovered his good humour. "You won't go before dinner?" he asked Boswell hospitably. The dinner was hearty, with many songs sung, and they remained at the table until after eleven at night; then Lonsdale invited Boswell to join him in his private dining-room for some fruit. Boswell "played the game all through and went, hugging myself at the thought of being free from him and setting out early the next morning." More wine appeared. Boswell was careful not to say anything that might give the slightest pretext for further delay. It was almost two when he returned to his lodgings, drowsy with the wine. After only a few hours' sleep, he set out early with Euphemia; they arrived in London two days later, driving all day and all night in the stage-coach from York. He had been Lonsdale's prisoner for exactly a month; at last he was free.

While he had been confined in Carlisle, Boswell had sent Malone a letter soaked in self-pity. "I do not think it is in the power of words to convey to you how miserable I have been since I left you," he bewailed. All his ambitions seemed at an end; his fortune was sadly encumbered; his children seemed a burden; his sore troubled him; he had been dragged away from his friend Temple. Perhaps worst of all, he had been forced to interrupt his *Life of Johnson*, "the most important, perhaps *now* the only concern of any consequence that I ever shall have in this world."[26]

STRUGGLE

—◀╍╍╢╟╍╍▶—

I am at last to deliver to the world a work which I have long promised, and of which, I am afraid, too high expectations have been raised.[1]

BOSWELL WAS PLEASANTLY SURPRISED to find that his *Life of Johnson* had advanced another twenty pages while he had been away, supervised by "my kind and active friend" Malone. He felt relief at being liberated from Lonsdale; it was a pleasure just to hold a proof-sheet, and to be able to call at Baldwin's to chat to the compositor and the corrector. Logically, he should now have concentrated on his book, taking advantage of whatever time remained before Malone left for Ireland. There was much remaining to be done, revising the first draft to feed the press at one end and correcting proofs as they emerged from the printer at the other. But Malone was often busy correcting the proofs of his own book, his edition of Shakespeare; and when he was alone, Boswell was too depressed to persevere. He had been scarred by his humiliating experiences with Lonsdale; his mind was "sore from the severe bruise it had suffered." His insignificance had been brutally emphasized; his ambition to become an MP had been crushed. Like a ship battered by a tremendous hurricane, he could now only drift, "conscious of being carried along the stream of life with no steady direction."[2]

Rather than knuckle down to work, Boswell grasped at any distraction. Though his spirits quickly recovered, he could not bear to remain long at home, now that he lacked the comforting presence of his wife. Almost every day, he would saunter out in search of company. He dined away from home four or five times a week; these dinners were usually convivial occasions, often lasting hours, and washed down by copious quantities of drink; he was seldom capable of any literary work afterwards. Despite the support of Malone, Reynolds, Courtenay, and other friends, Boswell was lonely; there was a sense of desperation in the way he ventured out time after time, looking for something—anything—to distract him. A week after his return from Carlisle, for example, he called at Baldwin's, and then dined at Dilly's; afterwards he called at four coffee-houses in succession without meeting anyone he knew. As he wandered the streets, his pocket was picked; he lost a proof-sheet of his *Life of Johnson,* and the accompanying manuscript; fortunately, all but two lines were already set in type, and he was able to supply the deficiency later from memory. Finally, he came to Reynolds's, where he found Malone; together the three men played whist and supped.

Even at Sir Joshua's, Boswell could sometimes be restless; he preferred hearty masculine society, and if there were ladies present, he was discontent, unless there was "something to *interest* me." One evening, after the ladies had left, Reynolds and Malone reproached him for showing an ungracious reluctance to join their guests in a hand of whist. Increasingly, he enjoyed formal occasions, such as those day-long City banquets, punctuated by toasts and speeches, when several hundred prosperous men sat down to stuff themselves with food and drink; he was a lively companion who could be relied upon to push the bottle about. Boswell and Reynolds formed an ambition of dining with all the City Companies of London; heroes of the table, they were "two inseparable companions of the illustrious Order of the Knife and Fork." Afterwards the befuddled Boswell often found himself in the arms of a whore.

He made no effort to revive his dormant legal practice. He would return to the law in earnest, he told himself, once the book was finished. When that would be was still uncertain. The end was like a mirage, vanishing as he approached; there seemed to be more and more material to insert, so that the book grew steadily in size. By the late summer, Boswell was forced to acknowledge that it would have to be published in two volumes after all, both of at least five hundred pages, each priced at a guinea. The printer had reached page 456 of the first volume; the backlog was such that two compositors were put onto the job. "When does your much desired, and long expected work come out?" inquired Barnard from Ireland. "If it does not soon appear we shall grow as outrageous as the galleries at Drury Lane. Shall we have it next season or not? Confess the truth."[3]

On the eve of his fiftieth birthday, Boswell wrote a note in his journal summing up his state of mind:

> My life at present, though for some time my health and spirits have been wonderfully good, is surely as idly spent as can almost be imagined. I merely attend to the progress of my *Life of Johnson,* and that by no means with great assiduity, such as that which Malone employs on Shakespeare. I am losing for myself and children all the benefits of a fine Place in the country. I am following no profession. I fear I am gradually losing any claim to preferment in the law in Scotland. But with the *consciousness* which I have of the nature of my own mind, I am sure that I am escaping innumerable hours of uneasiness which I should have were I in Scotland. I am in that great scene which I have ever contemplated with admiration, and in which there are continual openings for advantage.[4]

Boswell thought that he glimpsed such an opening later in the year, when a rumour spread that Sir Adam Fergusson, who had once again been elected MP for Ayrshire in the summer General Election, was about to resign from Parliament, to take up a post on the Government pay-roll. Boswell swung into action. He had long been convinced that Pitt and his ministers were indebted to him for writing his first *Letter to the People of Scotland* (1783), attacking Fox's East India Bill. Fox's attempted reform of the East India Company was indeed the issue that had precipitated the collapse of the Fox–North coalition nearly seven years before. Boswell's pamphlet had been a useful piece of propaganda against the outgoing coalition, though no more than that. At the time, Pitt had sent him a letter commending his "zealous and able support" of the public cause—a document Boswell thought worthy of quoting in a footnote to the *Life of Johnson.*[5] Dundas too had written to congratulate him. Over the years Boswell's pleasure at this attention had hardened into resentment at the Ministry's subsequent neglect. The moment had surely come to claim his reward. He dashed off a reminder to Dundas:

> I assure you *solemnly upon my honour* that in the year 1784 when I was of no inconsiderable service to the present administration, you gave me your *word* and *hand,* after dinner at Hillhead that you would give me your interest to be member for my own county, which has ever been and ever will be the fond object of my ambition. I have never claimed that *promise,* because it was made after we had participated largely of your generous wines . . .[6]

Dundas's reply suggested that Boswell's memory was at fault. The rumour that Fergusson was about to resign his seat turned out to be wrong anyway. And even if Dundas had made Boswell such a promise back in 1784, Boswell's second *Letter to the People of Scotland* the following year, attacking Dundas's plan to reduce the number of Lords of Session, had exhausted any credit his first pamphlet had earned him. It was no good expecting favours from the Government if you supported it one year and then attacked it the next.

A week or so before this, Boswell had attended the Lord Mayor's Feast at the Guildhall. Pitt was guest of honour; it seemed an ideal opportunity for Boswell to proclaim his loyalty to the Prime Minister. Knowing Pitt to be an honorary member of the Worshipful Company of Grocers, Boswell had composed a ballad, "The Grocer of London," celebrating Pitt's defence of British trade. (He had this printed and distributed as a broadside.) At some point in the proceedings, he stood up and burst into song. There were two stanzas, each followed by a chorus:

> There's a Grocer of London,
> A Grocer of London
> A Grocer of London who watches our trade,
> And takes care of th'estate of JOHN BULL.

The audience at the Lord Mayor's banquet liked Boswell's commercial sentiments, and encouraged him to recite the ballad no fewer than six times. By one eye-witness account, Pitt sat unsmiling through the performance, before relaxing and joining in the general laughter "at the oddity of Mr Boswell's character"; by another, he had left the table before the tribute was delivered. In any case, it was ineffective.[7]

One summer evening Boswell dined in fashionable company at No. 82 Piccadilly, in a room on the third floor commanding a spectacular view over Green Park, with the Queen's House (the London home of the Royal Family) and Westminster Abbey in the foreground and the Surrey hills in the distance. "How delightful it is to see the country and be sure you are not in it," he exclaimed. He found country life depressing, and he considered any possible move back to Auchinleck as a "retreat"; nevertheless, he had lost none of his feudal enthusiasm. Though he had not been to Auchinleck for nearly a year and would rarely go there again, he was determined to buy the adjoining property of Knockroon when it came up for sale in the autumn. Knockroon had been part of the Auchinleck estate until 1609, and had been owned by cousins ever since; Boswell could not bear to see "a piece of—as it were the flesh and blood of the family, in the hands of a stranger."[8] He paid over the odds—£2,500—to secure it, even though he was already encumbered with debt. This was the fourth parcel of land Boswell had purchased: the first, the moorland farm of Dalblair, as long ago as 1767. He regarded these purchases as an achievement, his own contribution to the Family of Auchinleck, even though the rent-roll from the land merely served to pay the interest on the sums he had borrowed to buy it in the first place. Boswell was haunted by the memory of his friend John Johnston, whose debts had been such that he was unable to hand over to his heirs the lands that he had inherited from his ancestors. He always referred to Johnston as "Grange," following the convention that a hereditary landowner was known by the name of his property. By surrendering his estate, Johnston had lost his identity.

To raise the purchase price for Knockroon, Boswell took out a mortgage for £1,500, but he was not at all sure how to find the other £1,000 which would become due in May 1791, especially as he would soon have to repay a further £500 that he had borrowed from a City merchant to lend to a cousin ten years earlier. He was tempted by an offer from George Robinson, a bookseller-publisher who mentioned to Malone his interest in buying the copyright in the *Life of Johnson*. "Only think of what an offer I have for it," Boswell boasted to Langton: *"A cool thousand."*[9] A thousand pounds was indeed a very handsome sum, perhaps five times the going rate for a quarto volume. "I am a bold man to have refused a cool thousand," he suggested to his cousin Robert Boswell. Growing bolder still, Boswell informed Forbes that he would not now accept £1,500 for the copyright in the book: "You cannot imagine what a rich treasure it will contain."[10]

Even at this late stage, Boswell was still soliciting more material for his *Life of Johnson*. Late in October, for example, he sought out Fanny Burney, Charles Burney's novelist daughter. Like her father, she had been a particular friend of Johnson's, whom she revered; unlike him, she was reluctant to entrust Boswell with Johnson's letters, still less to allow him to read extracts from her voluminous private diaries. As former friends of the Thrales, the Burneys were in a delicate position. Habitués of Streatham Park, they had been shocked by Mrs Thrale's decision to marry Piozzi, and had treated her coolly thereafter. Fanny Burney was a particular friend of the Thrales' eldest daughter, Hester Maria, known by Johnson's nickname for her, "Queeney," who had sought to deny her mother custody of her younger sisters after Mrs Thrale's involvement with Piozzi became known.

Fanny Burney's encounter with Boswell, memorably described in her posthumously published diaries, helped to establish the nineteenth-century image of him as a crank, obsessed to the point of absurdity with his *Life of Johnson*. Miss Burney was now one of the Queen's ladies-in-waiting; Boswell took advantage of a trip to nearby Eton, where he was visiting Sandy, in order to call on her at Windsor Castle. He found Miss Burney outside St George's Chapel, and asked for her help:

> "My help?"
>
>   "Yes, Madam; you must give me some of your choice little notes of the Doctor's; we have seen him long enough on stilts; I want to show him in a new light. Grave Sam, and great Sam, and solemn Sam, and learned Sam—

all these he has appeared over and over. Now I want to entwine a wreath of the Graces across his brow; I want to show him as gay Sam, agreeable Sam, pleasant Sam; so you must help me with some of his beautiful billets to yourself."

I evaded this by declaring I had not any stores to hand. He proposed a thousand curious expedients to get at them, but I was invincible . . .

He then told me his *Life of Dr. Johnson* was nearly printed, and took a proof-sheet out of his pocket to show me; with crowds passing and re-passing, knowing me well, for we were now at the iron rails of the Queen's Lodge.

I stopped, I could not ask him in: I saw he expected it, and was reduced to apologize, and tell him I must attend the Queen immediately . . .

Though Fanny Burney slipped through the gate and closed it behind her, Boswell was undeterred, and began to read aloud a letter from Johnson to himself "in a strong imitation of the Doctor's manner." But a crowd was gathering; the sight of a stranger declaiming through the railings presented a spectacle; the King and Queen were approaching from the terraces. Making a quick apology, Miss Burney scurried away. Boswell tried again the next morning, but she remained resolute:

I cannot consent to print private letters, even of a man so justly celebrated, when addressed to myself; no, I shall hold sacred those revered and but too scarce testimonies of the high honour his kindness conferred upon me.[11]

In mid-November 1790, a fortnight or so before his edition of Shakespeare was published, Malone left for Ireland. The two men had not yet finished revising the first draft of the *Life of Johnson,* though they had started more than a year earlier; indeed, they were still less than halfway through the second volume. From this point on, Malone could be of little editorial help to Boswell, beyond providing general advice: "Pray take care of colloquialisms and vulgarisms of all sorts. Condense as much as possible, always preserving perspicuity and do not imagine the *only* defect of style, is repetition of words."[12]

Two weeks after Malone's departure, Boswell wrote to him, quoting several favourable reactions to his Shakespeare. As for the *Life of Johnson,* he reported that Baldwin's compositors had reached page 216 of the second volume. He was still receiving new material, including three of Johnson's letters to Warren Hastings and a long account from Langton of Johnson's visit to Warley Camp in 1778, while Langton was serving there as a captain in the Lincolnshire militia. Boswell continued to send regular reports on his progress to Malone, and twelve days later he was able to announce that he had before him a proof of page 256. He was now hoping that the book could be published on 8 March 1791, Shrove Tuesday. On 17 December, he had a long session with Langton, reviewing and modifying the extensive "collectanea" Langton had given him to date.

Around the end of the year, Boswell took a house at No. 47 Great Portland Street, which was to remain his London address for the rest of his life. At about the same time, he sank into a new depression. Perhaps the house had something to do with his wretched spirits: his bedroom was in the front parlour, where he found it too noisy to sleep easily. He grumbled to Sandy that he was in "such bad spirits that I know not what to do"; he was dejected, fretful, full of woe. While before he had been content to drift, now he began to agonize that he was going nowhere. His money worries had become pressing. Forbes had refused him a loan; he feared that if he failed to raise the £1,000 needed to complete the purchase of Knockroon, he would lose both the property and his good name. "O, could I but get a few thousands," he lamented to Malone, "what a difference it would make upon my state of mind, which is harassed by thinking of my debts."[13] In early February Boswell purchased an expensive lottery ticket, costing more than £16 — a wild throw, and, as it turned out, a vain one. His brother and several of his friends advised him to consolidate, to give up the house in London and return to Auchinleck. But Boswell was not yet ready to entertain "provincial notions." He managed to postpone repayment of the £500 due at the beginning of the year by offering to pay the sum in instalments, with interest.

Boswell was missing Malone, whose good sense and practical advice were as valuable as his editorial help. "Your vigour of mind, and warmth of heart make your friendship of such consequence that it is drawn upon like a bank," he wrote to Malone at the end of January.[14] It was an appropriate metaphor, because Boswell was now desperate enough to ask Malone and even the penniless Courtenay to lend him money (neither was willing to do so). He hesitated whether or not to accept the offer from Robinson for the copyright: was it still open, would he perhaps pay more for two volumes? It was so hard to judge whether the book would sell; perhaps a bird in the hand was worth two in the bush? Over the next couple of months, Boswell timidly sought advice from all sides: some were confident that the book would sell, some less so. He was warned that interest in Johnson was waning; that the public would not pay two guineas* for any biography; and that nobody would read a biography in two thick quarto volumes. "I find so many people shake their heads at two quartos and two guineas," Boswell wrote anxiously to Malone.[15]

Still he laboured onwards. On 18 January 1791, he was able to tell Malone that he was expecting a proof of page 376 of the second volume that same night. He feared that those parts towards the end of the book which had not benefited from Malone's revision would be noticeably inferior, and that the late insertions would stand out awkwardly. The addition of so much extra detail meant that the second volume threatened to be as much as one hundred pages longer than the first. His progress had slowed, so that now only one compositor was required. Eleven days later, page 456 was in proof; one hundred pages of copy remained, and there were still many letters to insert; he had yet to write an account of Johnson's death. "Indeed I go sluggishly and comfortlessly about my work," he complained to Malone. "As I pass your door I cast many a longing look."[16]

On 3 February, Boswell received a visit from the actor, playwright, and manager of the Drury Lane Theatre, John Philip Kemble, who brought with him a note of Johnson's conversation in 1783 with his sister, the celebrated actress Mrs Siddons, which Boswell was to reproduce verbatim in his *Life of Johnson*. Kemble encouraged Boswell to believe that his book would have a great sale, "of which I was now despairing." Two days later, early in the morning, Boswell called on the

---

*Two guineas is forty-two shillings. By comparison, the price of *The Journal of a Tour to the Hebrides* was six shillings; Johnson's *Journey to the Western Islands of Scotland* was five shillings. Both were issued in the smaller octavo size. The normal price for a folio or quarto volume was ten to twelve shillings.

recently knighted Sir William Scott, seeking advice on how to handle a delicate topic: the failure of Lord Thurlow's application to the King for financial support to send Johnson to Italy. It was unthinkable to criticize the sovereign, but it was impossible to avoid the subject. Together they settled the matter: Boswell printed Johnson's spirited reply to the Lord Chancellor's apologetic letter, with only the following comment: "Upon this unexpected failure I abstain from presuming to make any remarks, or to offer any conjectures."[17]

After he left Scott, Boswell breakfasted with Dilly, who was pessimistic about the sale of his *Life of Johnson*. Afterwards Boswell called at a bookshop in St Paul's Churchyard, in order to check some quotations. The bookseller asked him when the book would be ready. "I told him in about a month, but that there would be too much of it. 'Oh no,' said he. 'It will be very entertaining.'"

Five days later Baldwin's compositor had reached page 488, and Boswell was wondering how to conclude his book. Should he print a version of the "Character" of Johnson he had used in the *Tour*? He consulted Malone. Yes, thought Malone, though he advised that it should be expanded and revised, emphasizing Johnson's piety and virtue, and omitting some less dignified details. One such that Malone particularly deplored was a quotation from Boswell's *louche* friend the Earl of Pembroke: "Dr Johnson's sayings would not appear so remarkable, were it not for his *bow-wow way*." Boswell deleted Pembroke's quip from the "Character," but sneaked it in elsewhere.[18]

The "Character" of Johnson in the *Life* was drawn from the *Tour*, but it was based on a much earlier model: Johnson's character-sketch of Savage, which concluded his life of the unhappy poet. Just as Johnson had done, Boswell began with a physical description of his subject, using Johnson's appearance as a key to unlock the secrets of his mind:

> His figure was large and well formed, and his countenance of the cast of an ancient statue; yet his appearance was rendered strange and somewhat uncouth, by convulsive cramps, by the scars of that distemper which it was once imagined the royal touch could cure, and by a slovenly mode of dress. He had the use of only one eye; yet so much does the mind govern and even supply the deficiency of organs, that his visual perceptions, as far as they extended, were uncommonly quick and accurate. So morbid was his

temperament, that he never knew the natural joy of a free and vigorous use of his limbs: when he walked, it was like the struggling gait of one in fetters; when he rode, he had no command or direction of his horse, but was carried as if in a balloon. That with his constitution and habits of life he should have lived seventy-five years, is a proof that an inherent *vivida vis* is a powerful preservative of the human frame.[19]

Boswell attended a meeting of the Club on 8 February 1791; among those present were several MPs, Courtenay, Fox, and William Windham. Boswell was so gloomy that he found even Fox's scintillating company insipid. It seems that at some point he discussed with the others a passage in the *Life of Johnson* that was troubling him, for two days later he wrote to Malone that he had decided to cancel it. "I wonder how you and I admitted this to the public eye for Windham etc. were struck with its *indelicacy* and it might hurt the book much. It is however mighty good stuff." The passage described a conversation between Boswell and Johnson held in 1779, on the subject of conjugal infidelity. During this period, while Boswell was in his late thirties, he had become obsessed with what he usually referred to as "concubinage," quizzing Johnson repeatedly on the matter. On this occasion, pressed by Boswell, Johnson had given his view that infidelity was less culpable in a husband than in a wife; and then had confided that Tetty had given him her permission to "lye with as many women as I pleased, provided I *loved* her alone." Boswell pursued this very interesting topic, and extracted from Johnson a further opinion: that if a woman was "of a very cold constitution," she had no right to complain if her husband went with other women. Boswell was obviously much taken with this line, suggesting that in such instances a husband might make a note in his pocket-book, and then do as he pleased. "Nay, Sir, this is wild indeed," said Johnson, smiling. "You must consider that fornication is a crime in a single man; and you cannot have more liberty by being married."

Following the advice of Windham and the others, Boswell rewrote this passage, removing altogether Tetty's remark that she did not care how many women Johnson went to if he loved her alone, and his own crude proposal for a husband to keep a note in his pocket-book each time his wife refused him. The leaf was cancelled, and a new one printed; but a few of the old leaves survived, to be bound into books, and 138 years later, the discovery of one of these was announced in a letter to the *Times Literary Supplement*.[20]

On 14 February, Boswell took tea with Baldwin's corrector, Thomas Tomlins, a former barrister who had fallen into debt, obliging him to quit the bar. They met to discuss the index, which Tomlins was preparing. Tomlins suggested a novel way to right the imbalance between the two volumes; instead of putting the index at the end, he would put it at the beginning. Boswell readily agreed to this unusual arrangement. Steering the conversation on to the topic of law, he spoke of his desire to get more practice, and Tomlins advised him to let it be known that he meant to apply himself to business as soon as his book was published, and to prove this by constant attendance at Westminster Hall. By studying the recent law-reports and legal textbooks, he might yet do well. Boswell was somewhat encouraged, though he shrank from the necessary labour. He had taken a lease on some chambers at No. 1 Inner Temple Lane, on the very staircase where Johnson had been living when Boswell first visited him in 1763.

Later that day, at a bookseller's in the Strand, he met the playwright Arthur Murphy, who had been commissioned to write a short life of Johnson to be prefixed to a new edition of his works—an honour Boswell had wanted for himself. His *Essay on the Life and Genius of Dr Johnson* was already written, Murphy told Boswell: he had received £200 in payment and it had taken him only a month. Boswell was by now "in great despondency" about the prospects for his book. During a walk in Lincoln's Inn Fields, Dilly advised him to sell the copyright. "I was unwilling to separate myself as an author from Dilly, with whom my name had been so long connected," ruminated Boswell, "though he in a friendly manner pressed it, notwithstanding he should lose seven and a half per cent agency on publication." Dilly confessed that George Steevens—another of his authors—had been talking the book down: maliciously, it seemed. "I believe that in my present frame I should accept even of £500," Boswell wrote despairingly to Malone, "for I suspect that were I now to talk to Robinson I should find him not disposed to give £1000. Did he absolutely *offer* it, or did he only express himself so that you *concluded* he would give it?"[21]

Though the end of his task was in sight, Boswell was still "sadly ill," "dejected and miserable," "sore and fretful." His friends tried to rally him for one last push. Malone again urged him to cut down his drinking: "Is not your depression entirely owing to yourself, I mean to your own almost uniform intemperance in wine?"[22] Temple offered to write every day if it would relieve his friend. "Poor Boswell is very low," Courtenay wrote to Malone,

> and dispirited and almost melancholy mad—feels no spring, no pleasure in existence, and is so perceptibly altered for the worse that it is remarked everywhere. I try all I can to rouse him but he recurs so tiresomely and tediously to the same cursed, trite, commonplace topics about death, etc.—that we grow old, and when we are old we are not young—that I despair of effecting a cure.

Boswell had written to Malone only a few days earlier expressing his concern about Courtenay, who had been declared a bankrupt, escaping imprisonment only because of his immunity as a Member of Parliament. Courtenay's cheerful defiance of his plight eventually shamed Boswell: "His manly mind conveyed to me some sympathetic force."[23]

Courtenay tried to fill the gap left by Malone. He lived only a few doors away in Great Portland Street, and he did what he could both to comfort Boswell and to encourage him forward. He extracted a promise from Boswell not to drink more than four glasses of wine at dinner, and not more than a pint afterwards—until the *Life of Johnson* was finished. He also gave him sensible editorial advice, of the kind that Malone had previously provided. On the evening of 22 February, for example, Courtenay arrived at Boswell's house at about ten o'clock in the evening; after a light supper he helped Boswell to tone down a long passage about Mrs Piozzi near the end of the book. At Courtenay's suggestion, Boswell deleted his emotional denunciations of her behaviour (including his irrational charge that she had made money out of Johnson by publishing his letters), retaining only his more measured criticism of her inaccuracies.

One morning in late February, Boswell woke feeling tearful, after dreaming that his youngest daughter was dead. He sent for her, and was reassured, both by her appearance and by her English accent. On the last night of the month, he had another vivid dream, this time benign: his wife appeared and "pointed out in her own handwriting the propitiation of our Saviour" (in Boswell's eyes, Margaret's handwriting added extra verisimilitude). He woke feeling miraculously recovered from the depression which had weighed on him since the beginning of the year. "Instead of a horror at getting up, I felt an alacrity and, what is truly *amazing,* my mind viewed without depression the very circumstances which had appeared ready to sink me in ruin."

One of those circumstances, his liquidity problem, was solved over the next few days. Baldwin and Dilly each advanced him £200 against expected earnings from the book, and Boswell found that he could borrow a further £600 from an Ayrshire bank against his rent income, due in the summer. As the mists clouding his mind cleared, he felt a surge of energy. One sign of his revival was that he called on Miss Upton, a young lady whom he had admired at church; sadly, she was not at home. Miss Upton and her mother called at Boswell's house later that day, while he was out. When he learned that she had called, Boswell was delighted: "How many *adventures* do I meet with or contrive! But to be *capable* of any at all, after my late wretchedness, is a wonderful change." In truth, he was not so interested in Miss Upton as to pursue her very actively; two years later he was still trying to arrange their first meeting. But the prospect cheered him.

Boswell's renewed vigour gave him strength to cope with "that nervous mortal," his fashionable second cousin, William Gerard Hamilton, who had become agitated about the Johnsoniana he had provided more than three years earlier. He was now asking for his name to be removed from these as the source. Boswell was annoyed, both because he had taken down Hamilton's stories from him in person, and because he disliked having to print material without attributing it to his informants, which he regarded as a mark of authenticity. Courtenay handled the tedious negotiations with Hamilton; it was agreed that Hamilton's name should be removed in several places, at his own expense (the bill for the cancels came to £2 16s).

Another last-minute complication was provided by a series of anxious letters from Percy, who begged and entreated Boswell "before it be too late" to look through his book and cancel any of Johnson's "severe censures on the personal characters of individuals." These were often "hasty escapes," Percy insisted, which if preserved in print would be injurious to the memories of both Johnson and the individuals concerned, and to the book which recorded them. "You know how liable he was to prejudice, and what severe things he would sometimes say of his nearest friends: such effusions he never did nor could seriously mean, should be recorded and transmitted to posterity, as giving their decided characters." Percy urged Boswell to make these cuts, not only out of regard to the memory of their revered friend, but also "out of regard to your own future comfort."

Percy's anxiety had been prompted by Boswell himself, who asked Malone to consult Percy about an allegation of Johnson's which he feared might be libellous. According to Johnson, the historian Richard Rolt had gone over to Ireland and published under his own name an edition of a book written by somebody else, Mark Akenside's *Pleasures of the Imagination*. Rolt had died in 1770, but Boswell was anxious to authenticate this charge of literary fraud, to avoid trouble with Rolt's family. "I would wish to avoid all cause of quarrel and even ill will," he wrote to Malone.[24] This was characteristically naïve; Boswell could never free himself from the delusion that people would not mind even the most unpleasant facts being published provided that they could be shown to be true. Percy advised him to omit the allegation, advice which Boswell decided not to take, though later he added a qualifying footnote to the second edition. Alerted to the nature of Boswell's book, Percy asked if there was anything in it about the poet Thomas Grainger, who had been much mocked by Johnson in his lifetime. Johnson had ridiculed Grainger's poem *The Sugar-Cane,* and ridiculed Percy for praising it. Percy suspected, rightly, that Boswell's book would make him look foolish. He asked, as a "particular favour," to be allowed to see what Boswell had written about Grainger. He offered to inspect the proof and to pay for any changes he might recommend. Replying, Boswell quoted a criticism of Grainger which he claimed to have suppressed in proof, but he was being disingenuous—the sentence appears nowhere in the manuscript.[25] He did in fact make some changes in response to Percy's defence of Grainger, but allowed most of Johnson's gibes at Percy himself to stand.[26]

On 4 March, Boswell dined with the Reverend George Strahan (son of the printer William Strahan), the clergyman who had attended Johnson in his last illness and who had edited Johnson's posthumously published *Prayers and Meditations*. Strahan gave Boswell some details which he was even now able to incorporate into the book. Ten days later he had some welcome news for Sandy: "I am now *writing* the *last sheet* of my Book. But the whole, including Dedication and Table of contents will not I imagine be *printed* sooner than this day fortnight." He was now hoping to publish in mid-April.

On 17 March, an announcement appeared in the *London Chronicle:* "Mr Boswell's Life of Johnson is positively finished, and the day of publication will be announced in the course of the present week." Two days later an advertisement predicted that the book would be published "next month." A newspaper called the *Oracle* joked that Boswell's own biography might have to be written before the much-postponed *Life of Johnson* could be published.

Early in March a satirical poem attacking Burke had appeared in the *Oracle,* credited to "Mr Boswell." The coolness between the two men arising from the publication of Johnson's remarks about Burke's wit in the *Tour* had never fully thawed, and Boswell was anxious not to allow the ice to re-form. He wrote to Burke denying authorship of these "impudent lines," and received a cordial enough reply. But Boswell was sufficiently annoyed to threaten legal action, forcing the paper to print a sarcastic retraction.[27]

He was again in poor spirits, fearing that the book in which he had invested so much effort would be a flop. On 6 April, he opened his heart to Temple:

> My *Life of Johnson* is at last drawing to a close. I am correcting the last sheet, and have only to write out an advertisement, to make out a note of errata and to correct a second sheet of contents, one being done. I really hope to publish it on the twenty-fifth current. My old and most intimate friend may be sure that a copy will be sent to him. I am at present in such bad spirits, that I have every fear concerning it—that I may get no profit, nay, may lose—that the public may be disappointed and think that I have done it poorly—that I may make many enemies, and even have quarrels. Yet perhaps the very reverse of all this may happen.[28]

The book did not appear on 25 April; in fact, it did not appear in April at all. But meanwhile Boswell published something else—a long poem entitled "No Abolition of Slavery, or, The Universal Empire of Love," a propaganda effort against the bill to abolish the slave trade which was about to be introduced into Parliament by the evangelical MP William Wilberforce. Boswell's sentiments could only be regarded as deplorable; but in truth, his pamphlet was a mere *jeu d'esprit,* the product of a whimsical mind. His poem defended the institution of slavery on the grounds that property rights were sacrosanct; the real point of the piece was an extravagant analogy between slavery and love. To be in thrall to one's beloved was a pleasure; subordination was the natural order of things. It was all nonsense, of course; fortunately, nobody took it seriously. It was odd, to say the least, that the man who had championed Corsican freedom and American independence should defend slavery. But Boswell's politics had never been consistent, as Burke had once pointed out: "You have the art of reconciling contradictions beyond any man."[29] At least nobody could accuse him of toadying to the powerful; among those attacked in the poem were Fox, Burke, and Pitt. Even Courtenay did not escape a stanza of censure— though this can hardly have been wounding, since Courtenay had written it for Boswell himself.

"When do we see your *Opus* magnum?" asked Joseph Warton on 9 April. He suspected that Boswell's "monument" to Johnson might take as long in making its appearance as the marble one, for which a committee was collecting subscriptions.[30] Boswell's Advertisement to the First Edition made use of the same metaphor, suggesting that the book had been so long delayed because so many people had been anxious to "share in the pious office of erecting an honourable monument" to Johnson's memory.

The *Magnum Opus* was almost ready. In order to protect his copyright, Boswell published (but did not distribute) two of its highlights, the letter to Lord Chesterfield and the minute of Johnson's meeting with the King. Under existing copyright law, anyone—newspapers and indeed other biographers, for example—was free to print extracts without permission, but forbidden from publishing any work in full. By publishing these two valuable items separately, Boswell ensured that he

could control their use. Advance interest in the book itself was encouraging; on 13 May, Boswell was able to report to Forbes that the London
booksellers had subscribed upwards of four hundred sets. He had
decided that the book should appear on the twenty-eighth anniversary
of his first meeting with his subject in Tom Davies's bookshop. At last,
on 16 May 1791, *The Life of Samuel Johnson, LL.D.* was published.

PART THREE

LIFE PUBLISHED

James Boswell

THIRTEEN

DESPAIR

I had no hope of happiness in this world, yet shrank from the thought of death.[1]

OF COURSE it was a success. Most of the reviews were favourable, and Boswell received a gratifying number of complimentary letters. The book sold steadily despite its high price, and soon it was evident that Boswell had been right to resist selling the copyright. By the end of August, 1,200 sets had been sold. One indication of the demand for the *Life of Johnson* was the speedy appearance of a cheap pirated abridgement.[2] Another good sign was the publication of several parodies, a mark both of the book's celebrity and of its distinctive style.

Boswell promoted the book by stirring up bogus controversies. He announced, for example (upon no foundation), that Mrs Piozzi was preparing to defend herself against his charges of inaccuracy; and proclaimed that, allowing for the difference in price, the *Life of Johnson* was selling better than the other book of the hour, Burke's *Reflections on the Revolution in France* (it was not).[3] In its May and June issues, the *European Magazine* published a flattering, two-part profile, "The Memoirs of James Boswell." These were written in the third person, by an anonymous hand—Boswell himself. They presented a generous assessment of his poetry, and an idealized version of his career. "Mr Boswell had not

been long at the English bar when he was elected Recorder of the
ancient city of Carlisle . . . Finding this Recordership, at so great a distance from London, attended with many inconveniences, Mr Boswell,
after holding it for about two years, resigned it." It was difficult to
explain why he had not been found a seat in Parliament, though perhaps
his "honest independence of mind" had something to do with this:
"indeed his not being amongst the Representatives of the Commons is
one of those strange things which occasionally happen in the complex
operations of our mixed Government."

The "Memoirs" contained a warm tribute to Margaret, whose acceptance of his offer of marriage was "the most fortunate circumstance of
his life." Very understanding of his "love of the fair sex," she was "the
constant yet prudent and delicate *confidante* of all his *égarements du coeur
et de l'esprit.*" Her melancholy death was "a severe affliction," which
"affected him very much; for it deprived him of the woman he loved,
and the friend he could trust." However, he did not resign himself to
unavailing grief, "but endeavoured to dissipate his melancholy by occupation and amusement in the metropolis, in which he enjoys perhaps
as extensive and varied an acquaintance as any man of his time." The
"Memoirs" concluded with a reference to "his great literary work in
which he was engaged for many years, *'The Life of Dr Johnson'* [*sic*],
which he has at last published, in two volumes quarto, and which has
been received by the world with extraordinary approbation."[4]

The world's response to the *Life of Johnson* was indeed favourable,
though perhaps not so favourable as might have been expected. The
book was too informal, too entertaining, too light to be taken seriously
as Literature. Criticism of the *Life of Johnson* echoed criticism of *The
Journal of a Tour to the Hebrides*: there were the same comments about
the author's indiscretions, his egotism, his eccentricity, his naïveté.
Some reviewers complained that Boswell had collected minutiae indiscriminately; others praised his indefatigable industry. In general, those
who liked Johnson liked the book. Those who disliked Johnson and
the principles he stood for were unlikely to appreciate the work of a
biographer who professed unabashed reverence for him. Such reviewers attacked Johnson for brutality and bombast; and condemned
Boswell for fawning and idolatry.

One of the first personal tributes to the *Life of Johnson* came from Vicesimus Knox, who only three years before had deplored the publication of works such as Boswell's *Tour* and Mrs Piozzi's *Anecdotes*. "I thank you for the very great entertainment your *Life of Dr Johnson* gives me," he wrote graciously to Boswell. "It is a most valuable work. . . . Yours is a new species of biography. Happy for Johnson that he had so able a recorder of his wit and wisdom." Knox's praise of the book was all the more remarkable because of the way he was portrayed in it: as a mere imitator of Johnson's style, as making a ludicrous mistake in one of his essays, and as having ungraciously attacked the University of Oxford, his *alma mater*.

Boswell might have expected a favourable response from his old friend Temple, but even so he must have glowed when he received Temple's letter. "Perhaps no man was ever so perfectly painted as you have painted your hero," enthused Temple. "You have given us him in every point of view and exhibited him under every shade and under every colour. We think we see him and hear him and are equally entertained whether he contend for truth or for victory." Temple was convinced that "your book must greatly raise and diffuse your reputation, as it also abounds with many ingenious observations of your own, shews your familiarity and acceptance with persons of the finest discernment and how eminently you were regarded and loved by such a judge as Johnson. Indeed, I can hardly express the pleasure I feel in considering the fame and profit it must procure you."[5] Another old friend, Dr Hugh Blair, was less certain of the benefit to Boswell himself. "I am not sure whether you have not depicted yourself sometimes too graphically and unnecessarily in your work. To me, who have known you so well and so long, the impression these passages leave is in no way unfavourable. But it is always a dangerous experiment for a man while he is living to exhibit himself too nakedly to the world."[6]

Dr Burney joined in "the general Chorus of your praise." His misgivings about Boswell's qualifications to write the life of Johnson were long gone; indeed, in keeping with Johnson's idea that "our Club should be composed of the heads of every liberal and literary profession," he judged that "*Biography* now claims you as her chairman." Burney believed that it was impossible to open either of the two volumes without finding "some sentiment of our venerable sage worth remembering." He had no doubt that Johnson's wit and wisdom would "become proverbial to Englishmen, and long continue to direct their taste as well as their morals. For my own part, I think myself infinitely obliged to you for embalming so many of his genuine sentiments which are not to be found in his works. Indeed, if all his writings which had been previously printed were lost, or had never appeared, your book would have conveyed to posterity as advantageous an idea of his character, genius, and worth as Xenophon has done of those of Socrates."* This was heady stuff, but Burney was sincere; years later, after Boswell's death, he gave his opinion to Malone that Boswell's memorabilia would "merit the gratitude of posterity as long as the language of our country shall be intelligible."[7]

After so much effort, and after enduring so much derision, Boswell's appetite for praise was hearty, and he tried to persuade several of those who spoke highly of the *Life of Johnson* in conversation to commit their opinions to paper. Wilkes, for example, told Boswell that it was "a wonderful book"; the next day Boswell solicited from him a letter of confirmation, "so as I may have your *testimonium* in my archives at Auchinleck."[8] No such letter has been found. He tried the same trick with Burke, who had delighted Boswell with a report on his conversation with the King. Like Burke, the King had been reading the book, and clearly both men had been enjoying it; indeed, Boswell had heard (from another source) Burke's comment to the King that "it was the most entertaining book he had ever read." Now Boswell asked Burke for a minute of his interview with the King. Burke's reply was cold. He disliked Boswell's habit of recording, and he felt that Boswell's request for a written report of a private interview with the sovereign was in poor taste. He claimed not to be able to recall the details of the King's remarks, beyond that he "seemed to be affected properly with the merit of your performance." Burke confirmed what he had said to the King, that he had not read any thing more entertaining; "though I did not say to his Majesty, what nothing but the freedom of friendship could justify in my saying to yourself, that many particulars there related

---

*Socrates' teachings are preserved only in the writings of his friends and followers; Xenophon's memoirs are the principal source for his life.

might as well have been omitted." Burke wished Boswell all happiness "whenever you retire to Auchinleck"; he was sure that "something original from you" would be well received. "Whether, in the present possession of the favourable opinion of the world as you are, it will be prudent for you to risk the further publication of anecdotes, you are infinitely more competent to judge than I am."[9]

There was no mistaking Burke's disapproval; any remaining intimacy between the two men was now at an end. Burke enjoyed the book, but he no longer trusted the author.

Percy was so deeply hurt by certain passages in the *Life of Johnson* that he could barely bring himself to speak to Boswell afterwards. Besides recording Johnson's sneers at him, Boswell had described two occasions on which Johnson had quarrelled with Percy in his presence: one in 1768, when Johnson had mocked Percy so harshly as to make him leave the company; and another in 1778, when Johnson and Boswell had been among the guests dining at Percy's house. This row between Johnson and Percy, both irascible men, makes one of the most vivid scenes in the *Life of Johnson;* it culminated in an explosion, with each man accusing the other of rudeness, before making up and shaking hands. But Percy had confessed to Boswell soon after this clash that he felt "very uneasy" at being treated so roughly by Johnson in the presence of the Reverend Robert Nichols, a clergyman who hoped to supplant him in the favour of his patron, the Duke of Northumberland, particularly since the quarrel had revolved around a description of the Duke's parkland at Alnwick Castle. Percy feared what might happen if the story reached the Duke. Boswell kindly offered to mention the matter to Johnson; and the upshot was that Boswell solicited a letter from Johnson in praise of Percy, which was subsequently read aloud in the presence of the Duke's heir. Percy had thanked Boswell in the warmest terms, being highly delighted by Johnson's letter: "I would rather have this than degrees from all the universities in Europe."

Boswell's aim in telling this story in his book was to illustrate two sides of Johnson's character: his rough treatment of even those of whom he was most fond, and his "tender and benevolent heart," which made him anxious to be reconciled, and to make ample reparation to any friend whom he had hurt "in his wrath." Johnson's roughness in conversation had been notorious; Boswell could not avoid the subject, but he was anxious to balance it by showing Johnson's other side—not least to provide a context for his behaviour to Boswell himself. The very day before Percy had confessed his uneasiness at Johnson's treatment of him, Boswell had been at the receiving end. Talking of Langton's extravagance, Boswell and Johnson had agreed that he must be persuaded to leave London. Johnson proposed sending Boswell to him: "if your company does not drive a man out of his house, nothing will." Boswell was stunned by this jibe, which he felt as a "horrible blunt shock." Perhaps perceiving that he had gone too far, Johnson afterwards spoke kindly to him, and disparaged Mrs Thrale, which always went down well with Boswell.[10]

So it was doubly important for him to record in his *Life of Johnson,* "the scene of too much heat" between Johnson and Percy, which otherwise "I should have suppressed." Boswell believed that his account of their quarrel showed Johnson's affection and esteem for Percy, just as other passages showed Johnson's affection and esteem for Boswell himself. But Percy did not see it that way; he was embarrassed and humiliated to find the story in print. In truth, he had been made to look foolish: absurdly anxious not to allow anything to his discredit to reach the ears of his patron, and absurdly gratified by Johnson's letter. Moreover, though Boswell's account was accurate insofar as it went (except that he condensed the action into a much shorter period), the story had not ended quite as Boswell described; he had glossed over the aftermath. In fact, Johnson had been angry with Boswell for giving Percy his letter and demanded its return, making it obvious that his sentiments expressed in it were not wholly sincere, and not ones that he wished to remain on record. Boswell was forced to retrieve the letter from Percy, who was left disgruntled; his well-meaning interference had deepened and perpetuated the quarrel between the two men he meant to reconcile.[11] It was not an episode that Percy liked to be reminded of, even in private. When it appeared in Boswell's book, he suspected Boswell of treacherous malice. And when he found an ostensible mistake there, he suspected Boswell of duplicity.

Johnson had been expert at writing dedications for other writers' books. It was a knack, he told Boswell: like writing an advertisement.

"He believed he had dedicated to all the Royal Family round." But those for whom he wrote these dedications were often very reluctant for this to be known—perhaps because the artificiality of the sentiments within them would be exposed, or perhaps because "they might be suspected of having received larger assistance."[12] Reynolds asked Boswell not to mention that Johnson had written the Dedication (to the King) for the collected edition of his *Discourses;* and Burney altered the copies of Johnson's letters that he sent to Boswell to hide the fact that Johnson had written the Dedication (to the Queen) for his *History of Music.* Boswell knew that Johnson had written the courtly Dedication to the Countess of Northumberland for the first edition of Percy's *Reliques of Ancient English Poetry,* and he put this in his book; but in deference to Percy's sensibilities, he took it out again. He failed, however, to alter the index accordingly, and after the *Life of Johnson* was published, Percy spotted that there was an index entry for his book referring to the page on which Boswell discussed Johnson's practice of writing dedications for other authors, many of whom were unwilling for this to be known. It was therefore evident that Percy was one of these. Percy believed this oversight to have been deliberate, and complained bitterly to Malone of this "very unfair and unpardonable proceeding."[13]

Percy's pain was still obvious seven years later, when he wrote that Boswell had been "studiously excluded from all decent and good company" after the publication of the *Life of Johnson,* because of "his violating the primary law of civil society in publishing in that work men's unreserved correspondence and unguarded conversation." Indeed, Percy declared, Boswell had been so much ostracized as to drive him to drink, which hastened his premature death. In fact, Percy was wrong: Boswell continued to move in some of the best circles for the remainder of his life—but the fact that he was accepted by some does not mean that he was not avoided by others.

An incident a few months after the publication of the *Life* shows how wary of him even some of those closest to Boswell had become. Hearing that several of his friends, including Reynolds and Malone, would be present at a dinner given by Sir William Scott, Boswell sent a letter suggesting that he should come, too; in reply, Scott said that he was always pleased to see Boswell,

. . . let me have what company I may. But excuse me if I state the true reason that makes [me] sometimes ask other friends of our connexion, when I
do not take the liberty of asking you. I have *other* acquaintance, men whom
I very much value on many accounts, but men who are perhaps more shy
and delicate than I am, and who, in my hearing, have often expressed a
proper respect for your talents but mixed with a good deal of censure upon
the practice of publishing without consent what has been thrown out in
the freedom of private conversation. I don't discuss the rectitude of their
opinion upon that matter, but I know they are sincere in it; and I really
have felt a repugnance in asking gentlemen to meet, whose company
might excite sentiments of unease or apprehension . . .

I shall be glad to see you, repeated Scott, "as *I* always am; but no *letter
press* upon the occasion!"

Boswell had long feared that his collecting so much of Johnson's
conversation had made some people shun him as a dangerous companion; now these fears had been confirmed. It was wounding to discover
that he was excluded (even if only occasionally) from those circles
within which he had felt most at home. Stung, he reacted scornfully: "I
should be curious to know *who* they are that are conceited enough to
imagine that I could take the trouble to publish *their* conversation,
because I have recorded the wit and wisdom of Johnson." It was the
same argument as the one he had made in the postscript to *The Journal
of a Tour to the Hebrides,* six years earlier.

In fact, as Scott delicately pointed out, Boswell had published some
of Scott's own conversation in the *Life of Johnson,* including a passage in
which he was quoted as recalling that the late Sir William Blackstone
had composed his *Commentaries* "with a bottle of port before him";
Scott's embarrassment on this account had caused him to apologize to
Blackstone's family. He could not grumble about it, however, because
he had approved the passage before publication. On his part, Boswell
was forced to concede that Johnson's was not the only conversation he
had recorded; "others, as well as myself, sometimes appear as shades to
the GREAT INTELLECTUAL LIGHT." Of course, this was not a role that
everybody might choose.

Boswell sulkily stayed away from the dinner, even though Scott
politely urged him to change his mind. Afterwards he made a point
of telling Scott that he had visited John Cator's fine country seat at

Beckenham instead. "I beg to be fairly understood," insisted Boswell, "that my recording the conversations of so extraordinary a man as Johnson with its concomitant circumstances was a *peculiar* undertaking, attended with much anxiety and labour, and that the conversations of people in general are by no means of that nature as to bear being registered and that the task of doing so would be extremely irksome to me."[14]

But in his letter soliciting details of the interview with the King, Boswell had informed Burke that he wished to resume "the anxious and laborious task of making minutes of conversations of value." The two statements were inconsistent. Burke might well have been one of the men Scott had been referring to, who felt pained by their conversation being brought out "into the glare of public light, when they supposed themselves to be merely discussing in a private society." Burke relished the cut-and-thrust of good conversation; he was a brilliant talker, often carried away by his own vehement rhetoric; he knew that his many enemies would seize on anything he said which could be used against him. In public, he was vilified as much as any other man of his time; in private, he liked to relax his guard. Hypocrisy is essential to politics, but crippling to the personality. Burke needed to be free to express himself openly to his confidants; to be constrained by the fear that his remarks might be published was intolerable.

It is impossible to know how many people avoided Boswell, and how much; he could not have known this himself. That there were *some,* however, was clear even to him. More than two years later, Boswell conceded to his son Sandy that "many foolish people" had been afraid to meet him, "vainly apprehending that *their* conversation would be *recorded*."[15]

In the euphoria following the publication of his book, Boswell placed a notice in the *Public Advertiser,* boasting of his social success: "Boswell has so many invitations in consequence of his *Life of Johnson* that he may be *literally* said to *live* upon his deceased friend."[16] He might have expressed himself differently had he been aware of Burke's aside to the bluestocking Hannah More, about Johnson's biographers: "How many maggots have crawled out of that great body!"[17]

• • •

Now that his *Magnum Opus* was published, Boswell began to cast around for other occupations. One of his several matrimonial schemes was the pursuit of Miss Milles, "a most agreeable woman *d'une certaine age,* and with a fortune of £10,000." Boswell tried to induce Miss Milles to commit to him before he declared his own feelings: a tactic which proved unsuccessful. Meanwhile, he amused himself with a "gay little Parisienne"—until she proved too expensive. London was full of French *émigrés,* many of them penniless. The revolt in Paris had led to nationwide disturbances; many Frenchmen had been too frightened to stay. In June 1791, the Royal Family tried to flee the country, reaching Varennes before being caught and brought back to Paris, escorted by a jeering mob. Across the Channel opinion was increasingly polarized, between those, like Fox, who thought the uprising in France the greatest and best event in the history of the world; and others, like his former ally Burke, who deplored what was happening there, and who feared that the revolutionary illness might infect Britain. Boswell was one of the latter; though he had welcomed "a rational and temperate reformation of the abuses of the French government," he was firmly opposed to the "barbarous anarchy" now raging through that country.[18]

In August Boswell revolved around the Home Circuit, without attracting a single brief; then he returned to Auchinleck, his first visit in two years, the first since Margaret's death. The house seemed deserted and melancholy; he missed his wife more than ever; and he sank into languor and gloom. "To escape from what I felt," he confessed to Temple, "I visited a good deal; but, alas, I could not escape from myself." A high point of his stay came when over one hundred "nominal and fictitious voters" were removed from the Ayrshire electoral roll, after Boswell had made a powerful speech against their retention; nobody, it seems, mentioned how vigorously he had defended the creation of such voters just across the border, at the behest of Lord Lonsdale. The eighteenth-century mind took a relaxed attitude to such inconsistencies. After eight weeks in Scotland, he returned to London, where he hoped to find relief, but his depression continued. He was saddened to find that Reynolds had gone into a decline. Now nearly seventy, Sir Joshua had been diagnosed as suffering from a "severe liver ailment"; he feared that he was losing the sight of his one remaining good eye. Reynolds, who had always been the most generous of hosts, began to withdraw from society, seeking solace in laudanum. Boswell visited him often, and tried to comfort his old friend. Otherwise he had very little to occupy him. Though he kept his chambers open and attended Westminster Hall, his practice remained dormant. "There is not the least prospect of my having business," he admitted to Temple.[19]

Still, he continued to attract plaudits from admirers of his work, which was cheering. One of the most perceptive of the many letters he received commenting on the *Life of Johnson* came from a stranger, the banker, painter, and scientist William Elford, who was later to become both a Member of Parliament and a Fellow of the Royal Society. Elford's excuse for taking the "undue liberty" of writing to him was his "invincible desire" to tell Boswell "how very great a pleasure I have received from the perusal of your *Life of Dr Johnson,* which to my great regret I have just finish'd." Elford had earlier read *The Journal of a Tour to the Hebrides,* "with an avidity, I had never experienc'd before."

> This kind of biography appears to me perfectly new, and of all others the most excellent—it constitutes a fund of the highest intellectual entertainment, by giving the portrait of the mind of perhaps the greatest man the world has produc'd—enliven'd with anecdotes, and conversations of most of the great literary characters of his time—and as these works of yours are, I believe, the first of their kind, so it will be long before your example will be follow'd, for your plan requir'd not only great ability, and capacity of selection, but a degree of labour and attention which very few persons will be found willing to submit to. In short instead of describing your characters, you exhibit them to the reader. He finds himself in their company, and becomes an auditor of conversations, which have all the dignity of the best moral writings, soften'd by the ease, the wit and the familiarity of colloquial manners.[20]

Over the next few years, Boswell received a continuous flow of correspondence concerning his book, including many letters suggesting corrections, additions, or deletions. Some of the letters drew attention to errors, of fact or of taste, some came from clergymen wishing to engage him in theological discussions. Boswell's replies were generally courteous, his responses to criticism gracious.[21] He presented a complimentary set of volumes to an unbeneficed clergyman who sent him a begging letter; and he cut out Johnson's signature from a letter and sent it to a fan—"no man, I think, is a greater, or more enthusiastic admirer of Johnson than myself"—who wrote soliciting some form of relic.[22]

The *Life of Johnson* continued to sell steadily, and by the end of the year 1,600 sets had been sold. Boswell reported on its success to Forbes, and received a letter in reply rejoicing at this "profitable issue." Forbes told Boswell that he had "derived a very high degree of entertainment" from a perusal of the book. "I found in it, indeed, several things that *might,* and some I must honestly confess, that I do humbly think *ought* to have been omitted." When Forbes heard that a second edition in three volumes was planned, he urged Boswell to look through the whole book with Malone, and to remove anything at which anybody might take offence or exception.[23]

Somebody who did take exception to something was the poet and philosopher James Beattie, whom Boswell had introduced to Johnson and the Thrales twenty years before. Beattie objected to a remark of Johnson's, mentioned in passing in the *Life,* which seemed to him to imply that when he first came to know his new London friends he had concealed from them the fact that he was married. He was naturally concerned at the insinuation that he was ashamed of his wife, especially since they were now living apart; and he asked Boswell to rectify the matter.[24] By this time, Baldwin had begun printing the second edition (in the smaller octavo size); as with the first edition, Boswell had started to feed copy to the printer as soon as it was ready, so that although he decided to include Beattie's letter as a corrective he could not insert it in the proper place, because the relevant passage was already printed.[25] At this late stage, he instituted an energetic search for new material, much of which had to be inserted after most of the book was printed. Impatience to begin, before he had made a proper assessment of the necessary work, would make a mess of the second edition.

Sir Joshua Reynolds died on 23 February 1792. His loss left a hole in Boswell's life that could not be filled. They had been friends for more than twenty years, and Boswell had enjoyed many happy hours of hospitality at Reynolds's house, "a common centre of union for the great, the accomplished, the learned, and the ingenious." In recent years Reynolds had been one of "the Gang" with whom Boswell spent so much of his time in London. He had encouraged Boswell by his very warm praise of the *Tour*, and contributed much to the *Life* itself; it was no accident that the latter was dedicated to him.[26] Indeed, he had given Boswell some fresh anecdotes since its publication, for inclusion in the second edition. Reynolds's passing cut a link to the past; he had founded the Literary Club with Johnson, and been one of its regular members. So many of those whose company had enlivened the Club during its heyday were now gone: Goldsmith, Garrick, Beauclerk, Johnson, Paoli, and now Reynolds. "This sad event dampens the spirits much," Boswell lamented to Sandy: "We shall never have his place supplied."[27]

In his will Reynolds left Boswell a legacy of £200, to spend at the anticipated dispersal sale of his paintings (not held until 1795). He had already given Boswell the first picture he had ever painted of Johnson—perhaps a *quid pro quo* for the Dedication—and waived the debt Boswell owed for his own portrait, which he had commissioned in a rush of enthusiasm back in 1785, on the strength of his expected future earnings at the English bar. Many people imagined that Boswell would now write a life of Reynolds, and indeed he toyed with the idea for some months, collecting notes on the subject; but in the end he decided against it. "Sir Joshua was indeed a man of pleasing and various conversation," Boswell acknowledged in a letter to Barnard, "but he had not those prominent features which can be seized like Johnson's."[28]

Boswell considered making a proposal of marriage to Reynolds's niece, Mary Palmer ("the fair Palmeira"), who had just inherited a fortune of £30,000 from her uncle; but Temple advised him that she would be after bigger game, and so it proved when she married the Earl of Inchiquin that summer. Still casting around for some occupation, he applied to join the entourage of the professional diplomat Lord Macartney (a fellow-member of the Literary Club), recently appointed as the first British Ambassador to China. Temple was appalled. "I trust you are not in earnest," he protested. "At our time of life the climate would kill you."[29] Frustrated of any useful activity, Boswell sought refuge in social life, going out so often that an obituarist was later able to write of him that he was "more absent from home than any man of his time."[30] Mostly—when he was not either depressed or boorishly drunk—he was a popular guest, with a gift for mimicry and a large stock of funny stories (told with a kind of whimsical serious-ness), vivacious, loquacious, and good-humoured, inspiring immedi-ate cheerfulness and mirth. "I *enjoy* a good deal in a somewhat feverish manner," he confided to his cousin Robert Boswell. But he was again drinking heavily, with sometimes unfortunate results. After behaving badly on a visit to Hatfield House, he was forced to send a formal letter of apology to Lord and Lady Salisbury. And his buffoonery at a City feast attracted so much newspaper attention that Sandy was moved to send him a letter of reproach from Eton. It seems that Boswell had mounted a stool to recite some lines of doggerel, and then launched into an impromptu speech, before being interrupted by the chairman. What little dignity remained to him was shredded by ridicule.

He suffered another reproof from one of his children, this time from his youngest daughter, Betsy, for his embarrassing behaviour with a fourteen-year-old schoolfriend. "It seems that after dinner, when I had taken too much wine, I had been too fond. Betsy told me the par-ticulars, of which I had no distinct recollection . . ."[31]

Boswell could not face going to Auchinleck that summer, so Sandy, who was about to go up to Edinburgh to read law, went in his place. Instead, Boswell decided to take up Temple's invitation to visit him in Cornwall. In mid-August, he set out, taking his two elder daughters with him. On the way down to the West Country, he called at Wilton, the magnificent home of his friend the Earl of Pembroke. They were received very politely; after dinner Boswell and the Earl joined the ladies in the magnificent Double Cube Room, designed by Inigo Jones to house the superb collection of family portraits by Van Dyck. "It was truly a *sight* to me, a man of *multitudinous imagination*, to behold *my daughters Veronica and Euphemia* sitting with the Earl of Pembroke in his immense drawing-room," mused Boswell. "How many *Scotch lairds* are there whose daughters could have such an honour?"[32]

In Cornwall he was lionized as the "Great Biographer," and received into some of the best homes—though he became aware of "a kind of apprehension that I might make a *book* of my tour." At Sir William Lemon's fine country seat, Carclew, he flirted with Miss Maria, Sir William's second daughter, whom he found so alluring that he fanta-sized about her for months afterwards. When he discovered that she had stood next to him at a party in London earlier in the year, he asked why she had not spoken to him. "What!" cut in her sharp-tongued mother. "Would you have her speak to the *great Boswell?*"[33]

Boswell and his daughters took in many of the sights, making an expedition to St Michael's Mount and another to Land's End, where Veronica ventured so near the edge of the cliff that he roared out for her to come back. One rainy day Temple produced two hundred or so of Boswell's letters, the earliest dating back as far as 1757. As he reviewed these, Boswell experienced "curious sensations." Despite all the changes he had been through, he could still recognize in some of these early letters the man he had become: "warmth of heart and imagination, vanity and piety." The two friends "laughed confidentially at my wonderful art of displaying extraordinary symptoms of learning and knowledge, when I had read so little in a regular way. Yet I had, as the French say, *feuilleté* a great many books, and had, like Johnson, the art of quickly seizing a general notion from perusing a small part."

The visitors stayed in Cornwall six weeks. One Sunday, as he and his host rode between two of the churches in Temple's parish, Boswell reflected that his friend "held a creditable actual situation in society, whereas I held none. Yet we both agreed that I was better as the distinguished biographer than as a Lord of Session. We recollected Dundas when our companion at college, when we thought him much our inferior, and wondered at his great preferment."[34]

"I have had a wonderful tour in Cornwall," Boswell wrote to Malone—but he did not disguise that he was looking forward to his return to London. As he noted in his journal, "My mind *rusts* very soon in the country, especially in damp weather."[35]

He came back to London at the end of September, just in time to set out on another Home Circuit, which yielded fees of £1 11s 6d against expenses of £3 5s 6d. Faced with this discouraging result, Boswell decided to give up his chambers in the Temple, which were costing him £40 a year. "I consoled myself with speculating that I should be as much a lawyer as was consistent with my various other circumstances as a gentleman of estate and extensive acquaintance—and as an author . . ."[36]

The second edition of the *Life of Johnson* was now well advanced; two of the three volumes were printed, and part of the third. But Boswell was still inserting corrections. In November he received a long list of these from Isaac Reed, editor of the *European Magazine,* who had assisted Johnson with his *Lives of the Poets*: a scholar "whose extensive and accurate knowledge of English literary history" was, Boswell thought, "wonderful."[37]

One Saturday in late November, Boswell walked briskly to Dilly's; it was the date they had fixed for settling the accounts for the quarto edition. After a hearty breakfast, Dilly produced the figures: a clear profit of £1,555 18s 2d.* The first run was almost exhausted, there being only a few copies remaining; eventually 1,689 sets were sold, the rest being given away as presents or entered at Stationers' Hall to establish copyright protection. Boswell was able to pay his debts to Baldwin and Dilly, with interest, and still collect a balance of £608. On the following Thursday, he gave a feast to celebrate the success of the first edition: present were Dilly, Baldwin, and members of their families, Reed, Malone, Nichols, Nichols's son-in-law the Reverend Mr Pridden, T.D., Veronica, Euphemia, and James. They drank "Health and long life to the *Life of Johnson,*" "To the pious memory of Dr Johnson," and, of course, the favourite Tory toast, "Church and King."[38]

It was an appropriate moment for all good men and true to pledge their loyalty. The upheaval in France had led to a fear of something similar happening in Britain; a Royal Proclamation on 1 December 1792 called on the militia to quell seditious activities. Boswell signed a Declaration of Loyalty drawn up by the Stationers' Company, and joined the Association for Preserving Liberty and Property against Republicans and Levellers, which met regularly at the Crown & Anchor Tavern in the Strand. Burke proposed a new toast: "Old England against New France." It was a tense time; those who sympathized with the revolutionaries were regarded as little more than traitors. Early in 1793, news arrived in England that Louis XVI had been guillotined; outraged, Boswell planned to publish an appeal to raise money for a monument to the French King in Westminster Abbey.

---

*No record remains of how this figure was reached, but it is possible to speculate: from each set priced at two guineas (forty-two shillings), the booksellers would have taken about one-third (fourteen shillings); as publisher, Dilly took a further 7½ percent commission (two shillings); and the costs of printing, paper, and advertising might have come to around £700 (eight shillings per set). Boswell would therefore have received about eighteen shillings for each set sold.

He drafted the appeal, and had it translated into French. But he dropped the idea when Dundas told him of Pitt's disapproval. This was no time for sentimental gestures; tension between Britain and France was high; Pitt was trying to avoid any provocation. A few weeks later, the French declared war.

Boswell was now drinking so much that he was often hung over in the mornings, despite sporadic attempts to go without alcohol. He stayed in bed late; when eventually he came downstairs he was listless and fretful, and he "breakfasted without appetite, having as it were a bitter taste which communicated itself to everything." He was suffering from "scorbutic eruptions" on different parts of his body, which he ascribed to scurvy, though these may have been a manifestation of repeated venereal infections. He felt himself painfully insignificant:

> I often called on Malone, and found him fully occupied in historical and biographical researches, on which he was intent while I had absolutely no pursuit whatever. The delusive hope of *perhaps* getting into some practice at the bar was *now* dead, or at least torpid. The printing of my second edition of Dr Johnson's *Life* was the only thing I had to do. That was little, and was now nearly ended. I hurried into the streets and walked rapidly, shunning to meet people as much as I could, my perceptions being liable to such soreness from even looks and manner that I suffered acute pain on being accosted, and this was augmented by an unhappy imagination that it must appear how inefficient and troubled I was.[39]

On 1 January 1793, in accordance with their custom, Boswell breakfasted with Malone and looked through the monthly publications. Then they walked together to a meeting of the Literary Club. Boswell did not much enjoy the gathering—except the wine. He reflected that he had lost his faculty of recording: perhaps a good thing, for among those present were Scott, Burke, and Percy. In mid-January Boswell again set out on the Home Circuit, and though his fees were higher than they had been the last time, they were still less than his expenses. Then, the following month, he returned to Auchinleck, to choose a new minister for the parish in place of the Reverend Dun, who had died the previous October. This responsibility invigorated him. "Only think, Temple, how serious a duty I am about to discharge," he bragged to his old friend: *"I James Boswell, Esq!"* From Auchinleck he wrote to Malone, enclosing the last revises to the second edition, including a new final paragraph. "I have been wonderfully active, and in health and spirits almost incredible," he informed Malone, "and never once drunk."[40] He was in such good form that he decided to risk a trip to Edinburgh, his first since 1786, where he was surprised to find himself cordially welcomed.

Boswell wrote to Temple that he had "lately received some more additions of great value," which he planned to include in the second edition.[41] Among them was Johnson's letter to the late Earl of Bute concerning his pension, which had been sent to Boswell by the new Earl, his companion on the Grand Tour, the former Lord Mountstuart. He had already received another letter from Johnson to Bute, transcribed by Lord Macartney. As it was too late to include these in their proper place without upsetting the pagination, Boswell grouped them, together with thirteen letters from Johnson to Langton, at the end of the second volume. It was not a satisfactory solution, but there was worse to come. Since the publication of the first edition, Boswell had received more Johnsonian reminiscences from Nichols, Reynolds, and Langton—and in May he received a fresh batch of Johnsoniana from the Reverend Dr William Maxwell. This material arrived too late to be included in the main text; Boswell decided that it should be added *en bloc* at the beginning of the first volume, before the pagination began (and just after the index), under the heading "Additions to Dr Johnson's Life Recollected, and Received after the Second Edition was Printed." There was also a mass of miscellaneous material under the heading "Corrections" and another headed "Additional Corrections." It was an extraordinary way to arrange a book.[42]

He added new material of his own to the second edition, much of it in lengthy (not always impressive) footnotes. He also took the opportunity to include some of the compliments he had received after the publication of the first edition. However, one of his additions prompted a strong protest from Malone. Boswell had composed a new Advertisement to the Second Edition; after a topical allusion to Johnson's principles as "an effectual anecdote to that detestable sophistry which has lately been imported from France," there followed several complacent paragraphs in which he compared his work to the *Odyssey*, and boasted that he had "*Johnsonised* the land." Towards the end he provided an account of his conversation with the King on 20 May 1785, when His Majesty had urged, "There will be many lives of Dr Johnson: do you make the best." After reproducing this remark, Boswell continued, "I flatter myself that I have obeyed my SOVEREIGN'S commands."

Quite apart from its general preposterousness, Boswell's Advertisement was a breach of the convention that the King's private comments should never be published. In a limited monarchy the privacy of the sovereign was sacrosanct.

Perhaps Boswell realized that Malone would not stomach his new Advertisement, because he did not show it to him in its final form; Malone chanced upon it by accident at Baldwin's. If so, Boswell was right to have been wary of Malone's reaction. He now received an ultimatum: if he persevered in printing this "wild Rhodomontade," Malone would insist on having his name removed from the book. "Poor Sir Joshua is in his grave, and *nothing can touch him further;* otherwise he could not but blush, that his name should appear at the head of a dedication, followed by such an Advertisement as the compositor now has in his hands."

Boswell was shocked by Malone's "strange letter": so much so, that he did not respond for a few days until tempers had cooled, in fact until Courtenay had come to assure him that Malone had written as he had done out of friendship. Boswell ascribed Malone's irritation to the "stabs" he was receiving from his rival Shakespearian, George Steevens. He disagreed with Malone's comments, but he offered to put the matter to a third party, his friend John Douglas, Bishop of Salisbury (another member of the Club), for him to decide. Eventually a compromise was reached: the conversation with the King was omitted, and Malone's name retained.[43]

The second edition of the *Life of Johnson* was published on 17 July 1793, its three octavo volumes priced at £1 4s, a little more than half the price of the first quarto edition. Within two weeks, four hundred sets had been sold. Boswell also issued a forty-two-page pamphlet of *Principal Corrections and Additions to the First Edition of Mr Boswell's Life of Dr Johnson,* which he distributed without charge, so that purchasers of the more expensive quarto edition might not lack his subsequent discoveries.

Boswell was delighted with the initial success of the second edition, but as sales slowed, his spirits drooped. The second edition was selling "*as well as could be expected*," he informed Malone in August. "The sale of my book was going on as might be expected," he noted five months later, when seven hundred sets had gone; two weeks afterwards he called at Dilly's, "and found that the sale of my *Life of Dr Johnson* had stagnated for some time, which discouraged me." Eventually 1,200 sets were sold; from the first and second editions combined Boswell earned about £2,500.[44]

In the October issue of the *Gentleman's Magazine,* Anna Seward, commenting on Boswell's *Corrections and Additions,* criticized his change of heart on the Sprig of Myrtle verses.* She now conceded that Johnson might have given these to Hector, but insisted that he had written them first for Lucy Porter. Miss Seward explained away Johnson's statement to the contrary as "a small untruth."

Boswell rose to the occasion in the next issue. The idea that Johnson might have written such tender verses for the daughter of the woman he was later to marry made "an awkward tale," he felt. In any case, Boswell had received a letter from Hector confirming that he had requested the verses from Johnson. "*Conjecture* must at once yield where a *fact* appears, and *that* we have from Mr Hector." He was indignant at Miss Seward's suggestion that Johnson might have been untruthful in this or in any other matter. "Dr Johnson's strict, nice and scrupulous regard to *truth* was one of the most remarkable circumstances in his career."

He pointed out that many of the anecdotes Miss Seward had sent him in 1785 had proved to be unreliable: for example, the story that, at the age of three, Johnson had written an epitaph on a duck that he had accidentally trodden on and killed—a story which Johnson himself had denied. "As my book was to be a *real history* and not a novel, it was necessary to suppress all erroneous particulars, however entertaining."

The controversy continued in subsequent issues of the *Gentleman's Magazine* until February, when the editor decided to call a halt to

*See page 215.

further discussion. Boswell was the clear winner; Miss Seward's arguments were shown to have been founded on her prejudice against Johnson.[45]

A few weeks before the second edition of his *Life of Johnson* was published, Boswell had been mugged. Returning home one June night, he was attacked in Titchfield Street, knocked down, robbed, and left lying stunned; until, with the help of a passing gentleman, who hailed the watchman and the patrol, he was led home. He was found to have a cut on the back of his head and contusions on both arms; he was confined to bed with a fever for several days, and he had still not fully recovered eight weeks later. Boswell confided to Temple that he had been drunk when the incident took place: "This, however, shall be a *crisis* in my life. I trust I shall henceforth be a sober, regular man."[46]

Boswell was gloomy that summer. Many of his friends were away from town: Malone, for example, who had gone to Stratford to pursue his Shakespearian researches. Boswell frequently sallied out, roaming the more fashionable thoroughfares of London in the hope of running into somebody who would invite him to dinner. On one such occasion, he was hailed by Lord Inchiquin, Mary Palmer's husband, and invited back to dine; when the Inchiquins went out to the theatre afterwards, Boswell found himself alone on the street at seven o'clock in the evening, warmed by the wine, without anybody on whom he could call. He stole home, and crept into bed. Two days later he called on Malone, who had just returned from Stratford, and was busy arranging old papers which he had found there. "I envied him the eagerness with which he examined them."[47]

Now that he no longer had a book to write, Boswell felt redundant. He was, in truth, a disappointed man. His fame as the "Great Biographer" contrasted painfully with his insignificance in the world of affairs. Again and again he reviewed his life, wondering where he had gone wrong, comparing notes with Temple. "How has Dundas overtop't us all?" Temple asked plaintively.[48]

As a young man, Boswell had set out the achievements for which he hoped to be remembered by his grandchildren: "He improved and beautified his paternal estate of Auchinleck; made a distinguished figure in Parliament; had the honour to command a regiment of foot-guards, and was one of the brightest wits in the court of George the Third."[49] Now, thirty years later, it seemed unlikely that any of these hopes would be realized.

Later in September, Temple arrived in London, where he had come in the hope of influencing Dundas, now Home Secretary as well as Trea-surer of the Navy, to make his midshipman son a lieutenant. The sight of Temple soothed Boswell's "weary soul." Temple saw how unhappy he was; together they reviewed all Boswell's obsessions: his disappoint-ment at not having achieved any high office, his failure to apply himself seriously to English law, his reluctance to return to the country, the pos-sibility of marrying an agreeable woman of fortune. The old dreams were fading; the years were rolling on and age was approaching. Yet friendship remained. "It was a valuable consolation to me to find that my old friend and I were as much attached to one another as ever, and that whenever I was alone with him in free conversation, I experienced a calm relief from my 'vexing thoughts.'"

Temple observed that Boswell was finding it difficult to manage his two elder daughters, Euphemia and Veronica; now nineteen and twenty, and lacking the steady control of their mother, they did much as they pleased. Removed from their home in Scotland, they had not enough polish for London society; even Nancy Temple, a country parson's daughter, found them vulgar and uncouth. Nor was Boswell the sort of parent who could introduce them into the right circles. They had learned to despise Ayrshire society without becoming equipped for London. Neither respectable nor fashionable, they were vulnerable. Provincial girls, marooned in the capital, they found themselves mixing with the most raffish company: fiddlers and singers and *émigrés,* for example. Temple remarked that they did not treat their father with the respect due to a parent. He spoke to them on Boswell's behalf, and an agreement was reached that they should go out no more than three days each week, and never on a Sunday.[50]

Like Boswell, Temple was now a widower; his wife had died in March, leaving him at first disconsolate, though during her lifetime he had complained continually about her peevishness and sexual unrespon-siveness. To help manage his children, he had employed a housekeeper, a twenty-eight-year-old dressmaker called Sukey Frood, and in no time at all he had become infatuated with her. After years of reading about Boswell's adventures, Temple was now involved in a drama of his own.

A couple of weeks after Temple had returned to Cornwall, Boswell received terrible news: Andrew Erskine was dead. As young men of genius and breeding, Erskine and Boswell had swaggered around London and Edinburgh together; they had published a book of facetious letters between them, the first publication that Boswell had acknowledged as his own. A poet with a minor talent (though considerably greater than Boswell's), Erskine had been an Army officer, a glamorous profession to which Boswell himself had once aspired (in peacetime only). Like Boswell, Erskine was melancholic, and also like Boswell, he occasionally suffered from a fevered imagination; the two of them had sometimes been so nervous as to resort to sharing a bed for mutual comfort. They had lost touch when Boswell began to spend more and more time in London (while Erskine remained in Scotland), but recently they had re-established contact. Erskine wrote to Boswell complimenting him on his *Life of Johnson*—"I am fond of your style, it is not like the solemn march of your friend, but the careless and easy walk of a gentleman"—and in his reply, Boswell had offered to send Erskine a set of the octavo edition when it was printed (it is not certain whether he ever did). Now Erskine had killed himself, filling his pockets with stones and walking into the sea near Leith, after a bad loss at whist. The shock was so great that Boswell could not bear to write Erskine's name in his journal, leaving a blank in its place.[51]

A month later, following a quiet Sunday, when he dined at home, Boswell was disturbed by a strange dream: a statue stepped down from its pedestal.* He ran from it in fear.[52]

Boswell was now drinking very heavily. One day he was so ill after "plying the bottle freely" the night before that he stayed in bed until half past three in the afternoon. Often he would importune his host to open another bottle; his dependence on drink was becoming embarrassingly obvious. He was getting fat. Several unsightly lumps appeared on his

---

*Mozart's *Don Giovanni* had first been performed in 1787, six years earlier. There is no evidence that Boswell ever saw the opera, in which a statue of a dead father comes to life.

forehead. The painter Joseph Farington, who had not seen him for nearly a year before they ran into each other in early October, noted in his diary that Boswell was "much altered for the worse in his appearance."[53] His drunkenness led him into scrapes; after one convivial dinner, he slipped while running in the street, and hurt his left elbow. At home he found he had misplaced £50 in banknotes; still intoxicated, he returned in a hackney-coach to the tavern where he had dined and made a search there, in vain. Vexed and confused, he tottered home and went to bed, only to find the notes in his cabinet the next morning.

Even now, he was still occasionally attending the sessions at Westminster Hall, donning the black barrister's dress, though his practice had completely ceased. In January 1794, he attended the Chelmsford sessions, without attracting a single fee. He felt worthless and unwanted. "My constant cause of repining is having indulged hopes of attaining both to consequence and wealth," he confessed, after a dinner with Malone, "and finding no prospect of attaining my ambitious objects, I tried to soothe myself with consideration of my fame as a writer . . ."[54]

Temple recognized what was wrong with his friend. "Your drinking is owing to want of employment and pursuit and the native activity of your mind." He advised Boswell to begin a new book, perhaps based on his travels during his Grand Tour, an idea Boswell had floated after the *Life of Johnson* was published.[55] But it was too late; he was no longer capable of the necessary sustained effort.

Suddenly an opportunity presented itself to him. The Corsicans had fallen out with the French, and appealed to the British for help. Somebody was needed to be British representative there. Surely there was nobody better qualified than himself? Boswell decided on one last throw. He wrote to Dundas offering his services; Dundas wrote back declining them.

Snubbed, Boswell spent the spring of 1794 rampaging around town, drinking, dining, card-playing, and whoring. He longed for some useful activity; but nobody wanted him.

There was always the estate, of course, where an increasing number of matters seemed to require his presence that summer. Thwarted of any employment in London, he could do his duty in Scotland. Perhaps he might save money by going there. He reluctantly decided that his two elder daughters should accompany him. In London they were in danger; in Scotland they might find more suitable society, perhaps even husbands.

On 26 June, the Boswell party left London, arriving at Auchinleck five days later. Sandy was walking in the park; when he saw them approach he came running, and greeted them on the green behind the house. He was now quite the young Scots gentleman, keen on shooting and horse-racing, with "a loud familiarity of manner and a very broad pronunciation which he has acquired by being so long in Scotland and so much of late among his inferiors." He referred to his father as "the old man."

For a while the two girls put on airs, affecting to look down on rural pursuits while "talking wild nonsense about London"; but soon they were caught up in a whirl of visiting and entertaining, house-parties, fêtes, and balls, gadding about with their brother and flirting with officers of the 4th Dragoons, conveniently stationed nearby at Kilmarnock.

Boswell passed the summer idly. He took no pleasure from entertaining, and found that he had little inclination to visit friends and neighbours. He admitted that he was "heartily weary." He tried to read, but could not summon up the energy even for that. He dealt with the necessary estate business, but without much relish: "I am continually fretted by hearing of trespasses upon my woods and lands, and tenants falling behind in their rents." The responsibilities he avoided in London were all too obvious here in Scotland. "How hard it is that I do not enjoy this fine place," he wrote to his brother. He sent regular letters to his younger son, James (his favourite), who had remained in London; in these he rarely failed to mention his "visionary, pleasing hope that I may obtain some preferment of consequence." He had promised to remain in Scotland until Christmas, but as he admitted in a letter to James on 6 October, "the time till Christmas seems very, very long."

James (then just sixteen years old) tried to rally his father:

Pray, Sir, do not suffer yourself to be melancholy. Think not on your having missed preferment in London or any of these kind of things, the unreasonableness of which you yourself upon reflection must be sensible of if you consider that your manner of living has never been that of a man of business and that, in short, you have been entirely different in every respect from those who have been (in that line) more successful—they who have obtained places and pensions etc. have not the fame of having been the biographer of Johnson or the conscious exultation of a man of genius. They have not enjoyed your happy and convivial hours. They have not been known to Johnson, Voltaire, Rousseau, and Garrick, Goldsmith, etc, etc. They have not visited the patriots of Corsica. In short, would you rather than have enjoyed so many advantages have been a rich, though dull, plodding lawyer? You cannot expect to be both at the same time.

But Boswell had sung the same refrain so long that he was incapable of learning any other. He promised James that he would try to avoid repining. "Yet at the same time I cannot be contented merely with literary fame and social enjoyments. I must still hope for some creditable employment, and perhaps I may yet attain it."[56]

His resilience was beginning to fail. In mid-November he sent a pathetic letter to Malone: "If I have been of consequence enough to you in my absence to make you think of me, you may possibly have wondered that you have not heard from me." It was an odd letter, written in a jerky style—not at all his usual confident prose. "I have little more business to transact here," he wrote to Malone. "But why go to London? What have I to do there? I can see no prospect in life but a thick fog. Could I but recover those pleasing delusions which braced my nerves when I first entered Westminster Hall! In short could I have any object!" He concluded with a touching message of gratitude that sounded almost like a farewell: "My Dear Malone, in whatever state I am I never forget your kindness to me, and the innumerable moments of happiness which I owe to you, and I ever am with unalterable regard your obliged, affectionate, and faithful friend . . ."[57]

He began to write a song, but abandoned it after only two lines:

'Tis o'er, 'tis o'er, the dream is o'er,
And life's delusion is no more.

Boswell remained in Scotland until the New Year, and returned to London in the middle of January. He was delighted to be back. After enduring Auchinleck for six months, he seemed to feel himself entitled to some indulgence. "The *intellectual* luxury of London, after so long an absence from it, has no doubt *occupied* me much—or *dissipated* me so much, I believe I should rather say," he wrote to Sandy, "—that I have not been able to settle either to read or write with composure. But *wine* has had its share in the effect."[58] His drinking now accelerated, as he hurtled towards the abyss.

On 14 April 1795, at a meeting of the Club, Boswell was taken ill with fever, shivering, headache, and vomiting. His kidneys had failed under the strain. The fever grew more alarming, and he became very weak; he was unable to keep down his food. Moreover, nineteen episodes of gonorrhoea had taken their toll; a swelling in his bladder was revealed as a tumour. He remained in bed a month, at home in Great Portland Street, tended by his brother and his son James. Early in the morning of 19 May, he died. He was fifty-four—just one year older than Johnson had been when the two men met for the first time. His body was taken to Auchinleck, where it was interred in the family vault.

FOURTEEN

POSTERITY

I tried to soothe myself with the consideration of my fame as a writer.[1]

BEFORE HE DIED, Boswell had begun preparing a new edition of the *Life of Johnson,* annotating a copy of the second edition, and indicating where addenda should be placed in the text of the third. Malone took over where Boswell left off. His conservative approach to the task reflected his habitual respect for an author's intentions. Three years after Boswell's death, Malone received a letter from one of his fellow-executors, Sir William Forbes, urging him (as Forbes had previously urged Boswell himself) to consider omissions from the next edition, on the principle that an author "ought scrupulously to take care not to say any thing that could prove injurious to the reputation of any person *dead,* or that could hurt the feelings of any one *living.*" He cited the example of Percy as one whose feelings had been hurt by Boswell's book. Malone's response was robust: changes of this nature were clearly unwarranted now that the author was dead. He claimed that the friendship between Boswell and Percy had been renewed as a result of revisions Boswell had made to the second edition. In fact, a letter of Percy's (presumably not seen by Malone), written on the very day that Forbes wrote to Malone, makes it obvious that he was still smarting from the sting of reading Boswell's book.[2]

The third edition was published in four octavo volumes on 18 May 1799, priced at £1 8s. This made a much more satisfactory book than its predecessor; order replaced the chaos of the second edition. The index now found its conventional place at the end.

As well as being responsible for Boswell's published work, Forbes and Malone, together with Temple, the third literary executor, were charged with deciding what to do with Boswell's enormous collection of papers. This comprised thousands of letters—not just Boswell's own correspondence, which was extensive enough, but also the many other letters that Boswell had accumulated by one means or another, particularly letters to and from Johnson; drafts, manuscripts, and proofs of Boswell's published and projected works, and of other men's works, including the proof-sheets of Johnson's *Lives of the Poets;* and Boswell's notebooks and journals—eight thousand pages of them. In his will Boswell left it to the discretion of the three literary executors to decide how much, if any, of this collection might be published: adding a later codicil expressing his wish that Malone should not divulge anything "which ought to be concealed." In his journal itself he had worried that its publication after his death might "hurt my children."[3]

The literary executors were widely scattered, Malone being in London, Temple in Cornwall, and Forbes in Scotland. The three of them were unable to meet before Temple died in 1796, only a year after Boswell—though Temple had discussed the issues involved with both Malone and Langton in London the previous year. Malone inspected the papers remaining in London and then sent them up to Forbes, who had already received a mass of papers from Auchinleck. There was nothing in them fit for publication, felt Malone, with the possible exception of Boswell's "extremely curious" journals. These, he thought, might some day be made into a book, though they would certainly need careful editing, "for in the freedom of his heart he put down many things both of himself and others that should not appear." Malone and Forbes agreed that no decision about the journals should be made for ten years or so, until Boswell's son James had finished his education: he would then be able to make a selection of what was fit to publish from them himself. Such a delicate task was best entrusted to a member of the family.[4]

Sandy, Boswell's heir, inherited the Auchinleck estate as entailed by Lord Auchinleck, and under the terms of Boswell's will he also inherited those lands purchased by his father. These were encumbered with the debts that Boswell had incurred to buy the land in the first place, and when they were added to Boswell's other borrowings, and the bequests due to members of the family, Sandy found that he was due to pay out over £10,000. The unentailed property was sold; Boswell's struggle to expand the estate had been in vain. Sandy would make many of the same mistakes as his father. He too would purchase large tracts of land with borrowed money, so that by the time of his own death he would be hopelessly insolvent.[5]

Boswell's second son, the studious James, was sixteen when his father died. After completing his education at Brasenose College, Oxford, he settled in London, becoming a close friend and protégé of Malone's. He remained a bachelor, devoted to his books; in time he became a considerable scholar. His eldest sister, Veronica, survived her father by only four months, succumbing to consumption, the same scourge which had carried away her mother and most of Margaret's family. Boswell's second daughter, Euphemia, quickly ran through her inheritance. Her subsequent behaviour was a trial to her relations, to Sandy in particular, as head of the family: she sent begging letters to prominent persons and succeeded in soliciting £50 from no less a person than His Royal Highness the Prince of Wales. She even advertised in the newspapers for charity. For a while she lived in London, where she wrote operas which were never performed. Fanny Burney described her as "dreadfully distressed and really crazy"; eventually she was placed in a lunatic asylum, where she remained nineteen years. She was discharged a year before her death in 1837. Boswell's youngest daughter, Elizabeth, married the advocate William Boswell, son of Boswell's cousin Robert. Sandy and his wife felt this to be an unsuitable connection, and shunned Elizabeth and her family thereafter.[6]

Under the terms of Boswell's will, the copyright in his work passed to James and his three sisters, and on their behalf Forbes sold the copyright in the *Life of Johnson* to the publishers Cadell and Davies, for the modest sum of £300. In due course the fourth (1804), fifth (1807), and sixth (1811) editions appeared, supervised by Malone with assistance from James. These two began the practice of including in the text letters from Johnson that had been unavailable to Boswell. The book continued to sell steadily; the fourth edition, for example, sold four thousand sets at a price of £1 16s each.

Though the *Life of Johnson* was increasingly praised, its author was not. Stories of Boswell's absurd behaviour circulated widely; the name Boswell could barely be mentioned without a smile. Anecdotes of his follies dotted the memoirs of the period. The very success of the *Life of Johnson* proved an embarrassment to the Boswell family. Readers of the Romantic era in literature admired the heroic figure that Boswell had so vividly evoked, but despised its humble attendant. His heir was said to be ashamed of his father's book, and to hate its being mentioned. Perhaps this was an exaggeration, but there can be little doubt that his father's notoriety caused Sandy pain. Sir Walter Scott remarked that Boswell's book, "though one of the most entertaining in the world, is not just what one would wish a near relation to have written." As a neighbour, moreover as a Scotsman of a similar social standing, Scott was in a position to judge how Sandy felt. Even as a schoolboy at Eton, Sandy had been teased about reports of Boswell's buffoonery. For a proud laird, to be constantly reminded that his father had abased himself before an uncouth Englishman, one who moreover delighted in baiting the Scots, was hard to bear. Sandy loved his father, and admired his work, but he hated the thought that Boswell had been laughed at by London society, and lampooned time and again in print; he wanted to reclaim the respect attaching to the name of Boswell in the time of his grandfather. He was therefore reluctant to countenance any further investigation of his father's journals, which were known to be damagingly indiscreet. He made little or no effort to ensure the return of the papers in Sir William Forbes's possession, and when several trunkloads of these arrived back at Auchinleck after Sir William's death in 1806, he failed to register that a large quantity had been overlooked. A rumour spread that Boswell's papers had been burned after his death, and the family did nothing to discourage the story. Reynolds's portrait of Johnson was banished to the attic at Auchinleck, and eventually sold, for much less than was hoped.[7]

Malone died in 1812, and afterwards James shouldered the task of editing his Shakespeare, just as Malone had taken on the task of editing Boswell's *Life of Johnson,* thus repaying in the next generation some of the debt incurred by his father. James's contribution was such that the Shakespearian edition became known as "Boswell's Malone." Perhaps this task distracted him from looking into his father's journals. He died suddenly in 1822, at the age of only forty-three.

Meanwhile, a succession of volumes had been offered to the public which plundered the *Life* and the earlier biographies for Johnson's most memorable sayings. The first of these, *The Witticisms, Anecdotes, Jests, and Sayings of Dr Samuel Johnson,* was published in 1791, within months of the *Life* itself; another, *The Beauties of Johnson,* followed the next year; *Dr Johnson's Table Talk* came out in 1798; and further similar volumes appeared on a regular basis. Within thirty years of the publication of the *Life of Johnson,* an anthology of Johnsoniana compiled from Boswell's book had been published in a series called "The English Prose Writers." Thus Boswell's record of Johnson's conversation became acknowledged as part of the Johnsonian canon.

Around the same time, Sandy had become Sir Alexander Boswell. From 1816 until 1821, he served as a Member of Parliament, for Plympton in Devon—perhaps a surprising seat for a Scotsman, but then James Macpherson had been MP for Camelford in Cornwall. Sandy purchased this seat at heavy expense, an extravagance that even his father had been sensible enough to resist. His fervent support of the Tory cause in the House of Commons was enough to earn him a baronetcy in 1821, and he retired from public life. Alexander Boswell was a literary man, a better poet than his father had been, and a keen antiquary, particularly interested in the Scots vernacular. He established a private printing press at Auchinleck, and put forward the idea of erecting a monument to Burns on the banks of the River Doon. Unfortunately, he shared his father's tendency to abuse his political opponents in the newspapers. When the victim of a series of such attacks, James Stuart of Dunearn, discovered that his anonymous antagonist was Sir Alexander, he called him out. Indeed, Stuart could hardly do otherwise, since Sir Alexander had accused him of being afraid to draw a trigger. The duel took place on 26 March 1822, on farmland in Fife. Honour was at stake, but it seems that neither man intended to hurt the other. Stuart fired without taking aim, and by an unlucky chance his shot hit Sir Alexander, who had fired into the air;

the baronet died of his wounds the next day, aged only forty-six. The distraught Stuart was charged with murder. A conversation between Boswell and Johnson recorded in the *Life of Johnson,* in which both men expressed their approval of duelling, was cited by the defence at his trial, and he was acquitted.[8]

Sir Alexander's son, another James, then only fifteen, succeeded to the title and inherited the estate: though his inheritance was so burdened by debt that he was advised to renounce the succession. Sir Alexander had left his affairs in even more of a mess than his father—much more so, in fact. Several years passed before Sir James was able to reach an agreement with Sir Alexander's creditors, and not before further sales had become necessary. Sir Alexander's widow, the Dowager Lady Boswell, lived on until 1864. She continued to discourage approaches from outsiders interested in looking at the family papers. Half a century after Boswell's death, she was still said to "dislike greatly any allusion to Dr Johnson," considering that her father-in-law had "degraded himself and his family by acting the toady" to him.[9] The family distaste for their famous ancestor if anything increased as the years passed; his great-granddaughter was said to encourage visitors to Auchinleck to take pot-shots at his portrait, so that it was shot practically to pieces.

The copyright in the *Life of Johnson* had lapsed in 1805. In 1829, the politician and essayist John Wilson Croker proposed to the publisher John Murray an entirely new edition, with much more extensive annotation. He planned to identify many of the anonymous individuals in the text, and to supply extensive notes "on the manners of the time, the state of society, the character of persons." Nearly seventy years had passed since the famous encounter in Tom Davies's bookshop, and much had changed in the meantime. By now, Croker argued, readers needed help to identify references that would have been familiar to Boswell's contemporaries. More controversially, Croker wanted to expand the text, to include not only *The Journal of a Tour to the Hebrides,* but also a mass of Johnsoniana not written by Boswell, including the whole of Mrs Piozzi's *Anecdotes,* much of Hawkins's *Life of Dr Johnson,* and extracts from the lesser works of Murphy, Tyers, etc. In fact, what Croker was proposing was a complete, scholarly, and respectable

equivalent to the unauthorized compilations that had been appearing
ever since the *Life of Johnson* was first published. Murray replied to Croker's letter the same night, agreeing to his proposals and offering him
one thousand guineas for his work as editor. This offer proved acceptable; Croker set to work assiduously, and his edition was published two
years later, in five large volumes. It contained plenty of new material,
including three hundred of Johnson's letters, a hundred of them
unearthed by Croker himself. He also contributed nearly 2,500 notes,
many of them contemptuous of Boswell.[10] Thus, paradoxically, the
appearance of a prominent new edition of Boswell's book contributed
further to the decline in his reputation. At the same time, Croker omitted, altered, or relegated to appendices much of what Boswell himself
had written.

One curious effect of Croker's approach was to imply that Boswell's
Life of Johnson encompassed all other books on the subject. It was as if
Boswell had taken complete possession of his master. His was now the
official biography, indeed the only biography; incidents originally
recorded by Hawkins or Piozzi were now to be found only in Boswell,
since Hawkins's and Piozzi's books had gone out of print long before.
Johnson's writings too had fallen out of favour; though twelve editions
of his collected works had been published between 1787 and 1825, after
that there would be no more for a century.[11] Johnson was known to the
Victorians principally in the works of Boswell.

Like Sir Alexander, Croker was a Tory, a friend of Canning's and
later of Peel's, credited with introducing the term "Conservative" into
politics. He was a regular contributor to the *Quarterly Review,* known
for his vicious attacks on writers of whom he disapproved; his review
of *Endymion* was said to have hastened Keats's death. As a result, he was
a much-hated man, caricatured in several novels of the period, most
famously as Rigby, political factotum to the Marquis of Monmouth, in
Disraeli's *Coningsby.*

The appearance of Croker's edition prompted the publication in the
Edinburgh Review of one of the most damning reviews ever published,
by the Whig essayist and historian Thomas Babington Macaulay. Like
Croker, Macaulay was a Member of Parliament; Croker had ridiculed
him on the floor of the House of Commons in the debate on the

Reform Bill, and Macaulay had developed a violent dislike, bordering on hatred, for his opponent. Now he savaged Croker for mutilating Boswell's text in "the most wanton manner." Croker's edition, according to Macaulay, was "ill-compiled, ill-arranged, and ill-printed," "swarming with monstrous blunders," "as bad as bad can be." It was, in fact, "worthless." Macaulay's devastating attack, combined with those of other reviewers who proved almost as critical, forced Murray to employ another editor to make radical revisions to the book before it could be reprinted.

But the most lasting effect of Macaulay's onslaught was not on Croker, or on Murray, but on Boswell. For the next hundred years or more, generations of schoolchildren brought up on Macaulay's collected works would form their opinion of Boswell from Macaulay, just as they would form their opinion of Johnson from Boswell. In 1910, Walter Raleigh would write that "For every reader of Johnson's works, there have been perhaps fifty readers of Boswell's Life, and a hundred of Macaulay's Essays."[12]

It suited Macaulay's purpose to praise Boswell as the *nonpareil* of biographers, comparing him to the champion race-horse Eclipse. "Boswell is the first of biographers," he wrote. "He has no second. He has outdistanced all his competitors so decidedly that it is not worth while to place them. Eclipse is first, and the rest nowhere." Even so, Boswell, according to Macaulay, was "one of the smallest men who ever lived . . . a man of the meanest and feeblest intellect . . . servile and impertinent, shallow and pedantic, a bigot and a sot, bloated with family pride, and eternally blustering about the dignity of a born gentleman, yet stooping to be a talebearer, an eaves-dropper, a common butt in the taverns of London." Macaulay's invective helps to explain why the Boswell family continued to feel so sensitive on the subject, so many years after the biographer's death. "He was always laying himself at the feet of some eminent man, and begging to be spat upon and trampled upon." Though he damned Croker for disfiguring Boswell's text, Macaulay united with Croker in denigrating Boswell himself. "There is not in all his books a single remark of his own on literature, politics, religion, or society," Macaulay continued, "which is not either commonplace or absurd."[13]

Almost everything that Macaulay said about Boswell was true, but he presented a one-sided picture. Nobody would have recognized from Macaulay's description the "man whom every body likes," the Boswell whom Burke described as "the pleasantest man he ever saw."[14] To Macaulay, Boswell was "a dunce, a parasite, and a coxcomb"; to Johnson, and to many others who had known him, he was a sweet-natured innocent, a man with no doubt ridiculous opinions but one whose zest and cheerfulness made his company a tonic. It is perhaps worth remembering that Boswell had shown both Macaulay's grandfather and his great-uncle to disadvantage in his *Journal of a Tour to the Hebrides*. Macaulay's grandfather had been revealed as the victim of one of Johnson's most famous rebukes: "Sir, are you so grossly ignorant of human nature, as not to know that a man may be very sincere in good principles, without having good practice?"

By implication, Macaulay's contempt reflected badly on Johnson as well as on Boswell. What kind of man was it who chose to keep company with a toady? For Macaulay, the answer was clear: Johnson was a diehard Tory, the intellectual defender of those brutal and illiterate squires left behind by the progress of history. Macaulay was the Whig historian *par excellence;* he specialized in attacks on Tory heroes, Dean Swift being another of his victims. In fact, the Johnson that Macaulay disliked so much was a caricature, his prejudices based not on Johnson's actual views, but on Johnson as portrayed by Boswell.

Macaulay's crushing polemic left a lasting wound on Boswell's reputation. It became the received wisdom to regard Boswell as an idiot who had somehow written a masterpiece. This seemed a paradox: how could such a fool have written such a book? Many years before, Thomas Gray had said of Boswell's *Account of Corsica:* "Any fool may write a most valuable book by chance." Surely it was stretching the bounds of credulity to suggest that a fool could have written not just one valuable book, but two—three, counting *The Journal of a Tour to the Hebrides*?

Macaulay believed that Boswell wrote the greatest of biographies *because* he was a fool: "If he had not been a great fool, he would never have been a great writer." Only a fool could have written such a book, because only a fool could have had the opportunity to do so: only a fool—"a man without delicacy, without shame, without sense"—would have been content to act as Johnson's whipping-boy, swallowing his pride to record the minutiae of Johnson's behaviour and conversation. This is Boswell as depicted by Mrs Piozzi and Fanny Burney, moving his chair up behind Johnson to catch his every word, leaning forward with eyes goggling.

Macaulay's notion that Boswell was a great writer because he was a fool implied that the greatness of his book was accidental, the result of circumstance rather than intent. Macaulay did not credit Boswell with literary skill, or even with any consciousness of what he was doing. Of course, Macaulay had no means of knowing how much of Johnson's conversation had been reconstructed or even "invented" by Boswell. His idea of Boswell's method followed Mrs Piozzi's misleading description; he assumed that Boswell had simply recorded what Johnson said verbatim.

"The work could never have been written if the writer had not been precisely what he was," observed Macaulay. "His character is displayed in every page, and this display of character gives a delightful interest to many passages which have no other interest." This again seemed a paradox. If Boswell was so despicable, how could the display of his character on every page be so delightful? Macaulay had identified one of the most endearing aspects of the *Life of Johnson*, though in doing so he blunted the thrust of his own polemic.

Macaulay helped to establish another orthodoxy, the idea first mooted by Burke, that Johnson "appears far greater in Boswell's books than in his own. His conversation appears to have been quite equal to his writings in matter, and far superior to them in manner. When he talked, he clothed his wit and his sense in forcible and natural expressions. As soon as he took his pen in his hand to write for the public, his style became systematically vicious." One is tempted to suggest that here Macaulay had glimpsed his own reflection, until it becomes clear that he meant only a "vicious partiality" for terms "borrowed from Greek or Latin" over "strong plain words, Anglo-Saxon or Norman-French." He complained that all Johnson's books were written in "Johnsonese": a mannered, stiff, and artificial prose very different from the language that anybody spoke.

"What a singular destiny has been that of this remarkable man!" concluded Macaulay: "To be regarded in his own age as a classic, and in ours as a companion." The reputation of Johnson's writings, Macaulay (echoing Burney) maintained, was "every day fading; while those peculiarities of manner and that careless table-talk the memory of which, he probably thought, would die with him, are likely to be remembered as long as the English language is spoken in any quarter of the globe." Thus, in Macaulay's opinion, Boswell's record of Johnson's conversation was *superior* to Johnson's writings. Boswell's Johnson had eclipsed Johnson himself.

In another review of Croker's edition, the historian and essayist Thomas Carlyle made much the same point. While he rated the *Life of Johnson* "beyond any other product of the eighteenth century," Johnson's own writings, he thought, stood "on a quite inferior level": already they were "becoming obsolete," and in the future might be "valuable chiefly as Prolegomena and expository Scholia to this *Johnsoniad* of Boswell." Yet though he disparaged the work, Carlyle idolized the man—the obverse of Macaulay's verdict on Boswell—for him it was Johnson's life, not his writing, that mattered. "Glory to our brave Samuel!" Carlyle rhapsodized. "Through long generations we point to him, and say: Here also was a man; let the world once more have assurance of a Man!" For Carlyle, the miracle of Boswell's book was to reverse the flow of time itself: "a revocation of the Act of Destiny; so that Time shall not utterly, not so soon by several centuries, have dominion over us . . . It was as if the curtains of the Past were drawn aside, and we looked mysteriously into a kindred country . . . which had seemed forever hidden from our eyes . . . wondrously given back to us, there once more it lay . . . There it still lies."[15]

Carlyle stressed the didactic importance of the *Life of Johnson:* "For as the highest Gospel was a Biography, so is the Life of every good man still an indubitable Gospel; and preaches to the eye and heart and whole man, so that Devils even must believe and tremble, these gladdest tidings: 'Man is heaven-born; not the thrall of Circumstances, of Necessity, but the victorious subduer thereof . . .'" Carlyle's prose was mannered, but intuitively he sensed why Johnson had been such a reassuring figure to his biographer.

By the mid-nineteenth century, Boswell's *Life of Johnson* had come to be recognized as one of the greatest books written in English. It had become a classic, part of the curriculum, a work that every educated man or woman was expected to read. But there remained a discrepancy between the reputations of the book and of its author. Boswell was evaluated not as Johnson's biographer, but as his companion. It was as if Shakespeare were judged as an actor in one of his plays, rather than as the playwright. Carlyle's assessment of Boswell's character was kinder than Macaulay's; Carlyle distinguished between sycophancy, a despicable quality, and reverence, which he considered admirable. The secret of Boswell's book, in Carlyle's view, was to be found in his character, "his open loving heart." Like Macaulay, however, Carlyle seemed oblivious to the skill with which Boswell had crafted his work; Boswell's talent, Carlyle declared, was "unconscious."

The perception of Boswell as a mere "stenographer" began to change in response to a series of sensational literary discoveries, spread out over more than a century. Sometime before 1850 (the exact date is unknown), a certain Major Stone, an Englishman in the East India Service, happened to be shopping on a visit to Boulogne. One of his purchases was wrapped in a piece of scrap-paper, which proved to be a fragment of a letter bearing Boswell's signature. Major Stone made inquiries at the shop, and more Boswell letters were produced, all of them addressed to his intimate friend Temple. Eventually Stone was able to retrieve ninety-seven such letters. He discovered that they had been supplied by an itinerant vendor of waste-paper who visited Boulogne irregularly. Though it was not apparent at the time how these letters should have found their way to France, it now seems likely that they travelled there in the possession of Temple's son-in-law, a spendthrift clergyman who fled England early in the century to escape his creditors.

The letters proved to be extraordinarily interesting and delightful, and in due course they were published, to general acclaim. As well as revealing much about Boswell himself, the letters were packed with references to his hopes, fears, and designs for the *Life of Johnson*. Readers of the letters began to glimpse that the book was more than just a

record of what Johnson had said: it was a carefully planned and con-
structed work in its own right.

In 1874, the Reverend Charles Rogers published *Boswelliana: The
Commonplace Book of James Boswell*, a collection of anecdotes and memorable sayings that Boswell had accumulated from at least as early as
1772, when his friend George Dempster had referred to it (perhaps
tongue-in-cheek) as "the greatest treasure of this age."[16] This manuscript had escaped the vigilance of the family, and had passed through
several hands after its purchase at the dispersal sale of the library of
Boswell's son James, following his premature death in 1822 (like so
many of the Boswells, James died insolvent). By comparison with Boswell's letters, the Boswelliana were unremarkable, though they were
of considerable biographical interest and, like the letters to Temple,
directed attention towards Boswell himself rather than Boswell as
Johnson's amanuensis. Moreover, though little of the Boswelliana had
served as material for the *Life of Johnson*, a couple of examples appeared
to show that he had conflated two separate remarks of Johnson's about
Burke, and rewritten one of Johnson's monologues to greater effect.[17]
These were among the first indications that Boswell's record of Johnson's conversation might be in any way artificial.

In the same year, Percy Fitzgerald, who was later to write the first
biography of Boswell, published a new edition of the *Life of Johnson*. This
represented a reaction against the tradition of bowdlerizing Boswell,
exemplified by Croker. Fitzgerald argued that Boswell's book should be
regarded not as a miscellaneous encyclopaedia of Johnsoniana, to be tinkered with as the editor saw fit, but as an artistic whole. He therefore
based his text on the first edition, incorporating the *Corrections and
Additions* that Boswell had published as a separate pamphlet in 1793.
Unfortunately, Fitzgerald's edition was full of inaccuracies.[18] And despite
posing as a purifier of Boswell's text, Fitzgerald was later to publish his
own anthology from the *Life of Johnson*, entitled *Gems from Boswell*
(1907). By contrast with Fitzgerald's edition, the same year saw the publication of *The Life and Conversations of Dr Samuel Johnson (founded
chiefly on Boswell)*, a rewritten and abridged *Life of Johnson* by Alexander
Main: with a preface by George Eliot's lover, the writer and critic
George Henry Lewes, who had suggested the underlying principle of

deleting the "thin soup of Boswellian narrative," retaining only "the solid meat of Johnson." The meat was dressed in a sauce of running commentary, described half a century later by Pottle as being written "in the goody-goody style of a Sunday-school tract: '*That* is the letter of a perfect gentleman'; 'Is that not a naïve resolution?'; 'Samuel Johnson is perfectly safe, then.'" It was a ridiculous piece of work, and dropped swiftly into obscurity.[19]

In 1887, George Birkbeck Hill published a new *Life of Johnson* in six volumes, which in its revised form has come to be regarded as the 'standard scholarly edition. Hill was sympathetic to Boswell; in 1878, he had published a revisionist work criticizing the judgements on Boswell and Johnson passed by Macaulay and Carlyle. In another book twelve years later, Hill deplored the effect of Macaulay's "nonsense" on "all those who have advanced as far as reading, but have not as yet attained to thinking."[20] Like Fitzgerald, Hill believed that Boswell's text should be presented as he had intended, not interpolated with Johnsoniana from other sources. But Hill's was very far from being the book that Boswell wrote. Hill seized on Boswell's boastful sub-subtitle—"The whole exhibiting a view of literature and literary men in Great Britain, for near half a century, during which he flourished"—and poured a lifetime's learning into the annotation, which became almost as extensive as the original text. Many pages had more Hill than Boswell, and each volume concluded in long appendices. Even his index was a dreadnought, occupying one whole volume of the six. Hill allowed that he was producing a reference work for scholars, not a book to read.

Like Fitzgerald, Hill stressed Boswell's achievement as a writer, rather than as a mere accumulator of Johnsoniana. He castigated Croker for his ignorance and insensitivity in producing "that monstrous medley." Only a "blockhead" (one of Johnson's favourite terms of abuse), Hill declared, "could with scissors and paste-pot have mangled the biography which of all others is the delight and the boast of the English-speaking world."[21] Yet even Hill, who was later to issue a scholarly edition of Johnson's collected letters (1892) and a collection of Johnsoniana entitled *Johnsonian Miscellanies* (1897), was to succumb to the temptation to compile a greatest-hits volume: *A Selection of the Wit and Wisdom of Dr Johnson,* published in 1888.

Boswell's biography had now sucked in everything else ever written about Johnson—not in the text, as in Croker's edition, but in the notes. This fact in itself could be confusing to the reader. The original notes written by Boswell and Malone appeared alongside Hill's notes, many of them based on diaries and other writings published later and never seen by either writer or editor of the *Life of Johnson*. For example, Fanny Burney had recorded in her diary Johnson's reference to Sir John Hawkins as "a most *unclubable* man!"[22] Boswell, of course, would have been delighted by this description of his rival, particularly as Johnson had described *him* as "clubable." But it is doubtful that he was ever aware of it; Fanny Burney refused him access to her diary, and it was published long after his death. Hill's inclusion of this extract from Miss Burney's diaries in his notes suggested the opposite to the casual reader—particularly since some subsequent editions have omitted the notes but included the reference in the index.[23]

Hill's edition, especially as revised in the twentieth century by L. F. Powell, brought the cycle of Boswell editions full circle. No longer would Boswell's text be regarded as a randomly collected store of Johnsoniana, to be raided at will: protected within a fortress of scholarly apparatus, it was now safe from further ravage. One of the most amusing aspects of Hill's work was his use of Johnson's writings in his annotation (thus fulfilling Carlyle's prediction that Johnson's writings would one day become "Prolegomena" and "expository Scholia" to "this *Johnsoniad* of Boswell"). Hill produced hundreds of footnotes demonstrating the similarities between what Johnson had written and what Boswell had reported him to say. In Hill's view such parallels buttressed Boswell's claim to authenticity. In fact, though much of Johnson's conversation was undoubtedly authentic, much of it had been reconstructed days, months, or even years afterwards, and both Boswell and Malone had used their familiarity with Johnson's writings to fill out the gaps in Boswell's record, paraphrasing what Johnson had written into direct speech. Without knowing it, Hill had found traces of the path they had followed, but it had taken him in the opposite direction.[24]

Like Croker before him, Hill made an approach to the Boswell family, in the hope that some papers had survived; and like Croker and no doubt several others, he was unsuccessful. The doors of Auchinleck remained closed to scholars.

Hill's *Wit and Wisdom of Dr Johnson* mixed quotations from Johnson's writings with quotations from Boswell, as if they were one and the same. Thus, a century after the publication of the *Life of Johnson*, Boswell had succeeded beyond even his wildest expectations. His writings were united with those of his master. The character he had created in his biography was assumed to be wholly authentic. Stealthily, imperceptibly, Boswell's Johnson had become one with Johnson himself.

Sir James Boswell had no sons, but two daughters, and he was determined that the Auchinleck estate should pass to them and their descendants. This meant breaking the terms of the entail drawn up by Lord Auchinleck, which stipulated that the estate should pass to the nearest heir male. When Sir James's lawyers scrutinized the deed of entail, they found one word that had been changed without being properly authenticated, and on the basis of this technicality Sir James was able to have the entail set aside. (Had he not succeeded, the present owner of the estate would have been an individual who is instead a retired dentist in North Somerset.) After his death in 1857, the estate therefore passed through his widow to his two daughters, one of whom married an Irish peer, Lord Talbot de Malahide. Their son, who was later to become the sixth Lord Talbot, eventually inherited the whole estate in 1905 following the deaths of both his mother and his childless aunt; but he continued to live in the Talbot family home at Malahide Castle, near Dublin. As a result the house at Auchinleck was left empty for long periods, and its contents gradually dispersed. Neglected, the house began to deteriorate. In 1918, it was sublet, and in 1920, the whole estate was sold to a distant relation, Colonel John Douglas Boswell of Garallan, ironically a descendant of the dancing-master cousin that Lord Auchinleck had been so anxious to exclude from the succession.[25] The new owners failed to maintain the house, and its long-term decline continued. Like so many large country houses, it was used to billet soldiers during the Second World War, and suffered further damage as a result. By the mid-1970s, it had become a mere shell, its inside gutted to prevent the spread of rampant dry rot.

There was another irony in the fate of the estate. Boswell and Johnson had frequently discussed the necessity of passing property through the male line, ridiculing their friend Langton, who planned to leave his estate to his daughters. Their conversations on the subject were recorded at length in the *Life of Johnson*. Indeed, for Boswell, the subject of male inheritance became an obsession; he could not bear the idea that the family property would pass into the control of an outsider, a man with a different name. So it was doubly ironic that Colonel Boswell should have bought the estate.

In 1905, the fifth Lord Talbot visited Auchinleck and spent some time rummaging through the Boswell family papers. He is said to have come down from the attic "as black as a miner." Afterwards the papers were packed up and shipped over to Ireland. A few years later his younger brother, Colonel Milo Talbot, was staying at Malahide Castle while Lord Talbot and his second wife were holidaying in South America. To pass the time, he read Boswell's journals, perhaps the first person to have examined them in any detail for more than a century. On his brother's return he recommended that they should be looked at by a publisher, and after some discussion an expurgated version of the journals was typed up and sent to Sir John Murray in London. Murray's reply indicated his "disappointment" or even "dismay" at what the journals revealed. "Many passages have been cut out, I presume on account of their immorality; but if they were worse than many which remain they must have been bad indeed." He regretted that he could not offer to publish the book.[26]

Murray's decision was understandable in the context of the time; it would have been impossible then for a respectable publisher to have issued Boswell's journals, except in a heavily expurgated form. But he justified his decision with contradictory logic; he quoted Macaulay's poor opinion of Boswell's character, and then went on to argue that if the journals were published, "Bozzy" would "inevitably fall very low in public estimation." How could he fall any lower? Murray was not thinking clearly, and his letter showed the continuing influence of Macaulay's diatribe seventy years on.

The Talbots took no further action. Murray's reaction reinforced their reluctance to allow the journals to pass out of the family's control.

Boswell's papers remained at Malahide Castle, in a fine ebony cabinet from Auchinleck that had once belonged to Boswell himself. Occasionally a letter or a journal would be fetched out and read to guests after dinner.

Professor Chauncey Brewster Tinker of Yale University devoted the best years of his life to the study of Boswell; he was, perhaps, the first exclusively Boswellian scholar. In 1922, he published *Young Boswell*, a series of linked biographical essays rather than a biography. In his Preface, Tinker asserted his belief that his subject had "fared rather badly" at the hands of his critics: "That Boswell was at times a very foolish young man any reader may see; but he was not, I think, as foolish as many of his critics have been." This was a sensible book, anticipating many of the conclusions reached by later scholars with far more information at their disposal. Tinker took an indulgent attitude towards Boswell's behaviour (one very different from that of Sir John Murray), and insisted on his genius as a writer.

Two years later Tinker issued a two-volume set of Boswell's letters, including more than one hundred previously unpublished. The edition was intended to be definitive: Tinker had drawn heavily on the collections of wealthy American collectors such as R. B. Adam of Buffalo, A. Edward Newton of Philadelphia, and J. Pierpont Morgan of New York. Morgan had acquired Boswell's letters to Temple, and Tinker was able to show that previous editions of these had been extensively bowdlerized. He now published them almost complete: "Only two or three phrases appeared to me unprintable."[27]

Tinker had placed an advertisement in the *Times Literary Supplement* asking for letters; one of the responses he received was a postcard from Dublin with an illegible signature, recommending him to "try Malahide Castle." He wrote to Lord Talbot accordingly, but his approach was rebuffed. This was the sixth Lord Talbot, a reserved, middle-aged bachelor, who had succeeded to the title at the age of forty-seven. Perhaps his full name provides a clue to his continuing reticence on the subject of his famous ancestor: James Boswell Talbot. In 1924, however, the year that Tinker's edition of the Boswell letters appeared, Lord Talbot married Joyce Gunning Kerr, a much younger woman, lively, intelligent, and attractive. She revived the proposal to publish Boswell's journals, and in 1925, the Talbots entered into discussions with another publisher, Eveleigh Nash of the firm Nash & Grayson. Reluctantly, Nash decided that the journal was too improper to publish unexpurgated. An expurgated edition would be interesting only to scholars, he thought, and this would be too costly to produce.

That summer Tinker tried again. Through the American Consul-General in Dublin he was able to arrange an introduction to Lord Talbot, and in due course he received an invitation to Malahide. There he was received politely by Lady Talbot. Over tea she confirmed that there were indeed Boswell papers at Malahide Castle, including two cases that had never been opened since arriving from Auchinleck. Tinker's immediate offer of editorial assistance was declined. He was led through into an adjoining room, until he found himself standing before the famous ebony cabinet. Opening some of its drawers, he saw that they were crammed with Boswell papers. "I felt like Sinbad in the valley of rubies." Tinker was allowed only a few moments to marvel at the contents of the ebony cabinet before being led away in a daze. He realized immediately that a new day had dawned for Boswellians. For Tinker himself, the discovery was "a dreadful crisis." His edition of Boswell's letters, on which he had built his reputation as a scholar, was hopelessly obsolete, only a year after its first publication. He did not sleep that night.

Tinker left Malahide in despair. He sent a postcard from Dublin to the collector A. Edward Newton: "Everything here and nothing to be touched. I have been on the rack." News of his find circulated quickly within the small circle of eighteenth-century collectors and dealers, and within weeks of Tinker's visit the Talbots received a telegram from America offering them £50,000 for the collection, sight unseen. This crude offer was spurned.

Crossing the Atlantic on the liner *Majestic,* Newton happened to meet his friend Lieutenant-Colonel Ralph Heyward Isham. He mentioned the papers, and suggested that Isham might go to Malahide in an attempt to secure them. Like Newton, Isham was a collector, but of a very unusual kind. Strikingly handsome, he had wit and style in abundance, and was an excellent raconteur; Newton enviously described him as "a fascinating devil." Moreover, despite his American birth, he spoke with an English accent, having enlisted as a private in the British Army at the start of the First World War and worked his way up to the rank of Lieutenant-Colonel. Afterwards he had made a successful business career in the United States. By the time he heard about the Boswell papers, he was at the height of his powers: thirty-five years old, wealthy, sophisticated, persuasive, tactful, energetic, and charming. If anyone could succeed with Lady Talbot, he could.

Isham was too canny to force his way into Malahide Castle waving his cheque-book. Instead, he began to court the Talbots indirectly, through intermediaries. It was a year before Isham himself went to tea with Lady Talbot, but once he had his foot in the door, his charm melted the family resistance. Soon after his first visit, he was able to buy from the Talbots a letter to Boswell from Oliver Goldsmith. In 1927, he spent three days with Lady Talbot sorting through a mass of Boswell letters and other papers, and agreed to purchase them for the sum of £13,585. Later he bought one of Boswell's journals, an account of the ten days Boswell had spent with Johnson at Ashbourne, for £1,250. Lord Talbot had been reluctant to allow any of the journals to pass outside the family's protection, but Isham reasoned that there was little danger in this case, because the Ashbourne journal had already been printed almost verbatim within the *Life of Johnson*. Subsequently, Isham was able to purchase the remainder of the Boswell journals from Lord Talbot— some four thousand pages—for a further £20,000. It was agreed that Lady Talbot should work through the journals, censoring particularly objectionable passages, before they were sent to him in relays.

Isham now began to lay plans to publish the Boswell papers, in an attempt to recoup his outlay. He was determined that the job should be done properly, as befitted papers of such importance. Tinker was the obvious choice to act as editor; he accepted Isham's invitation to pass a day looking through the papers in a room at Claridge's Hotel, but then shocked his host by declining the offer to edit them. Emotions ran high as Isham escorted Tinker out. In the hotel lobby, Tinker raised his fist and burst out angrily: "You have stolen my mistress!"

Isham's next choice was his friend T. E. Lawrence, who also declined, replying that he was not "a literary bird" and confessing that he had never read a line of any of Boswell's books. Another chance meeting led to a more suitable suggestion. Isham was lunching at Simpson's-in-the-Strand when he was clapped on the shoulder by Newton, who had returned from Europe only the previous day. Newton was naturally excited to hear about Isham's purchases, and came to his hotel suite that same evening to examine them. In the small hours of the morning, Isham outlined his difficulties in finding an editor; after a few moments' consideration, Newton recommended Geoffrey Scott, a young Englishman who had written a much-admired book about Boswell's friend Belle de Zuylen, *A Portrait of Zélide,* and who had already been asked by a publisher to write a life of Boswell. Two days later Scott arrived at Isham's hotel; the two men sat up all night looking through the papers, and the next day, at Isham's suggestion, Scott moved into Claridge's, working there until Isham left for New York. By the time of his departure they had agreed that Scott should edit the collection. This would appear in eighteen volumes, expensively produced in a limited edition for private subscribers in the eighteenth-century manner. Further funding would be obtained from the sale of subsidiary rights, and a biography written by Scott. Such was the commercial interest in this project that the projected publishers of the biography, Harcourt Brace, were able to sell serial rights in advance for $30,000.

When Isham began to receive portions of the journals from Lady Talbot, he was shocked by the extent of her deletions. It seemed that she had inked over even some passages which had already been printed within the *Life of Johnson.* But by holding the documents up to the light (and by various other methods) it proved possible to read the words that she had attempted to obliterate. Isham and Scott decided between them that if at all possible the journals should be published as they had been written, and after some persuasion the Talbots hesitantly agreed.

Scott's editing was exemplary and his introductions to each volume superb, but sadly he was able to edit only six of these volumes before his premature death in 1929. His successor as editor was Frederick A. Pottle, a former pupil of Tinker's who had already demonstrated his brilliance in a superb bibliography, *The Literary Career of James Boswell.* Pottle turned out to be another excellent editor; in 1931, he was able to crack the cipher used by Boswell to conceal some of the most sensitive passages of his journal (curiously enough, the very same as the one used by Pepys). But Isham's problems were multiplying. The Wall Street Crash had drastically reduced the value of his investments: by 1934, his income from the family trust had fallen to about one-quarter of what it had been in 1928. As a result of the financial crisis, subscriptions to his edition of the Boswell papers began to fall by the wayside. And in 1930, Isham received exciting but alarming news from Malahide: a croquet box had been found stuffed with more Boswell papers, including the original manuscript of *The Journal of a Tour to the Hebrides*. With borrowed money, Isham was able to secure this further hoard for £4,000, bringing his total investment in the Boswell papers near to £40,000—perhaps £1 million in today's money—and of course he had spent a great deal of money in producing the lavish private edition, perhaps twice as much again. In 1933, his second marriage collapsed. He was forced to sell both his beautiful Long Island home and most of his precious collection of rare books and manuscripts, at prices much lower than they would have been before the stock market collapse.

By 1936, however, the worst seemed to be in the past. Pottle had proved an efficient as well as a judicious editor, and only the index to Isham's edition of the Boswell papers remained to be published. Then, on 9 March, came another shock. A story in *The Times* announced the discovery at a house in Scotland of another stock-pile of Boswell papers: more than 1,000 letters, including 119 of Johnson's letters to various correspondents—letters that Boswell had borrowed for use in his biography and failed to return—and several missing portions of Boswell's journal. This was a literary discovery of the first importance, but for Isham it was almost a disaster.

These new Boswell papers had been found more than five years earlier by a lecturer at Aberdeen University, Claude Colleer Abbott, who was then carrying out research into Boswell's contemporary, the picturesque poet and philosopher James Beattie. Knowing that Sir William Forbes had written a biography of Beattie, Abbott was searching through Forbes's papers at Fettercairn House, in Kincardineshire, about twenty-five miles south-west of Aberdeen, when he stumbled across a package of letters from Sir Alexander Boswell and his brother. At the bottom of a stack of Sir William's manuscripts he found a faded and bat-tered volume, which proved to be one of Boswell's journals. Following this serendipitous find, Abbott had conducted a systematic search, and kept coming across more, including a loose packet labelled in Boswell's hand, "Concerning Ladies." Among its contents Abbott was startled to find a lock of fair hair. From the farthest corner of the attic, he dragged out a sack stuffed tight with Boswell's letters. His final haul was a collec-tion approximately half as much again as that already owned by Isham.

Abbott's momentous discovery had been kept secret at the wish of Lord Clinton, owner of Fettercairn House where the papers were found. In April 1931, he had consulted Humphrey Milford and R. W. Chapman, two senior officials of the Oxford University Press, about the possibility of publishing the manuscripts. They were in prin-ciple prepared to proceed, provided that the copyright issues could be resolved. It was by no means clear whether Lord Clinton was in a posi-tion to license the copyright, or even whether these papers of Boswell's belonged to him. Clinton wanted these questions answered before the discovery was made public, and the matter kept private until the papers had been catalogued and the catalogue published. Within the Claren-don Press (the academic arm of the OUP), the project was given the code-name "Operation Hush."

The delay was of course very damaging to Isham, who proceeded with his edition of the Boswell papers, ignorant of the existence of the Fettercairn find. Indeed, it compromised Chapman, who had sought Isham's assistance with his own edition of Johnson's letters, and who was due to publish the index to Isham's edition. Another kept in the dark all this time was L. F. Powell, who was engaged in revising Hill's six-volume edition of the *Life of Johnson* for the OUP. Not until after the fourth volume was published was he told of this important discovery, which had been known to his publishers almost five years.

Complex litigation followed over the next decade to determine the ownership both of the copyright in the Fettercairn papers and of the papers themselves. In the meantime, Isham had found more papers at Malahide: a tin dispatch-box containing fragments of Boswell's jour-nal, a diary of Johnson's, and various other papers. The Talbots agreed that he should have these for his collection without further payment.

By the time war broke out in Europe in 1939, Isham was exhausted and depressed. He had spent most of his fortune, and was living alone in a New York hotel. He had married again for the third time in 1937, but the marriage lasted only a few months. His beloved daughter died, leaving two children. His own health deteriorated. Relations with Pottle had frayed, after a succession of financial wrangles. The litigation over the Fettercairn papers was unresolved; claimants to the copyright included an ever-increasing number of Boswell's descendants, as well as Lord Clinton and even the Cumberland Infirmary. Without these his collection was incomplete. His whole effort had been devoted to bringing the Boswell papers together, and it seemed that events had conspired to thwart him.

He was therefore thunderstruck to receive a cable early in 1941 reporting the discovery of yet another cache of Boswell manuscripts at Malahide. At the outbreak of war, the local parish council had asked the Talbots if the loft of one of their farmyard buildings might be used as an emergency grain store. The loft was stuffed with old furniture, and to clear it a rotting staircase had to be replaced. In October 1940, workmen clearing the loft found two large packing-cases in the far corner: repositories for more Boswell papers, including most of the manuscript of the *Life of Johnson*. Isham was upset when the Talbots asked him to pay for these further manuscripts, not for their own benefit, but in aid of Ayrshire air-raid victims. He sent Lady Talbot an emotional letter which could easily have led to the breakdown of negotiations between them. Fortunately, she did not take lasting offence at his outburst, and after the war Isham was able to purchase the grain-loft cache to add to the Boswell manuscripts already in his possession, with the help of a generous interest-free loan from the collector Donald F. Hyde. Eventually too Isham managed to raise the money to buy out the remaining claimants to the Fettercairn find, which could now be reunited with the rest of the Boswell papers after a separation of more than 150 years. On 28 July 1948, the *Queen Mary* berthed in New York, bearing the Fettercairn manuscripts; their arrival was announced on CBS News, and Isham's photograph subsequently appeared on the front page of *The New York Times*. Sadly, Isham himself could not be present to greet them; he had been stricken by a serious illness, which kept him in bed for months. But he recovered sufficiently to complete the negotiations with Yale University for the purchase of the complete collection, negotiations which had been in train for some years and in which Hyde had played an important part. On 14 July 1949, the Boswell papers arrived at Yale University Library under armed guard. The name of one of the campus policemen escorting the eight Boswell trunks into their new home was Edmund Malone.[28]

Even then, the extraordinary story of the Boswell papers was not finished. In 1950, Lady Talbot produced a fresh suitcase full of "oddments," some five hundred or so items, which Yale University bought to add to its collection; and only a year afterwards, Isham heard that an old deed-box had been unearthed, containing more Boswell manuscripts. "My God!" he exclaimed, "is there no end to the Boswell saga?" A trickle of Boswell papers has continued ever since. In 1961, for example, the door of an old chest-on-chest, which had been stuck closed for many years, sprang open while being moved by workmen; inside was a drawer containing more of Boswell's vast archive.[29] Still remaining to be found are several important batches of Boswell papers, including those letters to Temple not retrieved by Major Stone, Boswell's journal in Holland, and, most important of all, his correspondence with Johnson.

At Yale an editorial committee was established, headed by Pottle, to oversee the publication of the Boswell papers. Its administrative offices within the university library soon became known as "the Boswell factory." The editorial committee was supported by a larger advisory committee, consisting of twenty-four scholars, half American, half British. Anticipating widespread interest, the editors decided to produce two editions, one for the general reader and one for scholars, totalling perhaps forty or fifty volumes. "The Boswell Papers," the publishers proudly announced, "are the largest and most important find of English literary manuscripts ever made." The first volume to be published, *Boswell's London Journal* (1950), was instantly recognized as a classic. Plaudits resounded around the world. Malcolm Muggeridge described it as "a unique book," and its publication as "a unique literary event"; Stephen Spender praised it as "an extraordinary work of art, as much an 'experiment in time' in its way as Proust's great work"; William Plomer hailed Boswell as "a great creative writer."[30]

As part of the Fettercairn find, *Boswell's London Journal* had not formed part of Isham's privately published edition of the Boswell papers, and was therefore being made available to readers for the very first time. The journal provided an account of Boswell's second visit to London, from the time he left Edinburgh in the autumn of 1762 until his departure for Holland in the summer of 1763. This was a particularly interesting period, encompassing Boswell's first meeting with Johnson and the formation of their friendship. It also marked the beginning of Boswell's experiment in keeping a fully written journal, which was to prove so important in his life. This particular journal exerted a special charm, written as it was by a young man in his early twenties, full of hope and vigour, experiencing life with corresponding freshness. It related his erotic escapades: his seduction of Louisa, for example, or his encounter with two "very pretty little girls" in a room at the Shakespeare's Head Tavern in Covent Garden. The public lapped up such detail; it was pleasant to be able to read about behaviour not normally described in respectable publications, in a work acknowledged as literature. Even today, the mention of Boswell's name is apt to provoke a smirk. Published in 1950, nearly two hundred years after it was written, *Boswell's London Journal* sold almost a million copies.[31]

After such a start, subsequent sales were bound to be disappointing, and so it proved, with the print-runs of later volumes in the series dwindling to only a few thousand copies. Nevertheless, Boswell had penetrated the public consciousness, and the effect was to create a new interest in him as an individual, distinct from Boswell the biographer of Johnson. In many ways, *Boswell's London Journal* was a more approachable book than Boswell's *Life of Johnson*, and the lively young man whose adventures it chronicled was a more attractive figure than the elderly, domineering, and sometimes cantankerous individual evoked in his biography. Attitudes had changed in the 120-odd years since Macaulay's slurs; conduct that had then seemed reprehensible now seemed forgivable, even admirable. Twentieth-century readers were less judgemental, more inclined to see personal failings as foibles: also less admiring, more inclined to scepticism about moralists and moralizing. Modern biography was revealing the lives of subjects as never before; and few heroes could survive such scrutiny unscathed. In this context Boswell's cheerful frankness appeared more sympathetic than Johnson's solemn reticence.

Of course, this contrast was to some extent misleading. Boswell had not written his journals for publication, while the Johnson known to the public was the one presented by his biographer.

Boswell's plain, direct prose was easy to read, and appealed to twentieth-century readers as Johnson's mannered, classical style never could. Moreover, Boswell's interest in himself, which seemed so peculiar to his contemporaries, was very much more acceptable two centuries later. Indeed, Boswell seemed to offer a unique combination: a writer who poured the contents of his mind freely into his journal, without either embarrassment or knowingness. At the beginning of the twentieth century, Freud had instigated a new era in autobiography, preaching the value of introspection and self-analysis, while showing what might lie below the surface of conscious thought. The knowledge was also a loss of innocence; after Freud, writing about oneself could never again be the same. Here was a miracle: a pre-Freudian autobiographer who revealed everything in his mind, without restraint, concealment, or distortion. Or so it seemed.

Half a century later, Isham and Pottle are gone, but new volumes in the Yale edition of the Boswell papers continue to appear at intervals. So much fresh material has proved a feast for academics. A Boswell industry has come into being, producing studies of Boswell's letters, journals, and manuscripts. In particular, Boswell scholars have dissected his technique, showing how carefully he wrote. There is an increasing emphasis on Boswell as a writer of skill and even genius; the old notion of Boswell as a mere recorder of Johnson's remarks has been obliterated. And in their analysis of Boswell's craft, Boswellians have shown how meticulously he worked his portrait. Now revealed for the first time is the extent to which Boswell manipulated his sources, to achieve the effects he wanted. As the respect for Boswell's literary abilities grows, so the authenticity of his creation is increasingly called into question.

Boswell scholarship now threatens to swamp Johnson's: some twenty-five years after Yale acquired the Boswell papers, the Johnsonian specialist Donald Greene complained in the *Times Literary Supplement* that an avalanche of Boswell minutiae continued to tumble from the presses, while a scholarly edition of Johnson's works was blocked by lack of funds. Boswell's reputation, Greene suggested, had become "preposterously inflated." Elsewhere Greene has argued that Boswell's *Life of Johnson* is really an autobiography; he proposed that it should be called the "Memoirs of James Boswell, concerning his acquaintance with Samuel Johnson." Greene has even asserted that the book is a disguised attack on Johnson, an attempt to cut him down to size, and to establish Boswell's superiority over him. Of all the Johnsonian scholars, Greene is the most hostile to Boswell; he condemns Boswell for making Johnson appear "stupidly pompous," by always affixing the title "Dr" to his name. In fact, it is easy to show that by the time Johnson died, most of his inti-mate friends—Reynolds, Langton, and Burke, for example—referred to him as "Dr Johnson."[32] But Greene is by no means alone among Johnson scholars in reacting strongly to the new emphasis on Boswell. Drawing partly on the Boswell papers themselves, a new wave of Johnsonian stud-ies has attempted to differentiate the real Johnson from the figure evoked so powerfully in Boswell's book, and to re-assert Johnson's status as a great writer, not just a great talker. Thus, the tendency of the rival camps has been the same: to prise Boswell and Johnson apart.

Writing only a few years after Boswell's death, William Wordsworth hailed the *Life of Johnson* as a new kind of biography, one which broke taboos that needed breaking.[33] What the young poet relished about the book was its emphasis on character. Boswell's portrait of Johnson was extraordinarily vivid; like the Flemish painters, he displayed his model distinct in every pore. In providing so much intimate detail about Johnson, Boswell tore down the wall between public and private, revealing his subject as no previous biography had done. Through Boswell, Johnson became one of the most recognizable characters in literature, and has continued as such, long after his own writings have sunk into relative obscurity. Though Johnson himself had championed values rejected by the Romantics, his passionate intensity was a trait that they cherished, his long struggle a saga which inspired them.

"I write therefore I am alive," the besotted, grief-stricken Johnson wrote to the dying Hill Boothby. Though a fool in so many ways, Boswell had the wit to recognize the greatness in this sad, lonely, shabby, quick-tempered, warm-hearted, difficult man. Mrs Piozzi once remarked dismissively that Johnson's life consisted of little more than talking and writing. But Boswell conceived of Johnson's life as a drama of epic, almost mythic proportions. He depicted Johnson as a hero who defied oblivion, who strove mightily to impose meaning on chaos, illuminating the darkness through the clarity of his intellect and the force of his mind. Boswell's Johnson was a solitary genius who grappled single-handedly with the universe: often neglected, but proud, defiant, and independent. His biography showed how the life of a writer—no less than that of a soldier or a statesman—could encompass every variety of human experience: disappointment, triumph, courage, despair, anger, tenderness, laughter, and tragedy.

The *Life of Johnson* was soon acknowledged as a masterpiece. Boswell had extended the form into new territory, borrowing techniques from the novel, the theatre, and the confessional memoir. With meticulous care, with long-practised skill, and with a generous imagination, he crafted a character who lived and breathed. He also set new scholarly standards; his verification of every possible detail, which seemed so eccentric to his contemporaries, would become the norm. In doing what he did, he relied mainly on instinct, his sense of what would serve his purpose best. Boswell was influenced by other biographers, by Johnson in particular, but his book was quite different from any that had gone before—or, indeed, any that would be published after. For though the *Life of Johnson* was a pioneering work which opened up new possibilities for biography, it was also unique: never again will there be such a combination of subject, author, and opportunity.

LIST OF ABBREVIATIONS
USED IN THE NOTES

—◄◄∩∩∩∩►►—

Full citations of works listed here can be found in the Select Bibliography (see page 333).

Anecdotes	Hester Thrale Piozzi, *Anecdotes of the Late Samuel Johnson, LL.D.*
BJTH	*Boswell's Journal of a Tour to the Hebrides* (edition of the unedited manuscript)
BP	*The Private Papers of James Boswell*
Corresp.	The Yale "research" editions of the Boswell papers (by volume number)
D'Arblay	Charlotte Barrett and Austin Dobson (ed.), *Diary and Letters of Madame D'Arblay*
Earlier Years	Frederick A. Pottle, *James Boswell: The Earlier Years, 1740–1769*
EM	Edmond Malone
JB	James Boswell
Jnl	Journal
Later Years	Frank Brady, *James Boswell: The Later Years, 1769–1795*
Letters	*The Letters of James Boswell*
Life	*Boswell's Life of Johnson* (six-volume edition)
Lit. Career	Frederick A. Pottle, *The Literary Career of James Boswell*
SJ	Samuel Johnson
Treasure	David Buchanan, *The Treasure of Auchinleck: The Story of the Boswell Papers*
WJT	William Temple

YALE "TRADE" EDITIONS OF BOSWELL'S JOURNALS

AJ	*Boswell: The Applause of the Jury*
BD	*Boswell for the Defence*
BE	*Boswell in Extremes*
BH	*Boswell in Holland*
BLJ	*Boswell's London Journal*
BSW	*Boswell in Search of a Wife*
EE	*Boswell: The English Experiment*
GB	*Boswell: The Great Biographer*
GTGS	*Boswell on the Grand Tour: Germany and Switzerland*
GTICF	*Boswell on the Grand Tour: Italy, Corsica & France*
LA	*Boswell: Laird of Auchinleck*
OY	*Boswell: The Ominous Years*

NOTES

INTRODUCTION

1. From the opening sentence to the *Life of Johnson*.
2. This expression appears in the chapter "Boswell's Colossal Hoard," in Ian Hamilton's *Keepers of the Flame: Literary Estates and the Rise of Biography*, London 1992, p. 70.
3. Donald J. Greene, "Johnson without Boswell," *Times Literary Supplement*, 22 November 1974, pp. 315–16.
4. Preface to *Man and Superman*.
5. The definitive biography is published in two volumes, by Pottle and Brady respectively (see Select Bibliography, page 333). There is also a lively and well-written short life by Iain Finlayson, *The Moth and the Candle: A Life of James Boswell*, London, 1984; and a more substantial general biography by Peter Martin, *A Life of James Boswell*, London and New Haven, 1999.

I. IMMATURITY

1. JB to WJT, 2 September 1775: *Letters*, I, pp. 240–41.
2. *Life*, V, p. 51.
3. "Sketch of my life," written for Rousseau, 5 December 1764, in *Earlier Years*, p. 4.
4. Jnl, 23 October 1762: *BP*, I, p. 112.
5. Jnl, 1 April 1773 and 10 November 1783: *BD*, p. 164; *AJ*, p. 169.
6. Jnl, 9 May 1767 and 10 July 1769; 10 February 1776, 10 January 1780: *BSW*, pp. 71 and 246; *OY*, p. 233; *LA*, p. 165.
7. Jnl, 1 August 1782: *LA*, p. 467.
8. Jnl, 10 February 1763: *BLJ*, p. 188.
9. WJT to JB, September 1758: *Corresp.*, 6, pp. 21–23.
10. Jnl, 20 January 1763: *BLJ*, p. 161.

11. "Sketch of my life," p. 5.

12. JB to WJT, 1 May 1761: *Corresp.*, 6, p. 33.

13. JB to Andrew Erskine, 1763: quoted in *Earlier Years*, p. 83.

14. Jnl, 27 November 1762: *BLJ*, pp. 51–52.

15. David Hume to JB, 24 February, JB to Hume, 1 March 1763: *BLJ*, pp. 206–9.

16. Jnl, 9 February 1763: *BLJ*, pp. 186–87.

17. Jnl, 1 December 1762: *BLJ*, p. 62.

18. Jnl, 21 November and 1 December 1762: *BLJ*, pp. 47 and 61–63.

19. SJ to Joseph Baretti, 10 June 1761: *Life*, I, p. 363.

20. Jnl, 8 December 1762: *BLJ*, pp. 71–72.

21. See the Introduction to *BLJ*, pp. 16–19, for a general discussion of this topic.

22. Linda Colley, *Britons: Forging the Nation 1707–1837*, New Haven and London, 1992, pp. 121–22.

23. Jnl, 14 May 1763: *BLJ*, pp. 258–59.

2. FORWARDNESS

1. *Life*, I, pp. 383–84.

2. Jnl, 21 September 1762: *BP*, I, p. 70.

3. *Life*, I, p. 224.

4. See Kernan, *Printing Technology, Letters and Samuel Johnson.*

5. Jnl, 18 January and 8 February 1763: *BLJ*, pp. 152 and 183.

6. *Life*, I, p. 392.

7. ibid., pp. 396–99.

8. ibid., p. 445.

9. JB to Sir David Dalrymple, 2 July 1763: *Letters*, I, pp. 16–17.

10. *Life*, I, pp. 423–25.

11. Jnl, 11 December 1762, 9 February and 28 March 1763: *BLJ*, pp. 76, 187, 227–28.

12. Brewer, *The Pleasures of the Imagination*, pp. 107–12.

13. JB to Lord Kames, 24 October 1762: see Ian Ross, *Lord Kames and the Scotland of His Day*, Oxford, 1972, p. 251; Jnl, 4 November 1762: *BP*, I, pp. 115 and 127–29.

14. Jnl, 14 January 1763: *BLJ*, pp. 142–43.

15. Jnl, 6 and 9 February 1763: *BLJ*, pp. 179 and 186–87.

16. Jnl, 19 October 1775 and 24–26 September 1793: *OY*, p. 168, and *GB*, p. 237.

17. *Life*, III, p. 288.

18. Lord Auchinleck to JB, 30 May 1763: *BLJ*, pp. 337–42.

19. Jnl, 14 April 1763: *BLJ*, p. 241n.

20. Jnl, 22 July 1763: *BLJ*, p. 319.

21. *Life*, II, p. 82.

22. ibid., I, pp. 471, 432.

23. ibid., II, p. 441.

24. ibid., IV, pp. 427–28.

25. ibid., I, p. 472.

26. ibid.

27. JB to John Johnston and WJT, 23 September and 16 August 1763: *BH,* pp. 6 and 7–8.

28. JB to WJT, 2 September 1763: *BH,* pp. 15–16.

29. *BH,* pp. 35, 33, and 375–78.

30. Jnl, 4 January 1776, 26 October 1775, and 31 July 1779: *OY,* pp. 214 and 171; *LA,* p. 126.

31. Jnl, 17 March 1776: *OY,* p. 265.

32. *Life,* V, p. 308.

33. Jnl, 9 November 1774: *OY,* p. 35.

34. Lord Auchinleck to JB, 10 August 1765: *GTICF,* p. 223.

35. Hume to the Comtesse de Boufflers, 12 February 1766: *GTICF,* p. 294n.

36. The great Boswellian scholar Frederick A. Pottle doubts some details of this story, but he produces no evidence to contradict the eye-witness account left by Lord Cadross (*Earlier Years,* p. 528).

37. Rogers (ed.), *Boswelliana,* p. 328.

3. SUBORDINATION

1. Jnl, 10 October 1783: *AJ,* p. 163.

2. Jnl, 19 January 1768: *BSW,* p. 129.

3. Jnl, 17 November 1774: *OY,* p. 39.

4. Jnl, 22 September 1774: *BD,* p. 302.

5. Jnl, 10 January 1775: *OY,* p. 54.

6. Jnl, 29 August 1782: *LA,* p. 477.

7. Jnl, 18 September 1774: *BD,* p. 335.

8. Jnl, 18 September 1774 and 3 November 1775: *BD,* p. 335, and *OY,* p. 174.

9. SJ to Mrs Thrale, 3 November 1773: *Letters of Samuel Johnson,* I, p. 385.

10. JB to WJT, 30 March 1767: *Letters,* I, p. 108.

11. JB to SJ, 3 March 1772: *BD,* p. 27.

12. Jnl, 20 April 1772: *BD,* pp. 137–38.

13. SJ to JB, early September 1772: *BD,* p. 151.

14. For a fascinating and full exploration of this idea, see the chapter "The Rambler and the Wanderer," in Pat Rogers's *Johnson and Boswell: The Transit of Caledonia,* pp. 139–70.

15. *BJTH,* pp. 35, 50.

16. ibid., pp. 23–24.

17. Jnl, 8 February 1763: *BLJ,* p. 182.

18. Fiona J. Stafford, *The Sublime Savage: A Study of James Macpherson and the Poems of Ossian,* London, 1988, p. 177.

19. Johnson, *Journey to the Western Islands of Scotland,* p. 108.

20. JB to SJ, 2 February, SJ to JB, 7 February 1775: *Life,* II, pp. 295 and 296–97.

21. Jnl, 6 and 21 March 1775: *OY,* pp. 73, 87.

22. *Life,* II, pp. 242, 159, and III, p. 347.

23. Jnl, 24 March 1775: *OY,* p. 94.

24. Jnl, 6 April 1772: *BD,* p. 103.

25. Jnl, "Review of My Life," summer 1775 and 11 March 1776: *OY*, pp. 158 and 250.

26. *Life*, V, p. 154.

27. Jnl, 19 March 1776: *OY*, pp. 276–77.

28. Jnl, 22 September 1777: *BE*, p. 181.

29. *Life*, IV, p. 71.

30. SJ to JB, 9 September 1769 and 20 June 1771: *Life*, II, pp. 70 and 140.

31. *D'Arblay*, II, p. 510.

32. *Life*, III, p. 64.

33. *BJTH*, p. 292.

34. *Life*, II, p. 326n.

35. *D'Arblay*, I, p. 509.

36. *Life*, III, p. 331.

37. ibid., II, p. 257.

38. *D'Arblay*, I, p. 511.

39. Jnl, 2–8 May 1778: *BE*, pp. 328–29.

40. *Life*, III, p. 198.

41. Jnl, 15 May 1781: *LA*, pp. 355–56.

42. Jnl, 27 December 1775: *OY*, p. 206.

43. Jnl, 9 August 1781: *LA*, pp. 389–90.

44. Jnl, 9 December 1784: *AJ*, pp. 267–68.

45. JB to WJT, 22 May 1775: *Letters*, I, pp. 224–26.

46. Brady, *Boswell's Political Career*, p. 13.

47. Jnl, 12 December 1784: *AJ*, pp. 269–70.

48. Jnl, 29 and 30 June 1784: *AJ*, pp. 253–55; *Life*, IV, pp. 336–39.

49. *Life*, IV, p. 360.

50. JB to WJT, 20 July 1784: *AJ*, pp. 261–62.

51. *Life*, IV, p. 379.

52. ibid., p. 380.

53. Jnl, 12 November 1784: *AJ*, pp. 263 and 263n.

4. INDEPENDENCE

1. JB to Thomas Barnard, 20 March 1785: *Corresp.*, 3, pp. 183–85.

2. Jnl, 17 and 18 December 1784: *AJ*, pp. 271–72.

3. WJT to JB, 6 January 1785: *Corresp.*, 2, p. 39.

4. Dilly's letters are summarized in Boswell's Register of Letters, quoted in *Corresp.*, 2, pp. liii–liv.

5. Jnl, 29 May 1785: *AJ*, p. 303.

6. JB to Sir Joshua Reynolds, 23 December 1784: *Corresp.*, 3, pp. 174–77.

7. *Life*, IV, pp. 401–5; Jnl, 28 December 1785: *AJ*, p. 274; Dr Richard Brocklesby to JB, 27 December 1784: *Corresp.*, 2, pp. 31–35.

8. Jnl, 28 December 1784: *AJ*, p. 274.

9. Steevens's letters to the *St James's Chronicle* are quoted in *AJ*, p. 279.

10. JB to Mary Cobb, 15 February 1785, quoted in *Corresp.*, 2, pp. 52–53.

11. Adams to JB, 17 February 1785: *Corresp.*, 2, pp. 56–63; *Life*, I, pp. 77–78.

12. Jnl, 30 September 1764: *GTGS,* pp. 114–16; *Life,* III, pp. 118 and 122n.
13. *Life,* I, p. 60.
14. Jnl, 31 March 1772: *BD,* pp. 86–87.
15. Jnl, 11 May 1772: *BD,* pp. 139–40.
16. JB to Garrick, 10 September 1772: *Corresp.,* 4, p. 45.
17. Jnl, 11 April 1773: *BD,* p. 183.
18. Jnl, 14 October 1773: *BJTH,* pp. 300 and 300n.
19. Jnl, 8 April 1775: *OY,* p. 135.
20. William Strahan to JB, 17 November 1778: *Corresp.,* 2, p. 12.
21. SJ to JB, 9 September 1769: *Life,* II, p. 70.
22. Jnl, 23 February 1785: *AJ,* p. 277.
23. *Life,* IV, pp. 482–83.
24. Boswell's dream is related in a notebook once in the possession of Professor Chauncey B. Tinker, now missing: quoted in *AJ,* p. 284.
25. JB to Thomas Percy, 20 March 1785: *Corresp.,* 2, pp. 75–76.
26. *BJTH,* p. 188.
27. ibid., pp. 193, 226, 188.
28. ibid., p. 241.
29. ibid., p. 245. In the printed version, this is changed to "a very exact picture of a portion of his life."
30. ibid., p. 341.
31. Boswell had referred to the possibility of Johnson's writing a book about the tour in his journal entry for the previous day (20 October), but he was usually several days behind in writing up his journal, and this must have been written after Johnson had disclosed his intention. Conceivably the same is true of Boswell's reference in the entry for 14 October to Johnson's being anxious to return to the mainland and start writing; but he may have meant that Johnson was anxious to obtain some paper there so that he could write some letters, which could only be sent from the mainland (see the entry for the following day, 15 October).
32. *BJTH,* p. 79n.
33. SJ to JB, 4 July, 1 October, and 26 November 1774: *Life,* II, pp. 279–80, 284–85, and 288.
34. Johnson, *A Journey to the Western Islands of Scotland,* p. 3; *Life,* V, p. 57.
35. Jnl, 11 February 1775: *OY,* pp. 63–64.
36. Sir William Forbes to JB, 6 January 1775: *OY,* p. 51n.
37. Jnl, 27 March 1775: *OY,* pp. 101–2. Boswell reflected bitterly in his journal for this day that Johnson "did not seem very desirous that my little bark [boat] should 'pursue the triumph and partake the gale,'" a quotation from Pope which he was eventually to use as an epigraph to his *Tour:*

> O! while along the stream of time, thy name
> Expanded flies, and gathers all its fame,
> Say, shall my little bark attendant fail,
> Pursue the triumph and partake the gale?

Boswell drew an analogy between himself and his book, attendant on Johnson and on his *Journey to the Western Islands of Scotland* (*Life*, III, p. 190).

38. JB to WJT, 10 May 1775: *Letters*, I, pp. 221–23.
39. Hester Lynch Thrale to JB, 18 May 1775: Hyde, *The Impossible Friendship*, p. 30.
40. SJ to Mrs Thrale, 22 May, 11 and 19 June 1775: *Letters of Samuel Johnson*, II,
     pp. 31–32, 43, and 47.
41. Jnl, 22 October 1773: *BJTH*, p. 346.

5. COLLABORATION

1.   JB to EM, 2 November 1785: *Corresp.*, 4, p. 266.
2.   See Robert E. Kelley and OM Brack Jr, *Samuel Johnson's Early Biographers*,
     Iowa, 1971.
3.   *D'Arblay*, II, p. 400.
4.   Jnl, 29 May 1785: *AJ*, p. 303.
5.   See Boswell's letter to WJT of 8 July 1784, quoted in *AJ*, pp. 259–60; and *LA*,
     p. 356.
6.   Hugh Trevor-Roper, "The Highland Tradition of Scotland," in *The Invention
     of Tradition*, ed. Eric Hobsbawm and Terence Ranger, London, 1983.
7.   Jnl, 11 August 1785: *AJ*, p. 336.
8.   *BJTH*, pp. 241–42.
9.   ibid., p. 47.
10. Jnl, 14–27 July 1785: *AJ*, pp. 323–30.
11. EM to JB, 5 October, JB to EM, 15 October 1785: *Corresp.*, 4, pp. 200 and 226.
12. Jnl, 15 August 1785: *AJ*, p. 337.
13. Revd Hugh Blair to JB, 7 March 1785: *Corresp.*, 2, pp. 71–73.
14. JB to EM, 30–31 October 1785: *Corresp.*, 4, p. 260.
15. *Life*, V, p. 19.

6. ANGER

1.   Lord Macdonald to JB, 27 November 1785: *Later Years*, p. 308.
2.   JB to EM, 29 October 1785: *Corresp.*, 4, p. 258.
3.   WJT to JB, 14 October 1785: quoted in *Later Years*, p. 322.
4.   EM to JB, 5 October and 5 November 1785: *Corresp.*, 4, pp. 201 and 271.
5.   Joseph Cooper Walker to JB, 13 November 1785: *Corresp.*, 2, p. 124.
6.   *Life*, V, p. 396n.
7.   John Wilkes to JB, 1 October 1785, after reading the *Tour*: *Corresp.*, 4, p. 217n.
8.   Jack Lee to JB, 3 October 1785: *Corresp.*, 1, p. 306n.
9.   Forbes, *An Account of the Life and Writings of James Beattie*, II, pp. 378–80;
     Forbes to JB, 6 December 1785: quoted in *Later Years*, p. 322.
10. Quoted in Tinker, *Young Boswell*, p. 216.
11. Revd Dr William Adams to JB, 17 November 1785: quoted in the Advertise-
     ment to the First Edition of the *Life of Johnson*.

12. *BJTH,* p. 202.
13. *English Review,* November 1785: quoted in *AJ,* p. 348.
14. *BJTH,* pp. 401–2.
15. JB to EM, 13 October 1785: *Corresp.,* 4, p. 210.
16. *BJTH,* p. 403.
17. Jnl, 12 January 1786: *EE,* p. 27.
18. JB to Edmund Burke, 20 December 1785 and 7 February 1786, and Burke to JB, 4 January and 9 February 1786: *Corresp.,* 4, pp. 147–53; Jnl, 7 February 1786: *EE,* p. 34.
19. Jnl, 13 June 1786 and 14 April 1787: *EE,* pp. 71 and 128–29; EM to JB, 14 September 1787: *Corresp.,* 4, pp. 329–30.
20. Jnl, 17 March and 11 April 1776 and 9 April 1778: *OY,* pp. 264 and 328, and *BE,* p. 257.
21. Alexander Tytler to JB, 24 November 1785: *Corresp.,* 4, p. 274n.
22. See Victor Kiernan, *The Duel in European History: Honour and the Reign of Aristocracy,* London, 1988.
23. JB to EM, 11 November 1785: *Corresp.,* 4, pp. 278–79.
24. Jnl, 27 November 1785: *EE,* p. 9.
25. See, for example, JB to EM, 13 January 1786: *Corresp.,* 4, p. 284.
26. *EE,* p. 20.
27. *Life,* V, pp. 417–19.
28. JB to EM, 13 October, EM to JB, 19 October 1785: *Corresp.,* 4, pp. 219 and 232.
29. Jnl, 21 and 22 December 1785: *EE,* pp. 18–19.

7. DISCRETION

1. *BJTH,* pp. 410–2.
2. Thurlow to JB, 5 January 1786, and Jnl, 9 January 1786: *EE,* pp. 291–92 and 28.
3. *Later Years,* p. 313.
4. *OY,* pp. 352–61.
5. Jnl, 26 February 1786: *EE,* pp. 43–44.
6. *Life,* I, pp. 261–62.
7. Paul Langford, *A Polite and Commercial People: England, 1727–1783,* Oxford, 1989, pp. 582–87.
8. *Life,* I, p. 266.
9. ibid., II, p. 34n.
10. Kernan, *Printing Technology, Letters and Samuel Johnson,* pp. 24–47.
11. Hyde, *The Impossible Friendship,* p. 105.
12. *Life,* II, p. 427.
13. Mrs Thrale to SJ, 18 September 1777: *Letters of Samuel Johnson,* II, p. 209.
14. *Life,* III, p. 316.
15. Jnl, 16 May 1784: *AJ,* p. 213.
16. JB to EM, 31 March 1786: *Corresp.,* 4, p. 314.
17. JB to EM, 22 March 1786: *Corresp.,* 4, pp. 303–5.

18. *Anecdotes,* p. 31.

19. Hyde, *The Impossible Friendship,* p. 107.

20. *Life,* II, p. 217.

21. ibid., pp. 371–72.

22. Jnl, 21 March 1783: *AJ,* p. 75.

23. *Life,* III, p. 270.

24. Geoffrey Scott, "The Making of the Life of Johnson as Shown in Boswell's First Notes," in Clifford (ed.), *Twentieth Century Interpretations of Boswell's Life of Johnson,* pp. 27–39.

25. Jnl, 25 October 1764: *GTGS,* p. 152.

26. *Life,* I, p. 421.

27. JB to EM, 31 March 1786: *Corresp.,* 4, p. 314.

28. *Anecdotes,* pp. 31–32.

29. Jnl, April–May 1776: *OY,* p. 351.

30. *Life,* III, p. 185; Jnl, 10 April 1778: *BE,* p. 264.

31. Sir John Hawkins, *The Life of Samuel Johnson LL.D.,* ed. and abridg. Bertram H. Davis, New York, 1962, pp. 271–72 (5 December 1784).

32. *Life,* IV, pp. 405–6. Boswell read Johnson's diary on 5 May 1776.

33. JB to Revd Dr William Adams, 21 January, 11 March and 22 December 1785, 5 May 1786; Adams to JB, 28 March 1785 and 12 July 1786: *Corresp.,* 2, pp. 42, 74, 128, 154, 82, and 159.

34. JB to Margaret Boswell, 18 May 1786: *EE,* pp. 63–65.

35. See Robert E. Kelley and OM Brack Jr: *Samuel Johnson's Early Biographers,* Iowa, 1971.

36. Revd Hugh Blair to JB, 4 May, JB to Thomas Percy, 12 July 1786: *Corresp.,* 2, pp. 153–54 and 162–63.

37. Jnl, 5 June 1786: *EE,* p. 67.

8. APPLICATION

1. JB to Margaret Boswell, 3 July 1786: *EE,* pp. 77–78.

2. Jnl, 27 June and 6 July 1786: *EE,* pp. 75–76 and 80.

3. JB to Margaret Boswell, 3 July 1786: *EE,* pp. 77–78.

4. Jnl, 8 July 1786: *EE,* p. 81.

5. *Life,* I, p. 164, and IV, pp. 395–98; Hawkins, *The Life of Samuel Johnson LL.D.,* ed. and abridg. Davis, pp. 30–31, 48–49.

6. See Frederick A. Pottle, "The Dark Hints of Hawkins and Boswell," in Hilles (ed.), *New Light on Dr Johnson;* and Davis, *Johnson before Boswell: A Study of Sir John Hawkins' Life of Samuel Johnson,* pp. 119–24, for two different interpretations of these facts.

7. *Rambler* No. 60; *Life,* V, p. 79 and I, p. 425.

8. Robert Folkenflik, *Samuel Johnson, Biographer,* Ithaca and London, 1978, pp. 19–21.

9. *Life,* I, p. 32.

10. ibid., II, p. 166.
11. Jnl, 16 September 1769: *BSW,* p. 311.
12. *Life,* III, p. 109; IV, p. 34; I, p. 25.
13. Jnl, 12 October 1780: *LA,* p. 260.
14. *Life,* I, p. 31.
15. *Later Years,* p. 428.
16. *Life,* I, pp. 29–30.
17. JB to WJT, 24 February 1788: *Letters,* II, pp. 342–45.
18. JB to Thomas Percy, 9 February 1788: *Corresp.,* 3, pp. 257–59.
19. *Corresp.,* 2, p. xxviii.
20. *Life,* I, p. 30.
21. ibid., V, pp. 340–41.
22. These paragraphs, including this phrase, draw heavily on Marshall Waingrow's introduction to his volume of the Boswell correspondence.
23. *Life,* IV, pp. 299–300, and II, pp. 106–7; *BSW,* p. 353.
24. *Public Advertiser,* 9 February 1787: quoted in Hyde, *The Impossible Friendship,* p. 116n.
25. JB to Thomas Barnard, 6 January 1787: *Corresp.,* 2, p. 197.

9. RIVALRY

1. Boswell's advertisement in the papers, May 1787: *Corresp.,* 2, p. lix.
2. *Later Years,* pp. 351–54.
3. *Life,* I, p. 28. Bertram H. Davis's *Johnson before Boswell* attempts to defend Hawkins from these criticisms (see also his Introduction to Hawkins's *Life of Samuel Johnson, LL.D.*). It is ingeniously done, but (to me) ultimately unconvincing. From Boswell's point of view, the important point is that most critics and friends of Johnson disliked Hawkins's book.
4. Edmund Hector to JB, 19 June 1787: *Corresp.,* 2, pp. 220–21.
5. JB to Francis Barber, Barber to JB, 29 June and 9 July 1787: *Corresp.,* 2, pp. 221–23 and 226–27.
6. JB to WJT, 5 March 1789: *Letters,* II, p. 361.
7. *Life,* I, p. 190, and III, p. 126.
8. JB to William Maxwell, 19 March, 10 June, and 4 July; Maxwell to JB, 29 March, 4 and 12 May, 16 June 1787: *Corresp.,* 2, pp. 209–10, 210–11, 213, 214, 215–16, 219, and 224–25.
9. Jnl, 11 May 1787: *EE,* p. 134.
10. Boswell's advertisement in the papers, May 1787: *Corresp.,* 2, p. lix.
11. EM to JB, 14 September 1787: *Corresp.,* 2, pp. 329–30.
12. Jnl, 28 October 1787: *EE,* p. 149.
13. Francesco Sastres to JB, *c.* February 1788; JB to Thomas Percy, 9 February 1788: *Corresp.,* 2, pp. 265–66, 270–71.
14. Jnl, 20 February 1788: *EE,* pp. 189–91.
15. Thomas Barnard to JB, 28 February 1788: *Corresp.,* 3, pp. 259–63.

16. Hyde, *The Impossible Friendship,* p. 126n.
17. EM to JB, 8 March 1788: *Corresp.,* 2, pp. 272–73.
18. Jnl, 15 and 18 March 1788: *EE,* pp. 199 and 201–2.
19. Hyde, *The Impossible Friendship,* pp. 150 and 157.
20. JB to James Beattie, 10 March 1788: *Corresp.,* 2, pp. 273–74.
21. R. W. Chapman, "Boswell's Revises of the Life of Johnson," in *Johnson and Boswell Revised by Themselves and Others,* Oxford, 1928, pp. 31–32.
22. See, for example, JB to William Bowles, after 14 November 1787: *Corresp.,* 2, pp. 258–59.
23. Roger Lonsdale, "Dr Burney and the Integrity of Boswell's Quotations," *Papers of the Bibliographical Society of America,* liii (1959), pp. 327–31.
24. Jnl, 25 April 1788: *EE,* pp. 217–18.
25. JB to EM, 12 July 1788: *Corresp.,* 4, pp. 341–46. A full account is given in Hyde, *The Impossible Friendship,* pp. 130–36; see also *LA,* pp. 316–21.
26. For an interesting and sympathetic portrayal of Anna Seward's views, see the chapter about her in John Brewer's *The Pleasures of the Imagination.*
27. Daniel Astle to JB, December 1786, JB to Anna Seward, and Seward to JB, 11 April and *c.* 3–4 May 1788: *Corresp.,* 2, pp. 190–92, 278–79, and 281.
28. Hawkins, *The Life of Samuel Johnson, LL.D.,* p. 70.
29. WJT to JB, 14 April 1788: *Corresp.,* 2, pp. 279–80.

10. BEREAVEMENT

1. Jnl, 10 July 1788: *EE,* p. 233.
2. JB to WJT, 22 May 1789: *Letters,* II, pp. 368–72.
3. Jnl, 15 March 1788: *EE,* pp. 198–99.
4. Jnl, 26 and 30 April, 1 May 1788: *EE,* p. 218 and pp. 220–21.
5. Jnl, 26 October 1777, 19 and 25 January 1778: *BE,* pp. 191, 205, and 207.
6. JB to EM, 2–5 June and 12 July 1788: *Corresp.,* 4, pp. 334–35 and 341–48.
7. EM to JB, 12 August and (with John Courtenay and Robert Jephson) 29 September, JB to EM, 18 September 1788: *Corresp.,* 4, pp. 347–58.
8. JB to Margaret Boswell, 9 November 1788, 9 and 25 March 1789: *EE,* pp. 253, 274, and 277–78.
9. *Life,* II, pp. 116–33 (Maxwell) and IV, pp. 1–33 (Langton).
10. ibid., II, p. 154.
11. ibid., IV, p. 320.
12. *BLJ,* p. 330n.
13. JB to Margaret Boswell, 9 November 1788: *EE,* pp. 252–55.
14. JB to Margaret Boswell, 28 November 1788: *EE,* pp. 258–59.
15. See Amanda Foreman, *Georgiana, Duchess of Devonshire,* London, 1998, p. 225, which provides a lucid account of the Regency crisis.
16. JB to WJT, 16 February and 31 March 1789: *Letters,* II, pp. 356–58 and 364–67.
17. JB to WJT, 10 January 1789: *Letters,* II, pp. 352–56.
18. JB to Margaret Boswell, 28 January 1789: *EE,* pp. 267–69.

19. JB to Margaret Boswell, 9 February 1789: *EE*, pp. 269–71.

20. JB to WJT, 10 January 1789: *Letters*, II, pp. 352–56.

21. JB to WJT, 5 March 1789: *Letters*, II, pp. 358–61.

22. Dr. John Campbell to JB, 8 March 1789: *EE*, p. 274.

23. JB to Margaret Boswell, 11 March 1789: *EE*, p. 276.

24. JB to WJT, 10 March 1789: *Letters*, II, pp. 362–63.

25. Foreman, *Georgiana, Duchess of Devonshire*, p. 224.

26. JB to WJT, 22 May 1789: *Letters*, II, pp. 368–72.

27. JB to WJT, 22 May 1789: *Letters*, II, pp. 368–72; and WJT to JB, 28 May 1789: cited in Brady, *Boswell's Political Career*, p. 158.

28. SJ to JB, undated letter between September and December 1782: *Life*, IV, p. 155.

29. JB to WJT, 23 July 1789: *Letters*, II, pp. 373–75.

11. HUMILIATION

1. JB to WJT, 21 June 1790: *Letters*, II, pp. 396–98.

2. Adapted from Marshall Waingrow's introduction to the first volume of the manuscript edition of the *Life of Johnson*, p. xxxiii.

3. Jnl, 15, 26, and 27 November and 21 December 1789: *GB*, pp. 16, 18, and 25.

4. JB to Mary Cobb, 14 and 27 March; Mary Cobb to JB, 18 and 29 March 1789: *Corresp.*, 2, pp. 286–90.

5. *Life*, I, pp. 154 and 534; and III, p. 344; see also James L. Clifford, "A Biographer Looks at Dr Johnson," in Hilles (ed.), *New Light on Dr Johnson*, pp. 127–28.

6. Lord Hailes to JB, 24 January 1790: *Corresp.*, 2, pp. 302–3.

7. JB to WJT, 28 November 1789: *Letters*, II, pp. 381–87.

8. Jnl, 12 and 13 January 1790: *GB*, pp. 32–33.

9. JB to WJT, 13 February 1790: *Letters*, II, pp. 389–90.

10. JB to WJT, 8 February 1790: *Letters*, II, pp. 387–89.

11. Revd Hugh Blair to JB, 18 March 1789; Langton to JB, 1 March, JB to Langton, 9 April 1790; Thomas Percy to JB, 19 March and 24 April, JB to Percy, 9 April 1790: *Corresp.*, 2, pp. 287, 308–9, 313, 310, 313–14, and 319–20.

12. EM to JB, 8 July 1790: *Corresp.*, 4, pp. 371–75.

13. JB to Sir John Dick, 26 February 1790: *GB*, p. 43.

14. Jnl, 9 January and 19 May 1790: *GB*, pp. 30 and 51.

15. WJT to JB, 11 March 1792: quoted in Frederick A. Pottle, "The Dark Hints of Sir John Hawkins and Boswell," in Hilles (ed.), *New Light on Dr Johnson*, p. 162.

16. ibid., pp. 153–62.

17. Peter Martin, *Edmond Malone, Shakespearean Scholar*, Cambridge, 1995, pp. 147–49.

18. Donald and Mary Hyde, "Dr Johnson's Second Wife," in Hilles (ed.), *New Light on Dr Johnson*, pp. 133–51.

19. *Life*, I, p. 234.
20. Jnl, 10 January 1784: *AJ*, pp. 176–77.
21. Jnl, 7 December 1789: *GB*, p. 22.
22. JB to WJT, 22 May 1789: *Letters*, II, pp. 368–72.
23. *Life*, I, p. 513.
24. JB to WJT, 21 June 1790: *Letters*, II, pp. 396–98.
25. Jnl, 7 July 1790: *GB*, p. 86.
26. JB to EM, 30 June 1790: *Corresp.*, 4, pp. 367–71.

12. STRUGGLE

1. The opening sentence of the Advertisement to the First Edition of the *Life of Johnson*.
2. Jnl, 21 August 1790: *GB*, p. 104.
3. Thomas Barnard to JB, 11 September 1790: *Corresp.*, 3, pp. 303–5.
4. Jnl, 10 September 1790: *GB*, p. 108.
5. *Life*, IV, p. 261n.
6. JB to Henry Dundas, 16 November 1790: *Letters*, II, pp. 524–25.
7. *Lit. Career*, pp. 141–44.
8. JB to EM, 29 January 1791: *Corresp.*, 4, pp. 393–96.
9. JB to Bennet Langton, 9 April 1790: *Corresp.*, 3, pp. 288–89.
10. JB to Robert Boswell, 28 September, JB to Sir William Forbes, 11 October 1790: *GB*, pp. 110–11.
11. *D'Arblay*, IV, pp. 430–33.
12. EM to JB, 23 December 1790: *Corresp.*, 4, pp. 385–87.
13. JB to EM, 10 February 1791: *Corresp.*, 4, pp. 398–401.
14. JB to EM, 29 January 1791: *Corresp.*, 4, pp. 393–96.
15. JB to EM, 12 March 1791: *Corresp.*, 4, pp. 414–16.
16. JB to EM, 18 and 29 January 1791: *Corresp.*, 4, pp. 388–91 and 393–96.
17. *Life*, IV, p. 350.
18. JB to EM, 10 February, EM to JB, 5 March 1791: *Corresp.*, 4, pp. 398–401 and 408–10.
19. *Life*, IV, p. 425.
20. *Life*, III, pp. 406–7; JB to EM, 10 February 1791: *Corresp.*, 4, pp. 398–401; see also *LA*, pp. 142–43.
21. JB to EM, 25 February 1791: *Corresp.*, 4, pp. 403–7.
22. EM to JB, 5 March 1791: *Corresp.*, 4, pp. 408–10.
23. John Courtenay to EM, 22 Feburary 1791: *GB*, p. 125; JB to EM, 18 January 1791: *Corresp.*, 4, pp. 388–91; Jnl 21 and 22 February 1791: *GB*, p. 127.
24. JB to EM, 25 February and 9 March 1791: *Corresp.*, 4, pp. 403–7 and 410–14.
25. JB to Thomas Percy, 10 May 1791: *Corresp.*, 2 (revised edition, in press), pp. 311–12.
26. Thomas Percy to JB, 12 and 24 March and 6 April, JB to Percy, 16–20 March 1791: *Corresp.*, 3, pp. 327–31 and 332–33.

27. JB to Edmund Burke, 5 March, Burke to JB, 7 March 1791: *Corresp.*, 4, pp. 157–59.

28. JB to WJT, 6 April 1791: *Letters*, II, pp. 430–34.

29. Jnl, 23 January 1790: *GB*, pp. 36–37.

30. Joseph Warton to JB, 9 April 1791: *Corresp.*, 3, p. 334.

13. DESPAIR

1. Jnl, 31 October 1792: *GB*, p. 190.

2. *Lit. Career*, p. 198.

3. *Later Years*, p. 453.

4. *Lit. Career*, pp. xxix–xliv.

5. Vicesimus Knox to JB, 1 June, and WJT to JB, 4 July 1791: *Corresp.*, 2, pp. 418–21 and 423–24.

6. Quoted in *GB*, p. 144.

7. Dr Charles Burney to JB, 16 July 1791, and Burney to EM, October 1798: *Corresp.*, 2, pp. 426–29 and 427n.

8. JB to John Wilkes, 25 June 1791: *Corresp.*, 2, p. 423.

9. JB to Edmund Burke, 16 July, Burke to JB, 20 July 1791: *Corresp.*, 4, pp. 159–63.

10. Jnl, 18 April 1778: *BE*, pp. 300–1.

11. *Life*, II, p. 64, and III, pp. 271–78; Jnl, 12, 20, 25, 28 April 1778: *BE*, pp. 272–75, 302, 310–11, 317–19.

12. *Life*, II, pp. 1–2.

13. See *Corresp.*, 3, pp. lxxxv–vi and 373, n. 12; JB to EM, 29 January 1791: *Letters*, II, p. 417, n. 2.

14. Sir William Scott to JB, 2, 4, and 5 August, JB to Scott, 1, 5, and 9 August 1791: *Corresp.*, 3, pp. 345–50.

15. JB to Alexander Boswell, 7 February 1794: *Corresp.*, 3, p. lxxxvii, n. 18.

16. *Public Advertiser*, 27 May 1791: quoted in *GB*, p. 288.

17. W. Roberts (ed.), *Memoirs of Hannah More*, 1834, II, p. 101.

18. JB to the Revd Andrew Kippis, 11 July 1791: *GB*, pp. 148–49.

19. JB to WJT, 22 August and 22 November 1791: *Letters*, II, pp. 438–41.

20. William Elford to JB, 16 March 1792: *Corresp.*, 2, pp. 474–75.

21. See, for example, JB to the Revd Ralph Churton, 5 April 1792: *Corresp.*, 2, pp. 476–77.

22. Revd Charles Edward De Coetlogon to JB, 15 September 1792, JB to De Coetlogon, 26 July 1793; Revd John Fawcett to JB, 22 September, JB to Fawcett, 12 October 1792: *Corresp.*, 2, pp. 488–89, 547, and 493–94.

23. JB to Sir William Forbes, 27 September, Forbes to JB, 13 and 29 October 1791: *Corresp.*, 2, pp. 446–47 and 448–49.

24. Dr James Beattie to JB, 3 May 1792: *Corresp.*, 2, pp. 482–83; see also *Life*, II, pp. 148–49.

25. *Lit. Career*, pp. 167–68.

26. *Life*, I, pp. 1–4.

27. JB to Alexander Boswell, 25 February 1792: quoted in *GB*, p. 154.

28. JB to Barnard, 16 August 1792: *Corresp.*, 3, pp. 370–75.

29. WJT to JB, 30 March 1792: quoted in *GB*, p. 155.

30. Quoted in *Later Years*, p. 459.

31. Jnl, 17 August 1792: *GB*, p. 159.

32. Jnl, 20 August 1792: *GB*, pp. 162–64.

33. Jnl, 29 August 1792: *GB*, p. 168.

34. Jnl, 29 August and 9 September 1792: *GB*, pp. 168 and 179–80.

35. JB to EM, 16 September 1792: *Corresp.*, 4, pp. 420–21; Jnl, 3 September 1792: *GB*, pp. 171–72.

36. Jnl, 5 November 1792: *GB*, p. 194.

37. *Life*, IV, p. 37.

38. Jnl, 29 November 1792: *GB*, p. 202.

39. Jnl, 21 December 1792: *GB*, pp. 207–8.

40. JB to EM, 20 March 1793: *Corresp.*, 4, p. 422.

41. JB to WJT, 26 February 1793: *Letters*, II, pp. 445–46.

42. *Lit. Career*, pp. 168–69.

43. EM to JB, 13 May, JB to EM, 17 May 1793: *Corresp.*, 4, pp. 423–24.

44. JB to EM, 22 August 1793: *Corresp.*, 4, pp. 425–26; Jnl, 11 and 28 January 1794: *GB*, pp. 276 and 281; *Lit. Career*, p. 168; *Later Years*, p. 577.

45. See *GB*, pp. 254–56.

46. JB to WJT, 21 June 1793: *Letters*, II, pp. 446–47.

47. Jnl, 4 and 6 September 1793: *GB*, p. 231.

48. WJT to JB, 7 September 1793: Brady, *Boswell's Political Career*, p. 179.

49. Jnl, 7 February 1763: *BLJ*, p. 181.

50. Jnl, 14, 16, 24, 25, 26 September 1793: *GB*, pp. 232, 233, and 235–37.

51. Andrew Erskine to JB, 14 January, JB to Erskine, 6 March 1793: *Corresp.*, 2, pp. 511 and 517–18; Jnl, 13 and 24 October 1793: *GB*, pp. 242 and 245.

52. Jnl, 25 November 1793: *GB*, p. 253.

53. Farington's diary, 5 October 1793: quoted in *GB*, p. 240n.

54. Jnl, 13 February 1794: *GB*, p. 287.

55. WJT to JB, 3 and 5 June 1794: quoted in *Later Years*, pp. 483–84.

56. JB to James Boswell Jr, 14 and 30 July, 12 September, and 21 November; JB Jr to JB, 18 October 1794: *GB*, pp. 300–7; JB to Thomas David Boswell, 13 October 1794: *Letters*, II, pp. 461–63.

57. JB to EM, 18 November 1794: *Corresp.*, 4, pp. 429–30.

58. JB to Alexander Boswell, 23 February 1795: *GB*, p. 310.

14. POSTERITY

1. Jnl, 13 February 1794: *GB*, p. 287.

2. Forbes to EM, 22 May, and EM to Forbes, 5 July 1798: *Corresp.*, 2, pp. 597–98; Thomas Percy to the Revd Thomas Steadman, 22 May 1798: *Corresp.*, 3, pp. lxxxvi–vii.

3. Jnl, 31 July 1779: *LA,* p. 126.

4. *Treasure,* pp. 175–203.

5. ibid., pp. 193–95, 204–5.

6. ibid., pp. 8–9.

7. ibid., pp. 5ff. Pottle does not agree with Scott's characterization of Alexander Boswell, and Buchanan goes along with him. I can only say that it makes sense to me. Sandy's love and respect for his father are in my view consistent with his unhappiness at the way Boswell was derided. His letter to Forbes of 21 October 1795 (quoted on p. 14 of *The Treasure of Auchinleck*) makes it clear that he was not particularly keen to have Johnson's portrait at Auchinleck.

8. *Treasure,* pp. 15–16.

9. ibid., pp. 204–7; Pottle, *Pride and Negligence,* pp. 61–62.

10. *Lit. Career,* pp. 177–80.

11. J. D. Fleeman, *A Bibliography of the Works of Samuel Johnson,* Oxford, 2000.

12. Walter Raleigh, *Six Essays on Johnson,* Oxford, 1910, p. 174.

13. Macaulay's review first appeared in the September 1831 issue of the *Edinburgh Review;* it was republished in his *Critical and Historical Essays,* ed. F. C. Montague, London, 1903, I, pp. 347–96.

14. SJ to JB, 3 July 1778: *Life,* III, p. 362; Sir Joshua Reynolds to JB, 1 October 1782: *Corresp.,* 3, pp. 127–28.

15. Carlyle's review first appeared in *Frazer's Magazine,* nos. 27 and 28, April 1832; reprinted in *Critical and Miscellaneous Essays,* 1869, IV, pp. 3–106.

16. Jnl, 22 March 1772: *BD,* p. 55.

17. *Life,* I, p. 454, and II, p. 450.

18. *Lit. Career,* pp. 186–88.

19. ibid., p. 203.

20. G. B. Hill, *Dr Johnson: His Friends and Critics,* cited in his *Life,* I, p. xxxiii, and *Footsteps of Dr Johnson* (1890), quoted in *Treasure,* p. 34.

21. *Life,* I, p. xli.

22. *D'Arblay,* I, pp. 58–69; *Life,* IV, p. 254n.

23. e.g. the OUP edition originally edited by R. W. Chapman, 1904, and most recently reissued in "The World's Classics" paperback series, Oxford, 1980, p. 1440.

24. See Paul J. Korshin, "Johnson's Conversation," in Clingham (ed.), *New Light on Boswell,* particularly pp. 188–90.

25. *Treasure,* pp. 25–26, 29–34.

26. ibid., pp. 39–45.

27. *Letters,* I, pp. vii–viii.

28. This whole section is based mainly on David Buchanan's *The Treasure of Auchinleck.*

29. Pottle, *Pride and Negligence,* pp. 195–96.

30. Reviews quoted on the jacket cover of *BH.*

31. Pottle, *Pride and Negligence,* pp. 206 and 214.

32. Donald J. Greene, "Johnson without Boswell," *Times Literary Supplement*, 22 November 1974, pp. 1315–16; "'Tis a Pretty Book, Mr Boswell, But—," in Vance (ed.), *Boswell's Life of Johnson: New Questions, New Answers*.

33. "Letter to James Gray," a review of a Life of Robert Burns, in W.J.B. Owen and Jane Worthington Smyser (ed.), *Prose Works of William Wordsworth*, Oxford, 1974, III, p. 170.

SELECT BIBLIOGRAPHY

A. BOSWELL'S PUBLISHED WORKS

The standard edition of the *Life of Johnson,* as edited by G. B. Hill and revised by
L. F. Powell, is *Boswell's Life of Johnson,* 6 vols., Oxford, 1934–50. This edition includes
as its fifth volume the published version of *The Journal of a Tour to the Hebrides with
Samuel Johnson LL.D.* The unedited manuscript of the latter has been published as
Frederick A. Pottle and Charles H. Bennett (ed.), *Boswell's Journal of a Tour to the
Hebrides with Samuel Johnson LL.D.,* New York and London, 1936, revised edition
New Haven and London, 1963. The manuscript of the *Life of Johnson* is being published in a projected four-volume edition in the Yale series (see below). The first two
volumes, edited by Marshall Waingrow and Bruce Redford respectively, have been
published as *James Boswell's "Life of Johnson": An Edition of the Original Manuscript
in Four Volumes 1709–1765* and *1766–1776,* New Haven and Edinburgh, 1994 and 1998.

B. BOSWELL'S LETTERS AND JOURNALS

Chauncey B. Tinker's edition of *The Letters of James Boswell,* 2 vols., Oxford, 1924, is
gradually being superseded by the Yale editions of the Boswell correspondence.
Boswell's notebook was published under the title *Boswelliana,* London, 1874, edited
by the Reverend Charles Rogers. The Boswell papers were originally published privately as *The Private Papers of James Boswell from Malahide Castle, in the Possession of
Lt-Colonel Ralph Heyward Isham,* 18 vols., Mount Vernon, N.Y., 1928–34, edited by
Geoffrey Scott and Frederick A. Pottle. This edition contains Boswell's earliest journal, not published in the Yale trade edition, and Geoffrey Scott's introductions.

C. THE YALE "TRADE" EDITIONS OF BOSWELL'S JOURNALS

Frederick A. Pottle (ed.), *Boswell's London Journal 1762–63,* New York and London,
　　1950.
——, *Boswell in Holland 1763–64,* New York and London, 1952.

——, *Boswell on the Grand Tour: Germany and Switzerland 1764*, New York and London, 1953.

Frank Brady and Frederick A. Pottle (ed.), *Boswell on the Grand Tour: Italy, Corsica & France 1765–66*, New York and London, 1956.

——, *Boswell in Search of a Wife 1766–69*, New York and London, 1957.

William K. Wimsatt Jr and Frederick A. Pottle (ed.), *Boswell for the Defence 1769–74*, New York and London, 1959.

Charles Ryskamp and Frederick A. Pottle (ed.), *Boswell: The Ominous Years 1774–76*, New York and London, 1963.

Charles McC. Weis and Frederick A. Pottle (ed.), *Boswell in Extremes 1776–78*, New York and London, 1971.

Joseph W. Reed and Frederick A. Pottle (ed.), *Boswell: Laird of Auchinleck 1778–82*, New York and London, 1977.

Irma S. Lustig and Frederick A. Pottle (ed.), *Boswell: The Applause of the Jury 1782–85*, New York and London, 1981.

——, *Boswell: The English Experiment 1785–89*, New York and London, 1986.

Marlies K. Danziger and Frank Brady (ed.), *Boswell: The Great Biographer 1789–95*, New York and London, 1989.

D. THE YALE "RESEARCH" EDITIONS
OF BOSWELL'S CORRESPONDENCE

Further volumes besides these six have been published, but they lie outside the scope of my work.

1. Ralph S. Walker (ed.), *The Correspondence of James Boswell and John Johnston of Grange*, New York and London, 1966.
2. Marshall Waingrow (ed.), *The Correspondence and Other Papers of James Boswell Relating to the Making of the Life of Johnson*, 2nd edition, New Haven and Edinburgh, 2001.
3. Charles N. Fifer (ed.), *The Correspondence of James Boswell with Certain Members of the Club*, New York and London, 1976.
4. Peter S. Baker *et al.* (ed.), *The Correspondence of James Boswell with David Garrick, Edmund Burke and Edmond Malone*, New York and London, 1987.
5. Richard C. Cole *et al.* (ed.), *The General Correspondence of James Boswell 1766–1769*, I, New Haven and Edinburgh, 1993.
6. Thomas Crawford (ed.), *The Correspondence of James Boswell and William Johnston Temple 1756–77*, New Haven and Edinburgh, 1997.

E. OTHER CONTEMPORARY WORKS

Charlotte Barrett and Austin Dobson (ed.), *Diary and Letters of Madame D'Arblay* (Fanny Burney), 6 vols., London, 1904–5.

Sir William Forbes, *An Account of the Life and Writings of James Beattie*, 2 vols., 1807.

Sir John Hawkins, *The Life of Samuel Johnson, LL.D.*, 1787.

Samuel Johnson, *A Journey to the Western Islands of Scotland*, 1775.

Hester Thrale Piozzi, *Anecdotes of the Late Samuel Johnson, LL.D.*, 1786.

——, *Letters to and from the Late Samuel Johnson, LL.D.*, 1788.

F. MODERN WORKS

This is a selection of the sources I have found most useful. Other references are given in the notes.

Walter Jackson Bate, *Samuel Johnson*, New York and London, 1977.

Frank Brady, *Boswell's Political Career*, New Haven, 1965.

——, *James Boswell: The Later Years, 1769–1795*, New York and London, 1984.

John Brewer, *The Pleasures of the Imagination: English Culture in the Eighteenth Century*, London, 1997.

Anthony E. Brown, *Boswellian Studies: A Bibliography*, 3rd edition, revised, Edinburgh, 1991.

David Buchanan, *The Treasure of Auchinleck: The Story of the Boswell Papers*, New York and London, 1975.

R. W. Chapman (ed.), *Letters of Samuel Johnson*, 3 vols., Oxford, 1952.

James L. Clifford (ed.), *Twentieth Century Interpretations of Boswell's Life of Johnson*, Englewood Cliffs, N.J., 1970.

Greg Clingham (ed.), *New Light on Boswell*, Cambridge, 1991.

Bertram H. Davis, *Johnson before Boswell: A Study of Sir John Hawkins' Life of Samuel Johnson*, New Haven, 1960.

Donald J. Greene, *The Politics of Samuel Johnson*, New Haven, 1960.

F. W. Hilles (ed.), *New Light on Dr Johnson*, New Haven, 1959.

Mary Hyde, *The Impossible Friendship: Boswell and Mrs Thrale*, Cambridge, Mass., and London, 1972.

Alvin Kernan, *Printing Technology, Letters and Samuel Johnson*, Princeton, 1987.

Frederick A. Pottle, *The Literary Career of James Boswell*, Oxford, 1929.

——, *James Boswell: The Earlier Years, 1740–1769*, New York and London, 1966.

——, *Pride and Negligence: The History of the Boswell Papers*, New York, 1982.

Johnson, Boswell and Their Circle: Essays Presented to L. F. Powell, Oxford, 1965.

Pat Rogers, *Johnson and Boswell: The Transit of Caledonia*, Oxford, 1995.

Chauncey B. Tinker, *Young Boswell*, Boston and London, 1922.

John A. Vance (ed.), *Boswell's Life of Johnson: New Questions, New Answers*, Athens, Ga., 1985.

INDEX

The Life of Samuel Johnson
James Boswell
Edited by Christopher Hibbert
A masterpiece that brims with wit, anecdote and originality, *The Life of Samuel Johnson* is a fascinating portrait of two friends—the author and the subject. Poet, lexicographer, critic, moralist, and Great Cham, Dr. Johnson had in his friend Boswell the ideal biographer. Notoriously and self-confessedly intemperate, Boswell shared with Johnson a huge appetite for life and threw equal energy into recording its every aspect in minute but telling detail. Considered a classic of the language, this shortened version is based on the 1799 edition, the last in which the author had a hand.

ISBN 0-14-043116-0

The History of Rasselas, Prince of Abissinia
Samuel Johnson
Edited with an Introduction by D. J. Enright
The classic story of Rasselas's and his companions' escape from the bland pleasures of their happy valley in Abissinia to Egypt is both a para-ble and pilgrimage novel in which all manner of subjects are discussed—flying machines, poetry, marriage, and madness. Rasselas embodies Dr. Johnson's most powerful and heart-warming qualities: his tragic sense of life, his justice, his wisdom which is never boring or solemn, and his miraculous ability to balance humor with sympathy in weighing up some of life's more mysterious problems—what is happiness, and how can we find it?

ISBN 0-14-043108-X

Johnson: Selected Writings
Samuel Johnson
Edited with an Introduction by Patrick Cruttwell
This excellent anthology contains generous selections from each period and includes *London, The Life of Savage, The Vanity of Human Wishes*, extracts from the English Dictionary, prefaces to *Shakespeare* and *Lives of the Poets*. Throughout, the editor has been concerned that his choices should illustrate the riches and brilliance of Johnson's literary personality, as well as allow Johnson's less known writings, such as his early journal-ism, his letters, and his prayers, a proper place. Johnson was a writer of vigor, power, passion and profundity, and this selection reveals all these intriguing traits of one of our greatest men of letters.

ISBN 0-14-043033-4

A PENGUIN READERS GUIDE TO

BOSWELL'S PRESUMPTUOUS TASK

Adam Sisman

AN INTRODUCTION TO
Boswell's Presumptuous Task

When it appeared in 1791, James Boswell's *The Life of Samuel Johnson* was the most innovative and most intimate biography ever written. It revealed its subject more fully, more dramatically, and more completely than any previous biography—and, arguably, more than any biography since.

Adam Sisman's *Boswell's Presumptuous Task* gives us an innovative and intimate account of the making of that book, a biography of Boswell's biography of Johnson. It reveals Boswell's literary methods, his personal foibles, and the widely varied critical reception his masterpiece has received over the past two centuries. In doing so, Sisman engages questions of essential importance to the biographical enterprise: Can the biographer ever truly understand another human being? Can a biography be fully accurate? How faithful should the biographer be to his/her source materials? How much of the biographer's own life inevitably intrudes into his or her work?

In Boswell's own case, Sisman shows that far from being a sycophantic recorder of Johnson's brilliant conversations, Boswell exerted a high degree of literary skill in crafting, editing, and in some cases altering his subject's remarks. Though he was scrupulous about checking his impressions against others who knew Johnson well, and tenacious about providing sources for all his material (a practice now standard but extraordinary at the time), Boswell was willing to sacrifice accuracy for aesthetic effect. The two men were friends for more than twenty years, yet there were sides to Johnson forever closed to Boswell. Sisman's book gives readers a clear and probing analysis of the ways in which Boswell knew Johnson, how that knowledge affected him, and how he shaped it into what is widely regarded as the greatest biography ever written. *Boswell's Presumptuous Task* gives us a vivid portrait of Boswell as a writer—

his inner turmoil, chaotic outer life, and heroic perseverance—struggling to do justice to his subject.

That portrait reveals not only Boswell the man and writer, but the very origins of modern biographical writing, for Boswell turned biography away from the kind of sloppy encomium then the norm towards the more rigorous, exhaustive, and balanced approach that we now take for granted. He was tireless in gathering up every letter to and from Johnson, in verifying what Johnson said and did, and in including as much material, both good and bad, as was humanly possible. Boswell professed to "write, not his panegyric, but his Life; which, great and good as he was, must not be supposed to be entirely perfect." To reveal Johnson's true character, he sought to include "shade as well as light" and to focus not only on the great events but also "the minute details of daily life." These were groundbreaking innovations in Boswell's time and paved the way for modern biography as we now know it.

Sisman also shows the degree to which Boswell prefigures modern autobiography. In his journals and diaries, Boswell was an unflinching examiner of his own behavior and, more importantly, of his own mind. Sisman suggests that Boswell anticipates Freud in the depth of his introspection and self-analysis, revealing "everything in his mind without restraint, concealment, or distortion." In many ways, our own age of self-searching memoir finds its origins in Boswell.

But *Boswell's Presumptuous Task* is not only an exploration of the beginnings of modern biography and autobiography. It is also a book about one of the most unlikely and fruitful friendships in English literary history. Sisman's account shows us the inner workings of that friendship, and elucidates the masterful work that resulted from it.

A Conversation with
Adam Sisman

1. How would you explain the ongoing interest, amongst both scholars and general readers, in Johnson and Boswell? What drew you to write about the making of Boswell's book?

The simple answer is that the two are perennially fascinating. Hundreds of books have been written about them, yet there is always more to say, as I hope I have demonstrated.

The recent discovery of Boswell's papers—his letters, manuscripts, and his extraordinary journals—has proved a gold-mine for scholars, and led to a complete reassessment of his work. He is now recognized as a writer of great skill, even genius: very different from the fool who merely copied down what people said, the image that prevailed for the first 150 years or so after his death. I was first drawn to the subject after writing a biography (of the historian A.J.P. Taylor, himself a biographer), in the process of which I became interested in biography itself. This led me on to Boswell's *The Life of Johnson*, the first and arguably the greatest of all biographies. And the more I learned about Boswell and Johnson, the more I wanted to know about these two unlikely friends. As A.J.P. Taylor once said, "When I want to find out about something, I write a book about it."

2. How would you describe Boswell's influence on biography? Has this influence been entirely positive?

It's hard to assess Boswell's influence. Undoubtedly his book was a landmark, "a new species of biography" as one contemporary called it; he set a new standard of verisimilitude. But there was no "school of Boswell"; his work stands alone. More generally, I argue in my book that Boswell's Johnson was a moral and intellectual hero, who inspired the young Romantic poets, and who continues to inspire readers to this day—especially, I think, in the United States.

3. How would you respond to those who, like Donald Greene, feel that Boswell's reputation has grown so much that it overshadows Johnson's? How would you answer Greene's charge that Boswell's apparent hero-worship of Johnson "is a mask, disguising from himself and others an unconscious wish to cut Johnson down to size and establish, in the end, the superiority of Boswell"?

Greene's charge seems to me a perverse misreading: far from wishing to cut Johnson down to size in his book, Boswell went to extraordinary lengths to defend him against what he saw as unfair criticism, for example from Mrs. Piozzi. I think it's quite clear that Boswell revered Johnson. I argue in my book that Boswell found it profoundly reassuring and indeed psychologically necessary to assert Johnson's superiority.

I do agree with Greene that there is a regrettable modern tendency to praise Boswell at Johnson's expense. But if Boswell's reputation now overshadows Johnson's, that is not his fault. Indeed, Boswell would have been horrified at the prospect.

4. You describe in great detail Boswell's method in writing The Life of Samuel Johnson. *Could you tell us something about your own way of working on* Boswell's Presumptuous Task?

I can't claim that my own way of working was as colorful as Boswell's! But there are certain similarities. Like him, I live in the countryside but am repeatedly drawn to the city; like him, I was distracted by domestic concerns, and by the need to pursue another career to provide essential income, so that there were periods of a year or more when I did no writing at all; and like him, I was plagued by anxieties of various kinds, including the fear that I

5

might be scooped by a competitor. I see now that these were misplaced; but I think such anxieties are common—perhaps universal—in writers.

5. What is your sense of the state of the art of biography now? Are there any recent literary biographies that approach the mastery of Boswell's The Life of Samuel Johnson?

Right now biography is going through an interesting stage, as biographers experiment with the form in playful and sometimes outlandish ways. Meanwhile fine biographies of the more conventional type are published every year. Michael Holroyd has described this as the "golden age of biography" (though I see that he has also said recently that "biography is dead").

But there is no biography, recent or otherwise, comparable to *The Life of Samuel Johnson.* As I write in the concluding sentence of my book, never again will there be such a combination of subject, author, and opportunity.

6. Would you agree with Carlyle's claim that Boswell's The Life of Samuel Johnson *is a book "beyond any other product of the eighteenth century"?*

No. How can you compare works as different as, say, *Tristram Shandy* and *The Life of Samuel Johnson*? I don't think it's profitable to rate books in this way. But I am sure that *The Life of Samuel Johnson* is a masterpiece, one of the outstanding books of its own or any century, a work that continues to delight and enrich readers more than two hundred years after it was written.

7. You argue that Boswell was a kind of pre-Freudian Freudian, "the first biographer to attempt to tell the whole truth about his subject, to portray his lapses, his blemishes, and his weaknesses as well as his great qualities: an aim we take for granted today, but in Boswell's time a startling innovation." What prompted Boswell to take such an unprecedented approach, and to persist in it? Why did he feel a similar need to expose himself so completely in his journals?

The prompt was Johnson himself, who in a famous essay on biography criticized the then prevalent view that the faults of the dead should be suppressed or glossed over. On the contrary, "if nothing but the bright side of characters should be shown, we should sit down in despondency, and think it utterly impossible to imitate them in any thing." Boswell quoted from this essay in his preamble to *The Life of Samuel Johnson*.

Early in their friendship Johnson encouraged Boswell to write a journal, but as Boswell then revealed, he was already doing so. One can only speculate on Boswell's motives for keeping such a frank and potentially damaging journal. He certainly believed that the act of writing regularly was beneficial in itself. He claimed that reading the journal would enable him to monitor and thus improve his own behavior; and also that it might serve as "a store of entertainment for my after life"—perhaps contradictory ambitions. Boswell was anxious that his journal might be used against him, but he was haunted by a morbid fear of evanescence and a sense that his life meant nothing unless it were recorded. He had to be completely open in his journals, because he used them as a means of exploring his own thoughts and feelings. Maybe only a man with such a combination of vanity and naïveté could have written so openly about himself.

Questions for Discussion

1. How has reading *Boswell's Presumptuous Task* changed your perception of Boswell? Of Johnson? Of the relationship between the two men?

2. Sisman argues that Boswell's *The Life of Samuel Johnson* was "a pioneering work which opened up new possibilities for biography" (p. 314). What did Boswell accomplish that had never been attempted in biography before? What is unusual in his approach to, and presentation of, his subject?

3. In a *Rambler* essay, Johnson wrote of biography that "no species of writing is more worthy of cultivation" (p. 153). Sisman suggests that Johnson esteemed biography because he "believed in the power of example, the value of learning about other men's lives so that one might live one's own life better" (p. 154). Is this still a major motive for reading biographies today? What other reasons draw people to the form? Does what Boswell learned about Samuel Johnson's life appear to have helped him to live his own?

4. In his introduction, Sisman suggests that, "the *Life of Johnson* can be read as an unending contest between author and subject for posterity. . . . Boswell will forever be known as Johnson's sidekick, remembered principally because he wrote the life of a greater man; Johnson is immortalized but also imprisoned by the *Life*, known best as Boswell portrayed him" (p. xviii). Some critics, most notably Donald Greene, have recently complained that Boswell's reputation has become "preposterously inflated," while a scholarly edition of Johnson's works remains unpublished for lack of funds. Who has won this contest for posterity? Has Boswell become a more important writer than Johnson? Is Boswell deserving of greater fame than the man he wrote about?

5. For the greater part of two centuries, Boswell was considered, at best, hardly more than a stenographer, merely copying down Samuel Johnson's brilliant conversations, and at worst, in the words of Macaulay, "a man of the meanest and feeblest intellect . . . servile and impertinent, shallow and pedantic, a bigot and a sot, bloated with family pride, and eternally blustering about the dignity of a born gentleman, yet stooping to be a talebearer, an eaves-dropper, a common butt in the taverns of London" (p. 293). In what ways does Sisman's book challenge both of these views? What more nuanced picture of Boswell, as both a writer and a man, emerges from Sisman's book?

6. How would you explain the relationship between Boswell's disordered life—his drunkenness, whoring, and professional failures—to his admiration of Johnson?

7. Boswell was attacked during his day for divulging too much of Johnson's private life. The Reverend Dr. Vicesimus Knox complained that "Instead of an instructive recital, [biography] is becoming an instrument to the mere gratification of an impertinent, not to say a malignant, curiosity" (p. 135). Is this charge in any way just, or merely a reflection of eighteenth-century prudishness? How would Knox, and others like him, react to today's tell-all biographies?

8. Sisman shows Boswell in relation to three powerful and domineering men: his father, Johnson, and Lord Lonsdale. What do we learn about Boswell through his interactions with these three figures?

9. Boswell appears to be trapped between the Scylla and Charybdis of inauthenticity on the one hand, and literary incompetence on the other. If he merely recorded Johnson's conversations, his *Life* is authentic but lacks literary sophistication.

If he manipulates Johnson's words for greater effects, he demonstrates his literary skill but renders his book less authentic. To what extent should the biographer remain faithful to his sources? To what extent should he/she massage those sources for aesthetic effects? Was Boswell right to rewrite and otherwise alter some of Johnson's remarks?

10. At the beginning of his book, Sisman asks: "Is it possible for a biographer to understand fully what it is like to be another human being? . . . Is biography science, or art? History or fiction?" (p. xv–xvi). Based on your reading of *Boswell's Presumptuous Task*, how would you answer these questions? How do you think Sisman would answer them?

For more information about or to order other Penguin Readers Guides, please call the Penguin Marketing Department at (800) 778-6425, e-mail us at reading@penguinputnam.com, or write to us at:

> Penguin Books Marketing Dept. CC
> Readers Guides
> 375 Hudson Street
> New York, NY 10014-3657

Please allow 4–6 weeks for delivery
To access Penguin Readers Guides online, visit the PPI Web site at www.penguinputnam.com